Ronald C. Fox, PhD
Editor

Current Research on Bisexuality

Current Research on Bisexuality has been co-published simultaneously as *Journal of Bisexuality*, Volume 4, Numbers 1/2 2004.

Pre-publication
REVIEWS,
COMMENTARIES,
EVALUATIONS . . .

"**F**INALLY, the subdiscipline of bisexual studies has moved forward. This book represents a greater breadth and depth of empirical research on bisexuality than any other work to date. It contributes greater insight into issues ranging from better understanding of the bisexual identity formation process, to friendship patterns, intimate relationships, and mental health. THE READER'S GUIDE ALONE IS WORTH THE PURCHASE PRICE."

Michele J. Eliason, PhD
Associate Professor
College of Nursing, University of Iowa

Current Research on Bisexuality

Current Research on Bisexuality has been co-published simultaneously as *Journal of Bisexuality*, Volume 4, Numbers 1/2 2004.

The *Journal of Bisexuality* Monographic "Separates"

Below is a list of "separates," which in serials librarianship means a special issue simultaneously published as a special journal issue or double-issue *and* as a "separate" hardbound monograph. (This is a format which we also call a "DocuSerial.")

"Separates" are published because specialized libraries or professionals may wish to purchase a specific thematic issue by itself in a format which can be separately cataloged and shelved, as opposed to purchas - ing the journal on an on-going basis. Faculty members may also more easily consider a "separate" for classroom adoption.

"Separates" are carefully classified separately with the major book jobbers so that the journal tie-in can be noted on new book order slips to avoid duplicate purchasing.

You may wish to visit Haworth's website at . . .

http://www.HaworthPress.com

. . . to search our online catalog for complete tables of contents of these separates and related publications.

You may also call 1-800-HAWORTH (outside US/Canada: 607-722-5857), or Fax: 1-800-895-0582 (out - side US/Canada: 607-771-0012), or e-mail at:

docdelivery@haworthpress.com

Current Research on Bisexuality, edited by Ronald C. Fox, PhD (Vol. 4, Nos. 1/2, 2004). *"Finally, the subdiscipline of bisexual studies has moved forward. This book represents a greater breadth and depth of empirical research on bisexuality than any other work to date. It contributes greater insight into issues ranging from better understanding of the bisexual identity formation process, to friendship patterns, intimate relationships, and mental health. The reader's guide alone is worth the purchase price." (Michele J. Eliason, PhD, Associate Professor, College of Nursing, University of Iowa)*

Bisexuality and Transgenderism: InterSEXions of the Others, edited by Jonathan Alexander, PhD, and Karen Yescavage, PhD (Vol. 3, Nos. 3/4, 2003). *The first book devoted exclusively to exploring the common ground–and the important differences–between bisexuality and transgenderism.*

Women and Bisexuality: A Global Perspective, edited by Serena Anderlini-D'Onofrio, PhD (Vol. 3, No. 1, 2003). *"Nimbly straddles disciplinary and geographical boundaries. . . . The collection's diversity of subject matter and theoretical perspectives offers a useful model for the continued development of interdisciplinary sexuality studies." (Maria Pramaggiore, PhD, Associate Professor of Film Studies, North Carolina State University)*

Bisexual Women in the Twenty-First Century, edited by Dawn Atkins, PhD (cand.) (Vol. 2, Nos. 2/3, 2002). *An eclectic collection of articles that typifies an ongoing feminist process of theory grounded in life experience.*

Bisexual Men in Culture and Society, edited by Brett Beemyn, PhD, and Erich Steinman, PhD (cand.) (Vol. 2, No. 1, 2002). *Incisive examinations of the cultural meanings of bisexuality, including the overlooked bisexual themes in James Baldwin's classic novels* Another Country *and* Giovanni's Room, *the conflicts within sexual-identity politics between gay men and bisexual men, and the recurring figure of the predatory, immoral bisexual man in novels, films, and women's magazines.*

Bisexuality in the Lives of Men: Facts and Fictions, edited by Brett Beemyn, PhD, and Erich Steinman, PhD (cand.) (Vol. 1, Nos. 2/3, 2001). *"At last, a source book which explains bisexual male desires, practices, and identities in a language all of us can understand! This is informative reading for a general audience, and will be especially valuable for discussions in gender studies, sexuality studies, and men's studies courses." (William L. Leap, PhD, Professor, Department of Anthropology, American University, Washington, DC)*

Current Research on Bisexuality

Ronald C. Fox, PhD
Editor

Current Research on Bisexuality has been co-published simultaneously as *Journal of Bisexuality*, Volume 4, Numbers 1/2 2004.

HPP

Harrington Park Press®
An Imprint of The Haworth Press, Inc.

New York • London • Victoria (AU)
www.HaworthPress.com

Published by

Harrington Park Press®, 10 Alice Street, Binghamton, NY 13904-1580 USA

Harrington Park Press is an imprint of The Haworth Press, Inc., 10 Alice Street, Binghamton, NY 13904-1580 USA

Current Research on Bisexuality has been co-published simultaneously as *Journal of Bisexuality*, Volume 4, Numbers 1/2 2004.

Cover design by Jennifer M. Gaska

Library of Congress Cataloging-in-Publication Data

Current research on bisexuality / Ronald C. Fox, editor.
    p. cm.
    "Current Research on Bisexuality has been co-published simultaneously as Journal of Bisexuality, Volume 4, Numbers 1/2 2004."
    Includes bibliographical references and index.
    ISBN 1-56023-288-9 (hard cover : alk. paper) – ISBN 1-56023-289-7 (soft cover : alk. paper)
    1. Bisexuality. 2. Bisexuals. I. Fox, Ronald C. II. Journal of bisexuality.
HQ74.C87 2004
306.76'5–dc22
                                                   2004002353

Indexing, Abstracting & Website/Internet Coverage

This section provides you with a list of major indexing & abstracting services. That is to say, each service began covering this periodical during the year noted in the right column. Most Websites which are listed below have indicated that they will either post, disseminate, compile, archive, cite or alert their own Website users with research-based content from this work. (This list is as current as the copyright date of this publication.)

(continued)

*Special Bibliographic Notes related to special journal issues
(separates) and indexing/abstracting:*

- indexing/abstracting services in this list will also cover material in any "separate" that is co-published simultaneously with Haworth's special thematic journal issue or DocuSerial. Indexing/abstracting usually covers material at the article/chapter level.
- monographic co-editions are intended for either non-subscribers or libraries which intend to purchase a second copy for their circulating collections.
- monographic co-editions are reported to all jobbers/wholesalers/approval plans. The source journal is listed as the "series" to assist the prevention of duplicate purchasing in the same manner utilized for books-in-series.
- to facilitate user/access services all indexing/abstracting services are encouraged to utilize the co-indexing entry note indicated at the bottom of the first page of each article/chapter/contribution.
- this is intended to assist a library user of any reference tool (whether print, electronic, online, or CD-ROM) to locate the monographic version if the library has purchased this version but not a subscription to the source journal.
- individual articles/chapters in any Haworth publication are also available through the Haworth Document Delivery Service (HDDS).

Current Research on Bisexuality

CONTENTS

ABOUT THE EDITOR

Ronald C. Fox, PhD, is a San Francisco-based researcher, author, educator, and psychotherapist. He conducted the first large-scale study of bisexual identity development and has contributed several chapters on bisexuality and bisexual issues to LGBT psychology books. He has presented workshops on sexual diversity and bisexual issues at professional conferences, graduate schools, and community agencies, as well as at U.S. and international conferences on bisexuality. Dr. Fox was a member of the Task Force that wrote the recently adopted American Psychological Association Guidelines for Psychotherapy with LGB Clients. He is Co-Chair of the Committee on Bisexual Issues in Psychology of the APA Division 44 (Society for the Psychological Study of LGB Issues).

About the Contributors

Mary Bradford, PhD, is a clinical psychologist in private practice in Berkeley, California, and is a faculty member of the Pacific Center for Human Growth in Berkeley and the Women's Therapy Center in El Cerrito.

Amity Pierce Buxton, PhD, is a researcher, educator, and author. Her writings include the book *The Other Side of the Closet: The Coming-Out Crisis for Straight Spouses and Families*, as well as the articles "The Best Interest of Children of Gay and Lesbian Parents," in *The Scientific Basis of Child Custody Decision*, and "Writing Our Own Script" in *Bisexuality in the Lives of Men: Facts and Fictions*. Executive Director of the international Straight Spouse Network, she counsels spouses in mixed-orientation marriages and lectures across the country and abroad. She has served on the board of the Family Pride Coalition and has led a support group in the San Francisco Bay Area for spouses for the past twelve years.

J. Fuji Collins, PhD, is a Core Faculty Member and Associate Dean for the School of Psychology at Fielding Graduate Institute in Santa Barbara, California. He has conducted research and clinical work in the area of biracial and bisexual identity.

Mary Crawford, PhD, is Professor of Psychology and former director of the Women's Studies Program at the University of Connecticut. She is a consulting editor for *Psychology of Women Quarterly* and *Sex Roles*, the U.S. editor of *Feminism and Psychology*, and a Fellow of both the American Psychological Association and the American Psychological Society. Crawford is the author of numerous research articles on gender as well as author or editor of eight books, including *Gender and Thought: Psychological Perspectives* (1989); *Talking Difference: On Gender and Language* (1995); *Gender Differences in Human Cognition* (1997); *Coming Into Her Own: Educational Success in*

Girls and Women (1999); *Innovative Methods for Feminist Psychological Research* (1999) and *Women and Gender: A Feminist Psychology* (4th ed., in press).

M. Paz Galupo, PhD, is Associate Professor of Psychology at Towson University. Her article on friendships across sexual orientations combines her interests in cross-category friendships, feminist psychology, and sexual orientation identity.

Robin Hoburg, PhD, received her doctorate in clinical psychology and is a Research Associate in the Department of Psychology at the University of Connecticut. Her research focuses on evaluation of mental health and addiction services, and issues related to sexual orientation and nontraditional gender expression, sexual identity development, multicultural counseling, and community psychology.

Tania Israel, PhD, is Assistant Professor in the Counseling, Clinical, and School Psychology Program at the University of California, Santa Barbara. Her professional interests include gender issues, feminist psychology, sexuality education and counseling, and diversity training. Her current research focuses on the development and assessment of counselor competence with lesbian, gay, bisexual, and transgender clients.

Julie Konik, PhD (cand.), is a graduate student in the Psychology and Women's Studies joint doctoral program at the University of Michigan. Her research interests include the creation and maintenance of social identities as well as the relationships among social identities, psychological and occupational well-being, and social networks. She is especially interested in studying sexual minorities and members of other social minority groups.

Kirsten McLean, PhD, is Lecturer in Sociology in the School of Political and Social Inquiry, Monash University, Australia. She teaches about gender and sexuality issues, and is currently completing research on the lives of bisexual men and women in Australia.

Jonathan J. Mohr, PhD, is Assistant Professor in the Department of Psychology at Loyola College in Maryland. He received his doctorate in counseling psychology from the University of Maryland, College Park, in 2001. His current research is focused on sexual orientation identity and attitudes, factors relevant to counseling process, and the intersection of these two areas.

Emily H. Page, PsyD, is a psychotherapist in private practice in the Boston area and a clinician at the Center for Family Development in Beverly, Massachusetts. She is Co-Chair of the Committee on Bisexual Issues in Psychology of the Society for the Psychological Study of Lesbian, Gay and Bisexual Issues (Division 44) of the American Psychological Association. She has participated in panels on recent research in bisexuality and on psychotherapy with bisexual clients in the Boston area, at annual conventions of the American Psychological Association, the Association of Women in Psychology, and at several U.S. and international conferences on bisexuality.

Carin A. Sailer, BA, received her bachelor's degree in psychology from Towson State University. She lives in Towson, Maryland, with her partner and their daughter.

Sarah Causey St. John, BS, received her bachelor's degree in psychology from Towson State University. She is the Site Coordinator for the Talent Search Program at Fort Lewis College in Durango, Colorado.

Michelle Williams, PhD, received her doctorate in clinical psychology and is Associate Professor in the Department of Psychology at the University of Connecticut. She is the Director of Clinical Training and holds a joint appointment with the Institute of African American Studies. Her research interests include ethnic and racial identity development, multicultural psychology, and issues related to domestic violence and sexual aggression.

Dan Clurman is a communications consultant in the S.F. Bay Area and teaches psychology at Golden Gate University. He is the author of *Floating Upstream,* a book of poetry. His forthcoming book of cartoons, *Suppose You Went to Heaven,* will soon be published.

Wayne Bryant is the author of *Bisexual Characters in Film: From Anais to Zee,* available from Harrington Park Press. He is the co-founder of Biversity Boston, President Emeritus of the Bisexual Resource Center and film editor for the Bisexual Recource Guide.

Larry W. Peterson is Professor of Music at the University of Delaware. His publications include an analysis of the Surrealist poetry of composer Olivier Messiaen, a study of the laments in Handel's operas and oratorios, and numerous articles on using technology to teach music. His multimedia work has won four national awards and is currently featured on a CD-ROM, *Technology Tools for Today's Campuses,* funded by Microsoft. He founded three listservs and managed a fourth devoted either to music instructions or to married bisexual/gay men.

Introduction

Ronald C. Fox

http://www.haworthpress.com/web/JB
© 2004 by The Haworth Press, Inc. All rights reserved.
Digital Object Identifier: 10.1300/J159v04n01_01

[Haworth co-indexing entry note]: "Introduction." Fox, Ronald C. Co-published simultaneously in *Journal of Bisexuality* (Harrington Park Press, an imprint of The Haworth Press, Inc.) Vol. 4, Nos. 1/2, 2004, pp. 1-6; and: *Current Research on Bisexuality* (ed: Ronald C. Fox) Harrington Park Press, an imprint of The Haworth Press, Inc., 2004, pp. 1-6. Single or multiple copies of this article are available for a fee from The Haworth Document Delivery Service [1-800-HAWORTH, 9:00 a.m. - 5:00 p.m. (EST). E-mail address: docdelivery@haworthpress.com].

The continued pursuit and publication of research on bisexuality in this first decade of the twenty-first century has grown out of several previous waves of theory and research on homosexuality and bisexuality. The concept of bisexuality, introduced into classical psychoanalytic theory in the 1890s and early 1900s, was used as a way of understanding evolutionary theory, developmental aspects of human sexuality, the balance of masculinity and femininity in the individual, and adult homosexuality (Angelides, 2001; Fox, 1996). From the 1940s through the early 1970s, post-Freudians rejected the bisexuality as a useful theoretical concept or descriptive term and instead viewed homosexuality and bisexuality as examples of individual and family psychopathology and arrested psycho-sexual development (Bieber et al., 1962; Rado, 1940; Socarides, 1978).

The first major more recent contribution to a more balanced and accurate understanding of homosexuality and bisexuality came about through the shift in attitudes and advocacy regarding homosexuality in society and through the development of more visible and vocal lesbian and gay communities, which supported and led to the declassification of homosexuality as a mental illness by the American Psychiatric Association in the 1970s (Bayer, 1981). This allowed for the emergence in the late 1970s and the 1980s of affirmative theory, research, and personal narratives, by and about the lived experiences of lesbians and gay men (Cass, 1979; Troiden, 1988).

The second major contribution to a greater understanding of bisexuality was the gradual shift in the 1980s away from a dichotomous view of sexual orientation. This movement toward a more open understanding of sexuality and sexual orientation was initiated by the work of Kinsey and his associates (Kinsey, Pomeroy, & Martin, 1948; Kinsey, Pomeroy, Martin, & Gebhard, 1952) and further encouraged by the development in the 1980s of more accurate conceptualizations of sexuality (Shively & DeCecco, 1977; Shively, Jones, & DeCecco, 1983, 1984; Storms, 1980) and the construction of a multidimensional model of sexual orientation and sexual identity, the Klein Sexual Orientation Grid (KSOG), that viewed sexuality along a continuum and as a combination of dimensions that may remain constant or may change over time, and that includes not only sexual attractions, fantasies, and behavior, but emotional attraction, lifestyle, and significantly self-identification as well (Klein, Sepekoff, & Wolf, 1985). In addition, there emerged in the 1980s and 1990s, more visible, vocal, and vibrant bisexual communities and community leaders. These parallel developments served to support and encourage the emergence of an affirmative and more balanced social science literature that includes information and input from theory, research, and personal narratives by and about bisexual women and bisexual men (Firestein, 1996; Fox, 1996).

Initially, research on bisexuality focused on the similarities and differences between bisexual identities and lesbian and gay identities as well as the sexual attractions and relationships of bisexual women and bisexual men. Findings from this research countered prevailing stereotypes about bisexuality and served to validate bisexuality as a distinct sexual orientation and identity that could be the legitimate subject of serious empirical research in its own right (Fox, 1996). The research that followed broadened in focus, including studies on bisexual youth, bisexuality in communities of color, bisexuality in cross-cultural perspective, and bisexuality and HIV/AIDS and more recently research on attitudes toward bisexuals and counseling and psychotherapy with bisexual women and bisexual men.

The contributions to this volume include research findings on bisexual identity development, bisexuality in college students, bisexual women's friendships with heterosexual and lesbian women, bisexual married women and their spouses, monogamy and polyamory in relationships of Australian bisexual women and men, and bisexual clients' experiences of mental health services. Also included are reviews of the literature regarding the experiences of bisexual people of color, attitudes toward bisexual women and bisexual men, and a comprehensive bibliography on bisexuality. All these contributions provide further understanding of bisexual peoples' life experiences.

Mary Bradford shares findings from her qualitative study of bisexual identity formation in "The Bisexual Experience: Living in a Dichotomous Culture." She describes the ways in which the twenty bisexual women and men that she interviewed experience their bisexuality, how their bisexual identities developed, and how they found and established a sense of community. The experiences of the participants in this study were contrary to the popular misconception of bisexual identity as a temporary phenomenon and led Bradford to propose an alternative, affirmative model of bisexual identity development.

In "Bisexuality Among Self-Identified Heterosexual College Students," Robin Hoburg, Julie Konik, Michelle Williams, and Mary Crawford describe a wide range of same- and other-sex feelings and an unexpectedly large proportion of same-sex feelings in two cohorts of self-identified heterosexual students. On the basis of their findings, the authors conclude that there is a significant variability in sexual attractions and sexual orientation labels in this population, which suggests the need for further study of the sexual attractions and relationships of young adults and college students.

In "Friendships Across Sexual Orientation: Experiences of Bisexual Women in Early Adulthood," Paz Galupo, Carin Sailer, and Sarah St. John examine the ways in which the bisexual identity of one of the members of a bisexual-lesbian or bisexual-heterosexual friendship pair affects the friendship relationship. Their findings point out the complexities involved in cross-orientation friendships and relationships and suggest another rich area for further research.

Amity Buxton, in "Works in Progress: How Mixed-Orientation Couples Maintain Their Marriages After the Wives Come Out" reports findings on her research on the experiences of bisexual and lesbian married women and their spouses. As in her prior research on men's mixed-orientation marriages (Buxton, 2001), she describes the strategies that her study participants have found most effective in maintaining their marriages.

In "Negotiating (Non)Monogamy: Bisexuality and Intimate Relationships," Kirsten McLean reports findings of her research with bisexual women and men in Australia. She provides an in-depth look at the experiences of monogamy and nonmonogamy in the relationships of her study participants and the communication and negotiation processes involved in defining and maintain both monogamous and polyamorous relationships.

Fuji Collins, in "The Intersection of Race and Bisexuality: A Critical Overview of the Literature and Past, Present, and Future Directions of the 'Borderlands,'" contributes a comprehensive overview of the literature on bisexuality, race, and ethnicity, providing insight and understanding of the multiple minority experiences of bisexual people of color in the United States.

In "Attitudes Toward Bisexual Women and Men: Current Research, Future Directions," Tania Israel and Jonathan Mohr provide a comprehensive review of the psychological literature on attitudes toward bisexual people. The authors clarify the key concepts in this area, looking at both theory and research, as well as describing those research findings that help us to understand the complexities of nonbisexuals' views of bisexual women and bisexual men.

Emily Page, in "Mental Health Services Experiences of Bisexual Women and Bisexual Men: An Empirical Study," shares findings from her research on the experiences of bisexual women and bisexual men as consumers of mental health services. She looks both at the factors involved in people seeking out mental health services, including the issues that bisexual people typically bring to psychotherapy. Her findings also highlight consumers' evaluations of the degree to which practitioners are aware and knowledgeable about bisexuality and bisexual issues, examples of affirmative and discriminatory practice on the part of providers, and consumers' suggestions for mental health providers in terms of providing affirmative and helpful mental health services.

In "Bisexuality: A Reader's Guide to the Social Science Literature," Ron Fox provides an overview of the social science literature on bisexuality in the form of a comprehensive reading list that includes books, journal articles, book chapters, theses, and dissertations. These materials provide a wealth of information on the life experiences of bisexual people from psychological, sociological, anthropological, and epidemiological points of view, as well as from personal, feminist, spiritual, queer theory, political, and bisexual community perspectives as well.

Taken together, the research findings, literature reviews, and reading list in this volume contribute further to our understanding of bisexuality. These resources can also serve as a basis for further research and education about bisexuality in the greater context of ongoing research, education, and advocacy regarding the concerns and life experiences of LGBTQI people.

REFERENCES

Angelides, S. (2001). *A History of Bisexuality*. Chicago: University of Chicago Press.

Bayer, R. (1981). *Homosexuality and American psychiatry: The politics of diagnosis*. New York: Basic Books.

Bieber, I., Dain, H. J., Dince, P. R., Drellich, M. G., Grand, H. G., Gundlach, R. H. et al. (1962). *Homosexuality: A psychoanalytical study*. New York: Vintage Books.

Buxton, A. P. (2001). Writing our own script: How bisexual men and their heterosexual wives maintain their marriages after disclosure. *Journal of Bisexuality, 1*(2/3), 155-189.

Cass, V. C. (1979). Homosexual identity formation: A theoretical model. *Journal of Homosexuality, 4*(3), 219-235.

Firestein, B. A. (1996). Bisexuality as paradigm shift: Transforming our disciplines. In B. A. Firestein (Ed.), *Bisexuality: The psychology and politics of an invisible minority* (pp. 263-291). Newbury Park, CA: Sage.

Fox, R. C. (1996). Bisexuality in perspective: A review of theory and research. In B. A. Firestein (Ed.), *Bisexuality: The psychology and politics of an invisible minority* (pp. 3-50). Thousand Oaks, CA: Sage.

Kinsey, A. C., Pomeroy, W. B., & Martin, C. E. (1948). *Sexual behavior in the human male*. Philadelphia: W. B. Saunders.

Kinsey, A. C., Pomeroy, W. B., Martin, C. E., & Gebhard, P. H. (1953). *Sexual behavior in the human female*. Philadelphia, PA: W. B. Saunders.

Klein, F., Sepekoff, B., & Wolf, T. J. (1985). Sexual orientation: A multi-variable dynamic process. *Journal of Homosexuality, 11*(1/2), 35-49.

Rado, S. (1940). A critical examination of the concept of bisexuality. *Psychosomatic Medicine, II*(4), 459-467.

Shively, M. G., & De Cecco, J. P. (1977). Components of sexual identity. *Journal of Homosexuality, 3*(1), 41-48.

Shively, M. G., Jones, C., & DeCecco, J. P. (1983/1984). Research on sexual orientation: Definitions and methods. *Journal of Homosexuality, 9*(2/3), 127-136.

Socarides, C. W. (1978). *Homosexuality*. New York: Jason Aronson.

Storms, M. D. (1980). Theories of sexual orientation. *Journal of Personality and Social Psychology, 38*(5), 783-792.

Sulloway, F. J. (1979). *Freud, biologist of the mind: Beyond the psychoanalytic legend*. New York: Basic Books.

Troiden, R. R. (1988). *Gay and lesbian identity: A sociological analysis*. Dix Hills, NY: General Hall.

The Bisexual Experience: Living in a Dichotomous Culture

Mary Bradford

http://www.haworthpress.com/web/JB
© 2004 by The Haworth Press, Inc. All rights reserved.
Digital Object Identifier: 10.1300/J159v04n01_02

[Haworth co-indexing entry note]: "The Bisexual Experience: Living in a Dichotomous Culture."
Bradform, Mary. Co-published simultaneously in *Journal of Bisexuality* (Harrington Park Press, an imprint
of The Haworth Press, Inc.) Vol. 4, Nos. 1/2, 2004, pp. 7-23; and: *Current Research on Bisexuality* (ed: Ronald C. Fox) Harrington Park Press, an imprint of The Haworth Press, Inc., 2004, pp. 7-23. Single or multiple
copies of this article are available for a fee from The Haworth Document Delivery Service
[1-800-HAWORTH, 9:00 a.m. - 5:00 p.m. (EST). E-mail address: docdelivery@haworthpress.com].

SUMMARY. This study examined how bisexually-identified individuals experience cultural attitudes toward bisexuality, how they establish a sense of community for themselves, and how their experience has affected their self-concept. Twenty self-identified bisexual women and men were interviewed for a descriptive study. The results indicate that cultural attitudes toward bisexuality affect sexual identity development, self-definition, visibility, and relationships. Three steps to establishing a sense of community included: perception of outsider status, location of bisexual individuals and community, and formation of new community. The effects on self-concept of forming and maintaining bisexual identity included: enhanced self-reliance, openness, and enrichment. Both gender and cultural minority status had an impact on the experience of bisexuality. On the basis of the findings, the author proposes a theory of bisexual identity development which includes the following stages: questioning reality, inventing the identity, maintaining the identity, and transforming adversity. *[Article copies available for a fee from The Haworth Document Delivery Service: 1-800-HAWORTH. E-mail address: <docdelivery@haworthpress.com> Website: <http://www.HaworthPress.com> © 2004 by The Haworth Press, Inc. All rights reserved.]*

KEYWORDS. Bisexuality, bisexual identity, sexual orientation, sexual identity, identity development

Dichotomies of exclusive hierarchical gender and sexual categories have long been generally accepted in our society. Like the division of gender, sexual orientation classifications have to do with separation and power. They also entail homophobia, which derives from erotophobia and sexism (Pharr, 1988; Weinberg & Williams, 1974). This kind of dichotomization assumes that people all fit into exclusive and separate categories. It allows no room for the variations, mixtures, and fluctuations that actually occur. The binary categorization of sexuality excludes the possibility of flexible, fluid sexuality because it associates bisexuality with conflict and confusion (Paul, 1985). The experience of bisexual people must be considered within the context of this dichotomy of sexuality, as well as in the atmosphere of negative cultural attitudes toward same-sex relationships.

BACKGROUND

Psychology has traditionally upheld the dichotomous view of sexual orientation. Until recently, heterosexuality has been viewed as the standard of nor-

mal functioning, with homosexuality seen as deviant behavior to be examined
and analyzed. The theoretical bases for approaching sexuality have reflected
this dichotomization and polarization. Specifically, the essentialist/social constructionist debate has dominated the field, with its focus on the origins and
development of sexual orientation and sexual identity. Biologically-oriented
psychological studies of sexual orientation (Dorner et al., 1975; Money, 1980)
considered homosexuality abnormal, and concentrated on the search for cause
and cure. Recently, influenced by the gay and lesbian political movement, the
focus has shifted from pathologizing homosexuality to investigating it as a
cultural phenomenon (Herek, 1984; Hopcke, 1989). While this research has
contributed to our knowledge of homosexuality, it has not enhanced our
knowledge of bisexuality. The binary categorization that omitted bisexuality
from consideration resulted in deficiencies in the findings of research on homosexuality as well as a lack of information on the full range of sexual behavior in relationships (Burr, 1993; MacDonald, 1981; Tripp, 1987; Weinberg &
Williams, 1974).

Over 45 years ago, the Kinsey studies (Kinsey, Pomeroy, & Martin, 1948;
Kinsey, Pomeroy, Martin, & Gebhard, 1953) provided information on the
broad range of sexual behaviors, not restricted to exclusive heterosexuality or
homosexuality. In 1985, Klein, Sepekoff, and Wolf developed the Klein Sexual Orientation Grid (KSOG), representing a multidimentional model of sexuality which further delineated the elements of sexuality by considering not
only behavior but attractions and lifestyle as well, and incorporating the important element of time, to depict the flexibility and complexity of sexuality.
This idea of a continuum of sexuality is now being explored in the literature,
with presentations of a more complex approach to the varieties of human sexual behavior and identity (Paul, 1985) and studies that reveal numerous variations in sexual lifestyles (Little, 1989).

Inspired by the gay/lesbian movement, many bisexual people have begun
to assert their distinct identity, and empirical research has emerged studying
bisexual women and men as such and tracing bisexual identity development.
The findings of this research have established that: bisexual people exist in
significant numbers (Klein, 1993; Zinik, 1985); they are a heterogeneous population with a wide variety of lifestyles (Galland, 1975; Harris, 1977); they
generally do not correspond with stereotypes (Ochs & Deihl, 1992); they demonstrate normal psychological adjustment (Harwell, 1976; Zinik, 1984); they
suffer discrimination from both heterosexual culture and within gay and lesbian communities (Rust, 1995; Rust-Rodriguez, 1989); and their identity development is similar to, though more complex and less linear than, gay and
lesbian identity development (Coleman, 1987; Fox, 1996; Rust, 1992; Shively
& De Cecco, 1977).

Research on bisexuality has provided descriptive data on personality characteristics, behavior, and identity development of bisexual people and has
documented the climate of prejudice they face (Blumstein & Schwartz, 1976a,

1976b, 1977; Fox, 1995; Galland, 1975; Rust-Rodriguez, 1989). Anecdotal reports have contributed experiential information on the lives and thoughts of bisexual women and men (Falk, 1975; Geller, 1990; Hutchins & Kaahumanu, 1991; Kohn & Matusow, 1980; Weise, 1992). However, we have as yet only limited qualitative research on the lived experience of self-identified bisexual women and men. George's study (1993) included information on the experience of others' responses to self-disclosure and on bisexual lifestyle for women in Great Britain. Little (1989), while focusing on defining female bisexuality, also provided data on community affiliation. Rust-Rodriguez (1989) and Rust (1995) revealed bisexual women's experience in regard to the lesbian community. Weinberg and Williams (1974) focused on lifestyle of bisexual men within the gay male culture. Weinberg, Williams, and Pryor (1994) focused on the experiences of bisexual women and men of the San Francisco bisexual community in the 1980s. We can now build on these studies and move into the next phase of research on bisexuality by directly addressing women's and men's experience of living in this culture as a part of an "invisible" minority.

This research sought to discover how bisexual people experience their identities once their identities are established, how they cope with stigma, form communities, and see themselves. It drew on feminist gender theory (which challenges the polarization of genders) and looked to deconstruction to provide theory for the breakdown of binary oppositions and the challenge to hierarchies assigned to them.

RESEARCH DESIGN

Research Questions

Three questions were considered in this study: (1) How do bisexually-identified individuals experience *cultural attitudes* toward bisexuality? That is to say, what is it like to live with this dichotomy and the invisibility that it entails? (2) How do they establish a sense of *community* for themselves, given the fact that they may not feel fully a part of either the dominant heterosexual community or the gay/lesbian subculture? (3) How has their experience affected their *view of themselves*? In other words, how do they internalize their experience as bisexual people and transform it into self-concept?

Research Methods

Twenty self-identified bisexual individuals (10 each women and men, aged 22 to 54) were selected and interviewed for a descriptive study based on the concepts of *naturalistic inquiry* (Lincoln & Guba, 1985). Participants who had established bisexual identities were chosen, and not those who might display bisexual attractions or behavior without identifying as such or those in process of grappling with self-definition. The study sought to learn from self-identified bisexual people what their experiences were of living with this identity.

The research method was qualitative, using open-ended-question interviews in an effort to obtain the rich subjective experience of a marginalized population. The questions were developed with the help of research assistants and pilot tested. A content/thematic approach was used to analyze the data (Patton, 1990). The participants collaborated in evaluating the findings by reviewing the written summary of findings and the researcher's analysis, and by providing feedback about the interpretations and conclusions.

DESCRIPTION OF THE SAMPLE

The participants live in 14 different cities and 7 different counties of the San Francisco Bay Area. The female participants range in age from 26 to 54, the males from 22 to 50. Their self-described racial/ethnic/cultural identities include Asian/Pacific Islander, African American, Latino, Bi-racial (Native American/Jewish, Native American/Caucasian), Jewish, and Euro-American (the majority). Levels of education range from high school to PhD. Length of time identified as bisexual ranges from 6 months to 24 years, the average being 9 years.

The sample represented a broad spectrum of relationship status, including single and celibate, "looking," or actively dating; legally married to other-sex partners and monogamous, in open marriages, in dual committed relationships, or separated; in nonmarital, committed, monogamous relationships with same-sex or with other-sex partners; and in nonmarital, committed, non-monogamous relationships that are open or dual.

FINDINGS

The findings will be described in terms of the three research questions: how cultural attitudes toward bisexuality affected participants, how participants established community, and how participants' experience as bisexual people affected their self-concept.

Ways Cultural Attitudes Affected Participants

Cultural attitudes affected the participants' sexual identity development, their self-definition, their ability to be visible, and their relationships.

Sexual identity development. When most participants were first aware of their attractions to both women and men (usually when quite young), they discounted one or the other and described being fraught with self-doubts and inability to make sense of their attractions. One participant reflected: "The difficulty is just coming to the realization that both feelings are very real, that they can co-exist, that you don't have to chose." Another man expressed it this way:

> I went through a really difficult time mentally because while, intellectually, I could say, "maybe I'm attracted to both," from a practical point of view it seemed like I should be one or the other. That's sort of how society divides it, but it seemed very difficult to me at the time to be able to think about just one or the other.

Many participants attributed the length of time coming to an acknowledgement of their bisexuality and the confusion along the way to the lack of models and to derogatory associations with the term "bisexual." One man remembered his difficulty with finding a congruent label:

> I didn't feel that I could consider myself gay because I had feelings and attractions to women, and by definition, that didn't fit being gay. At the same time, I was sexually involved with men, and that didn't fit the definition of heterosexual. I saw myself as neither one of those, but I didn't have a word to call where I was, and at the time, I didn't have any information about other people who might be identifying where I was.

One woman recalled having been influenced by a polarized view of sexual orientation:

> I associated [bisexuality] with people who were involved with men and women at the same time—some of the myths that I had heard and stereotypes. That didn't fit me. I tend to get involved with one person at a time. I was so much focused on this kind of dichotomous view: I can be gay or straight; those are my options. And neither of them fit.

Self-definition. Self-definition was an important issue for these participants. The discovery of a term to depict their identity was a pivotal experience in their development. They described confusion before hearing the word "bisexual" or associating themselves with it, and relief in finding the term and recognizing themselves in it. One woman expressed the confusion: "We really had no words for that experience or that concept. I think that was a big obstacle to us figuring out what was going on with us." Another remembered the relief at arriving at a sexual identity:

> It was truly a great relief to finally feel like I had an identity that I could call my own. It was wonderful. It felt like there was this internal struggle

that I'd been going through for so long, and I finally felt some relief and comfort. I had a name that fits me, which it felt I had been searching for so long.

Participants were asked the definition of "bisexual" that they had come to and gave many different answers. Most definitions were based on attractions to both women and men, such as this man's: "It means the capacity for same-gender or other-gender love, relationships, and sex." One woman put it this way:

> For me being bisexual means that sometimes I'm attracted to women; sometimes I'm attracted to men—that it doesn't seem to have to do with the person's gender as much as it has to do with the person themselves that I'm attracted to.

The broadest agreement was the concurrence that neither "heterosexual" nor "homosexual" (or straight or gay/lesbian) fit them. As one participant said, "Bisexuality says more about what you're not than what you are."

Visibility. The participants described being constantly met with assumptions that they were straight or lesbian or gay based on their partners' gender, so that their bisexuality was never seen unless they made a point of talking about it. One woman commented, "In the culture at large, since I'm mostly with [my husband] or by myself, I feel like people assume I'm straight." Another described her sense of invisibility as a bisexual woman:

> A lot of people have only known me since I met [my girlfriend] and so their belief is that I'm a lesbian. And the only time they'll ever find out otherwise is if they get in a conversation with me about it.

Another recalled her frustration in regard to others' conjectures about her sexual identity:

> What was frustrating was the only way a bisexual could be identified by the rest of the world as bisexual is if they were having a relationship with an hermaphrodite or something. If I was in a relationship with a man, everybody assumed I was straight. If I was in a relationship with a woman, everybody assumed I was a lesbian.

They all saw the absence of other visible bisexual people as a factor in their own ability to be visible as bisexual. For instance, one man said, "You don't really hear of any bisexuals running for office. You hear about gays running for office. You hear about gays in the military. But you don't hear about bisexuals."

As a result of this lack of visibility, many participants felt isolated. They described experiencing aloneness, without acknowledgement or support for their identity by community, friends, family, or, sometimes, even relational partners. Contributing to and reinforcing this invisibility is biphobia, a fear of and discomfort with bisexuality. Many statements were similar to this summation: "My experience is that most people that I've come in contact with, whether they're straight or gay, find bisexuality very disturbing, very distressing. They're very uncomfortable with it." A woman concluded: "Bisexuality means fear of rejection."

This experience with biphobia results in great caution regarding self-disclosure. When they did come out, most had experienced invalidation and denial of their existence as bisexual. Some were told they were "only going through a phase" or "bisexuality doesn't exist." One man who had felt his bisexuality was invalidated by gay men said, "If I tell my gay friends that I'm bi, they immediately say, 'Well, you just haven't figured it out yet,' or 'You want to hang on to the straight world,' or 'You're not ready to admit that you're gay.'"

Many of the women had experienced rejection from the lesbian community. One described being met with anger for having "heterosexual privilege":

> I was talking to some women who are lesbians and they told me that they thought that my being bisexual meant that I was hiding behind heterosexual privilege and that I was really a lesbian and that I just didn't want to come out with it and that they wouldn't ever trust someone who was a bisexual because I could give them a disease or I might go back to men again.

As one man summed it up: "Bi's are too straight for the gay community and they're too queer for the straight community."

Relationships. Participants described many ways in which their relationships were affected by cultural attitudes toward bisexuality. Some told of problems finding potential partners due to being bisexual (sometimes because of AIDS anxiety), having experienced homophobia from straight people, and biphobia from lesbian and gay people. The participants who chose non-monogamous relationships (25%) had an especially difficult time with the cultural bias against non-monogamy, which was described as an issue even more difficult and taboo than bisexuality. These people talked of both the problems of dealing with the world outside their relationships and the potential for fulfillment within them:

> I felt like I was the happiest woman in the world. I have this wonderful relationship with a beautiful woman, and I have this wonderful relationship with this beautiful man, and that's great. [However] it's very stressful when being true to yourself means challenging the culture.

They described suffering losses of friends and family due to their choice of nontraditional relationships and spoke of the constant stress of social prejudice, misunderstanding, and invalidation.

Establishing Community

Three steps in establishing a sense of community were illustrated: perception of outsider status, location of bisexual individuals and community, and formation of new community.

Perception of outsider status. The first experience for all the participants was their sense of being outsiders, of not really fitting into either the mainstream heterosexual culture or in the lesbian/gay subculture. One woman illustrated her sense of alienation this way:

> One day I had a gay man, who was talking about whether or not I, as a bisexual, had the right to speak at a gay meeting, say, "You're only a second class citizen here." And then, that same day, I was at a straight bar listening to them tell really horrifying gay jokes. No matter which side I went to, it didn't really feel comfortable.

Participants described the loneliness of not having a community at this stage and stressed the importance of having people to talk to who have shared similar experiences. As one man said:

> It's one thing to know in your mind you're bisexual. The part that is more important is being able to talk about it. Talking about it or having people to talk to about it and having kind of similar experiences is very important.

Location of others. The next step was locating other bisexual individuals and community. When this occurred, people described experiencing relief, a sense of kinship, validation, and support. One man spoke of the relief of "talking with someone who knows what I'm talking about," and one woman remembered that, "for the first time it felt like people really understood." Another woman described her experience of knowing other bisexual people: "I felt part of a group. I loved talking about people's experiences of bisexuality, their coming out, their discovery. It's been very rich." One man said, "It's been wonderful to go out and find that there are other people like me and it's okay . . . It's like finding a home." Another concluded, "It's easier to stand up when you're standing together."

Formation of new community. Finally, people moved toward forming their own communities. Some coped with the lack of given community by becoming active in forming bisexual community. Speaking of his involvement, a man said:

> I came out and started seeking other bisexuals and bisexual community and then I got pulled into the organizing, and I realized that there was a tremendous lack of community that I had. The more I tapped into it, the

hungrier I got, and the more I realized that what I wanted to do is build bi community.

Several of these participants had become bisexual activists, committed to acting as role models to make the way easier for others. One man related his reason for publicly revealing his bisexuality: "For me, it was really important because I recall that when I first started groping around for my identity, I wasn't seeing any people who identified as bisexual." Another spoke of how his own struggle with bisexual identity formation motivated his commitment to act:

> How horribly difficult it is in our culture because of not only homophobia, but the lack of acceptance of bisexual identity as a valid identity. I try not to dwell on those aspects, and I try to put my energies into the political community to deal with it.

Most participants had formed a sense of personal community for themselves, made up of an integration of different friends and colleagues. One woman described a sense of being bicultural:

> In one sense I feel like I belong almost anywhere, with heterosexuals, with gays, lesbians, with bisexuals. I can be comfortable anywhere. In another sense, it's like, well, it has to be a community that's open, that's inclusive and not exclusive, and that goes not just for sexual identity, but gender, age, ethnicity. I'm finding that I really ideally prefer communities that are very inclusive of a variety of identities and lifestyles.

One participant talked about still lacking a sense of community:

> I haven't ever had a strong sense of community anywhere. Whatever group I'm in, I always feel like there's that part of me there, and then there's this whole other part of me that's not seen. That's my consistent experience in community. I always feel like there's a part of me that fits and there's a big part of me that doesn't fit.

Effects on Self-Concept

The effects on self-concept of living with a bisexual identity were described in terms of self-reliance, openness, and enrichment.

Self-reliance. Nearly every participant related having gained strength, self-acceptance, and independence from the experience of coming to terms with a bisexual identity in this culture, so that they were more self-reliant than they might have otherwise been. One participant described the results of coming to terms with a bisexual identity this way: "I feel a little stronger, a little

more confident, and comfortable with who I am and all the parts of myself."
Another spoke of how having to stand alone had been strengthening:

> I don't get support from the main culture. I don't get that much support
> from the gay or lesbian community, relatively. So it has to come from ei-
> ther my very small community or myself. I think that one consequence
> of that is a strengthening of my character.

Openness. Many also spoke of feeling more open to and tolerant of others'
differences, more empathetic and compassionate towards others who are oppressed. As one participant said: "This experience has made me more open to
all peoples' sexuality and sexual orientation." Another, who emphasized that
his experience as a bisexual man had "broadened my horizons in terms of
things way beyond sexuality," explained by saying: "I know what it's like to
be ridiculed, because I'm not the most masculine, butch guy, and I got a lot of
ridicule. I think that made me empathetic, sympathetic, compassionate for
other people who were oppressed."

Enrichment. Nearly all described being personally enriched through their
struggles with coming to their sexual identity and affirming their bisexuality.
One participant claimed, "There is something so liberating about being bisexual." A woman spoke of claiming her bisexual identity as realizing her potential:

> Part of what's been so amazing to me about this whole experience is how
> it's opened my spirit. It's kind of like I've always known that there was
> some part of me sexually that wasn't being accessed. I could always feel
> that and I never knew why I felt blocked. Now I feel like I'm flowering.

Another spoke of her experience of bisexuality this way: "I feel really grateful
for it. I feel like I wouldn't have it any other way. Even though there's a way it
has put me on the outside. I feel so enriched by it."

Many talked of feeling that all their relationships were deepened by their
ability to love others in ways that went beyond gender. One woman said her
ability to relate intimately to both women and men "brings a kind of excitement and aliveness to all my relationships." Another recounted her discovery
that she was able to love deeply regardless of gender: "It made me feel good to
realize that I could love people to such a depth and not care about what gender
they were."

An ongoing process. Despite the positive nature of their responses regarding the effects of the experience, participants reflected that their journeys had
been difficult and that this is an ongoing process. A man remarked that although he celebrates his increased open-mindedness and ability to relate
deeply, there is always a battle with shame and self-doubt and work to do on
integrating the parts of himself that the culture tends to split off: "I think it's a

life-long process, that I'm still combating internalized homophobia." A woman who explained that she feels "more self-accepting and expansive" in settings where different sexualities are accepted, said she is "still very affected by prejudice" in less tolerant situations. Another concluded, "I'm happy with how I've turned out so far. I don't think it was easy, but I think it was a good process to go through. And it's still a process, and it's never going to stop."

Effects of Gender and Minority Cultural Status

Both gender and cultural minority status had an impact on the experiences of bisexuality for these participants. The males in the sample were more strongly affected by gender role restrictions and homophobia and the threats of AIDS and violence. They tended to describe their development in words such as "fight" and "battle," whereas the women tended to use terms such as "flowering" and "wholeness" for their experience. The women in this sample revealed a strong need for affiliation with the lesbian community and reported rejection by lesbian women as their greatest difficulty.

Members of minority racial, ethnic, and class groups described multiple layers of oppression which tended to intensify their experience of their bisexual identity. A Latina participant described her culture's response: "They think that people are sick if you are either [homosexual or bisexual], that you need help. There is only one way to be right. It's pretty rigid. They're very cruel with [homosexuals and bisexuals]. They make fun of them." An Asian American participant commented: "When you step out and become gay or lesbian as an Asian, you really step out. You're really going out of culture." She described the Asian/Pacific Islander lesbian community as colluding with the dichotomous view of sexuality and rejecting bisexual women, who find themselves "on the outskirts" of their community as well as its sexual minority subculture. This sense of outsider status was echoed by an African American participant who related facing biphobia in his community, based on "fear and misinformation:" "Being bisexual is tied into the spread of AIDS in the community." Some considered themselves better prepared to deal with the oppression and marginalization accompanying sexual minority status because of their previous experiences of grappling with racism, anti-Semitism, or classism. These people were often inspired to be role models to ease the way for others like them.

DISCUSSION:
STAGE THEORY OF BISEXUALITY

These findings suggest that bisexual identity involves a process of: *questioning one's own reality, inventing one's own identity,* and *maintaining that identity* through encounters with cultural bias, denial, and personal invalidation, which carry constant threats of isolation and invisibility (Table 1).

In the first stage the denial, or invisibility, of bisexuality in the culture results in doubting one's own experience of both same-sex and other-sex attractions. Under pressure to self-define as either heterosexual or homosexual, bisexual people must come to trust their own reality, despite cultural influence, in order to transcend this stage.

Those who are able to affirm the reality of both their attractions must then structure their reality and give it meaning by creating definition for it. This involves rejection of those definitions offered by the culture that are based on current relationship status and partner gender. Developing identity, however, is only the beginning for bisexual people. Once they come to terms with who they are, they are met with the challenge of preserving their identity against continual lack of acknowledgment. This period, which may be long-lasting, is marked by marginalization by both the straight and lesbian/gay communities, and calls on bisexual individuals to establish their own sense of community. For those who achieve and affirm bisexual identity despite these challenges, the experience is character-strengthening. Some *transform the adversity* of their experience into social action by continuing to participate in the community at large as bisexually-identified individuals. Many of these have become leaders in the formation of bisexual community and role models for others. They exhibit a sense of personal satisfaction.

This stage model of bisexual identity formation is in contrast to that proposed by Weinberg, Williams, and Pryor (1994). Theirs is a trajectory beginning with heterosexual identity and proceeding through four stages: initial confusion, finding and applying the label, settling into the identity, and continued uncertainty. By contrast, one-third of the participants in this study originally identified as homosexual. While the first two stages of questioning reality and inventing identity are similar to the first two of Weinberg, Williams, and Pryor (initial confusion and finding and applying the label), there are differences in the later stages. In their model, the period of settling into the identity involved increased self-acceptance and less concern with the negative attitudes of others,

TABLE 1. Stage Theory of Bisexual Identity

Stage	Characteristic	Successful Outcome
Questioning reality	Struggle with doubt	Belief in own experience
Inventing identity	Search for meaning	Creation of own definition
Maintaining identity	Encounter with isolation and invisibility	Sense of own community and increased self-reliance
Transforming adversity	Social action	Personal satisfaction

but also some ongoing absence of closure or lack of commitment to bisexual identity. They described the final stage as continued uncertainty, marked by periods of doubt about sexual identity. In the model presented here, the stage of maintaining identity is exemplified by the establishment of community and affirmation of bisexual identity despite encounters with marginalization, resulting in increased self-reliance. The final stage of transforming the adversity involves social action and leadership. While these participants acknowledged ongoing struggles with cultural prejudice, they expressed certainty about their bisexual identity.

CONCLUSIONS

To affirm a bisexual identity requires transcending the culture. It takes valuing one's own experience, and it takes courage and independence. It requires facing a constant struggle with isolation, prejudice, and invalidation. It is also a positive opportunity for personal and social progress. Perhaps the greatest contribution of these participants is in understanding and assisting those who have not yet made the achievements they demonstrate in forming their identities. By taking an affirmative approach to bisexuality and making knowledge and models visible, we may be able to support and inspire them to risk self-fulfillment. The lessons learned from these participants can help us in creating a society that is tolerant of and celebrates individual differences.

REFERENCES

Blumstein, P. W., & Schwartz, P. (1976a). Bisexuality in men. *Urban Life, V*(3), 339-358.
Blumstein, P. W., & Schwartz, P. (1976b). Bisexuality in women. *Archives of Sexual Behavior, V*(2), 171-181.
Blumstein, P. W., & Schwartz, P. (1977). Bisexuality: Some social psychological issues. *Journal of Social Issues, 33*(2), 30-45.
Burr, C. (1993, March). Homosexuality and biology. *The Atlantic Monthly*, 47-65.
Coleman, E. (1987). Assessment of sexual orientation. *Journal of Homosexuality, 14*(1/2), 9-24.
Dorner, G., Rohde, W., Stahl, F., Krell, L., & Masius, W. G. (1995). A neuroendocrine predisposition for homosexuality in men. *Archives of Sexual Behavior, 4*, 1-8.
Falk, R. (1975). *Women loving: A journey toward becoming an independent woman.* New York: Random House.
Fox, R. C. (1995). Bisexual identities. In A. R. D'Augelli & C. J. Patterson (Eds.), *Lesbian, gay, and bisexual identities over the lifespan: Psychological perspectives* (pp. 48-86). New York: Oxford University Press.
Fox, R. C. (1996). Bisexuality in perspective: A review of theory and research. In B. A. Firestein (Ed.), *Bisexuality: The psychology and politics of an invisible minority* (pp. 3-50). Thousand Oaks, CA: Sage Publications.

Galland, V. R. (1975). Bisexual women (Doctoral dissertation, The California School of Professional Psychology). *Dissertation Abstracts International, 36*(6), 3037B.

Garber, M. (1995). *Vice versa: Bisexuality and the eroticism of everyday life.* New York: Simon & Schuster.

Geller, T. (Ed.). (1990). *Bisexuality: A reader and sourcebook.* Ojai, CA: Times Change Press.

George, S. (1993). *Women and bisexuality.* London: Scarlet Press.

Harris, D. A. I. (1977). Social-psychological characteristics of ambisexuals (Doctoral dissertation, The University of Tennessee). *Dissertation Abstracts International, 39*(2), 574A.

Harwell, J. L. (1976). Bisexuality: Persistent lifestyle or transitional state? (Doctoral dissertation, United States International University). *Dissertation Abstracts International, 37*(4), 2449A.

Herek, G. M. (1984). Beyond "homophobia": A social psychological perspective on attitudes toward lesbians and gay men. *Journal of Homosexuality, 10*(1/2), 1-21.

Hopcke, R. H. (1989). *Jung, Jungians, & homosexuality.* Boston: Shambhala.

Hutchins, L., & Kaahumanu, L. (Eds.). (1991). *Bi any other name: Bisexual people speak out.* Boston: Alyson Publications, Inc.

Kinsey, A. C., Pomeroy, W. B., & Martin, C. E. (1948). *Sexual behavior in the human male.* Philadelphia: W. B. Saunders Company.

Kinsey, A. C., Pomeroy, W. B., Martin, C. E., & Gebhard, P. H. (1953). *Sexual behavior in the human female.* Philadelphia: W. B. Saunders Company.

Klein, F. (1993). *The bisexual option: A concept of one hundred percent intimacy* (2nd ed.). New York: Harrington Park Press.

Klein, F., Sepekoff, B., & Wolf, T. J. (1985). Sexual orientation: A multi-variable dynamic process. *Journal of Homosexuality, 11*(1/2), 35-50.

Kohn, B., & Matusow, A. (1980). *Barry and Alice: Portrait of a bisexual marriage.* Englewood Cliffs, NJ: Prentice-Hall, Inc.

Lincoln, Y. S., & Guba, E. G. (1985). *Naturalistic inquiry.* Newbury Park, CA: Sage Publications.

Little, D. R. (1989). *Contemporary female bisexuality: A psychosocial phenomenon.* Unpublished doctoral dissertation, The Union for Experimenting Colleges and Universities, Cincinnati, Ohio.

MacDonald, A. P., Jr. (1981). Bisexuality: Some comments on research and theory. *Journal of Homosexuality, 6*(3), 21-35.

Money, J. (1980). Genetic and chromosomal aspects of homosexual etiology. In J. Marmor (Ed.), *Homosexual behavior: A modern reappraisal* (pp. 59-72). New York: Basic Books, Inc.

Ochs, R., & Deihl, M. (1993). Moving beyond binary thinking. In W. J. Blumenfeld (Ed.), *Homophobia: How we all pay the price* (pp. 67-75). Boston: Beacon Hill.

Patton, M. Q. (1990). *Qualitative evaluation and research methods.* Newbury Park, CA: Sage Publications.

Paul, J. P. (1985). Bisexuality: Reassessing our paradigms of sexuality. *Journal of Homosexuality, 11*(1/2), 21-34.

Pharr, S. (1988). *Homophobia: A weapon of sexism.* Inverness, CA: Chardon Press.

Rust, P. C. (1992). Who are we and where do we go from here? Conceptualizing bisexuality. In E. R. Weise (Ed.), *Closer to home: Bisexuality and feminism* (pp. 281-310). Seattle, WA: Seal Press.

Rust, P. C. (1995). *Bisexuality and the challenge to lesbian politics: Sex, loyalty, and revolution.* New York: New York University Press.

Rust-Rodriguez, P. C. (1989). When does the unity of a "common oppression" break down? Reciprocal attitudes between lesbian and bisexual women (Doctoral dissertation, University of Michigan, Ann Arbor, MI). *Dissertation Abstracts International, 50*(8), 2668A.

Shively, M., & De Cecco, J. (1977). Components of sexual identity. *Journal of Homosexuality, 3*(1), 41-48.

Tripp, C. A. (1987). *The homosexual matrix.* New York: Meridian Books.

Weinberg, M. S., & Williams, C. J. (1974). *Male homosexuals: Their problems and adaptations.* New York: Oxford University Press.

Weinberg, M. S., Williams, C. J., & Pryor, D. W. (1994). *Dual attraction: Understanding bisexuality.* New York: Oxford University Press.

Weise, E. R. (Ed.). (1992). *Closer to home: Bisexuality and feminism.* Seattle, WA: Seal Press.

Zinik, G. A. (1984). The relationship between sexual orientation and eroticism, cognitive flexibility, and negative affect (Doctoral dissertation, University of California, Santa Barbara, 1983). *Dissertation Abstracts International, 45*(8), 2707B.

Zinik, G. (1985). Identity conflict or adaptive flexibility? Bisexuality reconsidered. *Journal of Homosexuality, 11*(1/2), 7-19.

Bisexuality Among Self-Identified Heterosexual College Students

Robin Hoburg
Julie Konik
Michelle Williams
Mary Crawford

http://www.haworthpress.com/web/JB
© 2004 by The Haworth Press, Inc. All rights reserved.
Digital Object Identifier: 10.1300/J159v04n01_03

[Haworth co-indexing entry note]: "Bisexuality Among Self-Identified Heterosexual College Students."
Hoburg, Robin et al. Co-published simultaneously in *Journal of Bisexuality* (Harrington Park Press, an imprint of The Haworth Press, Inc.) Vol. 4, Nos. 1/2, 2004, pp. 25-36; and: *Current Research on Bisexuality* (ed: Ronald C. Fox) Harrington Park Press, an imprint of The Haworth Press, Inc., 2004, pp. 25-36. Single or multiple copies of this article are available for a fee from The Haworth Document Delivery Service [1-800-HAWORTH, 9:00 a.m. - 5:00 p.m. (EST). E-mail address: docdelivery@haworthpress.com].

SUMMARY. Two large empirical studies examined bisexuality among self-identified heterosexual college students in three regions of the United States. For women college students, the rate of bisexuality was fairly consistent across both studies and the three geographic regions sampled with approximately 30% reporting same-sex feelings. The findings for heterosexually identified college women suggest considerable sexual variability exists for this population, thus challenging predominant constructs and measurements of sexual orientation. There was more variability in reports of same-sex feelings among heterosexually identified college men, with higher rates reported in the northeast and mid-Atlantic states than in the northwest. Further studies using larger samples of college men are needed to clarify these latter findings. *[Article copies available for a fee from The Haworth Document Delivery Service: 1-800-HAWORTH. E-mail address: <docdelivery@haworthpress.com> Website: <http://www.HaworthPress.com> © 2004 by The Haworth Press, Inc. All rights reserved.]*

KEYWORDS. Bisexuality, heterosexuality, sexual orientation, sexual identity

Although knowledge about the range of sexual experiences among self-identified lesbians and gay men has increased substantially in recent years (e.g., Blumstein & Schwartz, 1993; Fox, 1996; Rust, 2000; Weinberg, Williams, & Pryor, 1994), less is known about the range of sexual experiences among self-identified heterosexual persons (Rust, 2000). Relatively few studies have examined self-identified heterosexuals' reports of sexual attractions, fantasies, and behavior with persons of the same sex (Golden, 1987; Laumann, Gagnon, Michael, & Michaels, 1994; Lever, Kanouse, Rogers, Carson, & Hertz, 1992; Rust, 1992; Storms, 1980 are notable exceptions). Results from these few studies showed that identification as lesbian, gay, or heterosexual was not necessarily an indicator of exclusive same- or other-sex attractions and behavior. Expanding our knowledge of the variability of sexual experiences among self-identified heterosexual persons will inform theoretical models and measurements of sexual orientation, and clinical practices and public policy regarding human sexuality.

In this paper, we report on two independently conducted empirical studies that examined bisexuality among large convenience samples of college students reporting a heterosexual identification. The populations sampled across the two studies include college campuses in the midwest, northeast, and northwest regions of the United States. Both studies were part of broader studies investigating predictors and correlates of sexual identification (Hoburg, 2000;

Konik, 1999), and are reported together to allow for comparisons between rates of bisexuality using different operational definitions of bisexual feelings and heterosexual identification. For example, Study 1 assessed bisexual preferences while study 2 examined specific bisexual experiences. Note that, in this paper, "bisexuality" and "bisexual" refer to the existence of some degree of sexual feeling and/or some degree of sexual behavior with persons of the same and other sex.

STUDY 1

Method

Participants

Participants included 202 self-identified heterosexual (106 females and 42 male) undergraduate and graduate students primarily recruited from a midsize mid-Atlantic university; one participant was recruited from a conference and one participant was recruited from a listserv. The racial/ethnic composition of the sample was 86% European American, 7% African American, 2% Latino/Hispanic, 3% Asian American, and 2% Other. The sample consisted primarily of young adults with a mean age of 21.9 years (SD = 5.9).

Procedures

Participants were recruited via an Introductory Psychology participant pool and by inviting participants to complete the survey during the last 15 minutes of their class. All of the study materials allowed for anonymous participation. Participants interested in participating in follow-up interviews provided identifying information on a form that was kept separate from their survey questionnaire.

Measures

Sexual Identification. Participants were asked to self-identify their sexual orientation using the following five categories: heterosexual, homosexual (exclusively gay or lesbian), bisexual, chooses not to identify, and other (with space for a description of this response). For the purposes of the present report, only heterosexually identified participants were included in the analyses.

Sexual/Physical Preferences. Using an adaptation of the 2 X 2 sexual orientation grid proposed by Chung and Katayama (1996), participants were asked to rate the degree of their sexual/physical preferences for persons of the same and other sex along two 6-point Likert scales, each ranging from weak to strong. Because the scales used in this study did not allow for a "no preference" or "none" category, participants who endorsed the weakest category of sexual/physical preference (i.e., a score of "1") were considered to have reported "none" for that item. A sexual/physical preference was considered present if a participant scored two or higher on that item.

Results

Same-Sex and Other-Sex Sexual Preferences

All participants reported sexual/physical preferences for persons of the other sex, and 27% reported sexual/physical preferences for persons of the same sex (Table 1). Although 42% of women and 19% of men reported having some same-sex preferences, this difference was not significant ($\chi^2 = 1.791, p > .05$). Mean scores for other-sex preferences for women were 4.698 (SD = .525), and for men were 4.714 (SD = .596). Turning to same-sex sexual preferences, mean scores for women were 1.489 (SD = .748), and for men were 2.000 (SD = 1.60). These differences in means scores for other- and same-sex preferences were not significant (t = .160, $p > .05$; t = $-.330, p > .05$).

STUDY 2

Method

Participants

Participants (N = 528) were recruited from undergraduate courses at a large university located in the northeast (n = 423) and a large university in the north-

TABLE 1. Frequency of Sexual/Physical Preferences Among Self-Identified Heterosexual College Students

Responses	Same Sex				Other Sex			
	Females N = 160		Males N = 42		Females N = 159		Males N = 42	
	n	%	n	%	n	%	n	%
1 - Weak (none)	113	70.6	34	81.0	0	0.0	0	0.0
2	31	19.4	5	11.9	0	0.0	0	0.0
3	9	5.6	1	2.4	0	0.0	0	0.0
4	7	4.4	0	0.0	5	3.1	3	7.1
5	0	0	1	2.4	38	23.9	6	14.3
6 - Strong	0	0	1	2.4	116	73.0	33	78.6

west (n = 105). Participants ranged in age from 17 to 35 with a mean age of 18.74 (SD = 1.67). Seventy-three percent of the participants were female and 27% were male. The majority of participants, 75%, were White (N = 394). Ten percent were Asian or Pacific Islanders (N = 54), 5% were African-American or Black (N = 27), 4% were Latino/a or Hispanic (N = 22), 3% were Biracial (N = 18), and 2% listed their race/ethnicity as other (N = 12).

Participants sampled from the northeast and northwest varied in terms of ethnicity (χ^2 (5, 527) = 331.39, p < .01). There were more Asian/Pacific Islander participants from the northwest (N = 42, 40%) than the northeast (N = 12, 3%), and more Black and Latino participants from the northeast (N = 27, 6% and N = 20, 5%, respectively) than the northwest (N = 0, 0% and N = 2, 2%, respectively). There were no significant differences in age (F = 1.116, p > .05), gender (χ^2 (1, 526) = 331.39, p > .05), couple status (χ^2 (2, 522) = 3.208, p > .05), or income (χ^2 (3, 473) = 3.941, p > .05) between participants sampled in the northeast or northwest.

Procedure

Introductory Psychology students signed up for the study after reading a brief description of the study posted in the psychology department. Participants were asked to complete anonymous survey questionnaires in large group settings consisting of approximately 40 to 80 people. To enhance anonymity, they were seated at least one chair apart, instructed to place their surveys in a box with other surveys, and given tasks at the end of the survey (e.g., puzzles and games) to make survey completion time uniform.

Measures

Current Sexual Identity. Participants indicated their current sexual identity by choosing one of the following eight categories: exclusively heterosexual, predominantly heterosexual, bisexual, predominantly lesbian/gay/homosexual, exclusively lesbian/gay/homosexual, asexual, "not sure," and "other (specify)." For the purposes of the present report, only exclusively heterosexual participants were included in the analyses.

Sexual Feelings and Behavior. As shown in Tables 2 through 5, three items assessed same- and other-sex feelings (i.e., attractions, fantasies, and arousal to erotic material), and one item assessed same-and other-sex behavior. Sexual behavior was broadly defined to include open-mouth kisses, fondling, masturbation, oral sex, anal sex, vaginal penetration or use of objects for sexual pleasure. For the sexual arousal to erotic stimuli item, participants were provided with examples of erotic material, including pictures, magazines, books, movies, television programs and Internet material. Using a six-point Likert-type scale, participants were asked to indicate the total number of times they have ever had sexual feelings or behavior with persons of the other sex. By replacing the stem "other-sex" with the stem "same-sex," the same four items were used to assess for sexual feelings and behavior with persons of the same sex. In addition to lifetime prevalence of sexual feelings and behavior, participants were asked to indicate if a particular sexual feeling or behavior occurred within the past month. Same- and other-sex feelings were considered to be absent if the participant reported "none" across items that assessed a same- or other-sex feeling. For instance, if a participant reported "none" for sexual attractions, sexual fantasies, *and* sexual arousal for persons of the same sex, then same-sex feelings were considered "absent." Conversely, a same-sex feeling was considered present if the participant reported having at least one sexual attraction, sexual fantasy, or sexual arousal for persons of the same sex.

Results

Percentage of Other-Sex and Same-Sex Sexual Feelings and Behavior

All participants (N = 528) reported the presence of other-sex feelings, and 98% (N = 518) of these participants indicated that these feelings occurred within the past month. Both male and female participants reported high rates of other-sex attractions and fantasies, with relatively few reporting that they never had an other-sex attraction or fantasy (Tables 2 & 3). In contrast to male participants (2.7%), females were more likely to report never having other-sex arousal to erotic stimuli (20.5%). As Table 5 shows, the majority of participants (92.8% or more) reported engaging in sexual behavior with the other sex at some point in their lives, with a substantial percentage reporting engaging in other-sex behavior over 20 times (71% for females, 76.2% for males).

TABLE 2. Frequency of Sexual Attractions Among Self-Identified Exclusive Heterosexual College Students

Responses	Same Sex				Other Sex			
	Females N = 378		Males N = 143		Females N = 382		Males N = 145	
	n	%	n	%	n	%	n	%
None	333	88.1	134	93.7	7	1.9	0	0.0
One Time	14	3.7	5	3.5	14	3.7	1	0.7
2-5 Times	23	6.1	2	1.4	68	18.1	8	5.5
6-10 Times	6	1.6	1	0.7	47	12.5	7	4.8
11-20 Times	0	0.0	0	0.0	46	12.3	7	4.8
Over 20 Times	2	0.5	1	0.7	193	51.5	122	84.1

TABLE 3. Frequency of Sexual Fantasies Among Self-Identified Exclusive Heterosexual College Students

Responses	Same Sex				Other Sex			
	Females N = 374		Males N = 143		Females N = 382		Males N = 145	
	n	%	n	%	n	%	n	%
None	313	83.7	135	94.4	12	3.2	6	4.1
One Time	17	4.5	2	1.4	16	4.3	1	0.7
2-5 Times	31	8.3	3	2.1	85	22.6	10	6.8
6-10 Times	4	1.1	1	0.7	60	16.0	6	4.1
11-20 Times	4	1.1	1	0.7	63	16.8	11	7.5
Over 20 Times	5	1.3	1	0.7	140	37.2	112	76.7

As shown in Tables 2 through 5, participants reported having far fewer same-sex feelings than other-sex feelings. There were significant gender differences in reports of same-sex feelings (X^2 (1, 526) = 21.078, $p < .01$) with more females reporting the presence of same-sex feelings (N = 120, 32% of females) than males (N = 18, 12% of males). Thirteen percent of these female participants (N = 47) and 5% of these male participants (N = 7) reported experiencing same-sex feelings within the past month. Male participants from the northeast were twice as likely to report same-sex attractions, fantasies, or arousal to erotic stimuli (N = 16, 14%) than male participants from the northwest (N = 2, 7%). There were minimal differences in reports of same-sex feelings among female participants from the northeast (N = 90, 31%) and the northwest (N = 26, 34%).

Regarding the type of same-sex feelings reported, female participants were most likely to report sexual arousal to erotic material, with a relatively smaller proportion reporting sexual fantasy and sexual attraction (Tables 2-4). Male participants, on the other hand, were equally likely to report sexual attractions, fantasies, and arousal for persons of the same sex. In contrast to reports of same-sex feelings, both female and male participants reported lower frequencies of same-sex behavior (7.5% and 4.3%, respectively). In general, female participants reported a wider range of frequencies for both same- and other-sex feelings while male participants reported high frequencies of other-sex feelings and low frequencies of same-sex feelings (Tables 2-4).

Discussion

The findings of Study 1 and Study 2 show that 29% to 32% of women college students and 12% to 19% of men college students who self-identify as heterosexual or exclusively heterosexual report having sexual feelings or prefer-

TABLE 4. Frequency of Sexual Arousal to Erotic Stimuli Among Self-Identified Exclusive Heterosexual College Students

Responses	Same Sex				Other Sex			
	Females N = 374		Males N = 140		Females N = 370		Males N = 146	
	n	%	n	%	n	%	n	%
None	278	74.3	131	93.6	76	20.5	4	2.7
One Time	11	2.9	1	0.7	11	3.0	0	0.0
2-5 Times	38	10.2	2	1.4	109	29.5	7	4.8
6-10 Times	20	5.3	2	1.4	63	17.0	7	4.8
11-20 Times	13	3.5	2	1.4	46	12.4	7	4.8
Over 20 Times	14	3.7	2	1.4	65	17.6	121	82.9

TABLE 5. Frequency of Sexual Behavior Among Self-Identified Exclusive Heterosexual College Students

Responses	Same Sex				Other Sex			
	Females N = 372		Males N = 140		Females N = 373		Males N = 143	
	n	%	n	%	n	%	n	%
None	345	92.5	134	95.7	27	7.2	4	2.8
One Time	10	2.7	2	1.4	7	1.9	1	0.7
2-5 Times	10	2.7	0	0.0	23	6.2	11	7.7
6-10 Times	5	1.3	2	1.4	20	5.4	5	3.5
11-20 Times	1	0.3	0	0.0	31	8.3	13	9.7
Over 20 Times	2	0.5	2	1.4	265	71.0	109	76.2

ences for persons of the same and other sex. In addition to reporting higher rates of bisexuality, college women tended to report a wider range of frequencies of same- and other-sex feelings compared to college men. Thirteen percent of these women and 5% of these men report having current same- and other-sex feelings. Given that social desirability appears to play a role in reports of socially undesirable behaviors (Hoburg, 2000; Mensch & Kendel, 1988; Traugott & Katosh, 1979), results from the present studies most likely underestimate the rate of bisexuality among college students.

The rate of bisexuality reported among self-identified heterosexual college women appears to be fairly consistent across both studies and the three geographic regions sampled, providing strong support for the generalization of the results. In contrast, the rate of bisexuality among self-identified heterosexual college men was higher in the mid-Atlantic (19%) and northeast (14%) than in the northwest (7%). The smaller percentage of male students reporting bisexuality in the northwest may have been due to a small sample size (N = 30) in that region. Further studies are needed to clarify the findings for this population.

Study results suggest that sexual preferences appear to reflect sexual feelings for college women reporting a heterosexual identification, and that the labels "heterosexual" and "exclusively heterosexual" are fairly interchangeable for this population. Study 1 and Study 2 reported similar rates of same-sex feelings despite using different measurements of sexuality (i.e., sexual preferences in Study 1 vs. sexual attractions, sexual fantasies, and sexual arousal to erotic stimuli in Study 2). However, it appears that not all heterosexual identity categories are created equal. In her broader study of the predictors and correlates of sexual identification, Hoburg (2000) found that college students who label themselves as "predominantly heterosexual" report much higher rates of bisexuality (86%) than college students who identify as exclusively heterosexual (30%).

Results from the present studies suggest that research using measures of bisexual behavior and current sexual experiences as indicators of sexual orientation underestimate rates of bisexuality. Data from Study 1 and Study 2 show that the majority of college students do not act upon their feelings nor do they report that these feelings occurred within the past month, underscoring the importance of using measurements of sexual feelings (not just behaviors) and lifetime (not just recent) occurrence of sexual experiences. Results from Study 2 further suggest that studies of sexual orientation should include assessment of sexual arousal to erotic stimuli, particularly when examining rates of bisexuality for women. Same-sex arousal to erotic stimuli may occur more frequently than same-sex attractions or fantasies for college women.

It is hard to compare our results to other studies as few studies have assessed bisexuality among self-identified heterosexual college students, and even fewer studies have looked at bisexual attractions among this population. Moreover, given rapid change in the social visibility of diverse sexualities, comparisons with studies done in the 1980s may reflect differences in reporting over time as much as differences in bisexuality. However, our results generally confirm previous findings that show considerable bisexuality among college students (Golden, 1987; Storms, 1980) and are congruent with theories on the plasticity or fluidity of female sexuality (Baumeister, 2000). Our findings also support prior studies that show people's sexual identities do not always reflect the entire range of their sexual feelings and/or behavior (Golden, 1987; Laumann, Gagnon, Michael, & Michaels, 1994; Lever, Kanouse, Rogers, Carson, & Hertz, 1992; Rust, 1992). More studies examining same- and other-sex experiences among self-identified heterosexual college students are needed to further confirm our findings. Also, additional research is needed that investigates factors that impinge on people's ability or willingness to accurately report on their sexual experiences with persons of the same and other gender.

Study Limitations

The samples from Study 1 and Study 2 consisted of a broader range of ethnic-minority persons than other studies of bisexuality among self-identified heterosexual persons (i.e., 10% Asian or Pacific-Islander for Study 2 is a greater proportion than in studies reported by Golden, 1987; Laumann et al., 1994; Rust, 1992; Storms, 1980). However, as these studies sampled mainly young, White females living in the north and east, caution should be used when generalizing these results. Further research sampling more men, people from the south and west, and a more ethnically diverse population is needed to expand our results beyond young White women living in the north and eastern parts of the United States. In Study 2 participants were asked to report on feelings and behaviors that occurred over their lifetime. The retrospective nature of this task may have limited some participant's ability to answer questions accurately, especially participants with memory difficulties. Lastly, volunteer bias may have skewed the results. However, research suggests a minimal effect of volunteer bias on anonymous surveys of sexuality as virtually all college students express a willingness to participate in anonymous sex surveys (Wiederman, 1999).

Concluding Remarks

Together the findings of these two studies suggest considerable sexual variability exists among college students who identify with heterosexual or exclusively heterosexual labels, particularly college women. These results challenge predominant methods and constructs of assessing sexual orientation (Chung & Katayama, 1996; Kinsey, Pomeroy, & Martin, 1948). Our findings underscore the importance of using multiple measures of sexuality in studies of sexual orientation and suggest that, for certain populations, it may be normative to experience some degree of sexual feelings for more than one gender. Further research examining the prevalence of bisexuality across a wide cross-section of people identifying with broad range of sexual identity labels is needed to inform theoretical models and measurements of sexual orientation, and existing practices and policies regarding human sexuality.

REFERENCES

Baumeister, R.F. (2000). Gender differences in erotic plasticity: The female sex drive as socially flexible and responsive. *Psychological Bulletin, 126,* 347-374.

Blumstein, P., & Schwartz, P. (1993). Bisexuality: Some social psychological issues. In L. Garnet & D. Kimmel (Eds.), *Psychological perspectives on lesbian & gay male experiences* (pp. 168-183). Columbia University Press: New York.

Chung, Y., & Katayama, M.(1996). Assessment of sexual orientation in lesbian/gay/ bisexual studies. *Journal of Homosexuality, 30(4)*, 49-62.

Fox, R. (1996). Bisexuality in perspective: A review of theory and research. In B. Firestein (Ed.), *Bisexuality: The psychology and politics of an invisible minority*. (pp. 3-50). Thousand Oaks, California: Sage Publications, Inc.

Golden, C. (1987). Diversity and variability in women's sexual identities. In Boston Lesbian Psychologies Collective (Eds.), *Lesbian psychologies* (pp. 18-34). Urbana: University of Illinois Press.

Hoburg, R. (2000). Psychosocial and experiential factors relevant to discrepancies among the affective, behavioral and identity components of sexual orientation. *Dissertation Abstracts International*, 9968460.

Kinsey, A., Pomeroy, W., & Martin, C. (1948). *Sexual behavior in the human male*. Philadelphia: Saunders.

Konik, J. (1999). *Sculpting the sexual self: Exploring the relationship among sexuality, identity status, and cognitive flexibility*. Unpublished master's thesis, West Chester University, West Chester, Pennsylvania.

Laumann, E.O., Gagnon, J.H., Michael, R.T., & Michaels, S. (1994). *The social organization of sexuality: Sexual practices in the United States*. Chicago: University of Chicago Press.

Lever, J., Kanouse, D., Rogers, W., Carson, S., & Hertz, R. (1992). Behavior patterns and sexual identity of bisexual males. *The Journal of Sex Research, 29*, 141-167.

Mensch, B.S., & Kendel, D.B. (1988). Underreporting of substance use in a national longitudinal youth cohort: Individual and interviewer effects. *Public Opinion Quarterly, 52*, 100-124.

Rust, P.C. (1992). The politics of sexual identity: Sexual attraction and behavior among lesbian and bisexual women. *Social Problems, 39*, 366-386.

Rust, P.C. (2000). *Bisexuality in the United States*. New York: Columbia University Press.

Storms, M. (1980). Theories of sexual orientation. *Journal of Personality and Social Psychology, 38*, 783-792.

Traugott, M.W., & Katosh, J.P. (1979). Response validity in surveys of voting behavior. *Public Opinion Quarterly, 43*, 359-377.

Weiderman, M.W. (1999). Volunteer bias in sexuality research using college participation. *Journal of Sex Research, 36*, 59-66.

Weinberg, M., Williams, C., & Pryor, D. (1994). *Dual attraction: Understanding bisexuality*. New York: Oxford University Press.

Friendships Across Sexual Orientations: Experiences of Bisexual Women in Early Adulthood

M. Paz Galupo
Carin A. Sailer
Sarah Causey St. John

http://www.haworthpress.com/web/JB
© 2004 by The Haworth Press, Inc. All rights reserved.
Digital Object Identifier: 10.1300/J159v04n01_04

[Haworth co-indexing entry note]: "Friendships Across Sexual Orientations: Experiences of Bisexual Women in Early Adulthood." Galupo, M. Paz, Carin A. Sailer, and Sarah Causey St. John. Co-published simultaneously in *Journal of Bisexuality* (Harrington Park Press, an imprint of The Haworth Press, Inc.) Vol. 4, Nos. 1/2, 2004, pp. 37-53; and: *Current Research on Bisexuality* (ed: Ronald C. Fox) Harrington Park Press, an imprint of The Haworth Press, Inc., 2004, pp. 37-53. Single or multiple copies of this article are available for a fee from The Haworth Document Delivery Service [1-800-HAWORTH, 9:00 a.m. - 5:00 p.m. (EST). E-mail address: docdelivery@haworthpress.com].

SUMMARY. This research investigated women's friendships across sexual orientations as they relate to bisexual identity. Interviews were conducted with 28 female participants in close friendship pairs. Participants included 7 lesbian and 7 bisexual women, along with their heterosexual friends (n = 14). Participants ranged in age from 18-34, with a friendship duration of 1-12 years. Results of this study suggest that while cross-sexual orientation friendships serve a similar function as other friendships, sexual orientation does factor into the friendship dynamic. Analyses focused on the ways in which the difference in sexual orientation identity influenced friendship structure between bisexual-heterosexual pairs. Comparison with lesbian-heterosexual friendships allowed for an understanding of how bisexual friendship experience is unique. Heterosexual women perceived their bisexual women friends as less different from themselves when compared to lesbian friends. In addition, friends in bisexual-heterosexual friendship pairs perceived a shift in the friendship dynamic based on the sex of the bisexual friend's partner. *[Article copies available for a fee from The Haworth Document Delivery Service: 1-800-HAWORTH. E-mail address: <docdelivery@haworthpress.com> Website: <http://www.HaworthPress.com> © 2004 by The Haworth Press, Inc. All rights reserved.]*

KEYWORDS. Bisexuality, identity, friendship, sexual orientation, lesbianism, bisexual identity

Much of the research placing bisexuality in a social context has focused on understanding bisexual experiences in relation to a larger community. Because of the dichotomous conceptualization of sexual orientation (Fox, 1995; Rust 2000), bisexual experience is often narrowly defined in relation to both heterosexual and lesbian/gay experience, and bisexuality is not perceived by others as a valid and stable sexual identity. The personal consequences for individuals who identify as bisexual include a unique brand of discrimination or "bi-phobia" on the part of lesbian, gay and heterosexual individuals (Eliason, 1997; Fox, 1996; Herek, 2002; Ochs, 1996; Rust, 1995; Spalding & Peplau, 1997). Other research on community has identified the changing connections of bisexual women and men to a visible bisexual community (Weinberg, Williams, & Pryor; 1994, 2001).

Along with an understanding of community, research has emphasized the sexual relationships formed by bisexuals. Bisexuals have been classified into types based on their relationships to both men and women and on their identity and behavioral shifts across time (Klein, 1993). The nature of bisexual rela-

tionships has been debated in terms of the number and pattern of sexual partners (Vernallis, 1999) and of particular interest to researchers has been the
experience of bisexual women and men in heterosexual marriage and relationships (Buxton, 2001; Coleman, 1985; Hays, 1989; Higgins, 2002).

Implicit in our understanding of bisexuality in almost all areas of research is
the basic notion of how individuals with different sexual-orientation identities relate with one another. This basic question is implied when understanding bisexuality and its relation to community. It also underscores research on the sexual
relationships of bisexual women and men, as their sexual partners may or may not
share the same sexual orientation identity. Even bisexual identity research, which
posits that Western definitions of homosexuality and heterosexuality invalidate
bisexual existence (Rust, 2000), rests upon a tension between heterosexual, homosexual, and bisexual identities. Therefore, a better understanding of cross-sexual orientation interactions would have implications for a fuller understanding of
sexual orientation in general and of bisexuality in particular.

FRIENDSHIPS ACROSS SEXUAL ORIENTATION IDENTITIES

Friendships provide one arena in which to explore interactions between individuals with different sexual orientation identities, however there has been
little research to that end. Existing studies suggest overall that cross-sexual
orientation friendships are rare, and that when they do exist, they are tenuously
constructed around a number of barriers and conflicts (O'Boyle & Thomas,
1996; Price, 1999). In addition, much of this research has focused on the negotiation of difference in sexual orientation identity to the exclusion of other aspects of friendship, and has employed methodologies that limit understanding
of the intimate dynamics that exist in close friendships.

Earlier Research: Price

Price (1999) investigated male friendships across sexual orientation identities. Gay men with heterosexual male friends were identified and recruited
through the gay community. Individual interviews were conducted with 32
gay men and 24 of their heterosexually identified male friends. Price identified
three friendship types, which can be characterized by the way in which friends
negotiate their differences in sexual orientation, i.e., embracing differences,
ignoring differences, and struggling with differences. Although Price provides
an important classification of friendship types in cross-sexual orientation pairs,
a true portrait of the intimate dynamics within close friendships was not a focus
of her analysis as her sample included friends of varying closeness. In fact, a
third of the friendships included in her study were characterized as "struggling
with differences" and these "friends" were not intimate with one another in
emotional or personal terms, nor did they not spend much time together.

Earlier Research: O'Boyle and Thomas

O'Boyle and Thomas (1996) were the first to attempt to broadly characterize friendships between lesbian and heterosexual women. Data were collected using four focus groups (two composed exclusively of lesbian women and two composed exclusively of heterosexual women). The majority of focus-group discussion revealed significant barriers to the development of cross-sexual orientation friendships. These barriers included the associated stigma of having a lesbian friend, sexual tension, and reduced level of comfort on the part of the lesbian woman in disclosing personal information. Benefits of these friendships were not explicitly addressed. However, the researchers concluded that meaningful friendships between lesbian and heterosexual women, although rare, can and do exist.

The findings of O'Boyle and Thomas (1996) provide a beginning framework for understanding the issues relevant to cross-sexual orientation friendship development among women. However, their recruitment strategy ensured that their analysis remained general and less focused on the dynamics of existing close friendships. Many of the heterosexual participants in their study had never had a lesbian friend and were more likely to be describing how they felt about the possibility of such a friendship. Even for those participants who indicated having a close friend who differed in sexual-orientation identity, focus group discussions were more likely to elicit general feelings about cross-sexual orientation friendships than to allow for deep reflection of experiences within an existing close friendship.

Earlier Research: Galupo and St. John

Collectively, research of O'Boyle and Thomas (1996) and Price (1999) provide a general basis for understanding cross-sexual orientation friendship development. Neither study, however, included bisexually identified participants in their sample. Galupo and St. John (2001) describe a more in-depth examination of friendships across sexual orientation identities among adolescent women. For this study, researchers recruited bisexual and lesbian participants along with their close heterosexual friends. This approach allowed individuals to reflect upon an existing close friendship. Friends were interviewed both together and separately, and provided a more intimate portrayal of friendship dynamics. Analysis revealed that difference in sexual orientation identity between friends can impact their friendship in positive ways.

Positive aspects of cross-sexual orientation friendships were discussed in terms of the benefits afforded to heterosexual and sexual minority women (Galupo & St. John, 2001). Benefits included an increased closeness and trust within the friendship accompanying sexual orientation disclosure, providing objectivity in life due to the fact that cross-sexual orientation friends often conducted separate social lives, and breaking down stereotypes. In addition, heterosexuals reported an increased sensitivity to sexual minority perspectives, and increased flexibility in understanding their own personal sexual identity. Through their friendships with heterosexual women, lesbian and bisexual participants gained an understanding that acceptance from others is possible, and also reported increased self-acceptance and self-esteem.

Galupo and St. John (2001) provided the first research finding on friendships across sexual orientation identities that included bisexually identified individuals. Participants included both lesbian and bisexual women and their heterosexual friends. However, this initial analysis did not distinguish between bisexual-heterosexual and lesbian-heterosexual friendships (as data for bisexuals and lesbians were analyzed together as "sexual minorities"), nor did it allow for a comparison across the two.

Present Study

The present study is an extension of earlier work (Galupo & St. John, 2001) with a similar methodology and data set, with a focus on the experiences of bisexual women. Additional interviews were conducted to allow for a larger sample size with increased representation of bisexuals and racial diversity. In addition, the age range of participants was expanded to include women up through early adulthood. The present study was designed to explore the complex ways in which bisexual identity intersects with the intimate social dynamics within close cross-sexual orientation friendships.

METHOD

Design

The present study differs from past research in that our participants were recruited in close friendship pairs. This approach ensured that participants were answering questions about cross-sexual orientation friendships in the context of their experiences in a current stable friendship. In addition, participants were interviewed both individually and together in friendship pairs. This allowed for deeper reflection of the friendship but also ensured privacy in discussing potential sensitive topics.

Participants

The criteria for inclusion in the study were: (1) both individuals in the friendship pair agreed to participate in the study; (2) one friend identified as either bisexual or lesbian; (3) one friend identified as heterosexual; (4) participants were not related in any way and had considered themselves close friends for at least 1 year. The sample was composed of 14 pairs of volunteer participants ranging in age from 18-34 years at the time of interview. Friendship pairs reported a friendship duration of 1 to 12 years. All participants had either some college or had graduated from college. There was considerable racial and ethnic diversity among the 28 participants. Participants identified in the following way: 19 Caucasian, 4 African-American, 1 Asian-American, 1 Pacific Islander, 1 Hispanic, 1 Jamaican, and 1 Afghan. In addition, 2 participants identified as Jewish (1 Caucasian, 1 African American).

Our sample included 7 bisexual, 7 lesbian, and 14 heterosexual women. Bisexual and lesbian participants had comparable experiences as understood by a number of descriptive indices. Bisexual participants ranged in age from 18-30 years (mean = 23.0), while lesbian participants ranged in age from 19-34 years (mean = 23.0). Friendship durations for friendship pairs were 1-12 years (mean = 5.0) for bisexual participants, and 2-8 years (mean = 4.7) for lesbian participants. Bisexual participants reported having identified as such for 1 to 9 years (mean = 4.3), and lesbian participants reported having identified as such for 1 to 11 years (mean = 5.4).

Interview Method and Data Analysis

Three interviews were conducted for each friendship pair. Friends were interviewed first together and then individually, with all three interviews being conducted on the same day. Two researchers were present at the dyad interview. Following the dyad interview, each researcher conducted an individual interview with one of the participants. A semi-structured interview technique was used. Interviews were audio recorded and the content was later transcribed and verified across researchers and, in some cases, across participants. Each of the researchers independently reviewed interview transcripts and agreed upon the emergent themes presented in the results section.

RESULTS

All participants were asked to indicate the number of close friends that they had, and to describe those friendships. The number of total close friendships reported by participants ranged from one to eight. Because of the recruitment criteria for inclusion in the study, all participants indicated at least one cross-sexual orientation friendship. The number of reported cross-sexual orientation friendships, however, varied across sexual orientation identity. Heterosexual participants reported having between one and two cross-sexual orientation friendships, while bisexual and lesbian participants reported having substantially more cross-sexual orientation friendships, between two and six. All lesbian and heterosexual participants reported at least one close friendship with someone of the same sexual-orientation identity. None of the bisexual participants, however, indicated any close friendships with someone of the same sexual orientation identity. That is, bisexuals in this sample, experienced all of their friendships as cross-sexual orientation friendships.

Individual quotations from the interview transcripts are included in the discussion of the themes. However, many of these results were gleaned from a comparison of interview content across bisexual-heterosexual and lesbian-heterosexual friendship pairs. Because individuals were not recruited into the study based on having both friendship types, and because interview questions rarely focused on asking participants to make a direct comparison of heterosexual women's friendships with either lesbians or bisexual women, some of the results were not easily represented in individual quotations.

Thematic analysis of bisexual experiences in cross-sexual orientation friendships revealed three broad themes: (1) The overall friendship experience was similar to experiences in any other close friendship; (2) There was an emphasis on similarity between friends in heterosexual-bisexual friendship pairs; (3) There was a perceived shift in the friendship dynamic based on the sex of the bisexual woman's partner. Each of the three assumptions within the friendships has important implications for the social context in which bisexual identity is experienced and negotiated.

The Overall Friendship Experience Was Similar to Experiences in Any Other Close Friendship

Although the primary focus of this study was the impact of sexual orientation identity on friendship development, the close friendships reported here resemble women's friendships in general. Past research has established that the primary rewards of friendship are "being there when needed" and "having someone to talk to" (Rawlings, 1992). Our participants' descriptions of their friendships were overwhelmingly consistent with this finding. When asked to describe the benefits of their friendships, participants offered similar responses regardless of sexual orientation identity, age, race, ethnicity, or duration of friendship. Semantically equivalent phrases such as "Being there when needed" and "having someone to talk to" were mentioned in every participant's description of her friendship. When asked to describe how her 8-year friendship functioned in her life, one participant responded:

> It's my shield when I need it to be. It's my featherbed when I need it to be. You know, It's my warm cup of cocoa and a blanket when I need it to be. (She is) my therapist. My best friend . . . Just an ear when I need her to be. It's just that she's there for me. As a good friend would be. Someone to fool around with. Someone to depend on.

Her friend described their friendship in similar terms:

You know there is someone in the universe saying that everything is going to be OK and I'm always here for you. And, you know that, don't you? I think that that is major. I listen when she has her problems. I try to help her with whatever is going on. I sympathize and get upset if I'm supposed to be upset. And I'm indignant when she's been wronged. You know, that kind of thing.

Another participant describes her friendship in the following way:

Her friendship is of primary importance to me. It's essential to my well-being. I would feel a great sense of loss if we didn't have this friendship. (She's) someone that I can count on for good times, good laughs, a shoulder to cry on–to talk about all the things that are important.

When describing her friend, another participant says:

She really is the person I go back to, to unburden, you know. And then sometimes just to be there to fill the space. Just to hang out with. I don't know . . . I can tell her anything and she will not judge me. And she feels the same way, which I just love. And really intimate stuff too.

When participants discussed their friend and the friendship itself it became clear that sexual orientation was of ancillary concern. These friendships were experienced, first and foremost, as any other close friendship. In discussing the function of their friendships, no pattern of difference emerged in the friendship narratives between bisexual-heterosexual and lesbian-heterosexual pairs.

There Was an Emphasis on Similarity Between Friends in Heterosexual-Bisexual Friendship Pairs

Although cross-sexual orientation friendships were experienced similarly to other friendships, the difference in sexual orientation identity between friends did impact the friendship dynamic. Specifically, it often led to the perception and/or observation of difference between the two friends. However, in comparison to their perception of lesbian friends, heterosexual women perceived themselves to be more like bisexual women. This became apparent in the following ways.

Issues of Sexual Orientation in Bisexual-Heterosexual Friendships. When asked in the dyad interview how similar and different the friends were from one another, bisexual-heterosexual friendships pairs were less likely to bring up sexual orientation as an issue or difference. When asked the same question, lesbian-heterosexual friendships pairs almost always pointed to sexual orientation as a difference. In addition, throughout the interview, bisexual-heterosexual friends were less likely to openly talk about issues of sexual orientation or to acknowledge that it factored into their friendship. In fact, while interviewing one bisexual-heterosexual friendship dyad it was never clear which friend identified as bisexual until we asked pointedly near the end of the interview session. This never occurred in the lesbian-heterosexual friendship interviews. Even when participants downplayed the impact of sexual orientation identity on their friendship, the difference in sexual orientation identity was always acknowledged and discussed openly as a part of life and as a part of the friendship.

Focus on Mutual Attraction to Men. While bisexual-heterosexual friendship pairs did not often refer to the difference in sexual orientation, they almost always discussed their shared attraction to men. When asked what they talk about in their friendship, one bisexually identified woman simply answered A lot of guy stuff." This acknowledged similarity between friends had important implications for the friendships. For some, it structured not only their topics of discussions, but also how and when they socialized, and the way in which they imagined being involved in each other's future, e.g., one bisexual-heterosexual friendship pair spent a lot of time discussing their plans to be attendants at each other's weddings–with the assumption of marriage to men. Discussion of the bisexual woman's attraction to women was not discussed on equal par within the friendship.

Invisibility of Bisexual Identity. In some ways, it seems as though the bisexual-heterosexual friendship is ideal. We know there are potential benefits associated with cross-sexual orientation friendships (Galupo & St. John, 2001) and when compared to the lesbian-heterosexual friendship there is less discussion of sexual orientation difference and more focus on a shared interest (men). However, as described by our bisexual participants, these circumstances do not necessarily lead to an enhanced friendship experience. In fact, this alignment of male interest between friends had important psychological liabilities for the bisexual women interviewed. Many of our bisexual participants felt as though their bisexual identity was the cost of the friendship's primary focus on male attraction and interest. Bisexual women were much more likely than lesbians to feel as though their sexual orientation identity was invalidated within the friendship. Bisexual women in this sample felt as though their identity was ignored altogether or not taken seriously. One participant indicated, "I tend not to refer to it (bisexuality) a lot 'cause I don't want to freak her out." Within the context of her close friendship, this tendency to not discuss attraction to women was viewed by the bisexual participant as a routine sacrifice.

Lesbian participants, on the other hand, did not find common ground in male attraction with their heterosexual friends. Despite the fact that heterosexual women perceived their lesbian friends as different from themselves, lesbian identity was openly understood and acknowledged within the friendship.

Although bisexual women discussed a relative invisibility of their bisexual identities within the context of their friendship, they did so in very matter-of-fact terminology. It was never discussed in embittered terms, nor did they lay blame on their friends for a breech of understanding. Instead, it was most often discussed as a negotiation on their part (one which their friend was likely unaware of) that was built into the structure of their friendship. Even though bisexual participants noted a lack of acknowledgment of their identity within the friendship, it was not a point of contention that led them to question the closeness or importance of their friendship.

Perceived Shift in Friendship Dynamic Based on the Sex of Partner for Bisexual Women

There was a perceived shift in the friendship dynamic coinciding with the sex of partner for the bisexual woman. This perception held true on the part of both the friends in the bisexual-heterosexual friendship pair. Some bisexual participants had direct experience and contrasted their friendship at times when they had a female partner with times when they had a male partner. In some cases, the shift was hypothetical as in the case of a bisexually identified participant who had never had a woman partner but speculated that she would feel less comfortable discussing a same-sex relationship with her friend. In other cases the perceived shift in dynamics was hypothetical due to the stable partnership status of the bisexual during the friendship duration (i.e., a bisexual participant who had not dated anyone during the entire friendship period, or a bisexual participant who had maintained a monogamous relationship throughout).

None of the participants in our sample negotiated simultaneous sexual relationships with a man and a woman, despite the popular stereotype that characterizes the sexual behavior of bisexual women and men as such (Esterberg, 1997; Rust, 1995, 2000). This is consistent with current research which maintains that bisexually identified individuals do not require both female and male partners to find a bisexual identity label meaningful (Rust, 2001).

The perceived shift in friendship dynamic was conceptualized on a number of terms. First, bisexual-heterosexual friendship pairs felt as though the discussion of sexual and relational issues were different if the bisexual woman had a female versus male partner. Bisexual participants indicated that they discuss their sexual interest and behaviors more explicitly with their heterosexual friend when the partner is male. In addition, the way in which sexual behaviors were discussed differed. Bisexual participants indicated that they may describe their sexual activity with women, but were not likely to describe it in terms that would convey the importance of these relationships. In some cases the heterosexual friend was aware of the difference, in other cases she was not. Second, some bisexual participants felt as though their friend's support of the relationship was contingent upon the partner being male. This is illustrated in the following quotation:

I think if my choice winded up being a woman, I would see another aspect of (my heterosexual friend)–almost as if she would want to talk me out of it. So, in the back of my mind I know and feel that.

Third, both bisexual and heterosexual friends indicated that if/when the bisexual woman is partnered with a woman, the difference in sexual orientation identity becomes more apparent and acknowledged within the friendship. When bisexual participants were partnered with women, the friendship between bisexual-heterosexual friends became more similar to lesbian-heterosexual friendships, where sexual orientation identity was dealt with on more open terms. Fourth, bisexual women in this sample described that their bisexual identity shifted from invisible (when partnered with a man) to visible (when partnered with a woman) and vice versa. Within bisexual-heterosexual friendships, bisexual participants perceived a shift in the visibility of their bisexual identity along with sex of partner for the bisexual friend. Fifth, when the bisexual woman was partnered with a woman, the focus on shared interest in men diminished between the friends. Here again when the bisexual woman's partner was female there was a shift in the friendships' dynamic that mirrored the dynamic in lesbian-heterosexual friendship pairs. The salience of shared male attraction between friends was diminished with the bisexual's pairing with a female partner. And sixth, the heterosexual women indicated that some of the benefits of cross-sexual orientation friendships became more available within the friendship when the bisexual woman was partnered with a woman.

Galupo and St. John (2001) outlined the potential benefits of cross-sexual friendships among women. The benefits for heterosexuals included breaking down stereotypes about sexual minorities, increased sensitivity to sexual minority perspectives and increased flexibility in thinking about personal sexual identity. One heterosexual participant speculated that if her bisexual friend were partnered with a woman she would have an opportunity to learn new things from the friendship.

> If she had a girlfriend, I don't think our relationship would be different, but I think I'd learn a lot more. I wouldn't see it as a problem, but it would be something that I'd have to, like, kind of learn to deal with. But I wouldn't have a problem learning to deal with it. I almost would like to learn to deal with it.

In bisexual-heterosexual friendship pairs, these positive benefits for heterosexual women were associated with the bisexual friends' partnership with a woman.

DISCUSSION

This research is the first to focus on understanding bisexual experience in women's friendships across sexual orientation identities. At the outset, this research suggested that bisexual women may have a different friendship profile than lesbians or heterosexual women. O'Boyle and Thomas (1996) were the first to suggest that lesbians have more friendships with heterosexual women than heterosexual women have with lesbians. Similarly, the present findings suggest that bisexual women are even more likely to have friendships with women of different sexual orientation identities, than either lesbians or heterosexual women. In fact, while previous research has suggested that cross-sexual orientation friendships in general are relatively rare (O'Boyle & Thomas, 1996; Price, 1999) for bisexuals, cross-sexual orientation friendships (with either lesbians or heterosexual women) are common-place. Bisexual participants in this study experienced all of their friendships in a cross-sexual orientation context. Difference in sexual orientation identity can affect friendship dynamics in both negative (Price, 1999; O'Boyle & Thomas, 1996) and positive (Galupo & St. John, 2001) ways. Understanding the dynamics of cross-sexual orientation friendships for bisexual women, then, can be seen as an important model for understanding the social world in which bisexual women negotiate.

Findings from the present research suggest that cross-sexual orientation friendships are similar to other friendships in important ways. Close cross-sexual orientation friendships serve the common function of mutual support, just as any other close friendship. In addition, bisexual women are no less likely than lesbians to describe their friendships in social support terms.

Sexual orientation identity does, however, factor differently into the friendship dynamic for bisexual women and lesbians. There was an emphasis on similarity between friends in the heterosexual-bisexual friendship pairs. Issues of sexual orientation were brought up less frequently in bisexual-heterosexual friendships as compared to lesbian-heterosexual friendships. While bisexual-heterosexual friendship dyads found common ground in their mutual attraction to men, bisexuals experienced this focus, in part, as a de-emphasis and invalidation of their identity as bisexual.

In addition, the friendship dynamics of bisexual-heterosexual friendship pairs shifted based on the sex of partner of the bisexual friend. This perceived shift had important implications for disclosure within the friendship, acceptance of partner, and validation of bisexual identity.

SEXUAL EXPERIENCE AND BISEXUAL IDENTITY

One issue becomes particularly salient when placing the present findings in the larger context of research literature on bisexuality. Golden (1996) emphasizes that predictions about whether a woman considers herself heterosexual, bisexual, or lesbian cannot be made solely on the basis of past or present sexual attraction and involvement. Rust (2000) outlines the late 19th century emergence of sexual orientation identity categories and labels, and the implications that has on our current understanding of bisexuality. Previously, women were identified by their integration within a familial structure, namely their relationship to husbands and/or children (Katz, 1995). This identification took precedence over women's sexual behavior or emotional bonds to either women or men. Reconstruction of identity around the notion of sexual eroticism, together with the conceptualization of lesbianism and heterosexuality as polar opposites, has limited the degree by which bisexual expression is socially supported and has placed an emphasis on sexual experience with men and women as distinguishing bisexuality as unique from both lesbianism and heterosexuality.

In her 2001 study, Rust outlined the many paths by which individuals arrive at a bisexual identity, including feeling sexually attracted to both men and women; having the capacity to fall in love with men and women; having a willingness to act on sexual attraction with a man or woman; or adopting a bisexual identity which best reflects their political views on gender politics. An individual may rely on one of the above criteria in defining bisexual identity, or a combination of several, but it is clear that not all bisexually identified individuals require a behavioral litmus test to confirm or conceptualize their bisexuality. Contrary to cultural stereotypes, Rust (2001) found that many bisexual individuals do not feel a need to be equally attracted to men and women, or need to be sexually involved with both men and women in order to own a bisexual identity.

For many individuals, bisexuality is experienced as a stable end-point identity (Fox, 1995; Rust, 2001; Weinberg, Williams, & Pryor, 2001). In their longitudinal study Weinberg, Williams & Pryor (1994; 2001) followed bisexually identified individuals into mid-life. Across this time period, many of the bisexual men and women in their sample experienced monogamous relationships and in some cases became less identified with the bisexual community. This finding suggests that many individuals experience a stable and enduring bisexual identity.

The dichotomy between sexual experience and bisexual identity was not lost on the women in the present sample. Participants selected themselves into the present study based on their sexual orientation self-identification. Consistent with the findings of Fox (1995), Golden (1996), and Rust (2001), the identities of our participants did not always match the range of their sexual attractions and relationships experienced. One of our bisexually identified participants had never acted on her sexual interest in women. One of the heterosexually identified women had previously engaged in a sexual relationship with a woman, while maintaining a stable heterosexual identity, and another had indicated a sexual interest in women though she had not acted on it. We found a perceived shift in friendship dynamics based on the sex of partner of the bisexual woman even when sexual orientation identity was stable for both friends. The shift in friendship dynamic could not be explained by a shift in identity for the bisexual friend, nor could it be explained solely on the basis of sexual experience. The shift in friendship dynamic discussed by our participants was sometimes hypothetical in that participants speculated on potential changes in their friendships. The shift was associated most often with a change of perception of the bisexual friend based on the sex of her partner. The heterosexual woman's perception of her friend shifted with the sex of her partner for the bisexual woman, prompting a shift in friendship dynamic.

LIMITATIONS OF THE PRESENT STUDY
AND DIRECTIONS FOR FUTURE RESEARCH

The research reported here is an exploratory analysis of the relation between bisexuality and women's friendships across sexual orientation identities. The methodology for this study was unique in that friends were recruited and interviewed in close friendship pairs, which provided an in-depth analysis crucial for understanding the complex nature of this topic. However, because of the rather strict criteria for inclusion where both friends had to agree to be interviewed, and because participants represent a convenience sample from the east coast, generalizations from this research should be made cautiously and within the context of the noted demographics of this sample. Most notably, with regard to educational background participants represented a narrow range of experiences as they had all either graduated from college or had some college experience. And although the racial/ethnic background of the participants was quite diverse, differences in experiences across race or ethnicity was not considered in this analysis. In addition, further research will be necessary to determine whether male friendships across sexual orientation identities are similarly experienced.

The psychological implications for the impact of sexual behaviors in shifting friendship dynamics in bisexuals are likely to be complex. In our study, we found that even within a close friendship, the visibility of sexual orientation identity for bisexuals shifted based on sex of current partner. Our findings suggest that bisexual women are more likely to experience all or most of their friendships in cross-sexual orientation friendships with either heterosexual or lesbian women. Although this research explored cross-sexual orientation friendships of bisexual-heterosexual pairs, it is likely that similar shifts in friendship dynamics would occur in bisexual-lesbian pairs. Past research has documented the often negative attitudes of lesbians towards bisexuals (Esterberg, 1997; Rust, 1995) and lesbians' change of perception toward bisexuals when they are dating men versus women (Esterberg, 1997). Whether or not close friendships between bisexual-lesbian pairs would reflect this same shift in dynamic has yet to established. Additional research is necessary to fully understand bisexuals' experience of friendship.

Pursuing a better understanding of bisexual women's friendships with lesbians and heterosexual women could potentially allow a broader understanding of women's sexuality in general. Rust (2000) indicated that cultural constructions of lesbian and heterosexual experience have framed our current understanding of bisexuality. Considering the intimate dynamics that structure close friendships between women of different sexual orientation identities may allow a better understanding of the way in which lesbians and heterosexual women define themselves against bisexual experience in order to establish and maintain meaning in their own sexual orientation identities. In addition, continued research in the area friendship and bisexual identity may provide a model for understanding the ways in which bisexual women and men negotiate a larger social world dependent upon interacting with individuals with different sexual orientation identities.

REFERENCES

Buxton, A. (2001). Writing our own script: How bisexual men and their heterosexual wives maintain their marriages after disclosure. *Journal of Bisexuality*, 1(2/3), 155-189.

Coleman, E. (1985). Bisexual women in marriages. *Journal of Homosexuality*, 11(1), 87-99.

Eliason, M. J. (1997). The prevalence and nature of biphobia in heterosexual undergraduate students. *Archives of Sexual Behavior*, 26, 317-326.

Esterberg, K. G. (1997). *Lesbian and bisexual identities: Constructing communities, constructing selves*. Philadelphia, PA: Temple University Press.

Fox, R. C. (1995). Bisexual identities. In A.R. D'Augelli & C. Patterson (Eds.), *Lesbian, gay and bisexual identities over the lifespan* (pp. 48-86). New York: Oxford University Press.

Fox, R. C. (1996). Bisexuality in perspective: A review of theory and research. In B. A. Firestein (Ed.), *Bisexuality: The psychology and politics of an invisible minority* (pp. 3-50).Thousand Oaks, CA: Sage.

Galupo, M. P., & St. John, S. (2001). Benefits of cross-sexual orientation friendships among adolescent females. *Journal of Adolescence*, 24(1), 83-93.

Golden, C. (1996). What's in a name? Sexual self-identification among women. In R. C. Savin-Williams, & K. M. Cohen (Eds.), *The lives of lesbians, gays, and bisexuals: Children to adults* (pp. 229-249). Ft. Worth, TX: Harcourt Brace.

Hays, D. (1989) Heterosexual women's perceptions of their marriages to bisexual or homosexual men. *Journal of Homosexuality*, 18(1-2), 81-100.

Higgins (2002). Gay men from heterosexual marriages: Attitudes, behaviors, childhood experiences and reasons for marriage. *Journal of Homosexuality*, 42(4), 15-35.

Herek, G. M. (2002). Heterosexuals' attitudes toward bisexual men and women in the United States. *The Journal of Sex Research*, 39(4), 264-274.

Katz, J. N. (1995). *The invention of heterosexuality*. New York: Plume.

Klein, F. (1993). *The bisexual option: A concept of one hundred percent intimacy, 2nd edition*. New York: Harrington Park Press.

O'Boyle, C. G. & Thomas, M. D. (1996). Friendships between lesbian and heterosexual women. In Jacqueline S. Weinstock and Esther D. Rothblum (Eds.), *Lesbian friendships*. New York: New York University Press.

Price, J. (1999). Navigating differences: Friendships between gay and straight men. New York: Harrington Press.

Rawlings, W. K. (1992). *Friendship matters: Communication, dialectics, and the life course.* New York: Aldine DeGruyter.

Rust, P. C. (1995). *Bisexuality and the challenge to lesbian politics: Sex, loyalty and revolution.* New York: New York University Press.

Rust, P. C. (2000). Bisexuality: A contemporary paradox for women. *Journal of Social Issues, 56*(2), 205-221.

Rust, P. C. (2001). Two many and not enough: The meanings of bisexual identities. *Journal of Bisexuality, 1*(1), 31-68.

Spalding, L. R., & Peplau, L. A. (1997). The unfaithful lover: Heterosexuals' perceptions of bisexuals and their relationships. *Psychology of Women Quarterly, 21*(4), 611-625.

Ochs, R. (1996). Biphobia: It goes more than two ways. In B. A. Firestein (Ed.), *Bisexuality: The psychology and politics of an invisible minority.* Thousand Oaks, CA: Sage.

Vernallis, K. (1999). Bisexual monogamy: Twice the temptation but half the fun? *Journal of Social Philosophy, 30*(3), 347-368.

Weinberg, M. S., Williams, C. J., & Pryor, D. W. (1994). *Dual attraction: Understanding bisexuality.* New York: Oxford University Press.

Weinberg, M. S., Williams, C. J., & Pryor, D. W. (2001). Bisexuals at midlife: Commitment, salience, and identity. *Journal of Contemporary Ethnography, 30*(2), 108-208.

How many bisexuals does it take to change
a light bulb? As many as you want.

http://www.haworthpress.com/web/JB
© 2004 by The Haworth Press, Inc. All rights reserved.
Digital Object Identifier: 10.1300/J159v04n01_05

[Haworth co-indexing entry note]: "How Many Bisexuals Does It Take?" Clurman, Dan. Co-published simultaneously in *Journal of Bisexuality* (Harrington Park Press, an imprint of The Haworth Press, Inc.) Vol. 4, Nos. 1/2, 2004, p. 55; and: *Current Research on Bisexuality* (ed: Ronald C. Fox) Harrington Park Press, an imprint of The Haworth Press, Inc., 2004, p. 55. Single or multiple copies of this article are available for a fee from The Haworth Document Delivery Service [1-800-HAWORTH. 9:00 a.m. - 5:00 p.m. (EST). E-mail address: docdelivery@haworthpress.com].

Works in Progress: How Mixed-Orientation Couples Maintain Their Marriages After the Wives Come Out

Amity Pierce Buxton

http://www.haworthpress.com/web/JB
© 2004 by The Haworth Press, Inc. All rights reserved.
Digital Object Identifier: 10.1300/J159v04n01_06

[Haworth co-indexing entry note]: "Works in Progress: How Mixed-Orientation Couples Maintain Their Marriages After the Wives Come Out." Buxton, Amity Pierce. Co-published simultaneously in *Journal of Bisexuality* (Harrington Park Press, an imprint of The Haworth Press, Inc.) Vol. 4, Nos. 1/2, 2004, pp. 57-82; and: *Current Research on Bisexuality* (ed: Ronald C. Fox) Harrington Park Press, an imprint of The Haworth Press, Inc., 2004, pp. 57-82. Single or multiple copies of this article are available for a fee from The Haworth Document Delivery Service [1-800-HAWORTH, 9:00 a.m. - 5:00 p.m. (EST). E-mail address: docdelivery@ haworthpress.com].

SUMMARY. In up to 2 million marriages in the United States, current or former, one spouse is bisexual, gay, or lesbian. When the spouse comes out, the marriage is threatened because of scant information about mixed-orientation marriages (especially those with disclosing wives), misconceptions about sexual orientation, and the myth that post-disclosure marriages are doomed, particularly when wives disclose. Bisexual-heterosexual couples face the dichotomous view of sexual orientation as gay or straight. About a third of known post-disclosure couples try to stay married, and roughly half do so for three or more years. This study looks at strategies, supports, and deterrents in enduring marriages of 40 bisexual wives, 47 lesbian wives, 27 heterosexual husbands of bisexual women, and 22 husbands of lesbian women. Helpful strategies common to all samples include honest communication, taking time, and finding peers. Peer support and counseling are supports. These findings echo those of bisexual and gay husbands and heterosexual wives of bisexual or gay men. Others reveal personal qualities and parental caring. Compared to their counterparts, more bisexual wives and heterosexual husbands of bisexual women mention love and emphasize the couple relationship. Fewer report deterrents, and families of origin support more. Like bisexual husbands and heterosexual wives of bisexual men, they expanded their concept of sexual orientation to encompass dual attraction and assume marital sex as a given. *[Article copies available for a fee from The Haworth Document Delivery Service: 1-800-HAWORTH. E-mail address: <docdelivery@haworthpress.com> Website: <http://www.HaworthPress.com> © 2004 by The Haworth Press, Inc. All rights reserved.]*

KEYWORDS. Bisexual wives, lesbian wives, heterosexual husbands of bisexual wives, heterosexual husbands of lesbian wives, bisexuality, mixed-orientation marriages

Life is not a problem to be solved, but reality to be experienced.

–Soren Kierkegaard

INTRODUCTION

Mixed-orientation marriages have quietly existed for centuries. In the United States alone, up to 2,000,000 bisexual, gay, or lesbian persons in the

United States have been or are married (Buxton, 2001), although not all have come out or may ever do so. In the wake of socio/political liberation movements of the last quarter of the 20th century, more and more have disclosed their sexual orientation. Internet subscription mailing lists for spouses in such marriages grow daily, as do calls to the Straight Spouse Network, a worldwide organization for heterosexual spouses whose mates have come out. Among disclosing spouses, the number of wives seems to be increasing more rapidly than that of husbands.

As disclosures increase, so does the spread of the myth that such marriages are doomed. The reality is that about half of the couples who commit to maintaining their marriages stay together three or more years after disclosure (Buxton, 1994, 2001). Yet the myth lives on, due to many factors. Mixed-orientation couples are indistinguishable from heterosexual couples and remain invisible. As detailed in "Writing Our Own Scripts" (Buxton, 2001), the prevailing notion that sexual orientation is solely a matter of sexual behavior precludes the possibility that someone who marries and has children might not be heterosexual. This false assumption is reinforced by an either/or mindset based on "fixed societal and psychological ontologies" (Martin & Sugarman, 1999) that makes it impossible to conceive that someone could be *both* married *and* gay or lesbian, much less bisexual. Many research studies of spouses in mixed-orientation marriages have been conducted within this dualistic framework, combining data about bisexual spouses with those about gay or lesbian spouses.

Scant literature on spouses in mixed-orientation marriages reinforces the idea that these marriages do not last. The studies and trade books most often focus on husbands who are closeted or come out. Few look at lesbian or bisexual wives, heterosexual spouses, or couples who maintain their marriages after disclosure.

From the start of my study of spouses' disclosure in 1986, couples who stayed married compelled my interest in how they bridged the divide of sexual orientation. As Executive Director of the Straight Spouse Network, I put spouses in touch with one another for peer support, and, in 1996, initiated a research project to gather data systematically about spouses whose marriages endured. The first report on the research, focused on bisexual and gay husbands and heterosexual wives of bisexual or gay men, reinforced some findings from prior research and added insights. Honesty and communication, found previously, were common to all samples, and they revealed three new factors as essential: taking time, the quality of a couple's relationship, and deterrent factors within the marriage. Most important, they emphasized the process of reconstructing their marriages, rather than the structure.

The second part of the project, focused on spouses in marriages in which the wives come out, is reported here. The study fills the gap in the literature about bisexual/lesbian-heterosexual marriages and expands our understanding of post-disclosure marriages that last.

THE STUDY

The present study focused on how strategies, supports, and deterrents worked together as spouses in bisexual- or lesbian-heterosexual marriages reconfigured their relationship. To grasp the import of their reported experience, their reports need to be framed within the family and community setting. A married person's disclosure impacts everyone in the immediate family. "The Other Side of the Closet" (Buxton, 1994) and "The Best Interest of Children of Gay and Lesbian Parents" (Buxton, 2001) describe in detail the overlapping stages of family members' dealing with the disclosure: First, the coming out of the disclosing spouse, next, the processing of that information by his or her heterosexual spouse, and, finally, their children's sorting out meaning for them and their growing up.

The immediate family's processing of the disclosure is, in turn, affected by diverse concepts of homosexuality and bisexuality and varied views about marriage held by members of their extended families, gay and straight friends, and groups with whom they interact, work, play, and often worship (Buxton, 2001). Few therapists knowledgeable about mixed-orientation relationships are available for both spouses, while community and Internet support resources for the gay, lesbian, or bisexual spouses far outnumber those for their heterosexual spouses. Given the lack of outside support and understanding, each gay/bisexual-heterosexual couple in my previous study developed their own "context" for rewriting their marriage script to create an enduring marriage. The question the present study raised was how similar or different were the "contexts" created by spouses in marriages in which the wives came out.

The goals of the study were to illuminate characteristics of spouses in bisexual/lesbian-heterosexual marriages, to provide real-life examples for other such couples, and to expand our understanding of bisexual spouses and of post-disclosure marriages that endure. Rather than the structure of a couple's relationship, i.e., monogamous or polyamorous, the study aimed to discern the process by which the spouses redefined their relationship. Of interest were individual perceptions, couple interaction, and family and societal factors that impacted their work.

The primary objective was to identify which strategies spouses used to maintain their marriages and factors that fostered or hindered their work. A second objective was to determine if any characteristics were distinctive of marriages in which the wives were bisexual, compared to lesbian/heterosexual marriages. A third objective was to see if the bisexual-heterosexual couples or bisexual wives shared any singular characteristics with bisexual-heterosexual couples or bisexual husbands in the first study, compared with lesbian and gay spouses and their respective spouses. A fourth was to identify any differences between spouses in marriages in which the wives came out and those in marriages in which the husbands disclosed.

Methodology

Since the study focused on the experience of spouses over time, the investigation was primarily qualitative but included enough quantitative work to reveal patterns of experiences. Using a phenomenological approach (Merleau-Ponty, 1962), the study proceeded without a priori hypotheses. Self-reports provided data, out of which the findings emerged.

Announcements of the project were emailed to Internet mailing lists. Questionnaires were emailed to Internet respondents who chose to participate and mailed by post to known spouses and to support group leaders of the Straight Spouse Network and those listed in The Bisexual Resource Directory. Roughly half of the Internet members returned surveys, and a handful of support group members. All but one spouse directly contacted responded. The response ratio from support group members is unknown.

The questionnaire asked for demographic information and responses to four open-ended topics: *Three coping strategies, individual and couple, that were the most helpful for maintaining the marriage and/or a positive relationship? Circumstances that supported your staying together? External factors that worked against or interfered with the continuation of the marriage or maintenance of a positive relationship married? Advice you would give a couple when one of the spouses comes out?*

Examination of the self-reports proceeded against a cumulative database gathered from 7,000 spouses in the United States and fifteen foreign countries since 1986. Augmenting these data were a continuing review of the literature; thirteen years of leading a straight spouse support group; participation in seven Internet mailing lists of spouses (heterosexual, bisexual, gay, and lesbian); and work with spouses and couples through the Straight Spouse Network.

Analysis occurred in four steps. First, a content analysis was applied to spouses' reported strategies, circumstances, negative factors, and advice. Second, these self-reports were grouped into clusters of similar content and ranked in terms of "frequency of mention." The third step was to compare the clusters of strategies, circumstances, and negative factors with the clusters of advice to see which factors, if any, reappeared as advice, thereby suggesting a greater saliency, and what advice was freshly mentioned, implying a particular import. The fourth step was to compare and contrast proportions of respondents in the four samples who reported the most helpful strategies, supports, and negative factors and most-advised factors. Finally, strategies, supports, and negatives most frequently cited by spouses in this study were compared with those cited by spouses in the prior study of bisexual/gay-heterosexual marriages.

The Spouse Samples

Of the 200 questionnaires returned, 137 respondents qualified as having disclosed to their husband their orientation or same-sex activity after marriage and deeming the current status of their marriage to be "stable" or "unclear," but not "heading toward separation." The spouses were grouped into four samples defined by self-identity, not by sexual behavior or any other dimension of the Klein Sexual Orientation Grid (Klein, 1993), whether or not they acted on their same-sex attractions or continued sexual relations with their husbands. Spouses in bisexual-heterosexual marriages included 40 bisexual wives and 27 heterosexual husbands of bisexual women. Two wives completed questionnaires twice over the research period, one of whom shifted from self-identifying as lesbian to bisexual. Since 10 husbands and 10 wives were married to each other, the two samples represent 57 bisexual-heterosexual couples. Their counterparts included 47 lesbian wives and 22 heterosexual husbands. Four wives and two husbands responded two or three times during the research period; two of the wives came out initially as bisexual. Since seven spouses from each sample were married to each other, the two samples represent 62 lesbian-heterosexual couples.

These samples do not include spouses who are not on Internet lists, in support groups, or in contact with SSN; those who never heard of the survey; or those who remain private or chose not to participate. Yet, as the largest and most recent study of "still married" bisexual/lesbian-heterosexual post-disclosure couples to date, the findings offer the best information we have and are consistent with anecdotal evidence gathered from thousands of spouses since 1986.

The respondents present a varied demographic picture. Most were Caucasian and middle-class, lived in the United States, and worked in diverse jobs, including stay-at-home mother. The largest clusters were in their 30s or 40s, while bisexual wives and husbands of bisexual women were slightly younger on average than their counterparts. Each sample had a sizeable group who lived in small towns or midsize cities, with the fewest living in metropolitan cities. The bisexual wives were fairly evenly divided across these three locales and the suburbs, while a large group of husbands of bisexual women were suburbanites. The largest proportion of lesbians lived in midsize cities.

Spouses had been married from six months (a bisexual wife) to 45 years (a lesbian wife). The bisexual wives and husbands of bisexual women had been married on average for fewer years (11 and 13 and a half years) than their counterparts (22 years). The largest group in each sample married in the 1980s, and many more bisexual wives and husbands of bisexual women married in the 80s and 90s than did their counterparts. Only one bisexual wife married before the 1969 Stonewall Inn uprising, and one husband of a bisexual woman married between 1970-1973, when the American Psychiatric Association removed homosexuality from the *Diagnostic and Statistical Manual*. In contrast, several lesbians wedded before 1969 and slightly more husbands of lesbians married between 1970 and 1973.

The wives had come out or the husbands had "found out" from three weeks to 32 years before the survey. The bisexual wives had the largest cluster "out" for up to a year; the husbands of lesbians, the most who had known for two years. Contrasted to their counterparts, slightly fewer bisexual wives and husbands of bisexual women had passed the three-year mark that seems to be the pivotal point for deciding whether or not to stay married. However, bisexual wives had the largest proportion of any sample of those still married seven years or more after disclosing.

The number of children of these spouses ranged from none to five, and more than half of every sample had minor children. Slightly fewer bisexual wives and husbands of bisexual women were parents on average than their counterparts, and had more with none or one child.

HELPFUL COPING STRATEGIES, SUPPORTIVE CIRCUMSTANCES, AND NEGATIVE FACTORS

The four samples reported diverse coping strategies, supports, and negative factors. Some were common to large groups in every sample. In several cases, self-reports of one sample revealed a singular pattern. Other configurations varied from sample to sample.

Helpful Coping Strategies

The spouses were helped by a host of strategies. Four were common across the samples: communication, honesty, finding peer support, and receiving counseling (Table 1). Communication, mentioned by the most spouses of each sample, meant both spouses' expressing feelings, wants, and needs and listening to the other spouse's concerns. "Honesty" usually referred to wives' being candid to themselves or their husbands about their same-sex attractions, feelings, or relationships; or husbands' openly expressing their hurt, concerns, or self-concept to themselves and their wives. "Peer support" came via Internet and/or face-to-face groups or gatherings. Counseling was done by therapists or other types of counselors, such as clergy.

Bisexual Wives and Heterosexual Husbands of Bisexual Women. For a majority of the bisexual wives, communication helped them cope, and a large number advised listening as well as talking and expressing feelings, such as fear or anger, hurt, and questions. Communication was "compassionate," "caring," "supportive," or "intimate." Some wives shared information with their husbands about their girl friends or lovers. Others discussed with their husbands the past, present and future of the marriage or talked about their love or alternatives to a traditional marriage. One wife told her husband what she

TABLE 1. The Most Helpful Post-Disclosure Coping Strategies Ranked by Frequency of Mention Per Spouse Sample

Frequency Rank	Bisexual Wives N = 40	Husbands of Bisexual Women N = 27	Lesbian Wives N = 47	Husbands of Lesbians N = 22
Most Cited Strategy	Communication 22 / 55%	Communication 17 / 63%	Communication 25 / 53%	Communication 10 / 45%
2nd Most Cited Strategy	Honesty; Peer Support Tied: 11 / 28%	Honesty 8 / 30%	Counseling/ Therapy 14 / 30%	Peer Support 9 / 41%
3rd Most Cited Strategy	Commitment/Work on Relationship 9 / 23%	Counseling/ Therapy 6 / 22%	Honesty; Personal Space Tied: 13 / 28%	Counseling/ Therapy 8 / 36%
4th Most Cited Strategy	Mutual Respect 8 / 20%	Love/ Reassurance; Peer Support Tied: 5 / 19%	Focus on Children 10 / 21%	Marital sex/ Physical Intimacy 7 / 32%
5th Most Cited Strategy	Counseling/Therapy; Focus on Children; Books/Online Information Tied: 6 / 15%	Open Mind; Mutual Support Tied: 4 / 15%	Peer Support 9 / 19%	Honesty; Redefinition of Relationship 5 / 23%
6th Most Cited Strategy	Love/Reassurance; Mutual Support Tied: 5 / 13%	Personal Space; Outside Support; Negotiation/ Rules; Trust; Understanding Tied: 3 / 11%	Outside Support; Acceptance/ Open Mind; Redefinition of Relationship/ Rules Tied: 6 / 13%	Commitment/ Work on Relationship 4 / 18%
7th Most Cited Strategy	Taking Time/ Patience; Personal Space Tied: 4 / 10%		Mutual Support; Friendship Tied: 5 / 11%	Acceptance/ Open Mind; Friendship Tied: 3 / 14%

would like and did not like about sex with him, something that she had never been comfortable doing. "Now he's as good a lover as I ever had," she wrote. A wife who left her marriage for three years and had been back for four stated, "I have learned to speak up and ask for what I need rather than expect that my husband (or others) will know. He has learned to listen and seriously consider what I say, because he has learned the consequences."

Specific tools included ways to say things or what information to convey. One wrote, "Sometimes it just takes saying something in a different way for it to click for the other person." Her husband had said he did not like her spending so much time with her girl friend. She thought he wanted her to cut back the time, until he explained, "he just wanted to see me making as much effort to spent time with him." Another wife cautioned, "Don't make your partner listen to all of it. Get outside support, or even just a diary, so you don't wear them down."

Taking time and being patient helped several wives, alone of all samples, and many more advised taking time. "Think things out in your own mind," one advised, "without rushing ahead." Another wrote. "It (dealing with my bisexuality) never goes away, but sometimes you need a break from the roller coaster ride."

Both honesty and peer support helped a number. Advised by just as many, honesty was often entwined with "open communication." One wife told her husband her sexual fantasies. For others, being candid kept their trust alive or confirmed who they were. "Trying to be 'nice' doesn't work," a wife wrote. "It can wear down a relationship because a partner is trying to be someone she is not." Peers were a major part of the outside support that many wives advised. They found peers mainly online (SSML, SOTTS, and Wombats) or in face-to-face support groups, including PFLAG (Parents, Families, and Friends of Lesbians and Gays). Commitment, which helped about as many and was advised by a number of wives, focused on the spouses to each other; the priority of the marriage; or constructive problem solving.

Mutual respect uniquely helped some women and was also advised. They seemed keenly aware of how they and their husbands treated one another. Respect included "tolerance," being careful of the other spouse's feelings, kindness, and consideration, or attending to, but not judging, the other spouse's concerns, such as, "outbursts of anger (husband) or exhilaration (wife)." One wife advised, "Be prepared for and patient with their pain and anger. Understand where the anger comes from." Another wrote, "If one feels sad, mad, detached, the other should respect that without passing judgment and blaming themselves." The wife who returned after separating wrote, "My husband . . . never blamed me for leaving so he has always kept the door open. Blame just poisons the relationship when those hurtful angry words are spoken. It is difficult to overcome later and can create a barrier." Yet another said, "I have always tried to honour his feelings by not acting on my attraction I might have felt for other women."

Several wives educated themselves and/or their husbands about bisexuality and mixed-orientation marriages (through reading, Internet lists, or the gay community); by counseling; or by concentrating on the children. One wrote, "I am a sponge absorbing . . . all that I can in order to better understand myself." Others were helped by impartial, caring counselors who were "good communicators," though several encountered therapists who were biased toward divorce. Parenting helped in different ways. One wife and her husband put a priority on "creating a positive environment for the kids." Others "focused on being a good wife and mother," considered "the effect on divorce on the kids and baby," or "shared the responsibility of household and children with my husband."

Feeling and expressing love, couple's reassuring each other of their love, and mutual support helped some wives. Comments included "Love was our priority," "Remembering our love," and "Once all was said and done we knew we still loved each other and wanted our marriage to last and work." One reflected, "You have to feel loved and valued for any relationship to work, but in one with the added complexity of mixed-orientation/polyamory, it's seems doubly important."

Mutual support ranged from "supporting each other's emotional and physical needs" to "trying not to hurt my husband." One wife reflected, "My husband took a look at himself and our relationship and how could he be a better person and more supportive . . . I was always impressed with his love and support. Friends had tried to convince him that he needed to get mad at me and that he was making a mistake letting me back." Another advised, "Realize they are reeling too–if you can, hold onto each other and help each other out. It is soooo much harder to go it alone."

Like the bisexual wives, the largest clusters of the husbands of bisexual women found communication and honesty helpful, and almost half advised both strategies, more than any other sample. One wrote, "Find out what common vision, if any, they (wives) have about their family's future together and talk about how to get there. Thinking about the future helps ease the pain of the present and motivates you into thinking about how you can get there . . . Talk about the possibilities of divorce, opening their eyes to what may happen between you. It might influence their attitude to understand how this has hurt you and why and what it would cost."

Honesty worked closely with communication. Husbands described "utterly honest and searching" discussions or "unabashed honesty." One "made clear my bottom line" about what he needed and wanted in the relationship. Two men described the price of not being honest: "My wife's trying to suppress her feelings toward women and trying not to act on it was a hindrance to our process," and "Don't try denying your own feelings . . . I have seen it come out as anger. Let you and your wife be honest and you will find it much more peaceful."

Love or the reassurance of love, counseling, and peer support helped proportionately more men than bisexual wives. One defined love as a "spiritual connection flowing love through me, despite the pain, to help my spouse in her confusion and guilt." Another advised, "Remember why you fell in love with your partner, often." For them, love was a verb, seen in the number who advised, "Love each other."

Counseling was advised by as many as found it helpful, for example, "Take what he or she says with a grain of salt because there are few experts in this field and even fewer that most insurance companies will pay for. But you may have to do this to start a dialog." Peer support came from spouses on Internet discussion lists (SSML or HUGS) and face-to-face contacts.

Open-mindedness or acceptance helped a number of men. The largest proportion of any sample advised being open to alternatives. Accepting included the wife's same-sexual attractions and the concept of bisexuality. Several created a personal space for one or both spouses to enable each or both of them to pursue their own interests and/or think through issues or the wife to be with her girl friend.

Unlike bisexual wives, some men coped by negotiating the relationship. One man spoke of the couple's nightly check in "on how we were doing and what we discovered or experienced (good or bad) about ourselves and each other during the day." The two also took walks to talk. "(That) time, commitment, and physical activity, seems to allow a slower and more relaxed processing of sharing of issues."

Three strategies were unique. Several husbands spoke of and advised seeking outside support (other than peers), understanding and trust. Trusted, impartial friends provided a reality check and an audience for the men's fears and concerns. Many men, the most of any sample, advised, "Take your time," and a large number counseled, "Get a perspective."

Lesbian Wives and Heterosexual Husbands of Lesbians. Communication helped the largest cluster of lesbian wives, and a number advised, "Talk, talk, talk." Helpful communication was "open and direct" and included "expressing and empathetic listening in areas of thoughts, feelings, and wants/needs." One wrote, "Allow yourself time to feel and express the worst while not judging the emotions of the other. Their fear and anger are legitimate even if they hurt you."

Three large clusters found counseling or therapy, honesty, or making personal space helpful. Honesty was advised by even more and included being candid with themselves as well as with their husbands. "It is VITAL," one advised, "that you be as honest as possible . . . but not brutally honest. In other words, be sensitive to where each of you are at." Another explained, "I want my husband to know that he can trust me as he always had. I do not hide my plans with my lover from him." While counseling helped a number, fewer advised it. Creating a personal space ranged from pursuing lesbian interests while the husband was engaged in his military service to living on a separate floor in the home. Several wives compartmentalized their life into two lives: one as a lesbian and the other as a wife and mother.

Two coping strategies addressed these separate lives: attending to the children's needs or engaging in family life and spending time on Internet mailing lists or with lesbian friends or lovers. One wife and her husband made "a special point of doing things as a couple and as a family to reinforce that we are a functioning and thriving unit. It helps when things get tough to have the base be as strong as possible." Another focused on "what we do have–child, home, friendship–rather than what we don't have–a sexual marriage." For others, it helped to communicate with peers, most often through online lists or discussion groups, such as SSML, SOTTS, or MaRBLs.

Two clusters were helped by outsiders' support or their husbands' acceptance and open-mindedness. A number advised such acceptance. For one, her husband's acceptance of "where I am at emotionally, physically, etc., only strengthened the bonds between us." Another wrote, "Without his reassurance that God loves me just the way I am, I don't believe I would have had the courage to actively engage in a relationship with another woman, with his reassurance that I wasn't cheating if he was aware of it." A husband's acceptance often extended to his wife's lesbian friends or lover. One wife, who took limited visits with her long distance lover of six years, said that her husband "had (over time) accepted it as an unchangeable reality and decided to make the best of it."

Several wives were helped by redefining the marriage or setting ground rules with their husbands (usually through compromise), mutual support, or the couple's friendship. The wife who traveled to be with her lover did so only a few times a year, for a few days at a time, and never overnight. Two wives continued marital sex for their husbands' sake, not their own pleasure. Mutual support included caring for each other's needs and showing interest in his or her concerns. "Knowing that my husband is truly interested in my well-being and care," one wife wrote, "has made us much closer because I feel like he has been so supportive. That has been a major reason why I have never acted on feelings in the 6 years since I came out to him, despite his encouraging me to find someone."

Among the husbands of lesbians, communication helped the largest cluster and was advised by many. Communicating provided answers to questions about their wives' lesbianism or desire to explore or express it, helped solve problems, and produced facts. One husband, whose wife initially self-identified as bisexual, denied the disclosure for six months. She waited until she felt he could handle her bringing it up and then they shared feelings regularly. "It has helped a great deal," he explained, "to just be able to tell her that 'today I am very depressed/angry/whatever' and have her acknowledge that that is just where I am today." Another husband did a periodic "pulse-checking" with his wife, when each asked the other, "How are you doing–concerning our relationship?"

More husbands than spouses in any other sample were helped by peer support and counseling. One wrote, "Finding out that we weren't alone was crucial to keeping our relationship together. Support group, mailing list, polyamory workshop, HUGS gathering." Another described his first talk with another straight spouse: "I could look in that person's eyes and see they really understood. This was more important to me than I can describe." For yet another, discovering an online group was a turning point. "I was able to connect with a larger community of people who were asking the same questions I was asking."

Sex or nonsexual physical intimacy with their wives helped a number. "We adapted our sex life to fit her desires," one man wrote. "I almost always perform oral sex on her. She almost always uses her hands on me." Another said, "I believe our relationship will stay together as long as we can be together sexually . . . we will eventually split up if our sexual relationship ends." Still another wrote, "She still has sexual intimacy with me (after 15 months) though she indicates frequency will decrease."

Honesty helped fewer husbands than lesbian wives, but more advised candor, often mixed with communication. One wrote that self-honesty "is as important as being honest with your spouse . . . Was/is it (the marriage) worth saving without considering the sexual orientation of the spouse?" Another advised, "Be open . . . even if you think it will hurt them. The straight spouse will have his imagination run wild unless this is done." Yet another wrote, "Allow yourself to express feelings and fears you have hidden inside all your life. If she doesn't know what you are feeling or thinking, she will assume the worst." One man cautioned, "Do this even if either or both spouses know, or feel, that the question, or answer, will cause temporary pain for one, or both, of the spouses."

Compared to the other samples, more husbands of lesbians found negotiating rules, like "non-monogamy ground rules," helpful. One advised, "Look into the possibility of open marriage. But this needs to be a very slow and mutual decision." Another worked out a "new paradigm of the heart": "Inclusivity" of loved ones for each spouse, rather than "Exclusivity" of the couple within the traditional framework of monogamy.

For several, activating the couple's friendship or explicit acceptance helped. Their friendship motivated joint activities, such as, Friday nights out. "We didn't institute this for several months. When we did, it restored a certain amount of order and stability." One man accepted his wife's lesbianism in four weeks: "My wife is gay. Now, let's figure out how to integrate her homosexuality in our life together." Most took longer. One explained, "Accepting that for her to be happy staying with me, I would have to accept her needs being met." Another said, "She's the same woman I have loved and continue to love." Accepting meant not judging, as one wrote, "When it comes to our sexual orientation there is no such thing as blame or fault. These things can only apply if there is dishonesty somewhere along the way." Several husbands, alone of all the samples, advised understanding.

Supportive Circumstances

Supportive circumstances were aspects of the spouses' lives that facilitated their creating an enduring marriage (Table 2). Spouses reported many more factors than the examples offered on the questionnaire, and many did not cite any of them. Each sample reported a distinct set of supports, though they all cited children and family life among the three most frequently mentioned sup-

TABLE 2. Supportive Circumstances for Maintaining Post-Disclosure Marriages Ranked by Frequency of Mention per Spouse Sample

Frequency Rank	Bisexual Wives N = 40	Husbands of Bisexual Women N = 27	Lesbian Wives N = 47	Husbands of Lesbians N = 22
Most Cited Support	Children/Family Life 15 / 38%	Friends; Our Love Tied: 8 / 30%	Finances 21 / 45%	Children/Family Life; Job Tied 11 / 50%
2nd Most Cited Support	Our Love 14 / 35%	Quality of Relationship; Children/Family Life; Peer Support Tied: 5 / 19%	Children/ Family Life 18 / 38%	Friends; Wife's Lover Tied: 5 / 23%
3rd Most Cited Support	Finances 10 / 25%	Active Sex Life; Family of Origin; Finances; Job Tied: 3 / 11%	Quality of Relationship 14 / 30%	Closet/Privacy; Our Love Tied: 4 / 18%
4th Most Cited Support	Lover 8 / 20%		Closet; Friends Tied: 13 / 28%	Faith Community 3 / 14%
5th Most Cited Support	Family of Origin; Friendship Tied: 7 / 18%		Faith Community 8 / 17%	
6th Most Cited Support	Friends 6 / 15%		Friendship 7 / 15%	
7th Most Cited Support	Peer Support 5 / 13%		Lover; Our Love Tied: 5 / 11%	
8th Most Cited Support	Closet/Privacy; Faith Community; Job Tied: 4 / 10%			

ports. Common to smaller clusters were the couple's love and the wife's lover. All other supports related to day-to-day exigencies of living, couple or social interactions, or the relationship.

Bisexual Wives and Heterosexual Husbands of Bisexual Women. For a majority of the bisexual wives with minor children, children and family life supported their staying married. A number felt supported by "our love," far more than their counterparts. Love as a support, in contrast to its expression as a coping strategy, continued in their lives. "A lot of things . . . kept us together," wrote one, "most importantly, the faith in each other and our love." Another advised, "Learn to see the love in the marriage as a gift rather than given: don't take it for granted."

Finances influenced almost as many, usually because the couple could not afford two households or the wife was a stay-at-home mother. Most other supports came from people: the wife's lover or their family of origin, the couple's friendship, friends, peers, or members of their faith communities. A number of wives advised seeking outsiders' support. "Take some calculated risk," one advised. "I know it seems a little scary. Severe isolation is even more harmful." Outside support more often was directed at continuance of the marriage than the wife's same-sex attractions. "My sisters," wrote another, "two of which are lesbian, very much support us staying together . . . They do not believe I should have a girl friend because they love my husband and they believe I'm cheating."

Jobs, their faith community, or being closeted supported several wives. For one and her husband, "being in our careers always made us feel that each of us were in the relationship because we want to be not because we need financial support." Staying in the closet or keeping their bisexuality private supported some wives also. By avoiding pressures to divorce or negativity toward their lesbianism or staying married, they could concentrate on support from the three sources most meaningful: husband, marital relationship, and lover.

Among the husbands of bisexual women, "our love" and friends supported the largest group. "Love" referred to the core of their relationship. One wrote simply, "We love each other," and another, "I'm very much in love with her." Yet another said, "My wife loves me no less than before she came out, and as long as her relationship with her other lover does not adversely affect us, we will remain together." Although some men did not dare tell others, a number advised reaching out. "We have found such support from that side we did not expect," another commented. "Our friends were great. Some are still looking for girl friends for us."

Smaller clusters were supported by peers (mostly online), the quality of the couple's relationship, or their children and family life. The husband whose wife came back elaborated, "The interpersonal skills that we'd developed during the marriage (i.e., respect, honesty, compassion, support) were instrumental in preserving the communication during the coming out and three years of separation." Love and caring for children and/or participating in family activities held various meanings. One wrote, "Hetero spouse working. Homo spouse working at home taking care of the kids. The children are a major part in holding the marriage together." Another said, "We also want to provide a stable environment for the last kids as they finish out their high school years."

A continuing sex life, finances, job, or support from their families of origin reinforced the marriage for several husbands. Alone of the samples, one cluster found the couple's active lovemaking to be a key support, reinforcing their marital satisfaction. One man noted, "My wife doesn't feel that her orientation is solely lesbian, or that it is a problem sharing her life and bed with me." Another said, "Commitment to our vows and to monogamy so far has been enough to prevent her from acting upon her sexuality. For right now, her fantasies are enough for her, and I accept and perhaps actively encourage these fantasies."

Support that some found from families of origin mirrored the experience of some bisexual wives. One husband wrote, "I'm liked by my sister-in-law and they were hoping we would work our marriage out." Another commented, "her family is very supportive of her." Jobs, too, supported the same proportion of husbands as bisexual wives. Finances supported fewer. Reasons were either that no financial concerns interfered with the marriage or, for two who worked with their wives, both spouses gained personal reward from work or a continued married let them provide for their employees and their own financial interests.

Lesbian Wives and Husbands of Lesbians. Children and family life supported the largest cluster of lesbian wives to stay married. Finances, supports for a large number, held diverse meanings. One wife was changing jobs to move ahead in her career, though it paid less money. For another, the couple's finances were intertwined, making separation difficult. "But," she explained, "that hasn't been the real factor . . . I have a good job and I'm not financially dependent on my husband."

For nearly half of mothers of minor children, children were a key reason to continue the marriage out of love and caring for them, parental responsibilities, and concerns about effects of divorce. "I don't want to rock their perfect little world," one wrote, "and my husband feels the same way." Another did not want her children "living in an atmosphere of hostility or resentment. So I've been determined not only to stay with my husband but to try to nurture a healthy relationship with him. Oddly enough, our relationship has actually grown stronger since I've come out."

The quality of the couple's relationship supported a number of wives, underscored by advice like, "pay attention to the quality of the relationship." One stated, "We have always had a strong bond and this seems to be the glue to hold us together." Several spent time thinking to put their relationship into perceptive or change their attitudes toward their husbands or themselves, for example, "I made a conscious effort to stop blaming my husband for the lack of intimacy in the marriage because I read that that is a universal complaint of married lesbians. Eventually that led to accepting and predicting the level of intimacy between us is what is right for me in this relationship, and that I want more, deeper, or maybe specifically women intimacy somewhere in my life."

Two supports seem contradictory: the closet and support of selected friends. Some closeted wives wanted to avoid rejection by important people in their lives, though the closet had its price. One wrote, "His family is Muslim and we were afraid they would no longer let us see our nephews if I came out to them, so we pretended everything was fine." Another said, "I hate the fact that I have to hide, that people would revile me if they knew. I do not like living this way. I hate society for making this so damn hard, even though I swear, I would not have chosen to be lesbian." Yet another was not out to any relatives, because "my parents supported me to slam the door tightly to my closet years ago, before my marriage." Closeted wives found support from a few trusted friends, and a number advised seeking such support. "Our friends and family know about our open marriage," one wrote, "Although they think we're weird, they support us."

Religion or members of their faith communities supported several wives. "Strong religious beliefs," wrote one in a 13-year-long lesbian relationship, "have contributed to our attempts to maintain the marriage, to put the extra effort into it." Church members or clergy encouraged the marriage and/or supported the lesbianism of some wives. One attended an "affirming church," where members helped her confront being lesbian but then pressured her to "not be gay, to not want a girl friend, to not talk about it, to not rock the boat and to not break my marriage covenant." When she came out to fellow congregants, she felt pressure "to get on with my life and be fair to my husband to get on with his." For another wife, a gay Unitarian minister affirmed the couple's decision to stay married.

The couples' friendship provided support for other wives. One wrote, "We were friends long before we were married and we HAD to get back to that place to find the ability to continue to live together." She advised, "Find a place inside your soul that reminds you of why you did marry this person so that you can build a friendship from there."

The couple's love or the wife's lover supported others. For one, love was part of her value system. "My faith calls me to love my husband and others. When I think of this instead of 'making the marriage work,' it does work (at least for now)." Another wife and her husband reflected, "We've always had a strong bond." Some simply said that they and their husbands loved each other," one clarifying, " I'm not in love with him." Several supportive lovers insisted that they did not wish to break up the marriage.

Among the husbands of lesbians, children and family life were a key support for the largest proportion overall and of parents of minor children among all the samples. Jobs, too, supported a half. Friends or their wives' lover supported smaller clusters. As one husband wrote, "Support from lover is practically unheard of in the lesbian community." Another spoke of the couple's telling a friend about the disclosure and trying to sort out what it meant, "His simple acceptance was balm to us from all the nonacceptance we had been experiencing in our other friendships."

A smaller number of men felt supported by the couple's love, while more advised paying attention to "our love." One stated, "Family and our knowing we love each other was the main factor," and advised, "Keep telling your spouse you love them, and tell them why!" Another wrote, "Give concrete examples of why you love them every day."

Staying in the closet supported several. "Her unwillingness to come out probably helped," one wrote. Another said, "We don't feel comfortable with our employers knowing anything. Our temple supports the glbt community but no mixed-orientation marriages or anything that would involve a polyamorous situation." For some, members of their faith communities supported their marriage, though not always the wife's homosexuality. One felt "pressure from our friends from the church community that divorce is wrong and we 'should' find a way to remain married (in a traditional heterosexual marriage) no matter what." Another noted that he and his wife attended "a very anti-homosexual church (Mormon) and although we have many friends this is not an issue that we can share with them."

Negative Factors

The survey question about negative factors aimed to discover external obstacles to continuing the marriage. However, many spouses mentioned factors internal to the marriage (Table 3). More important, a number did not cite any deterrent or wrote "None" or "N.A.," and those who cited negatives mentioned fewer of them than they did of coping tools or supports. Most deterrents came from outside the family circle. Common to all samples was negativity from their families of origin or the gay and/or lesbian community.

Bisexual Wives and Heterosexual Husbands of Bisexual Women. The bisexual wives were adversely affected by more factors than any other sample and faced the most distinctive pattern of obstacles. Alone, they were negatively affected by societal expectations or assumptions about lesbian relationships; a lover's negativity toward the marriage or husband; or martial relationship problems.

The largest cluster felt pressured by societal views about traditional marriages, an assumed inevitability of divorce after a disclosure, or bisexuality itself. One wife wrote of "our erroneous preconceived ideas, learned through socialization, of the nature of bisexuality [and a] lack of sources of accurate information and support for our situation." Another cited society's not "seeing the fluidity of sexuality and women's later sexual development (compared to men's)." Other deterring assumptions were that women should not have lesbian relationships and women with "lesbian attractions" cannot be parents.

Wives' or their husbands' troublesome feelings included guilt or disloyalty from wanting to be with another person, religious judgments "to batter" them into changing; emotional dependency; fear of rejection or failure; lying; feeling isolated or lonely; jealousy; or resentment toward the husband's representing "the marriage." One felt jealous when she saw her husband with "the other woman" in their polyamorous arrangement. Another non-monogamous wife

TABLE 3. Negative Factors that Interfered with Maintaining the Post-Disclosure Marriage Ranked by Frequency of Mention per Spouse Sample

Frequency Rank	Bisexual Wives N = 40*	Husbands of Bisexual Women N = 27*	Lesbian Wives N = 47*	Husbands of Lesbians N = 22*
Most Cited Negative Factor	Social Expectations 8 / 20%	Family of Origin Negativity 4 / 15%	Family of Origin Negativity 11 / 23%	Family of Origin Negativity 7 / 32%
2nd Most Cited Negative Factor	Negative Feelings; Lesbian Relationships Tied: 7 / 18%	Negativity of Gay Community; Wife's Lesbian Feelings; Lack of Information/ Models; Negative Feelings Tied: 3 / 11%	My Lesbian Feelings 6 / 13%	Negativity of Lesbian Community 6 / 27%
3rd Most Cited Negative Factor	Relationship Problems 6 / 15%		Negative Feelings 5 / 11%	Negativity of Straight Community 3 / 14%
4th Most Cited Negative Factor	Family of Origin Negativity; Lover's Pressure; Negativity of Gay Community Tied: 4 / 10%			
***No Negative Factor Cited**	"None"/ NR/"NA" 9 / 23%	NR/"NA" 15 / 56%	"None" 4 / 9%	"None" 3 / 14%

wrote, "When I'm feeling healthy I don't have a problem with jealousy, but when I start to have self-doubts, I can fall apart easily."

"Lesbian relationships" concerned several wives. Dates with girl friends took time away from their husbands, or their husbands did not like their being with a lover. Smaller clusters were hampered by their lovers' pressure to divorce, isolation from or pressure to divorce by members of the gay community, or negativity about lesbian feelings and/or activities from their families of origin.

Among the husbands of bisexual women, less than half cited deterrents to staying married. Family negativity impacted the most, as parents or in-laws spoke against their wives' lesbianism and/or sex-sex activities or expressed doubts about the marriage's survival. Their wives' lesbian feelings threatened some. "I'm not particularly concerned about my wife's bisexuality," one wrote, "but about her need to express it physically and emotionally with another person." Negative feelings of one or both spouses included anger, sadness, frustration, fear of a third person in the relationship, or insecurity about the future. One said, "I'm scared that ultimately she may be gay, and I'm sad that we stand a chance of losing all we have. She tries to reassure me, but it's only words. Until a genuine third party exists, even she won't know how she'll react." Lack of information or role models was unique to several.

Also unique to these husbands, members of the gay community discouraged some from staying married. "The official 'politically correct' 'gay community,'" wrote one, "did the very best they could to separate us and convince my wife that she was REALLY lesbian. We lost a large number of lesbian friends when my wife came out as bi." Another stated, "I strongly feel that if everything were out . . . the pressure from friends, neighbors and family would be extremely difficult to ignore. (I did not want to experience) public rejection without the support of the gay community (or the positive tangible benefit of another positive relationship) to help sustain me. My personal ego was and is still so totally destroyed, that that may have pushed me to leave just to prove to others that I can. That I am a man. That I'm not so needy that I can't walk away from such a 'terrible' person and situation."

Lesbian Wives and Heterosexual Husbands of Lesbians. All but four lesbian wives reported deterrents, though they noted only three of them. Most felt family negativity. "My mother especially putting a lot of pressure on me" one wrote, "not necessarily to get a divorce more like not to be lesbian. Any type of pressure increases my overall stress level which is off the scale these days and that makes the married and gay status harder to cope with." Another said, "My religiously-stepped mother was more concerned with the fact that I would be committing adultery than that I was a lesbian."

A number were deterred by their lesbian feelings, and others by their own or their husbands' negative feelings. One spoke of "bitterness, anger, hurt at first, our fears." Another knew how unhappy her husband was and "how unfair it was to him," while yet another "hated the fact I have to hide." For still another, it was difficult for her and her husband to overcome jealousy, anger, and guilt. "We have to watch for them when we talk." Yet another wife spoke of the negative aspect of her determination to make the marriage work "because it's the right thing to do. I feel caught in a strait jacket and want out."

Like the lesbian wives, the husbands of lesbians identified only three obstacles. Family negativity affected the largest group. One commented, "My family, her family, most everyone that has an opinion says–it won't work." The other clusters encountered negativity from members of the gay community, who were against lesbians' staying married, or some in the straight community who did not accept homosexual persons. One wrote, "We live in a small town. Two years ago a man at the mill . . . came out to his wife, family, and friends. He was socially ostracized by the entire community. (For me) it would be difficult to maintain an open marriage, without constantly facing the judgments of others."

DISCUSSION

This portrait of bisexual and lesbian wives and heterosexual husbands of bisexual or married lesbians confirms the thesis of the previous study of bisexual and gay husbands and heterosexual wives of bisexual or gay men: communicating candidly, loving and being friends with each other, caring for their children, finding peers and supportive friends, getting effective counseling, and taking time characterize couples who maintain their marriages after disclosure. Most important, the findings disprove the assumption that wives, especially lesbians, inevitably leave their marriages after coming out.

Honest communication lies at the core of any ideal relationship, but speaking honestly and keeping love and friendship alive while dealing with disclosure issues is remarkable. As a husband of a bisexual woman wrote, "Being honest with one another as to what we need and want, we have developed a stronger bond." Many echoed another husband's words: "We made time to talk . . . in a nonjudgmental way, speaking out of love not fear."

External factors both supported and deterred spouses. Peers supported the most. Counselors helped a number, although others found no therapists knowledgeable about mixed-orientation relationships. Children were among the most frequently mentioned supports, and "our love" or friends supported smaller clusters. Though many spouses identified no obstacles; those who did so cited far fewer than the strategies or supports they reported. Most came from the societal context. Given the smaller number of respondents and the fewer deterrents cited, these negative factors very likely represent the most critical.

The small proportion who identified obstacles also suggests that the challenge to maintain a post-disclosure marriage is so formidable and the stakes so high that spouses minimize any inhibiting factor, lest it weaken their resolve. The singular mark of the spouses is their ability to withstand deterrents and to break through polarized views of sexuality and habitual patterns of interacting. That took considerable cognitive, psychological, and for some, spiritual work.

The spouses reinforced the three core components of that work that the spouse revealed in the earlier study in which husbands came out: the quality of the relationship, taking time, and facing negatives within the relationship. They also added illustrative details to these key elements and contributed two more. At the same time, discussed later, they differed in several ways from spouses in marriages in which the husbands came out.

The greater number of reflective comments in the present study further clarifies what is meant by "quality of the relationship." Many spouses analyzed their behaviors, their partners' qualities, or the couple relationship and rebuilt their marriages accordingly. Several reflected on themselves and made personal changes for the sake of the relationship or to strengthen the couple's joint work toward mutual understanding. A bisexual wife advised communicating to discover the other spouse's needs so that the couple could grow together, instead of "heading off each in your own direction without considering the needs of the other one." The husband of a bisexual woman cautioned: "It is amazing how often people just assume they know what their spouse's real needs are, only to be shocked with the divorce because they did not have a clue what the other person really needed."

Most important, many spouses specified why taking time was critical. "Think things out in your own mind," advised a bisexual wife, "before coming out. Your wants, needs, the possible reactions of the other spouse, and the risks. Can you prepare so you are able to take the risk and handle that possibility." Some spouses took time to broaden their perspective on the disclosure or life's cycles, such as the pain that comes with loss and birth. A lesbian wife advised, "Know there will be ups and downs and that a river of tears will be shed." Another advised, "Be prepared for a period of disorientation, as the gay/bi spouse discovers the other side, the excitement of the discoveries my blind the spouse for a while to the positives of the heterosexual relationship. If the straight spouse can hold it together and remain open and love at this crucial time, when the gay/bi partner calms down, the marriage will be better than ever."

The first component that these spouses contributed to our picture of the post-disclosure process is a personal dynamic comprised of empathy, compromise, resilience, and flexibility of individual spouses. These features, revealed in comments or described actions, played key roles in couples' reconfiguring their relationship and handling obstacles. Many spouses demonstrated empathy, the ability to sense the other spouse's pain but not to assume responsibility to resolve it. Compromise by both spouses was evident, as was resilience in overcoming deterrents. Flexibility was obvious as spouses modified previous concepts of sexual orientation, accepted the new identity of the disclosing spouse, and changed patterns of interaction and time/space scheduling. A husband of a bisexual woman wrote, "I compare my wife and me to a glove with fingers that fit absolutely perfect. It's the thumb that is just wrong. The more we struggle to make the thumb fit, the worse off we make the fingers. If we free ourselves to find adjust the gloves for our thumbs, then the fingers return to their old wonderful fit." This finding may be a function of the greater expressiveness of these spouses, compared to those in the prior study. Yet I have observed such characteristics over the years and at least two previous studies of spouses in post-disclosure gay/bisexual-heterosexual marriages note one or more of them (Buxton, 1994, 2001; Coleman, 1981; Gochros, 1989; Matteson, 1985; Reinhardt, 1985; Whitney, 1990; Wolfe, 1985).

The second new component is possibly a mark only of marriages in which wives come out. Caring about their children, parenting concerns, and pleasure in family activities were palpable in the responses of a large number of both mothers and fathers of minor children. The maternal love and parental responsibility of the wives, complemented by the caring of the heterosexual husbands, played a major role in their working hard to stay married.

Aside from these contributions to the overall picture of post-disclosure marriages, the present study presents a distinctive array of strategies, supports, and obstacles among the four samples. The bisexual wives, heterosexual husbands of bisexual women, and their respective spouses differed on many counts from the lesbian wives, heterosexual husbands of lesbians, and their respective spouses. Their coping strategies more often focused on the couple's interaction and each spouse's part of relationship work, whereas their counterparts more often focused on individual needs, through counseling or peer support, or their children. More advised taking time than did their counterparts, often referring to the difficulty of understanding bisexuality within a marriage. "(It needs) most of all communication and LOTS of patience," wrote a wife. "It takes a long time for things to smooth out, and we aren't there yet. I think it is just a smooth bit of pavement." Expressed love and the reassurance of love helped more of them cope, rather than friendship that motivated more of their counterparts.

While jobs and finances supported more bisexual wives and husbands of bisexual women than their counterparts, they also developed a unique support system composed of themselves, bound by love and sex, families of origin, peers, and, for some, the wife's lover. In contrast, more lesbian wives and heterosexual husbands of lesbians and their respective spouses found support in their children and the closet. Fewer felt supported by "our love," and few were supported by their families of origin.

The bisexual wives and the husbands of bisexual women present a strikingly singular pattern of deterrents, too. Fewer reported obstacles than their counterparts, but there were many more obstacles. Negative feelings of one or both spouses in their marriages were troubling, as were pressures to divorce from members of the gay community. Fewer than their counterparts encountered negativity from families of origin, and no husbands felt pressured by the straight community.

Many of these characteristics resemble those of the bisexual husbands and their heterosexual wives in the prior study. The most prominent is their ability to expand their concept of sexual orientation so that the bisexual spouses can integrate the two sides of their sexuality and the heterosexual spouses can comprehend their mate's dual attraction. More of them than spouses in gay- or lesbian-heterosexual marriages emphasized the couple relationship, rather than their children and family life. Demonstrated love enhanced the relationship for a number and was a major reason to maintain their marriage for many, illustrating the power of the continued sexual attraction of both spouses in a bisexual-heterosexual relationship to intensify a loving bond and commitment.

More similarities appear when we look at only the bisexual wives and bisexual husbands in the two studies. More than their counterparts found love to be both a coping strategy and support. They alone had several who coped with mutual respect, possibly a function of the dual sexuality of the bisexual spouses that made them more aware of their heterosexual spouses' concerns. Families of origin and peers supported more of them than their counterparts, perhaps because of the heterosexual facet of their orientations and a wider acceptance of marriage among bisexuals. Finally, none of them mentioned marital sex as a coping tool or support, since lovemaking with the opposite gender is integral to bisexuality.

Several differences between the present study in which wives came out and the prior study, in which husbands came out, call for more research but are worth noting. More bisexual and lesbian wives, compared to gay or bisexual husbands, felt part of two worlds, gay and straight, and rejected by both. Contrasted with the denial and sense of imprisonment that the closet symbolized for some spouses after the husband came out, "the closet" supported lesbian and bisexual wives and husbands of lesbians, possibly because more were bothered by negativity from their families of origin. The closet let them to work on their relationship without outside criticism. For some heterosexual husbands, marital sex or physical intimacy, rarely cited in the prior study, was a coping tool (husbands of lesbians) or a support (husbands of bisexual women).

Regardless of differences among the spouses, their striving in the face of internal and external obstacles is extraordinary, seen alongside divorces of heterosexual couples who do not face such challenges. Their achievement results from interplay of individual personalities, the couple's relationship, and dealing with reactions from family and community. Among the bisexual wives and husbands of bisexual women and their respective spouses, unique nutrients of demonstrated love, sexual intimacy, and mutual sexual pleasure validated the sense of self-worth of the individual spouses and reinforced their joint commitment to develop a relationship that reflected the needs, wants, and values of each. As a bisexual wife stated, "I don't think my marriage would survive without sex."

Faith in themselves and their partners colored the self-reports, but most spouses were also realistic in acknowledging that their marriage was a work in progress and that they might eventually have to separate in order to maintain the quality of their relationship. Should that come to pass, they knew that the relationship that they and their spouse had wrought together would be an invaluable gift for each.

REFERENCES

Buxton, A. P. (1994). *The other side of the closet: The coming-out crisis for straight spouses and families.* New York: John Wiley & Sons.

Buxton, A. P. (2000). The best interest of children of lesbian and gay parents. In R. Galatzer-Levy & L. Kraus (Eds.), *The scientific basis for child custody decisions* (pp. 319-346). New York. John Wiley & Sons.

Buxton, A. P. (2001). Writing our own script: How bisexual men and their heterosexual wives maintain their marriages after disclosure. In B. Beemyn & E. Steinman (Eds.), *Bisexuality in the lives of men: Facts and fiction* (pp. 157-189). New York: Harrington Park Press.

Coleman, E. (1981/1982). Bisexual and gay men in heterosexual marriages: Conflicts and resolutions in therapy. *Journal of Homosexuality, 7*(2/3), 93-103.

Gochros, J. S. (1989). *When husbands come out of the closet.* New York: Harrington Park Press.

Hays, D., & Samuels, A. (1988). Heterosexual women's perceptions of their marriages to homosexual or bisexual men. *Journal of Homosexuality, 17,* 81-100.

Klein, F. (1993). *The bisexual option,* Second edition. New York: Harrington Park Press.

Martin, J., & Sugarman, J. (1999). *The psychology of human possibility and constraint.* Albany, NY: State University of New York Press.

Matteson, D. R. (1985). Bisexual men in marriage: Is a positive homosexual identity and stable marriage possible? *Journal of Homosexuality, 11*(1/2), 149-173.

Merleau-Ponty, M. (1962). *Phenomenology of perception* (C. Smith, trans.). London: Routledge.

Reinhardt, R. U. (1985). Bisexual women in heterosexual relationships: A study of psychological and sociological patterns. Unpublished doctoral dissertation: The Professional School of Psychological Studies, San Diego, CA.

Whitney, C. (1990). *Uncommon lives: Gay men and straight women.* New York, Plume Books.

Wolf, T. J. (1985). Marriages of bisexual men. *Journal of Homosexuality, 11*(1/2), 135-118.

Negotiating (Non)Monogamy: Bisexuality and Intimate Relationships

Kirsten McLean

http://www.haworthpress.com/web/JB
© 2004 by The Haworth Press, Inc. All rights reserved.
Digital Object Identifier: 10.1300/J159v04n01_07

[Haworth co-indexing entry note]: "Negotiating (Non)Monogamy: Bisexuality and Intimate Relationships." McLean, Kirsten. Co-published simultaneously in *Journal of Bisexuality* (Harrington Park Press, an imprint of The Haworth Press, Inc.) Vol. 4, Nos. 1/2, 2004, pp. 83-97; and: *Current Research on Bisexuality* (ed: Ronald C. Fox) Harrington Park Press, an imprint of The Haworth Press, Inc., 2004, pp. 83-97. Single or multiple copies of this article are available for a fee from The Haworth Document Delivery Service [1-800-HAWORTH, 9:00 a.m. - 5:00 p.m. (EST). E-mail address: docdelivery@haworthpress.com].

SUMMARY. Based on Australian research on 60 bisexual men and women, this article examines the variety of ways participants arranged their intimate relationships. While some participants were monogamous, others had negotiated some level of 'openness' in their relationships. Those who chose to have open relationships did so in a variety of ways; however, issues such as jealousy, setting boundaries, and communicating needs to partners often arose. Nonetheless, participants worked hard to overcome these difficulties through honesty and communication, and as such these findings go some of the way in addressing the common stereotypes of bisexual men and women as dishonest, untrustworthy partners. *[Article copies available for a fee from The Haworth Document Delivery Service: 1-800-HAWORTH. E-mail address: <docdelivery@haworthpress.com> Website: <http://www.HaworthPress.com> © 2004 by The Haworth Press, Inc. All rights reserved.]*

KEYWORDS. Bisexuality, relationships, monogamy, nonmonogamy, open relationships, polyamory

INTRODUCTION

While there has been wider acknowledgement of bisexual lifestyles over the past two decades, bisexuality is often still represented in stereotypical ways in popular discourses on sexuality. In particular, the intimate relationships that bisexuals form are often misrepresented, with bisexuals constructed as promiscuous, deceptive and unable to commit to long-term relationships. Much of this has to do with contemporary understandings of sexuality that construct it as a dichotomy between heterosexuality and homosexuality, with little or no room for bisexuality. However, stereotypes of the relationships of bisexual people are also influenced by the powerful Western cultural ideal of monogamy, which is rarely questioned by the media or society.

Effectively, this means that relationships falling outside of the (hetero)normative 'coupled' arrangement are rendered invisible, and in turn, delegitimised. Therefore, bisexual people, many of who form a variety of relationship types, of which some are not monogamous, are ostracised not only for falling in between or outside a dichotomous model of sexuality, but also for failing to conform to the accepted monogamous relationship structure of society.

Robinson (1997) argues that the ideology of monogamy forces us to "fit into neat, well-defined categories which don't allow for the complexity and reality of the diverse ways in which human beings relate" (p. 145). Not only must we fit into an explicitly heterosexual model of relationships, but one that defines the 'right' and 'proper' relationship as an intimate and closed union between one person and another. Defining intimacy in this way means that romantic and/or sexual activity outside the primary relationship is always constructed as a negative–hence our fixation on affairs, infidelity and sexual exclusivity. As a result, many people who have open relationships may find themselves being accused of all sorts of crimes against monogamy: legitimate outside sexual relationships are represented as 'affairs,' implying some sort of secrecy of the union, and primary partners are pitied for having to 'tolerate' acts of infidelity by their partners. Those who defend their rights to have open partnerships or form "multipartner relationships" (Pallotta-Chiarolli, 1995) are constructed as foolish or immature. The association between nonmonogamy and infidelity means that many find it difficult to accept nonmonogamy as a conscious choice to construct one's relationships along different lines (Robinson, 1997).

Following on from the misrepresentation of nonmonogamy as infidelity is the association between bisexuality and infidelity. Cultural constructions continually imply that those who identify as bisexual will always cheat on their partner. George (1993) argues that:

> People with no personal knowledge of bisexuality are likely to assume that bisexuals want multiple relationships; that one lover, male or female, can never be enough because a bisexual has needs which cannot be met by one sex or the other. (p. 83)

Such assumptions lead to the belief that bisexuals, as a result of their overwhelming desires for both men and women, will have to cheat on a partner to have their needs met. Rarely is it acknowledged that there are other options for bisexuals in relationships other than deception or infidelity.

Furthermore, the connection between bisexuality and infidelity means that bisexuals are believed to be 'incapable of monogamy, and by extension of commitment and deep feeling' (George, 1993, p. 83). In effect, then, ideas about the 'commitment-phobic' bisexual result from cultural understandings about bisexuality that see nonmonogamy as a necessary condition of being bisexual and the further association between nonmonogamy and infidelity, ideas that are both embedded in and articulated through contemporary discourses of love and romance that reinforce outside sexual relationships as immoral. These associations lead to a mistrust of bisexuals in relationships, and are fuelled by stereotypes in both the popular media and society that bisexual people need to have simultaneous relationships with men and women to be truly satisfied, and sensational media images depicting bisexuals as swingers or in the stereotypical 'ménage a trois' (Rust, 1996).

Such discourses and representations not only create suspicion amongst the wider community but may also impact on bisexuals themselves. Bisexual people often spend considerable time defending themselves against these misrepresentations and stereotypes. In an episode of *The Oprah Winfrey Show* in

1995, a statement by an audience member that she was bisexual and in a monogamous marriage was met with confusion by some other members of the audience. Trying to clarify this confusion, Oprah stated to the woman: 'If you are bisexual, and you are married, and you are monogamous, you are not bisexual' (Hudson, 1995). While this was met with disagreement from both the woman and many others in the audience, and was debunked as a myth by one the panel experts, the argument that one's bisexuality is erased when one chooses a single partner delegitimises bisexuality as a valid sexual identity, 'proving the point that bisexuals cannot be monogamous' (Rust, 1996, p. 128). As a result, those coming to terms with attractions to both men and women may feel that they are destined for a life of promiscuity and short-term relationships (Rust, 1996), or feel that they must commit to a life of nonmonogamy to be 'really' bisexual, despite a desire for monogamous relationships.

Constructing bisexuality using a singular model of nonmonogamy as infidelity does not allow us to recognise and represent the diverse ways bisexuality can be enacted in everyday life. Moreover, associating nonmonogamy with infidelity also does little to assist an understanding of the multiple ways nonmonogamy can be performed in relationships and the variety of relationships structures and arrangements that bisexual people may choose.

THE RESEARCH

This research forms part of a larger study on the lives of 60 bisexual men and women living in Australia. The data was collected using in-depth interviews where I asked participants about their bisexual self-identity, coming out, their relationships with partners, friends, family and their participation in gay, lesbian and bisexual communities. The majority of participants (60%) were aged between 21 and 29 so it was a very young sample. Despite this, the age range is from 21-66. As well as this, participants were mostly from urban centres in Australia (82% from capital cities of Australia), and mostly from East Coast states. Seventy-two percent were Australian born. The following discussion looks firstly at the relationship contexts of participants in the research–how many were in relationships, and the gender of their partners, then examines some of the issues and challenges faced by bisexual men and women when negotiating the level of monogamy in their intimate relationships.

Relationship Contexts

I asked participants if they were currently in a significant relationship. Of the 60 bisexual men and women interviewed, 42 were in a relationship, 16 were not currently in a relationship, and 2 chose not to answer questions on relationships. For those who were not in a relationship, I asked them to reflect on the last relationship they had been in. Of the 60 participants, most of them were, or had recently been, in a relationship with someone of the other sex. Of the 40 female participants, 75% were, or had recently been, in a relationship with a man, 17.5% were, or had recently been, in a relationship with another woman, and 7.5% gave no response for this question. For the male participants the figures were similar: 80% were, or had recently been, in a relationship with a woman and 20% with another man. These findings concur with figures reported by Weinberg, Williams and Pryor (1994, p. 79) who found that over three-quarters of the bisexual men and women interviewed in 1983 were in relationships with someone of the other sex. Overall, while identifying as bisexual implies an ability to form intimate relationships with men or women, these patterns indicate that most bisexual men and women tend towards primary relationships with the other sex.

Monogamy in Bisexual Relationships

Weinberg et al. (1994) found that in their sample of bisexuals living in San Francisco, nonmonogamy was a common factor in their intimate relationships:

> It took various forms: swinging, sexual triads, group sex parties, multiple involved partners, casual sex with friends, and anonymous sex at places such as bath houses or through pick-ups at gay and lesbian bars. (p. 107)

In another study on bisexual relationships, Rust found many of these varieties of nonmonogamy, but also found that some respondents had romantic relationships with partners considered 'non-sexual lovers,' or maintained sexual friendships that didn't become romantic. Another option was a group of friends who had sex with each other (Rust, 1996).

Despite these varieties of nonmonogamy, most bisexual people tend to prefer, and form, significant primary relationships with one partner and then arrange an open relationship in which they can explore a variety of sexual options (Weinberg et al., 1994; Rust, 1996). Similarly, my research found that while a few participants did seek out triad or multipartner relationships, more often than not participants formed intimate relationships with one person as their primary partner but often made the decision to be nonmonogamous within this relationship. They described this primary relationship in terms of being 'open' to a variety of nonmonogamous arrangements. Others had monogamous or exclusive relationships in which having outside sexual experiences was not an option. Of the 60 participants, many were in open relationships rather than monogamous relationships. Sixty percent of the bisexual men and 52.5% of the bisexual women indicated that their relationship fell into a category that could be broadly described as 'open' while a smaller proportion indicated their relationship was monogamous. Twenty-five percent of the bisexual men interviewed and 35% of the bisexual women were in what was defined as an exclusive relationship. A small number of participants claimed the issue of monogamy was still being negotiated within their relationship. Several others indicated that they were in new relationships where the issue of monogamy was yet to be discussed, or in relationships that they felt were not serious enough to warrant such a discussion. While women were *slightly* more likely to be in a monogamous relationship, the gender of the participants was not a major factor in whether or not participants were in a monogamous relationship in my research.

Relationship Arrangements

Monogamous relationships. As previously discussed, at least a quarter of the bisexual men and women interviewed were in monogamous relationships. Participants in these types of relationships had generally agreed to keep the relationship monogamous and were happy with this arrangement. At the time of the interview, Miranda was living with her heterosexual male partner and said:

> We are monogamous. He made it clear he wasn't interested in a nonmonogamous relationship and I was happy with that. I have no interest in a nonmonogamous relationship at all.

Others agreed to be monogamous for the sake of their partners. Michael was married for 38 years until his wife passed away, and told his wife he was bisexual just before she died:

> Our relationship was completely monogamous on my behalf. I was absolutely faithful to my wife and chose to be so off my own back. I've only had sex with other people since she passed away.

Sometimes participants identified external challenges to their commitment to monogamy when starting relationships. When starting her relationship with her lesbian partner, Sarah claimed:

> When we met, Kelly had only ever been in long-term relationships with other lesbians, so I think she had some initial concerns about being with someone bisexual. I think she became comfortable with the relationship and knew I was monogamous so I wasn't really looking for anyone else.

Kelly's concerns about forming a relationship with a bisexual woman indicate that misconceptions about bisexuality are also present within the lesbian community. Ault found this in her research on lesbian discourse about bisexuality. Quoting a lesbian participant in her research, Ault (1994) demonstrates how lesbian discourse constructs bisexuality in particular ways:

When I think of 'bisexual' I think of bedhopping . . . They not only cannot commit to being one or the other, but probably can't commit to whoever they're with, be it male or female. How could someone who wants to be in a long-term committed relationship still call themselves bisexual . . . without some infidelity coming into the picture? (p.117)

The belief that bisexuals are inevitably unfaithful and unable to commit to a partner are evident in this quote, and as Sarah found out, this often results in having to defend one's commitment to monogamy if one identifies as bisexual. Luckily for Sarah, the discussion about this issue in the early stages of the relationship challenged these misconceptions and the relationship was able to continue.

Being in a monogamous relationship did not always guarantee the relationship would be trouble-free, nonetheless. Two participants identified problems with their own commitments to monogamy. Colin was married with one son, and neither his wife nor his son knew he was bisexual:

In the eyes of my wife, we have a monogamous relationship. But I have a female lover at the moment and I've had numerous male sexual partners.

Tara was in a monogamous relationship with a heterosexual man at the time of being interviewed:

I told him that I was monogamous, but I broke the trust by going off with a woman. It's affected our relationship, because I think now he sees everyone as a potential threat. Now when we look at pictures of women together he gets insecure about it. My partner is monogamous, but now he's suggesting he should reconsider that because of what I did.

Generally, monogamous relationships were modelled heavily on the principles of sexual and emotional exclusivity. Despite some participants having difficulties with their own commitment to monogamy, most of those in monogamous relationships were satisfied with this arrangement. The issue of monogamy was often discussed quite early on in the relationship, often because discourses on bisexuality that construct bisexuals as untrustworthy meant that monogamous bisexuals had to defend themselves against accusations of potential infidelity in the future.

Open relationships. Previous research by Weinberg et al. (1994) on bisexual men and women in open relationships has found that there were a variety of ways they arranged their relationships:

Open relationships meant different things to different people. One type of relationship was very open, permitting emotional as well as sexual involvement. The person was free to fall in love with others and be open to the affectional feelings of others. A second type of relationship was more narrow, permitting only *sexual* relationships with others. A third type was similar to the second in that sex with others was allowed, but there were specific ground rules that defined who were acceptable partners, how much time could be spent with them, etc. (pp. 107-108)

My research also found a variety of arrangements within participants' open relationships: while some had relationships where both partners were able to have a variety of outside sexual and/or romantic experiences, others only shared sexual experiences with their primary partner and did not have separate outside partners. Very few had two partners at the same time; nonmonogamy was more likely to take the form of outside sexual/romantic/emotional relationships within the context of a committed primary relationship with one person. Very few also seemed to have secondary relationships or experiences that were more than sexual. In addition, many had established conditions or rules about how the open relationship would operate.

Negotiating (Non)Monogamy: Issues and Challenges

Agreeing to be monogamous can be relatively clear-cut, provided both partners agree, of course; however, negotiating an open relationship can be more challenging. For participants in open relationships, the process of negotiating the degree of openness in the relationship was by no means an easy process. Many couples established 'ground rules' to avoid some of these problems. Establishing ground rules often involved negotiating the extent of sexual experiences outside the relationship, the gender of outside partners, and the disclosure of experiences happening outside the relationship (Rust, 1996). Even when the ground rules were the same for both partners, they needed to be agreed upon and sometimes involved placing limits on what each partner could do. Many also renegotiated the ground rules when issues arose for one or more partners during the relationship.

One of the main ground rules for those in open relationships was honesty and communication. Sam identified this when discussing his relationship with his wife, who was also bisexual:

Technically it's an open relationship but it's situationally monogamous because of children, life, etc. The only condition is that we are completely open and honest with each other. Our partners can be of either gender.

Christine and David, another married bisexual couple, also had similar rules in their relationship:

Christine: We have an open marriage on both sides. The condition is that nothing is hidden between us. We both must know everything.

Most of the time we do things together, but if not, we are both aware of what's going on.

David: I've had outside sexual experiences with both men and women. Christine doesn't say anything except we always discuss it afterwards.

Megan, who had two concurrent relationships, a primary relationship with a heterosexual man and a secondary relationship with a bisexual woman, said:

> I came into my primary relationship stating that I didn't want to be monogamous. The rules are honesty, and preferably knowing experiences will happen in advance. I also have a secondary partner who is female. I'm able to have experiences outside of my two relationships but at the moment I don't do anything.

Others defined the ground rules in terms of the timing of and types of sexual experiences that could be engaged in. For example, Wendy and her male partner, who was also bisexual, had negotiated a relationship that was opened up only for an annual event:

> We are mostly monogamous, except for during [the Sydney Gay and Lesbian] Mardi Gras when we both play with other lovers. The rule is, however, no penetrative sex, especially as we only really want to have outside experiences with the same sex.

Several participants specified rules about the gender of any partners outside the relationship. For example, Martine, who had recently been in a relationship with a married woman whose husband was aware of and supported the relationship, said:

> I could see other men, but not other women, and the same for her–she couldn't see other women.

Alison, discussing her relationship with her bisexual male partner, said:

> I am slightly more restrictive in him than he is on me. I can sleep with both men and women, but he can only sleep with other men.

Ruth, who was married to a heterosexual man, had negotiated an open relationship with her husband and they were both nonmonogamous. They often attended swingers' parties together:

> We are both able to take other partners. I can have both male and female partners, and my husband can have female partners. Joe is happy for me

to have outside relationships. I currently have a boyfriend, who is a friend of Joe's. Joe is very supportive of this. Joe's had some experiences with men and women at couple's parties, but hasn't really been with anyone on his own.

Others had rules both about the gender of outside partners and the types of experiences that could be undertaken outside of the relationship. Sofia discussed the rules that she and her heterosexual male partner had settled on for their relationship:

I can't have a lover of my own even if I wanted to. We are currently involved together with another woman though. Mark is my number one soul mate, and he's heterosexual so we don't share male partners.

Christina, in a relationship with a heterosexual man, called her relationship 'semi-open,' and had a special condition attached to her outside liaisons:

I have the freedom to go outside of the relationship on the condition that my partner knows the person first. I haven't had any male lovers and I don't really want to, and my partner would probably be offended if I did.

As evidenced by many of the above quotes, it was common for some participants to agree only to have same-sex lovers (if their partner was of the other sex) and for them to indicate they were more comfortable with their partners having same-sex lovers too. Female participants often indicated that their male partners were more comfortable with them having outside experiences with women rather than men, and they also indicated their preference for male partners to not have outside liaisons with other women. For example, Peita, who was in a long-term relationship with a heterosexual man, said:

I have my partner's support and permission to be with women (even with men) but I wouldn't be OK if he went off with another woman—even though I know it's a double standard.

Negotiating the ground rules in open relationships often resulted from open discussions about certain situations and deciding which activities partners would feel comfortable with. Sometimes these ground rules were established early on in the relationship before any outside experiences had occurred. Other rules were established after one or both partners expressed concerns about outside experiences that had occurred or issues that had come up such as jealousy, insecurity or fear.

For others, jealousy occurred for a number of reasons and made the relationship rather difficult. At the time of being interviewed, Richard was in a relationship with a heterosexual woman:

Our relationship is open but we've had problems because my partner has a bit of a jealous streak and is perhaps more insecure about it all.

Jeanette was in a relationship with a heterosexual man:

We have an open relationship and talk about our other partners–that's part of the policy of it. I've had one-night stands with one other guy and one other woman. But it affected my relationship with my partner because of the honesty issue–it threw our open relationship into doubt. When my partner had sex with another woman, I was jealous and had hang-ups about it.

Jacinta was in a relationship with a woman who identified as a lesbian. They were still in the process of negotiating their relationship when I interviewed her:

Our relationship is constantly being negotiated. I wanted a nonmonogamous relationship and brought up issues such as safe sex with her. But it's created problems. She gets jealous if I kiss other women.

Another issue that arose was insecurity–many of those interviewed either identified feelings of insecurity expressed by their partners, or identified their own feelings of insecurity within the relationship. Barbara and Michael were married and had had several shared experiences in threesomes with both women and men:

In the early days our open marriage affected our relationship. There was insecurity, bad experiences. We worked through them, but it took 2 or 3 years.

Michelle had recently been in a relationship with a heterosexual man and they had had a number of shared sexual experiences with other individuals and couples. They did not have liaisons outside of these shared experiences. She said:

Our relationship was monogamous except for experiences we had as a couple. During one foursome with another couple my partner felt really left out because the other couple concentrated on me.

Nadine was married to a heterosexual man, Stephen. They had an open relationship, but her husband had not had any sexual experiences other than within the marriage at the time of the interview. She said:

I can have sex with other women if I want to, and Stephen actually initiated this. He said he would support my need to discover things about myself. I've been with women once or twice, but I've found that I often can't act out my desires because I think about my husband and this stops me! I get the big guilt trips because I feel like I'm cheating on him.

Matthew and Anne were one of several bisexual couples I interviewed. They had negotiated an open relationship that wasn't without its own difficulties:

> *Matthew:* We agree that we can't penalise half of our lives because we're in a heterosexual relationship. We are both free to have other lovers. I don't believe I have ownership over my partner. Anne does have a bit of a problem with me being with other women, but we are working through it.

> *Anne:* I'm free to have sex with other men, but I've chosen not to. I'm also more comfortable with Matthew having experiences with other men than with women, but I guess it also depends on the context.

The above quotes demonstrate that negotiating an open relationship with one's partner was not a straightforward process. Many participants identified a number of issues and challenges that had forced them to rethink the terms of the relationship, and for some, spend considerable time working on the primary relationship. For many, this was achieved by a commitment to honesty and through communicating about each partners' changed needs and expectations, and then setting clearer boundaries about what each partner could and could not tolerate within the relationship.

Others, however, found that negotiating the terms of the relationship was not a difficult process, and sometimes improved the relationship. For Tom, the renegotiation of his marriage came soon after he told his wife that he was bisexual:

> We've only recently renegotiated our relationship. I can now have sex with other men and women. I've only started having other sexual experiences since telling her I'm bisexual. I could actually see myself having a second relationship whilst still being married . . . Renegotiating our relationship has improved things immensely, as she has reached menopause and isn't as interested in sex–so now she knows that I don't expect sex when I hug her, which is a relief for her! She has been really supportive since I told her.

Tom found that rather than continuing to hide his bisexuality, being honest about his sexual needs and desires meant an improvement of the relationship not only for him, but also for his wife–and he said his marriage was better because he and his wife were no longer frustrated by their differing sexual needs.

DISCUSSION

While being bisexual does not automatically mean a person desires an open relationship, Trnka (1992) claims that 'bisexuality often brings nonmonogamy up as an issue' (p.106). It is evident from my findings that to be bisexual brought with it a necessity to reconcile one's attractions to both men and women with the desire for a committed relationship, and this often resulted in many choosing to be in some type of open relationship. Nonetheless, whether participants were in monogamous or open relationships, most put consider- able time and effort into negotiating their relationships in order to come to an arrangement that suited all parties involved, and such negotiations were not al- ways easy. Furthermore, some found that the demands of life, such as chil- dren, ageing, or other factors, often changed the meanings of fidelity and monogamy in their relationships.

As this research was exploratory qualitative research and used a small sam- ple of participants, it is difficult to know how typical of the wider bisexual population these findings are. What was discovered from this research, how- ever, was the diversity in the types of relationships that participants entered, and the distinctive processes of negotiating monogamy that occurred within these relationships. Further research using a combination of quantitative and qualitative methods, and a larger sample of bisexual men and women, could draw upon these findings and examine the broader patterns of relationships entered into by bisexual men and women, as well as the issues they face in both monogamous and nonmonogamous relationships.

Despite the stereotypes that claim that bisexuals are deceitful, unfaithful and untrustworthy in relationships, most of the bisexual men and women I in- terviewed demonstrated a significant commitment to the principles of trust, honesty and communication in their intimate relationships and made consider- able effort to ensure both theirs and their partner's needs and desires were ca- tered for within the relationship. More often than not, despite challenges that came with negotiating an open relationship, many participants worked hard to overcome any problems that arose. They discussed the issue of monogamy early on in their relationships, and were committed to communicating with partners about any jealousies, insecurities or other issues that arose. Such find- ings indicate that stereotypes that construct bisexuals as dishonest, and discourses that create a fear of both nonmonogamous relationships and rela- tionships with bisexual people, are not accurate. These views assume that nonmonogamy is the same as infidelity, or that nonmonogamy necessarily means dishonesty. Equally important, the findings of this study strongly confirm that bisexual men and women can and do participate in healthy, committed intimate relationships that are sometimes, but not necessarily or always, monogamous.

REFERENCES

Ault, A. (1994). Hegemonic discourse in an oppositional community: Lesbian feminists and bisexuality. *Critical Sociology*, *20*(3), 107-122.

George, S. (1993). *Women and bisexuality*. London: Scarlet Press.

Hudson, D. (Executive producer). (1995). *The Oprah Winfrey show*. [Television series]. Chicago: Harpo Productions.

Pallotta-Chiarolli, M. (1995). Choosing not to choose: Beyond monogamy, beyond duality. In K. Lano & C. Parry (Eds.), *Breaking the barriers to desire: New approaches to multiple relationships* (pp. 41-67). Nottingham: Five Leaves Publications.

Robinson, V. (1997). My baby just cares for me: Feminism, heterosexuality and non-monogamy. *Journal of Gender Studies*, *6*(2), 143-157.

Rust, P. C. (1996). Monogamy and polyamory: Relationship issues for bisexuals. In B. Firestein (Ed.), *Bisexuality: The psychology and politics of an invisible minority*. (pp. 127-148). Thousand Oaks: Sage Publications.

Trnka, S. (1992). A pretty good bisexual kiss there . . . In E. R. Weise (Ed.), *Closer to home: Bisexuality and feminism* (pp. 103-113). Seattle: Seal Press.

Weinberg, M. S., Williams, C. J., & Pryor, D. W. (1994). *Dual attraction*. New York: Oxford University Press.

The Intersection of Race and Bisexuality: A Critical Overview of the Literature and Past, Present, and Future Directions of the "Borderlands"

J. Fuji Collins

http://www.haworthpress.com/web/JB
© 2004 by The Haworth Press, Inc. All rights reserved.
Digital Object Identifier: 10.1300/J159v04n01_08

[Haworth co-indexing entry note]: "The Intersection of Race and Bisexuality: A Critical Overview of the
Literature and Past, Present, and Future Directions of the 'Borderlands.'" Collins, J. Fuji. Co-published simultaneously in *Journal of Bisexuality* (Harrington Park Press, an imprint of The Haworth Press, Inc.) Vol. 4,
Nos. 1/2, 2004, pp. 99-116; and: *Current Research on Bisexuality* (ed: Ronald C. Fox) Harrington Park Press,
an imprint of The Haworth Press, Inc., 2004, pp. 99-116. Single or multiple copies of this article are available
for a fee from The Haworth Document Delivery Service [1-800-HAWORTH, 9:00 a.m. - 5:00 p.m. (EST).
E-mail address: docdelivery@haworthpress.com].

SUMMARY. There has been significant growth in the past two decades in the psychological literature exploring sexual orientations from gay, lesbian, and bisexual perspectives, as well as the role of culture and ethnicity on human development. However, the research on sexual orientation has been predominantly focused on gays and lesbians from an overwhelmingly White, middle-class population. Additionally, the research on ethnic minority groups rarely acknowledges differences in sexual orientation of group members. Despite the expanding empirical research, scant attention has been given to bisexuals who are members of ethnic minority groups. Hence, there has been a lack of research in the exploration of the complex interaction between a bisexual identity and ethnic identity development. Sexual identity research on ethnic minorities has outlined how a person of color establishes a dual identity as a sexual minority and as a person of color. However, surprisingly little research has investigated the influences of ethnicity on sexual identity development. Various studies have examined the identity development of persons with dual minority status. But, again these studies have predominantly focused on gays and lesbians. Such research obscures many issues relevant to ethnic minorities who are bisexual. This article explores the research on bisexual identity development and how it intersects with people of color. It reviews previous theoretical and empirical research on bisexuality development, the impact of bisexual identity and ethnic identity, ethnic/sexual identity integration, and the current research being conducted in this area which has received little attention, an area this author refers to as the "borderlands." *[Article copies available for a fee from The Haworth Document Delivery Service: 1-800-HAWORTH. E-mail address: <docdelivery@haworthpress.com> Website: <http://www.HaworthPress.com> © 2004 by The Haworth Press, Inc. All rights reserved.]*

KEYWORDS. Bisexual, ethnic minority, race, identity development

Recently, C. C. I. Hall (1997) discussed the need for psychology to address issues of ethnicity/culture, gender, and sexual orientation. She avowed that it is time for the American Psychological Association (APA) to take action to improve the profession before it becomes obsolete and irrelevant to diverse populations in the United States. The demographic changes in the United States (U.S.) will demand changes in psychology. By the year 2050, it is expected that the U.S. population will be 50% people of color; many cities and states are currently at or near this percentage (U.S. Bureau of the Census, 1995). Current estimates of gay men and lesbians in the U.S. tend to hover around 10%-12% (Crooks & Baur, 1990; Gagnon,1977). Gebhart (1972) suggested approximately 25 million Americans may be bisexual, and the rising acceptance of bisexuality among the youth of America (Leland, 1995) will require the psychology profession to reconsider this misunderstood phenomenon. This article will cross the "borderlands" of bisexuality and people of color.

According to the psychological literature, homosexuality and bisexuality were assumed to be mental illnesses for over a century. The second edition of the *Diagnostic and Statistical Manual of Mental Disorders* (DSM-II; American Psychiatric Association, 1973) listed homosexuality as a diagnostic category, and the psychological literature focused on homosexuality as pathology. Articles focused on the assessment of homosexuality, causes of homosexuality, and "reorientation" of lesbians and gay men to become heterosexual (Rothblum, 1994). Homosexuality began to be depathologized by the American Psychiatric Association (ApA) in 1973 when they officially removed this classification from their list of mental disorders (Bayer, 1981). Then in 1975, the APA (American Psychological Association) adopted a resolution stating, "homosexuality per se implies no impairment in judgment, stability, reliability, or general social or vocational capabilities" (Conger, 1975, p. 633). Further, the APA urged psychologists to "take the lead in removing the stigma of mental illness that has long been associated with homosexual orientations" (Conger, 1975, p. 633). The focus of research and theory moved towards an understanding of lesbian and gay identity development, discrimination, homophobia, coming-out processes, and to a smaller extent, mental health and treatment issues. Now all major American mental health associations have affirmed that homosexuality is not a mental illness (American Association for Marriage and Family Therapy, 1991; American Counseling Association, 1996; American Psychological Association, 1992; Canadian Psychological Association, 1995; National Association of Social Workers, 1996). In fact, the American Psychological Association adopted specific guidelines for psychotherapy with lesbian, gay, and bisexual clients (APA, 2000).

Since the late 1970s there have been many empirical studies and theoretical writings that have focused on the process by which an individual develops a gay or lesbian identity. In the past fifteen years, there has been significant growth in the psychological literature that appropriately explores gay and lesbian sexual orientations from affirmative perspectives (Greene, 1997). As one reviews the literature, one finds that the majority of the empirical research on or about lesbians and gay men have been conducted with overwhelmingly White, middle-class participants (Chan, 1992; Eliason, 1996; Greene, 1994, 1996; Morales, 1992). Unfortunately, there has been scarce attention paid to lesbians and gay men who are members of ethnic minority groups. Most notable in this area of inquiry is Greene (1986, 1990, 1994, 1996, 1997). Greene (1997) discusses how research on ethnic minority groups rarely acknowledges differences in sexual orientation among group members and that there has been little exploration of the complex interaction between sexual orientation and ethnic identity development. She does, however, present a framework from which to begin examining clinical work with ethnic minority gay men and lesbians, but not with bisexuals.

Research on homosexuality in people of color has been touched upon by several researchers: African American (Boykin, 1996; Greene, 1986, 1990, 1994, 1996, 1997; Gutierrez & Dworkin, 1992; Icard, 1986; Loiacano, 1989; Sears, 1991, 1995; Wade, 1996), Asian American (Chan, 1989, 1992, 1995; Horn, 1994; Leong, 1996), Latino/Latina (Carrier, 1989, 1992; Diaz, 1998; Espin, 1987; Hidalgo, 1984; Morales, 1992), and Native Americans (Allen, 1984; Brown, 1997; Jacobs, Thomas, & Lang, 1997; Williams, 1986). Other research include the comparative analysis of Latino, Black, and Asian men who have sex with men and how the intersection of cultural background, race, and ethnicity influence comportment and identity formation over time (Manalansan, 1996), as well as understanding how young gay people of color negotiate disclosure of their homosexuality to family members (Merighi & Grimes, 2000; Savin-Williams & Dube, 1998).

So what about bisexuals? An exhaustive review of the current literature on lesbian, gay, and bisexual identities was presented by D'Augelli and Patterson (1995) in a collection of 15 chapters (Strader, 1996). The reviews were comprehensive. Two of the most notable were Fox's chapter on bisexual identities and Chan's chapter on sexual identity in Chinese Americans, which was the only chapter to deal with a specific ethnic minority group. Fox (1995) presented an overview of bisexuality which provides the reader with a theoretical perspective on bisexuality and bisexual identities, bisexuality in research on homosexuality, and research on bisexuality and bisexual identities. He combines the research from several disciplines into a comprehensive summary not heretofore seen in the literature (Strader, 1996). Chan (1995) presented a chapter that concerns sexual identity formation in the context of a bi-cultural background in which one of the cultures is non-Western. She indicates that theoretical models of sexual identity development have come from a Western approach and have not accounted for cultural differences. Clearly, the "borderlands" are within view.

THE PAST

During the past two decades researchers have used identity models generally based on a single social identity (e.g., race, gender, sexual orientation). These models suggest a universal, unidimensional (i.e., along a continuum of intensity or difficulty of acceptance) sequence of events. However, recent research (Dube & Savin-Williams, 1999) suggests these models require modification to accurately represent the experience of lesbians and bisexual women

(Diamond, 1998), and younger cohorts of gay and bisexual men (Dube, 1997; Savin-Williams, 1998).

Several theorists have developed identity models related to race, ethnicity, gender and sexual orientation (Atkinson, Morten, & Sue, 1989; Banks, 1981; Cass, 1979; Collins, 1996, 2000; Cross, 1991; Helms, 1986, 1990). Many of these identity models suggest a linear process, although some theorists (Collins, 1996, 2000; Parham, 1989) suggest that individuals recycle through identity stages/phases in an ongoing process.

Until recently, most identity theories and models have been based on single social identities (Fukuyama & Ferguson, 2000). They have generally examined a specific social identity as if the group members were homogeneous, monolithic and lacking multiple identities. This type of framework does not address nor acknowledge the multiple and complex identities that bisexual people of color must integrate. Thus, individuals who are bisexual and also a member of a minority group must deal with a dual or multiple minority status. Just as models have been developed to describe the process of lesbian and gay identity and, to a lesser extent, bisexual identity, researchers who have focused on ethnicity have proposed models such as the Minority Identity Development Model (Atkinson et al., 1989) which is quite similar to lesbian and gay identity models (Bohan, 1995). Poston (1990) developed a five-stage biracial model that may have relevance to the experiences of bisexual persons. Though this model was not formulated based on sexual identity development, there are parallels in the processes that may accurately describe the coming-out processes for bisexuals (Fukuyama & Ferguson, 2000). Previous literature on sexual identity development among ethnic minorities has outlined how members of ethnic groups establish a dual identity as a sexual minority and a person of color. They have emphasized the incompatibility between homosexuality and traditional values prevalent in ethnic-minority communities (Bhugra, 1997; Chan, 1997; Icard, 1986; Manalansan, 1996; Morales, 1990; Savin-Williams, 1996, 1998). Where does that place a bisexual person of color?

THE PRESENT-MOVING INTO THE "BORDERLANDS"

It appears that bisexual identity development has not received the attention that lesbian and gay identity models have (Collins, 2000). This relative lack of theoretical work is compounded by the general lack of attention among queer theorists to the bisexual theory and writing that does exist (Phelan, 1997). Further, because of the complexities of the interaction of sexuality to race, ethnicity, and gender, surprisingly little research has investigated the influences of ethnicity on sexual identity development. According to Dube and Savin-Williams (1999), the lack of empirical research may be due to the inherent difficulties of studying ethnic minorities. Further, Soto (1997) conducted a 10-year review of gay, lesbian, and bisexual publications and less than 5% of the journal articles focused primarily on the area of race or ethnicity. This statistic clearly shows how bisexual people of color are often hidden within their communities. Is it because bisexuality may be laden with societies stereotypes and misconceptions (Fox, 1995)?

It is believed the contributing variable to the marginalization of the bisexual population is the socially constructed assumption that sexual orientation is dichotomous (Guidry, 1999). This simple dichotomy–either one is heterosexual or homosexual–hampers understanding the full range of sexuality. It exacts a toll on many who find their identity invalidated by society's propositions about sexual orientation. This outlook fails to take into account the experiences of bisexual individuals who understand their sexuality as existing on a fluid and flexible continuum or as a choice that supports and complements their self-identity (Guidry, 1999). Therefore, bisexuals stand outside of the normative sexual dichotomy. This perspective has further fueled numerous disparaging claims against bisexuality made by early researchers on sexual orientation. Zinik (1985) found that many professionals branded bisexuals as adolescent and undifferentiated and at worst, as fraudulent and dangerous. Others view bisexuals as those who are conflicted, are in denial of their "real" homosexual identity, are indecisive, confused, are ambivalent fence-sitters, in transition, are attempting to be trendy, have retarded sexual development, are shallow and lack the capacity for true love, or are wanting the best of two worlds (Fox, 1995; Guidry, 1999; Nichols, 1994). Bisexuals are also subject to an oppressive environment. Despite this, bisexuality is becoming more and more acceptable as a legitimate and enduring sexual orientation (Coleman, 1987; Fox, 1995).

Recent scholarship on biracial (Daniel, 1994, 1996; Root, 1992, 1996) and bisexual (Fox, 1993; Young, 1992) identity development has begun to question the old theoretical frameworks. Both old and new paradigms permit researchers to test, label, systematize, and make sense of the truly dynamic and complex worlds of the biracial and bisexual individual (Collins, 2000). The old views provide an understanding of how they have suffered (e.g., social misidentification and psychological confusion) while new frameworks highlight the complex realities of these individuals. It becomes clear that almost all bisexual and biracial identity models involve interaction with an oppressive society.

Current literature has discussed the integration of sexual orientation and ethnic minority group membership as dealing with multiple oppressed-group memberships (Bohan, 1995; Fukuyama & Ferguson, 2000; Rothblum, 1994). Bohan (1995) has suggested that bisexuals of color are caught in the margin between identities, living in crisis; and, many experience a sense of invisibility and marginality. If someone identifies with a minority culture (e.g., Asian American), that someone must confront and cope with one or more forms of oppression (e.g., sexism, racism) each day. Compound that with being a sexual minority and a culture that fosters a collective sense of identity rather than an individualistic identity which is more likely with a person of color, then they truly are in the borderlands, a place where they are marginalized due to their ethnic background, and then marginalized by heterosexuals and homosexuals alike. Identity theories do not acknowledge concurrent multiple identities which obscures the complexity of integrating multiple social identities and coping with multiple forms of identity (Collins, 2000; Fukuyama & Ferguson, 2000). Thus, using a single identity framework may not help in the affirmative understanding of bisexual people of color.

Models of bisexuality must be able to incorporate more than one social identity. Oetting and Beauvais (1990) suggested that individuals may identify with more than one cultural group and that these identities may function independently of each other; in other words, that one can have a multicultural identity. Fox (1995) suggested that bisexual identity development is complex and is affected by multiple factors, one being ethnicity. McCarn and Fassinger (1996) proposed a model which includes group membership identity as well as individual sexual identity development. Walters (1997) also incorporated a group membership and individual membership model which focused on urban, gay, American Indians. Finally, Collins (2000) proposed a model of biracial/bisexual identity development which focuses on an individual being truly multi-ethnic and bisexual. It is clear that theories are moving toward understanding the complexity of multiple identities, those with multiple group memberships and identities subsumed by various sources of oppression.

INTEGRATION OF IDENTITIES IN THE "BORDERLANDS"

Few researchers have assessed whether individuals are able to accept their ethnic and sexual identities simultaneously and how this process occurs within the development of a sexual identity (Dube & Savin-Williams, 1999). Studies of identity development for ethnic minorities, and for lesbians, gays, and bisexuals have previously been examined in the context of ethnic minority and lesbian or gay identity models (Espin, 1987; Wooden, Kawasaki, & Mayeda, 1983). These studies used Cass's (1979) model of homosexuality identity formation. Espin (1987) used the Minority Identity Development model (Atkinson et al., 1989) as a foundation in understanding Latina lesbians. Espin (1987) noted that these models of identity development are quite similar in portraying a process that "must be undertaken by people who must embrace negative or stigmatized identities. This process moves gradually from a rejected and denied self-image to the embracing of an identity that is finally accepted as positive" (p. 39). Each model presents a process for understanding identity development of either a homosexual or ethnic minority identity. Instead of having fragmented literature regarding identity development, there may be a need to develop an inclusive model of minority development that reflects dual or multiple identities. Collins (2000) proposed such a model which describes individuals who have two distinct identities that place them in a position of self-devaluation. From there they move to a position where there is a positive perception of identity based on the coexistence of their identities. Collins (2000) suggests four phases in the development of a positive biracial/bisexual identity. These phases are: Phase I–Questioning/Confusion; Phase II–Refusal/ Suppression; Phase III–Infusion/Exploration; and Phase IV–Resolution/Acceptance.

In Phase I, Collins (2000) states that individuals who have two distinct identities must endure the same developmental markers such as color differentiation, racial and sexual awareness, self- and race identification, and self-evaluation, as all individuals do. However, the awareness of differentness appears to be compounded for those who have a dual minority status due to the perceived lack of full affiliation. This appears to be an uncomfortable, confusing, and negative experience. Phase II is a period of self-identification, and a crucial period. It is a period when an individual selects one identity over the other, and attempts to suppress or deny what they have rejected. It is a phase that individuals either attempt to maintain a certain reference group or look for the possibilities of other reference groups. Phase III finds many individuals choosing one identity, but the result is confusion and sometimes guilt; it is during this phase where they choose a group, but are uncomfortable with it. As a result, they reach out to others in an attempt to integrate the part of them that appears to be missing. They move from the dominant identity toward their previously rejected identity. Finally, in Phase IV, individuals acknowledge both components of their identity as significant yet equal parts of themselves.

Collins (2000) further discusses the development of a "double" sense of identity. The term denotes those who have a positive reflection of their identity based on the coexistences of their identities (no matter what those identities are). Double moves beyond the social interaction of a biracial/bisexual reference group to a more multiple identity. He believes that this is true integration. A multiple or double identity is where biracial or bisexual individuals can recognize and value all of their identities and develop a secure and integrated identity (Collins, 2000, p. 246).

Bisexual individuals of color are triumphs produced through the discourse between the margins of sexuality and understanding the extremes of race. It is suggested that bisexuals of color have identities that are fluid, multidimensional, personalized social constructions that reflect the individual's current context and sociocultural position (Collins, 2000; Rust, 1993).

"THE BORDERLANDS"

Bisexual people of color are the blending of subcultures based on race, ethnicity, gender and sexual orientation. There is a lack of research in this "borderland" (Alquijay, 1997; Fukuyama & Ferguson, 2000; Soto, 1997; Stokes,

Damon, & McKirnan, 1997), the intersection of sexuality and ethnicity. There are a few researchers who have provided a concise overview of African American, Asian American, Hispanic, and Native Americans (Bohan, 1995; Fukuyama & Ferguson, 2000; Greene, 1994, 1997; Herdt, 1990; Morales, 1990; Rust, 1996). This research generally focused on how the experiences of persons of color dealt with either being gay or lesbian; rarely did it discuss the intersection with bisexuality. So, the majority of the research was constructed to explain how lesbian and gays construct their identity, rather than bisexual identity. Some researchers have maintained that its structure is ill-suited in describing bisexual identity (Blumstein & Schwartz, 1993; Diamond, 1998; Rust, 1993). This research takes only one step in the process of understanding diversity and marginalized sexual identity.

The literature indicates there is potential for internal conflict between ethnic and sexual identities, yet it should be acknowledged that the integration of multiple identities is also a possible source of strength (Patterson, 1995). Collins (2000) suggests there is a need for more fluid and comprehensive models of development that examine the interrelatedness of the various aspects of identity that reflect dual or multiple social group memberships. This supports Frable (1997) in that sexual identity theory is now on the cutting edge of understanding the intersection of identity, social forces, cultural diversity and individual lives.

THE VISIBILITY OF BISEXUAL PEOPLE
IN POPULAR LITERATURE

The bisexual movement is gaining visibility in the popular literature beyond the erotic and cultural arena. In the anthology compiled by Hutchins and Kaahumanu (1991), they were among the first to present stories about bisexual people, their experiences, and how they took pride in who they were. They believed bisexuals function as bridges between two opposed camps (e.g., gay and straight, people of color and white people). Because of public scrutiny (e.g., disease statistics, HIV/AIDS), discrimination and misunderstanding, the bisexual community needed to organize and come to terms with their collective identity.

Initially, Hutchins and Kaahumanu (1991) were considering focusing on feminist bisexuality but realized since it was going to be a first book of its kind, they decided to represent the bisexual experiences of both men and women. As a result, their anthology set the foundation in this arena. They were told by several women's presses that they would not be interested in a book that included men, because they wanted to focus their resources on women. But, just as is now true in the empirical literature, they felt it was necessary to have both sexes represented, and also determined to present combinations and contrasts of experiences and different perspectives from people of color.

Some of the crossing of bisexuality and color presented included Rios (1991) who discussed what it is to be both bisexual and Native American, how sexuality is based on clan and tribal customs, how they conflict with traditional Christian attitudes, and how Native Americans have to fathom their own sexuality alone. A poem was written by Kaahumanu (1991) who presents what it is like to be biracial-bisexual; another discusses what it is like to be a married bisexual man with HIV (Stewart, 1991) and, a feminist Japanese bisexual woman discusses sexuality, loving and respecting people (Uwano, 1991). Alexander (1991) speaks about the intersection of religion and bisexuality and his relationships with a man and woman; another describes what it is like being bisexual in a Chicano and Latino environment (Leyva, 1991), and Sheiner (1991) talks of being a lesbian with bisexual tendencies. Thus, Hutchins and Kaahumanu (1991) made a significant step in the nonempirical literature by sharing the stories of bisexual people.

Garber (1995) discusses how bisexuality has moved steadily into the mainstream, through videos, talk shows, sitcoms, advertising, and practice. Biographies of individuals such as Marlon Brando, Marlina Dietrich, Leonard Bernstein, talk shows such as Oprah, television shows such as L.A. Law, and advertising campaigns, such as Calvin Klein's, are indicators of border crossings. In her text, Garber (1995) attempts to answer the question of whether bisexuality is a type of identity, whether it puts into question the concept of identity, and if bisexuality has something fundamental to teach us about human eroticism. To further support the notion that bisexuality is rapidly gaining recognition and visibility, Tucker, Highleyman, and Kaplan (1995) demonstrate through interviews, poems, and articles a commitment to understand how it is to cross borders. It is clear through both of these texts show how contemporary gay, lesbian and queer theories marginalize or silence bisexuals.

Rose, Stevens, and the Off-Pink Collective (1996) presented a review of the politics, histories and lives of bisexual people of color. Barlow (1996) presented bisexuality and feminism from a Black woman's perspective. This includes how one must deal with a "mosaic of oppression" and move forward using foundations of feminism, socialism and other liberation philosophies; bisexuality in the Arab world (Gollain, 1996); on being bisexual and Black in Britain (Paul, 1996), and being bisexual and a person of mixed-race (Prabhudas, 1996). Storr (1999) published a critical reader which only touches the borders of bisexuality and people of color by reprinting Prabhudas' (1996) article on what it is like being bisexual and a person of mixed-race.

It is clear that the overlap of bisexuality and people of color has been progressing slowly in publications which focus on personal and political perspectives. All of the submissions are only a few pages in length, which does not give an adequate grasp of the complexities of being bisexual in this world. Reviews such as those presented by Kent (1998) will further elaborate the necessity of more elaborate, descriptive and informative stories of those who dare cross the boundaries of bisexuality and color.

THE FUTURE

In the past decade, there has been some growth in the psychological literature that appropriately explores bisexual orientation from an affirmative perspective (Fox, 1995; Stokes, Damon, & McKirnan, 1997). Although the current theories of bisexual identity offer some valuable insights, they are limited. Research needs to move beyond what has been a normative middle-class (and primarily white Western) standard. It is important to develop interdisciplinary models that will draw upon the diverse experiences of being an "other" and elucidate these into a new inclusive paradigm. Collins (2000) proposed a model which is a theory of development that is more fluid and comprehensive in that it proposes an interrelatedness of various aspects of the individual identity and the role of sociohistorical context in which bisexual and biracial individuals negotiate their identities. He combines biracial and bisexual literature into a comprehensive model of identity development for those who are marginalized by more than one culture or ethnic group.

Bisexuals are now able to disprove the prior images that have tarnished them. As society becomes more multiracial and multiethnic, bisexual people of color are finding a much larger reference group with which to compare and identify themselves. Cultures do not stand still, nor do the generations of bisexual individuals. The self is usually understood in relation to society, and its importance is found in the individual's interaction with others. Bisexuality identity development can only be understood in such a social context.

It is hoped that the integration of bisexual and biracial literature in the academic and popular literature can promote the concept of an integrated identity development model that incorporates neglected groups, for all those individuals appear to be the products of the same search. The "borderlands" are growing and the individuals within it are becoming more visible, and with that, our understanding of bisexual people of color.

REFERENCES

Allen, P. G. (1984). Beloved women: The lesbian in American Indian culture. In R. Darty & S. Potter (Eds.), *Women-identified women* (pp. 83-96). Palo Alto, CA: Mayfield.

Alexander, C. (1991). Affirmation: Bisexual Mormon. In L. Hutchins & L. Kaahumanu (Eds.), *Bi any other name: Bisexual people speak out* (pp. 193-197). Boston: Alyson Publications.

Alquijay, M. A. (1997). The relationships among self-esteem, acculturation, and lesbian identity formation in Latina lesbians. In B. Greene (Ed.), *Ethnic and cultural diversity among lesbians and gay men* (pp. 249-265). Newbury Park, CA: Sage.

American Association for Marriage and Family Therapy (1991). *AAMFT code of ethics.* Washington, DC: Author.

American Counseling Association (1996). ACA code of ethics and standards of practice. In B. Herlihy & G. Corey (Eds.), *ACA ethical standards casebook* (5th ed., pp. 26-59). Alexandria, VA: Author.

American Psychiatric Association (1973). *Diagnostic and statistical manual of mental disorders* (2nd ed.). Washington, DC: Author.

American Psychological Association (1992). Ethical principles and code of conduct. *American Psychologist, 47,* 1597-1611.

American Psychological Association Division 44/Committee on Lesbian, Gay, & Bisexual Concerns Task Force (2000). Guidelines for psychotherapy with lesbian, gay, and bisexual clients. *American Psychologist, 55*(12) 1440-1451.

Atkinson, D. R., Morten, G., & Sue, D. W. (Eds.). (1989). *Counseling American minorities: A cross-cultural perspective* (3rd ed.). Dubuque, IA: William C. Brown.

Banks, J. A. (1981). The stages of ethnicity: Implications for curriculum reform. In J. A. Banks (Ed.), *Multi-ethnic education: Theory and practice* (pp. 129-139). Boston: Allyn & Bacon.

Barlow, V. (1996). Bisexuality and feminism: One Black women's perspective. In S. Rose, C. Stevens, & The Off-Pink Collective (Eds.), *Bisexual horizons: Politics, histories, lives* (pp. 38-40). London: Lawrence & Wishart.

Bayer, R. (1981). *Homosexuality and American psychiatry.* New York: Basic Books.

Blumstein, P., & Schwartz, P. (1993). Bisexuality: Some social psychological issues. In L. D. Garnets & D.C. Kimmel (Eds.), *Psychological perspectives on lesbians and gay male experiences* (pp. 168-183). New York: Columbia University Press.

Bohan, J. S. (1995). *Psychology and sexual orientation: Coming to terms.* New York: Routledge.

Boykin, K. (1996). *One more river to cross: Black and gay in America.* New York: Doubleday.

Brown, L.B. (1997). Women and men, not-men and not-women, lesbians and gays: American Indian gender style alternatives. In L. B. Brown (Ed.), *Two spirit people: American Indian lesbian women and gay men* (pp. 5-20). New York: Harrington Park Press.

Buhgra, D. (1997). Coming out by South Asian gay men in the United Kingdom. *Archives of Sexual Behavior, 26,* 547-557.

Canadian Psychological Association (1995). *Canadian code of ethics for psychologists.* Ottawa, Ontario, Canada: Author.

Carrier, J. M. (1989). Gay liberation and coming out in Mexico. *Journal of Homosexuality, 17,* 225-252.

Carrier, J. M. (1992). Miguel: Sexual life history of a gay Mexican American. In G. Herdt (Ed.), *Gay culture in America: Essays from the field* (pp. 202-224). Boston: Beacon Press.

Cass, V. C. (1979). Homosexual identity formation: A theoretical model. *Journal of Homosexuality, 7,* 219-235.

Chan, C. S. (1989). Issues of identity development among Asian-American lesbians and gay men. *Journal of Counseling and Development, 68,* 16-20.

Chan, C. S. (1992). Cultural considerations in counseling Asian American lesbians and gay men. In S. H. Dworkin & F. J. Gutierrez (Eds.), *Counseling gay men and lesbi-*

ans: Journey to the end of the rainbow (pp. 115-124). Alexandria, VA: American Association for Counseling and Development.

Chan, C. S. (1995). Issues of sexual identity in an ethnic minority: The case of Chinese American lesbians, gay men, and bisexual people. In A.R. D'Augelli & C. J. Patterson (Eds.), *Lesbian, gay, and bisexual identities over the lifespan.* New York: Oxford University Press.

Chan, C. S. (1997). Don't ask, don't tell, don't know: The formation of a homosexual identity and sexual expression among Asian American lesbians. In B. Greene (Ed.), *Ethnic and cultural diversity among lesbians and gay men* (pp. 240-248). Thousand Oaks, CA: Sage.

Coleman, E. (1987). Bisexuality: Challenging our understanding of human sexuality and sexual orientation. In E. E. Shelp (Ed.), *Sexuality and medicine* (pp. 225-242). New York: Reidel.

Collins, J. F. (1996). *Biracial Japanese American identity: Hapa, double, or somewhere in between.* Unpublished doctoral dissertation, Fielding Institute, Santa Barbara, CA.

Collins, J. F. (2000). Biracial-bisexual individuals: Identity coming of age. *International Journal of Sexuality and Gender Studies, 5,* 221-253.

Conger, J. (1975). Proceedings of the American Psychological Association, Incorporated, for the year 1974: Minutes of the annual meeting of Council of Representatives. *American Psychologist, 30,* 620-651.

Crooks, R., & Baur, K. (1990). *Our sexuality.* Redwood City, CA: Benjamin/Cummings.

Cross, W. E. (1991). *Shades of Black.* Philadelphia: Temple University Press.

Daniel, G. R. (1994). *Two parent ethnicities and parents of two ethnicities: Generational difference in the discourse on multiethnic identity: A preliminary study.* Unpublished manuscript.

Daniel, G. R. (1996). Black and White identity in the new millennium: Unserving the ties that bind. In M. P. P. Root (Ed.), *The multiracial experience: Racial borders as the new frontier.* Thousand Oaks, CA: Sage.

D'Auguelli, A. R., & Patterson, C.J. (Eds.). (1995). *Lesbian, gay, and bisexual identities over the lifespan.* New York: Oxford University Press.

Diamond, L. M. (1998). The development of sexual orientation among adolescent and young adult women. *Developmental Psychology, 34,* 1085-1095.

Diaz, R. M. (1998). *Latino gay men and HIV: Culture, sexuality and risk behavior.* New York: Rutledge.

Dube, E. M., (1997). *Sexual identity and intimacy development among two cohorts of gay and bisexual men.* Unpublished master's thesis, Cornell University. Ithaca, NY.

Dube, E. M., & Savin-Williams, R. C. (1999). Sexual identity development among ethnic sexual-minority male youths. *Developmental psychology, 35,* 1389-1398.

Eliason, M. J. (1996). Identity formation for lesbian, bisexual, and gay persons: Beyond a "minoritizing" view. *Journal of Homosexuality, 30,* 31-57.

Espin, O. M. (1987). Issues of identity in the psychology of Latina lesbians. In Boston Lesbian Psychologies Collective (Eds.), *Lesbian psychologies: Explorations and challenges* (pp. 35-51). Urbana: University of Illinois Press.

Fox, R. C. (1993). *Coming out bisexual: Identity, behavior, and sexual orientation self-disclosure.* Paper presented at American Psychological Association Annual Convention, Toronto, Ontario, Canada.

Fox, R. C. (1995). Bisexual identities. In A. R. D'Augelli & C. J. Patterson (Eds.), *Lesbian, gay, and bisexual identities over the lifespan* (pp. 48-86). New York: Oxford University Press.

Frable, D. E. S. (1997). Gender, racial, ethnic, sexual, and class identities. *Annual Review of Psychology, 48,* 139-163.

Fukuyama, M. A., & Ferguson, A. D. (2000). Lesbian, gay, and bisexual people of color: Understanding cultural complexity and managing multiple oppressions. In R. M. Perez, K. A. DeBord, & K. J. Bieschke (Eds.), *Handbook of counseling and psychotherapy with lesbian, gay, and bisexual clients.* Washington, DC: American Psychological Association.

Gagnon, J. (1977). *Human sexualities.* Glenview, IL: Scott Foresman.

Garber, M. B. (1995). *Vice versa: Bisexuality and the eroticism of everyday life.* New York: Simon & Schuster.

Gebhart, P. H. (1972). Incidence of overt homosexuality in the U.S. and Western Europe. In J. M. Livinggod (Ed.), *NIMH Task Force on homosexuality: Final report and papers,* (DHEW Publications No. HSM 72-9116, pp. 22-30). Rockville, MD: National Institute of Mental Health.

Gollain, F. (1996). Bisexuality in the Arab world. In S. Rose, C. Stevens, & The Off-Pink Collective (Eds.), *Bisexual horizons: Politics, histories, lives* (pp. 58-61). London: Lawrence & Wishart.

Greene, B. (1986). When the therapist is White and the patient is Black: Considerations for psychotherapy in the feminist heterosexual and lesbian communities. *Women & Therapy, 5,* 41-66.

Greene, B. (1990, December). African American lesbians: The role of family, culture and racism. *BG Magazine, 6,* 26.

Greene, B. (1994). Lesbian women of color: Triple jeopardy. In L. Comas-Diaz & B. Greene (Eds.), *Women of color: Integrating ethnic and gender identities in psychotherapy* (pp. 389-427). Thousand Oaks, CA: Sage Publications.

Greene, B. (1996). The legacy of ethnosexual mythology in heterosexism. In E. Rothblum & L. Bond (Eds.), *Preventing heterosexism and homophobia* (pp. 59-70). Thousand Oaks, CA: Sage Publications.

Greene, B. (1997). Ethnic minority lesbians and gay men. In B. Greene (Ed.), *Ethnic and cultural diversity among lesbian and gay men.* Thousand Oaks, CA: Sage Publications.

Guidry, L. L. (1999). Clinical interventions with bisexuals: A contextualized understanding. *Professional Psychology: Research and Practice, 30,* 22-26.

Gutierrez, F. J., & Dworkin, S. H. (1992). Gay, lesbian, and African American: Managing the integration of identities. In S. H. Dworkin & F. J. Gutierrez (Eds.), *Counseling gay men and lesbians: Journey to the end of the rainbow* (pp. 141-156). Alexandria, VA: American Association for Counseling and Development.

Hall, C. C. I. (1997). Cultural malpractice: The growing obsolescence of psychology with the changing U.S. population. *American Psychologist, 52,* 642-651.

Helms, J. E. (1986). Expanding racial identity theory to cover counseling process. *Journal of Counseling Psychology, 33*, 62-64.

Helms, J. E. (1990). *Black and White racial identity: Theory, research, and practice.* New York: Greenwood Press.

Herdt, G. (1990). Developmental discontinuities and sexual orientation across cultures. In D. P. McWhirter, S. A. Sanders, & J. M. Reinisch (Eds.), *Homosexuality/heterosexuality: Concepts of sexual orientation* (pp. 208-236). New York: Oxford University Press.

Hildago, H. A. (1984). The Puerto Rican lesbian in the United States. In T. Darty & S. Potter (Eds.), *Women-identified women* (pp. 105-115). Palo Alto, CA: Mayfield.

Horn, A. Y. (1994). Stories from the homefront: Perspectives of Asian American parents with lesbian daughters and gay sons. *Amerasia Journal, 20*, 19-32.

Hutchins, L., & Kaahumanu, L. (Eds.). (1991). *Bi any other name: Bisexual people speak out.* Boston: Alyson Publications.

Icard, L. (1986). Black gay men and conflicting social identities: Sexual orientation versus racial identity. In J. Gripton & M. Valentich (Eds.), *Social work in practice in sexual problems* (pp. 83-93). New York: Haworth Press.

Jacobs, S. E., Thomas, W., & Lang, S. (1997). *Two-spirit people: Native American gender identity, sexuality, and spirituality.* Chicago: University of Illinois Press.

Kaahumanu, L. (1991). Hapa haole wahine. In L. Hutchins & L. Kaahumanu (Eds.), *Bi any other name: Bisexual people speak out* (pp. 306-307). Boston: Alyson Publications.

Kent, K. R. (1998). Let me count the ways: Reviewing bisexuality. *Journal of Lesbian and Gay Studies, 4*, 487-498.

Leland, J. (1995, July 17). Not gay, not straight: A new sexuality emerges. *Newsweek, 126*, 44-50.

Leong, R. (1996). *Asian American sexualities: Dimensions of the gay and lesbian experience.* New York: Routledge.

Leyva, O. (1991). Que es un bisexual? In L. Hutchins & L. Kaahumanu (Eds.), *Bi any other name: Bisexual people speak out* (pp. 201-202). Boston: Alyson Publications.

Loiacano, D. K. (1989). Gay identity issues among Black Americans: Racism, homophobia, and the need for validation. *Journal of Counseling and Development, 68*, 21-25.

Manalansan, M. R. (1996). Double minorities: Latino, Black, and Asian men who have sex with men. In R. C. Savin-Williams & K. M. Cohen (Eds.), *The lives of lesbians, gays, and bisexuals: Children to adults* (pp. 393-415). Fort Worth, TX: Harcourt Brace College Publishers.

McCarn, S.R., & Fassinger, R. E. (1996). Revisioning sexual minority identity development formation: A new model of lesbian identity and its implications for counseling and research. *The Counseling Psychologist, 24*, 508-534.

Merighi, J. R., & Grimes, M. D. (2000). Coming out to families in a multicultural context. *Families in Society, 81*, 32-41.

Morales, E. S. (1990). Ethnic minority families and minority gays and lesbians. *Marriage and Family Review, 14*, 217-239.

Morales, E. S. (1992). Latino gays and Latina lesbians. In S. H. Dworkin & F. J. Gutierrez (Eds.), *Counseling gay men and lesbians: Journey to the end of the rain-*

bow (pp. 125-139). Alexandria, VA: American Association for Counseling and Development.

National Association of Social Workers (1996). *Code of ethics of the National Association of Social Workers.* Washington, DC: Author.

Nichols, M. (1994). Therapy with bisexual women: Working on the edge of emerging cultural and personal identities. In M. P. Mirkin (Ed.), *Women in context: Toward a feminist reconstruction of psychotherapy* (pp. 149-169). New York: Guilford Press.

Oetting, E. R., & Beauvais, F. (1990). Orthogonal cultural identification theory: The cultural identification of minority adolescents. *International Journal of the Addictions, 25,* 655-685.

Parham, T. A. (1989). Cycles of psychological nigrescence. *The Counseling Psychologist, 17,* 187-226.

Patterson, C. J. (1995). Sexual orientation and human development: An overview. *Developmental Psychology, 31,* 3-11.

Paul, N. (1996). On being bisexual and Black in Britain. In S. Rose, C. Stevens, & The Off-Pink Collective (Eds.), *Bisexual horizons: Politics, histories, lives* (pp. 95-99). London: Lawrence & Wishart.

Phelan, S. (1997). *Playing with fire: Queer politics, queer theories.* New York: Routledge.

Poston, W. S. (1990). The biracial identity development model. *Journal of Counseling and Development, 69,* 152-155.

Prabhudas, Y. (1996). Bisexuals and people of mixed-race: Arbiters of change. In S. Rose, C. Stevens, & The Off-Pink Collective (Eds.), *Bisexual horizons: Politics, histories, lives* (pp. 30-31). London: Lawrence & Wishart.

Rios, J. (1991). What do Indians think? In L. Hutchins & L. Kaahumanu (Eds.), *Bi any other name: Bisexual people speak out* (pp. 37-39). Boston: Alyson Publications.

Root, M. P. P. (1992). *Racially mixed people in America.* Newbury Park, CA: Sage.

Root, M. P. P. (1996). *The multiracial experience: Racial borders as the new frontier.* Thousand Oaks, CA: Sage.

Rose, S., Stevens, C., & The Off-Pink Collective (Eds.). (1996). *Bisexual horizons: Politics, histories, lives.* London: Lawrence & Wishart.

Rothblum, E. D. (1994). Introduction to the special section: Mental health of lesbians and gay men. *Journal of Consulting and Clinical Psychology, 62,* 211-212.

Rust, P. C. (1993). Coming out in the age of social constructionism: Sexual identity formation among lesbians and bisexual women. *Gender and Society, 7,* 50-77.

Rust, P. C. (1996). Managing multiple identities: Diversity among bisexual men and women. In B. A. Firestein (Ed.), *Bisexuality: The psychology and politics of an invisible minority* (pp. 53-83). Newbury Park, CA: Sage.

Savin-Williams, R. C. (1996). Ethnic- and sexual-minority youth. In R. C. Savin-Williams & K. M. Cohen (Eds.), *The lives of lesbians, gays, and bisexuals: Children to adults* (pp. 393-415). Fort Worth, TX: Harcourt Brace.

Savin-Williams, R. C. (1998). *". . . and then I became gay": Young men's stories.* New York: Rutledge.

Savin-Williams, R. C., & Dube, E. M. (1998). Parental reactions to their child's disclosure of a gay/lesbian identity. *Family Relations, 47,* 7-13.

Sears, J. T. (1991). *Growing up gay in the South: Race, gender, and journeys of the spirit*. New York: Haworth Press.

Sears, J. T. (1995). Black-gay or gay-Black?: Choosing identities or identity choices. In G. Unks (Ed.), *The gay teen: Educational practice and theory for lesbian, gay and bisexual adolescents* (pp. 135-158). New York: Rutledge.

Sheiner, M. (1991). The foundations of the bisexual community in San Francisco. In L. Hutchins & L. Kaahumanu (Eds.), *Bi any other name: Bisexual people speak out* (pp. 203-204). Boston: Alyson Publications.

Soto, T. A. (1997). Ethnic minority gay, lesbian, and bisexual publications: A 10-year review. *Division 44 Newsletter, 13*, 13-14.

Stewart, H. (1991). A healing journey. In L. Hutchins & L. Kaahumanu (Eds.), *Bi any other name: Bisexual people speak out* (pp. 147-150). Boston: Alyson Publications.

Stokes, J. P., Damon, W., & McKirnan, D. J. (1997). Predictors of movement toward homosexuality: A longitudinal study of bisexual men. *The Journal of Sex Research, 34*, 304-312.

Storr, M. (1999). *Bisexuality: A critical reader*. New York: Rutledge.

Strader, S. C. (1996). Lesbian, gay, and bisexual identities over the lifespan [Book review]. *Journal of Sex Research, 33*, pp. 82-84.

Tucker, N., Highleyman, L., & Kaplan, R. (Eds.). (1995). *Bisexual politics: Theories, queries & visions*. Binghamton, NY: Haworth Press.

U.S. Bureau of the Census. (1995). *Statistical abstracts of the U.S.* (115th ed.). Washington, DC: Author.

Uwano, K. (1991). Bi-loveable Japanese feminist. In L. Hutchins & L. Kaahumanu (Eds.), *Bi any other name: Bisexual people speak out* (pp. 185-187). Boston: Alyson Publications.

Wade, J. C. (1996). African American men's gender role conflict: The significance of racial identity. *Sex Roles, 34*, 17-33.

Walters, K. L. (1997). Urban lesbian and gay American identity: Implications for mental health service delivery. In L. B. Brown (Ed.), *Two spirit people: American Indian lesbian women and gay men* (pp. 43-65). New York: Harrington Park Press.

Williams, W. L. (1986). *The spirit and the flesh: Sexual diversity in American Indian culture*. Boston, MA: Beacon.

Wooden, W. S., Kawasaki, H., & Mayeda, R. (1983). Lifestyles and identity maintenance among gay Japanese-American males. *Alternative Lifestyles, 5*, 236-243.

Young, S. (1992). Breaking the silence about the "B-word": Bisexual identity and lesbian feminist discourse. In E. R. Weise (Ed.), *Closer to home: Bisexuality and feminism* (pp. 75-90). Seattle, WA: Seal Press.

Zinik, G. (1985). Identity conflict or adaptive flexibility? Bisexuality reconsidered. *Journal of Homosexuality, 11*, 7-19.

Attitudes Toward Bisexual Women and Men: Current Research, Future Directions

Tania Israel
Jonathan J. Mohr

http://www.haworthpress.com/web/JB
© 2004 by The Haworth Press, Inc. All rights reserved.
Digital Object Identifier: 10.1300/J159v04n01_09

[Haworth co-indexing entry note]: "Attitudes Toward Bisexual Women and Men: Current Research, Future Directions." Israel, Tania, and Jonathan J. Mohr. Co-published simultaneously in *Journal of Bisexuality* (Harrington Park Press, an imprint of The Haworth Press, Inc.) Vol. 4, Nos. 1/2, 2004, pp. 117-134; and: *Current Research on Bisexuality* (ed: Ronald C. Fox) Harrington Park Press, an imprint of The Haworth Press, Inc., 2004, pp. 117-134. Single or multiple copies of this article are available for a fee from The Haworth Document Delivery Service [1-800-HAWORTH, 9:00 a.m. - 5:00 p.m. (EST). E-mail address: docdelivery@haworthpress.com].

SUMMARY. This article describes research on attitudes toward bisexual women and men. The authors describe types of attitudes toward bisexual individuals in terms of heterosexism, questions of authenticity, focus on sexuality, concerns about loyalty, and positive attitudes. Empirical research pertaining to these attitudes is summarized, and the results of survey, psychometric, experimental, and analogue studies are described. Recommendations for future research on attitudes regarding bisexuality are identified in the areas of conceptualization and measurement of attitudes, attitudes in communities and interpersonal relationships, and interventions designed to change attitudes. The authors conclude by discussing ways in which research on attitudes toward bisexual women and men can benefit from and extend knowledge gained through research on attitudes toward lesbians and gay men. *[Article copies available for a fee from The Haworth Document Delivery Service: 1-800-HAWORTH. E-mail address: <docdelivery@haworthpress.com> Website: <http://www.HaworthPress.com> © 2004 by The Haworth Press, Inc. All rights reserved.]*

KEYWORDS. Bisexuality, attitudes regarding bisexuality, biphobia, binegativity, monosexism

Negative attitudes create a context of hostility for bisexual women and men that can affect many areas of their lives. Bisexual individuals have reported lack of validation, isolation, and ostracism from both heterosexual and lesbian/gay communities (Hutchins & Ka'ahumanu, 1991). Such experiences with negative attitudes may adversely affect the mental health and well-being of bisexual individuals. Furthermore, therapists' negative attitudes may lead to biased assessment and treatment of bisexual clients (Division 44/Committee on Lesbian, Gay, and Bisexual Concerns Joint Task Force on Guidelines for Psychotherapy with Lesbian, Gay, and Bisexual Clients, 2000). Internalization of such negative attitudes by bisexual individuals may create a barrier to developing a positive bisexual identity (Fox, 1991; Ochs, 1996).

Data are needed to document these potentially powerful effects of attitudes in the lives of bisexual women and men. Relatively little empirical investigation of attitudes toward bisexual women and men has been conducted, however, particularly in comparison to the now substantial literature on attitudes toward lesbian women and gay men (Eliason, 2001; Mohr & Rochlen, 1999). Nonetheless, research in this area has grown considerably over the past decade. This article will review this emerging literature and provide suggestions for future research on this topic. The first section describes types of attitudes toward bisexuality that have been reported in the literature. The second section identifies and reviews the empirical research on attitudes toward bisexuality. Finally, directions for future research are discussed.

THE NATURE OF ATTITUDES
TOWARD BISEXUAL WOMEN AND MEN

Theoretical and anecdotal writings on bisexuality have made it evident that attitudes toward bisexual women and men are anything but simple. Part of the complexity of these attitudes may stem from the challenge that bisexuality presents to fundamental assumptions about sexual orientation–assumptions that are held not only by heterosexual individuals but also by lesbian women and gay men. For example, in disputing the assumption that sexual orientation is a dichotomous construct, bisexual women and men raise questions about the fundamental nature of sexual attractions and romantic relationships that some individuals may find disconcerting. Furthermore, lesbian, gay, and heterosexual people may find it difficult to place bisexual individuals within a neatly defined sociopolitical category, which can introduce uncertainty about the political allegiances of bisexuals.

In this section, we have organized some of the ideas that have been proposed regarding the many types and sources of attitudes regarding bisexuality. In reviewing the literature, it became clear that even the language used to describe these attitudes was varied. The language of attitudes toward lesbian women and gay men has expanded from the use of "homophobia" (Weinberg, 1972) to inclusion of terms such as "homonegativism" (Hudson & Ricketts, 1980) and "heterosexism" (Neisen, 1990). Similarly, the language of attitudes toward bisexuality is in the process of evolution. Biphobia (Ochs, 1996) has been joined by "binegativity" (Eliason, 2001) and "monosexism" (Nagle, 1995), although the later two have not yet been used widely in the professional literature. In this article, we will discuss these constructs mostly in terms of attitudes toward bisexual women and men.

Heterosexism

One reality that lesbian, gay, and bisexual individuals must all face is the fact that same-sex desire is viewed negatively by a large number of individuals and communities. Similar to lesbian women and gay men, bisexual individuals are targeted for prejudice and discrimination based on beliefs about the superiority of one pattern of loving (opposite-sex partners) over another (same-sex partners). Thus, one source of negative attitudes regarding bisexuality is the heterosexism that also fuels negative attitudes regarding homosexuality. This source of marginalization and oppression of bisexual individuals contributes to the overlap between homophobia and biphobia (Ochs, 1996).

Authenticity

Several types of attitudes are related to questioning the authenticity or existence of bisexual women and men (Mohr & Rochlen, 1999a). For example, some negative attitudes are based on the belief that bisexual individuals are really lesbian or gay individuals who are in transition or in denial about their true sexual orientation. Proponents of these views may say that people who identify as bisexual lack the courage to come out as lesbian or gay (Eliason, 2001) or are trying to maintain heterosexual privilege (Ochs, 1996; Rust, 1993). The view of bisexuality as a transitional stage in the development of sexual orientation identity may be reinforced by the personal histories of lesbian- and gay-identified individuals who identified as bisexual at some point in their coming-out process (Fox, 1991). Some negative attitudes are based on the view that people who claim to be bisexual are simply confused about their sexuality or unable to decide their sexual preference (Bronn, 2001; Eliason, 2001; Zinik, 1985). Also, some individuals may question the legitimacy of bisexuality because of an understanding of bisexuality as a pure 50/50 split. If a person believes that bisexuality is defined as having equal attraction to both sexes, then it would not be surprising for such a person to expect that few people truly fit this label (Mohr & Rochlen, 1999b; Ochs, 1996).

Ochs (1996) attributed such denial of the existence of bisexual people to "the fact that we live in a culture that thinks in binary categories" (p. 224) and noted that the relative invisibility of bisexual individuals may be due to the tendency to assume a person's sexual orientation based on the sex of his or her current romantic partner. Gay men's and lesbian women's fear of being bisexual is another reason that some may deny the existence of bisexuality (Ochs, 1996; Udis-Kessler, 1990). The possibility of being bisexual may threaten the sense of self and community for individuals who have based their social identity on a lesbian or gay sexual orientations. Bisexuality may present such individuals with the possibility that the pain of being lesbian or gay in a homophobic society could have been avoided (Udis-Kessler, 1990) or fear that they would need to go through the difficulty of coming to terms with a new identity all over again if they were actually bisexual. This is not unlike the belief that homophobia is sometimes motivated by fear that one might be gay or lesbian (Herek, 1984b).

Sexuality

Some attitudes toward bisexual women and men are focused on sexuality. Perhaps even more than lesbian and gay male sexual orientations, bisexuality is associated with deviant sexuality; thus, some of the negativity directed toward bisexual individuals is related to the prevalence of erotophobia in our society (Ochs, 1999; Queen, 1999). Some people believe bisexual men and women are obsessed with sex (Eliason, 2001), a perspective that dates back at least as far as Freud's (1905/1962) view of adult bisexuality as a continuation of the "polymorphous perversity" of infancy. This stereotype of bisexuality as a form of unbridled, immature sexuality is clearly negative, but it used to humorous effect in the title of a popular magazine targeted to a bisexual audience called "Anything that Moves."

Also related to sexuality is the belief that bisexual women and men cannot or will not be monogamous (Eliason, 2001; Spaulding & Peplau, 1997). For some, this belief rests on the assumption that bisexual individuals must have concurrent lovers of both sexes, or the view of bisexuality as the "requirement-for-both" rather than the "potential-for-either" (Udis-Kessler, 1990). Such beliefs are supported by media portrayals of nonmonogamous bisexual individuals (Ochs, 1996). Although bisexual individuals are more likely to value nonmonogamy as an ideal compared to lesbian, gay, and heterosexual individuals, research clearly indicates that some bisexual-identified individuals prefer monogamous relationships (Rust, 1996). Perhaps in part because of the stereotypical association of bisexuality and nonmonogamy, bisexual women and men are often viewed as vectors of transmission of HIV and other sexually transmitted infections (Eliason, 2001). The fear that bisexual men are secretly having sex with men and infecting their unsuspecting wives and children is supported by media portrayals of such incidents (Ochs, 1996; Spaulding & Peplau, 1997). Additionally, lesbian women may express the concern that bisexual women are bringing HIV from the heterosexual to lesbian communities. This attitude is based on an assumption that lesbian women have not had sex with men and are thus otherwise "safe" from HIV, although the reality is that most women who identify as lesbian have had sex with men (Ochs, 1996).

Loyalty

Some negative attitudes regarding bisexuality are based on beliefs that bisexual women and men may be less trustworthy and loyal than others (Mohr & Rochlen, 1999a; Ochs, 1996). For example, as noted above, some individuals may assume that bisexual romantic partners cannot be trusted to be monogamous. Beliefs about bisexual individuals in relationships go beyond concerns about nonmonogamy, however, to a more general belief that bisexual women and men are untrustworthy and are not dependable as romantic partners and friends (Eliason, 2001; Spaulding & Peplau, 1997). Furthermore, some lesbian women and gay men may believe that a same-sex relationship cannot possibly offer the benefits of a "heterosexual" one, and thus fear that a bisexual partner would leave them for a person of the other sex if given a choice (Ochs, 1996).

Lesbian women and gay men may fear that bisexual individuals are not committed to the lesbian and gay community and politics (Mohr & Rochlen,

1999; Ochs, 1996; Udis-Kessler, 1990). Some of these concerns are best understood within the context of the history of lesbian feminist communities that developed as resistance to sexism and patriarchy (see Rust, 1995, for a comprehensive account of this historical context). This political aspect of lesbianism led to the view of relationships with men as "sleeping with the enemy." Also, some lesbian women and gay men may resent bisexual individuals' unwillingness to stand in solidarity with the lesbian and gay communities by coming out as lesbian or gay. Furthermore, bisexual individuals are suspected of trying to get the best of both worlds by benefiting from the support and civil rights developed by the labor of the lesbian and gay rights movement without giving up their heterosexual privilege. Such loyalty concerns may be related to the concept of authenticity described earlier as well as to the need of the lesbian and gay communities to create safety by establishing an "us/them" boundary (Ochs, 1996). Bisexuality may also pose a threat to the political strategy of framing lesbian and gay rights within an essentialist context and linking it conceptually with civil rights for ethnic minorities (Rust, 1995; Udis-Kessler, 1990).

Positive Attitudes

Not all beliefs about bisexual men and women have negative connotations. In fact, some attitudes toward bisexuality are quite positive and affirming. Generational changes may contribute to the emergence of these positive views as youth become more bi-accepting in the wake of challenges to heteronormativity by the lesbian and gay rights movements (Herdt, 2001). In contrast to the dichotomous view of sexual orientation that underlies the denial of bisexuality, some people situate bisexuality on a continuum of sexual orientation (Bronn, 2001). Such a view allows for various degrees of bisexuality and diverse experiences of bisexuality. From this perspective, bisexual individuals may be viewed as cognitively and interpersonally flexible, and may be admired for their attraction to personal qualities rather than simply to the gender of a partner (Zinik, 1985). This conceptualization may lead individuals to view bisexuality as the most natural or ideal state (Mohr & Rochlen, 1999b).

Although bisexual individuals are sometimes admired for their sexuality–e.g., for being sexually active and talented (Spaulding & Peplau, 1997) or sexually open (Bronn, 2001)–it is important to note that such views may become objectifying when directed toward bisexual women (Eliason, 2001). For example, the demand for bisexual women expressed in personal ads seems to be motivated by the desire of heterosexual men to have sex with two women rather than by an appreciation for the diversity of bisexual women in their sexual interests.

EMPIRICAL RESEARCH ON ATTITUDES
TOWARD BISEXUALITY

As noted above, research on attitudes toward bisexuality is a relatively new development. Until recently, the literature on attitudes regarding bisexuality consisted mostly of anecdotal writings (e.g., Hutchins & Ka'ahumanu, 1991; Weise, 1992). Although these personal accounts articulated the effects of negative attitudes toward bisexuality on bisexual individuals, rigorous empirical investigation of such attitudes was largely absent until the last few years. The studies described below constitute what may come to be viewed as the first wave of empirical research on biphobia. This research has produced useful knowledge about the measurement of attitudes regarding bisexuality, as well as the correlates of attitudes in lesbian, gay, and heterosexual populations.

Several studies have constructed instruments to evaluate the extent to which individuals adhered to beliefs about bisexuality that were identified in the anecdotal literature. Rust (1993) developed what may have been the first survey to evaluate lesbian women's beliefs about bisexual women. The content of the survey was based on interviews with lesbian and bisexual women, and the survey was administered to a primarily White sample of 346 lesbian-identified women. Results indicated that lesbian women believed (a) it was more likely for bisexuality than for lesbianism to be a transitional sexual orientation, (b) bisexual women were more likely than lesbian women to deny their true sexuality, (c) bisexual women had a greater desire and greater ability to pass as heterosexual than did lesbian women, and (d) bisexual women's personal loyalty to friends was more questionable than their political trustworthiness.

According to Rust, lesbian women's attitudes toward bisexual women were significantly correlated with sexual feelings (attraction exclusively to women versus attraction to women and men), role of bisexual identity in their own lives (whether or not they had identified as bisexual and whether bisexuality was a transitional identity), and social class. Attitude differences did not exist based on variables of age, race, educational status, income, history of relationships with men, or current relationship status. The author concluded that "most lesbians in this sample believed that there are differences between lesbians and bisexual women, but that these are differences of degree rather than kind and that the degree of these differences is moderate" (Rust, 1993, p. 225).

Eliason (1997, 2001) developed a survey that asked participants to agree or disagree with 23 statements describing common stereotypes about bisexuality. Additionally, participants rated single-item attitude scales targeting lesbian women, gay men, bisexual women, and bisexual men. These instruments were administered to 229 primarily White, heterosexual undergraduate college students. Participants felt more disapproval and disgust toward bisexual men compared to lesbian women, gay men, and bisexual women; and over three-quarters of the participants felt it was "very" or "somewhat" unlikely that they would have a sexual relationship with a bisexual partner. A majority of the participants endorsed the stereotypes that "bisexuals have more flexible attitudes about sex than heterosexuals," but most participants disagreed that "bisexuals are just gay and lesbian people who are afraid to admit they are gay" (Eliason, 2001, p. 146). Many of the items did not receive clear endorsement or disapproval, and the participants frequently used the "don't know" response category, leading the author to conclude that "heterosexual students do not have clear-cut beliefs about bisexuals" (Eliason, 2001, p. 146). Male participants were more likely than female participants to endorse some of the stereotypical beliefs about bisexuality, and they were more likely to report that they would have a sexual relationship with a bisexual (female) partner. In a multiple regression analysis, the greatest unique contribution to binegativity was made by homonegativity, followed by lack of bisexual friends and acquaintances, younger age, belonging to a conservative religion, and male gender (for negativity toward bisexual men only).

Mohr and Rochlen (1999a) contributed to the literature by constructing a scale assessing multiple aspects of attitudes regarding bisexuality, testing the measure with both heterosexual and lesbian/gay samples, and holding the measure up to rigorous psychometric scrutiny. In the initial test development studies, the Attitudes Regarding Bisexuality Scale (ARBS) was administered to 1,184 participants from two samples of lesbian and gay male college students and three samples of heterosexual college students. Two factors emerged from research on the ARBS: tolerance and stability. Tolerance was described as the degree to which bisexuality is viewed as a moral, acceptable sexual orientation. Results suggested that, among heterosexual individuals, moral tolerance for bisexuality overlaps strongly with positive attitudes toward lesbian women and gay men. Relatedly, in heterosexual samples, tolerance was correlated with a range of variables known to be related to attitudes regarding homosexuality (e.g., race, religiosity, political ideology, tolerance for ambiguity and complexity, and personal contact with lesbian, gay, and bisexual individuals; Herek, 1994). Also similar to findings on attitudes toward homosexuality was the result that heterosexual women were more tolerant of male bisexuality than heterosexual men were, although lesbian women and gay men did not differ on this dimension of attitudes regarding bisexuality. Correlations with tolerance were particularly strong in heterosexual samples, suggesting that this dimension of attitudes may be generally most salient for heterosexual individuals.

The other subscale of the ARBS, stability, assesses the degree to which bisexuality is viewed as a stable, legitimate sexual orientation, as well as the degree to which bisexual individuals are stable and trustworthy in their romantic, erotic, and affiliative relationships (Mohr & Rochlen, 1999a). Although these diverse aspects of attitudes regarding bisexuality may be conceptually distinct, analyses suggested that they are highly interrelated and constitute a single attitude dimension. Whereas correlations with tolerance were found to be strongest in heterosexual samples, correlations with stability were strongest in the lesbian and gay male samples. Lesbian women and gay men who viewed bisexuality as a legitimate sexual orientation were more likely than others to be willing to date bisexual individuals and have a bisexual best friend, to have had personal contact with a bisexual individual, to interact on a regular basis with heterosexual individuals, and to view themselves as not exclusively lesbian or gay. The research provided evidence of some differences between lesbian women and gay men related to the stability dimension of attitudes. First, lesbian women were more likely than gay men to view male bisexuality as a legitimate sexual orientation. Second, whereas lesbian women viewed male bisexuality as more legitimate than female bisexuality, the reverse was true for gay men. Finally, among those with negative attitudes regarding bisexuality, lesbian women were more likely than were gay men to limit interactions with heterosexual individuals and to exclude bisexual individuals as possible best friends.

Herek (2002) conducted a national telephone survey that included items evaluating heterosexuals' attitudes toward bisexual men and women. Of the 1,338 total respondents, 1,283 heterosexual participants were included in the analyses. Ratings on a feeling thermometer were used to compare attitudes toward bisexuals to attitudes toward a variety of groups (e.g., religious denominations, ethnic groups, pro-choice and pro-life individuals, and lesbians and gay men). Ratings indicated that participants held less favorable attitudes toward bisexual women and men than toward all other groups assessed, except for injection drug users. More negative attitudes toward bisexual women and men were associated with higher age, less education, lower annual income, residence in the South and rural areas, higher religiosity, political conservatism, traditional values regarding gender and sexual behavior, authoritarianism, and lack of contact with gay men or lesbians. Whereas male participants' attitudes differed according to the sex of the target (i.e., lower ratings for gay and bisexual men than for lesbian and bisexual women), female participants' attitudes differed according to the target's sexual orientation (i.e., lower ratings for bisexual women and men than for lesbian women and gay men), leading the author to speculate that the function of attitudes toward bisexuals may be different for heterosexual women versus men.

Spalding and Peplau (1997) used an experimental design to evaluate heterosexual college students' attitudes related to romantic relationship functioning. The participants received stimulus material that varied the sexual orientation of the target (heterosexual or bisexual) and the gender of the partner (same- or other-gender) and rated each partner and the relationship in terms of monogamy, sexual riskiness, trust, sexual talent, and relationship quality. In a comparison of bisexual and heterosexual individuals in mixed-sex relationships, there were no differences in terms of trust or relationship quality. However, bisexual individuals were seen as less monogamous, more likely to cheat, and more likely to give their partner a sexually transmitted disease than were heterosexual individuals. In addition, the authors identified a trend in which partners of bisexual individuals were seen as more sexually satisfied than were partners of heterosexual individuals. Spalding and Peplau (1997) also compared scenarios of bisexual individuals in same-sex and other-sex relationships. Results indicated that bisexual individuals were seen as more likely to cheat on a heterosexual than a lesbian or gay partner, and heterosexual partners were seen as more sexually satisfied by a bisexual partner than were lesbian or gay partners. A comparison of bisexual versus lesbian/gay individuals in same-sex relationships showed that bisexual women and men are seen as more likely than lesbian women and gay men to give their partner a sexually transmitted disease and less likely to satisfy their partner sexually. No differences were found between perceptions of male and female bisexual individuals.

Finally, attitudes toward bisexuality have been investigated as predictors of counselors' clinical response to a client (Mohr, Israel, & Sedlecek, 2001). This study used an analogue design that described a bisexual-identified female client and asked participants to indicate their views of the client on a number of measures. The authors found that counselors with positive attitudes were more likely than others to view the bisexual client in a positive light, rate the client as having high levels of psychosocial functioning, and avoid applying bisexual stereotypes to the client. The aspect of biphobia that overlapped with homophobia (i.e., intolerance of same-sex attractions) was most predictive of counselors' judgments of the client's overall psychological functioning and counselors' tendency to impose personal values on the client. The aspect of biphobia distinct from homophobia (i.e., the view that bisexuality is not a legitimate or stable sexual orientation) was most predictive of counselors' personal reaction to the client and their judgments about the degree to which the client suffered from intimacy problems. These results provided support for the assertion that counselors' attitudes regarding bisexuality may influence their clinical reactions to bisexual clients even above and beyond the effects of attitudes regarding homosexuality.

FUTURE DIRECTIONS

Conceptualization and Measurement of Attitudes

Research on attitudes regarding bisexuality can benefit from consideration of the foundation laid by research and conceptualization regarding attitudes toward lesbian women and gay men. For example, Herek (1984b) suggested that attitudes toward lesbian women and gay men serve a variety of functions, including helping individuals make sense of past experiences related to lesbian/gay individuals, cope with personal insecurities with gender or sexuality, and express personal values important to self-concept. As suggested earlier, negative attitudes among lesbian women and gay men may serve to communicate a sense of loyalty to their communities (Ochs, 1996; Rust, 1995; Udis-Kessler, 1990). This function of binegativity was aptly expressed by a gay male participant in Mohr and Rochlen's attitude study: "I think bisexuals who avoid the self-designation 'gay' or 'lesbian' are hurting the cause" (1999a, p. 366). Furthermore, negative attitudes toward bisexual women and men may have different motivations, depending on the gender of the respondent and target (Herek, 2002). Development and evaluation of a functional model for attitudes regarding bisexuality may provide directions for investigating and altering such negative beliefs.

The measurement of attitudes regarding bisexuality may benefit from greater attention to affect. Just as with measures of homonegativity such as the Attitudes Toward Lesbians and Gay Men Scale (Herek, 1994), most measures of attitudes toward bisexual women and men focus on the cognitive components of attitudes (i.e., opinions and beliefs) about bisexual individuals rather than affective components such as disgust, fear, and enthusiasm. It may be beneficial to develop a measure of affective attitudes, or personal discomfort, to more fully capture the multidimensional nature of attitudes toward bisexual women and men. Such a measure might be modeled on the Index of Attitudes toward Homosexuals (Hudson & Ricketts, 1980).

Future research may also profit from increased focus on measurement of positive attitudes. Attitudes toward bisexuality, like attitudes toward homosexuality, have typically been conceptualized as the degree of adherence to negative views about the target population. As noted earlier, however, some individuals have been found to hold quite positive views of bisexuality. Development of a measure of positive attitudes could provide valuable information about the degree of relationship between positive and negative attitudes. Furthermore, it seems possible that the correlates of positive and negative attitudes differ, particularly with regard to aspects of relationships with bisexual individuals. For example, behavior that is especially affirming of bisexual individuals' sexual orientation may be better predicted by positive attitudes than negative attitudes. Although there appears to be no published measure of positive attitudes toward bisexuality, Worthington, Savoy, and Vernaglia (2000) developed a measure of LGB affirmativeness that could be used as a starting point for researchers who wish to create a similar measure specific to bisexuality. This measure moves the concept of attitudes into an affirming realm that goes beyond the notion of positive attitudes as the absence of negative attitudes.

Additionally, researchers should consider the role of social desirability in shaping individuals' responses to bisexual attitude measures. Although some communities may accept or even encourage negative attitudes toward bisexual individuals, people who see themselves as liberal or diversity-minded may be reluctant to express disapproval toward any marginalized individuals. Thus, particularly when studying populations who believe they should be sensitive to disenfranchised groups (e.g., lesbian women and gay men; counselors; feminists), researchers should attempt to find ways of accounting for underreported negative attitudes. Although research has suggested that general social desirability is unrelated to attitudes regarding bisexuality (Mohr, Israel, & Sedlecek, 2000; Mohr & Rochlen, 1999a), binegative attitudes may be related to forms of social desirability specific to sexual orientation. The measure of political correctness for sexual orientation developed by Brittan-Powell, Bashshur, Pak, and Meyenburg (1999) could serve as a starting point for efforts to assess this type of social desirability in studies of attitudes regarding bisexuality.

In addition to evaluating heterosexual and lesbian/gay individuals' attitudes regarding bisexuality, it may be useful to evaluate the internalized biphobia or binegativity of individuals who identify as bisexual. Although studies have evaluated the self-esteem of bisexual individuals (Fox, 1996), no published studies thus far have evaluated bisexual individuals' adherence to stereotypical views of bisexuality or rejection of their own bisexuality. Research on the experiences of bisexual individuals can help determine the psychological consequences of a biphobic environment for bisexual women and men. Instruments that have been developed to measure internalized homophobia (e.g., Mohr & Fassinger, 2000a; Ross & Rosser, 1996; Shidlo, 1994) may provide guidance for the development of measures of internalized biphobia. Indeed, Mohr and Fassinger (2000b) have revised their Lesbian and Gay Identity Scale (2000a) to be inclusive of bisexual individuals, and preliminary data based on this measure suggests that bisexual individuals' rejection of their own sexual orientation is linked to higher levels of distress (Balsam & Mohr, 2002).

Attitudes in Communities and Interpersonal Relationships

Given the conflicts about bisexuality in lesbian feminist communities, feminist identity may be a key variable in understanding lesbian women's attitudes toward bisexual women. According to Downing and Roush (1985), feminists progress through five stages of identity development. In the revelation stage, women tend to see men as negative and women as positive. Feminists, particularly lesbian feminists, in the revelation stage may have negative feelings about bisexual women, especially those who are in relationships with men. Similarly, feminists in the embeddedness-emanation stage may be more likely to question the loyalty of bisexual women to interpersonal relationships and political communities. This possible relationship between stage of feminist identity and attitudes regarding bisexuality has yet to be studied directly, although lesbian women's willingness to interact with heterosexual individuals (which may be related to feminist identity) has been found to be significantly associated with positive attitudes toward bisexual attitudes (Mohr & Rochlen, 1999a). Given the degree to which lesbian feminist identities have changed over the past several decades, it seems likely that the strength of the relationship between feminist identity and attitudes may vary according to the historical period in which lesbian women developed their identities.

The study of attitudes regarding bisexuality may also provide greater understanding of dynamics related to romantic and sexual relationships with bisexual individuals. As noted earlier, some research has indicated that attitudes are related to willingness to date bisexual women and men. More information is needed, however, about how the attitudes of heterosexual and lesbian/gay individuals affect relationship functioning, satisfaction, and stability with bisexual partners. Relevant data could be easily obtained by replicating Spaulding and Peplau's (1997) analogue study (described earlier) and assessing attitudes regarding bisexuality in participants. Analyses could help to determine the degree to which attitudes explain the romantic relationship differences associated with sexual orientation that Spaulding and Peplau found. Ideally, though, future research in this area will include studies of actual romantic and sexual relationships with bisexual individuals.

Attitudes and Interventions

Given the prevalence of misinformation and negative attitudes toward bisexual women and men and the potential damaging effects of such attitudes, it will be important to conduct research on attitude change interventions. Given the different types of attitudes toward bisexual individuals that are expressed by various populations (e.g., heterosexual individuals, lesbian women, gay men), such interventions should likely be targeted to particular populations. For example, interventions for heterosexual men might focus on changing sexual objectification of bisexual women, whereas interventions for lesbian women may attempt to heal historical personal and political rifts with bisexual women. Interventions for bisexual individuals could explore ways to overcome internalized binegativity.

Furthermore, helping professionals such as counselors, social workers, nurses, and doctors may benefit from interventions designed to improve attitudes toward bisexuality. Because counselors may associate bisexuality with particular presenting issues (Mohr, Israel, & Sedlecek, 2001), interventions that help counselors make more accurate judgments of bisexual individuals may contribute to appropriate diagnosis and treatment of bisexual clients. Also, given the view of bisexual individuals as vectors of transmission for sexually transmitted infections, interventions addressing health care professionals' attitudes regarding bisexuality may improve health care delivery. Research documenting both helping professionals' attitudes and the efficacy of attitude change interventions is clearly needed.

CONCLUSION

The small but growing literature on attitudes regarding bisexuality has demonstrated both similarities to and differences from research on attitudes regarding homosexuality. As Ochs (1999) noted, sanctions against same-sex desire affect lesbian women, gay men, and bisexual women and men alike. The research reviewed in this article suggests that this basic intolerance for same-sex sexuality constitutes an important aspect of attitudes regarding bisexuality, particularly among heterosexual women and men. Correlates of this dimension of attitudes appear to be similar to those of intolerance of homosexuality (e.g., religious fundamentalism, political conservativism, gender). It seems likely that many of the developments in research on homonegativity (e.g., focus on affective, cognitive, and behavioral aspects of attitudes; focus on internalized homonegativity) can be applied to research on this aspect of binegativity.

Research has also shown, however, that some attitudes toward bisexual women and men are based on beliefs and sociopolitical dynamics that are unrelated to attitudes toward lesbian women and gay men. Some negative attitudes are fueled by questions about the legitimacy of bisexuality as a sexual orientation and the trustworthiness of bisexual individuals. Such attitudes have been found to be related to the desirability of bisexual women and men as romantic partners and friends, as well as to the capacity for intimacy in such individuals. Furthermore, research has indicated that these attitudes may be particularly salient in understanding the ways that lesbian women and gay men relate to bisexual individuals. Such findings indicate that to fully understand the effects of stigma on the interpersonal relationships of bisexual individuals, it is critical to examine the influence of attitudes related to the legitimacy and stability of bisexual orientation and identity.

We believe that research on attitudes regarding bisexuality can both profit from and extend knowledge gained through research on attitudes toward lesbian and gay individuals. Just as bisexuality challenges dichotomous notions of sexual orientation, research on attitudes regarding bisexuality can increase the complexity of our understanding of attitudes toward sexual minority individuals. Documentation of attitudes in different social, political, and professional communities may provide greater understanding of the contexts of bisexual individuals' lives, the role of stigma in the identity development process of bisexual individuals, and the means by which negative attitudes can be reduced and positive attitudes increased. Conducting such research is now more feasible than ever due to advances over the past decade in both theory and measurement on attitudes regarding bisexuality. We look forward to the new insights that research in this area brings over the coming decade.

REFERENCES

Balsam, K. F., & Mohr, J. J. (2003). *Adaptation to antigay stigma and psychological distress in lesbian, gay male, and bisexual individuals.* Manuscript in progress.

Brittan-Powell, C., Bashshur, M., Pak, E. H., & Meyenburg, T. (1999, August). *A measure of political correctness for issues of sexual orientation.* Paper presented at the annual convention of the American Psychological Association, Boston, MA.

Bronn, C. D. (2001). Attitudes and self-images of male and female bisexuals. *Journal of Bisexuality, 1* (4), 5-29.

Butt, J. A., & Guldner, C. A. (1993). Counselling bisexuals: Therapists' attitudes towards bisexuality and application in clinical practice. *Canadian Journal of Human Sexuality, 2* (2), 61-70.

Division 44/Committee on Lesbian, Gay, and Bisexual Concerns Joint Task Force on Guidelines for Psychotherapy with Lesbian, Gay, and Bisexual Clients (2000). Guidelines for psychotherapy with lesbian, gay, and bisexual clients. *American Psychologist, 55,* 1440-1451.

Downing, N. E., & Roush, K. L. (1985). From passive-acceptance to active commitment: A model of feminist identity development for women. *The Counseling Psychologist, 13,* 695-709.

Eliason, M. (2001). "Bi-negativity: The stigma facing bisexual men." *Journal of Bisexuality, 1* (2/3), 137-154.

Eliason, M. J. (1996). A survey of the campus climate for lesbian, gay, and bisexual university members. *Journal of Psychology & Human Sexuality, 8* (4), 39-58.

Eliason, M. J. (1997). The prevalence and nature of biphobia in heterosexual undergraduate students. *Archives of Sexual Behavior, 26* (3), 317-326.

Fox, A. (1991). Development of a bisexual identity: Understanding the process. In L. Hutchins & L. Ka'ahumanu (Eds.), *Bi any other name: Bisexual people speak out* (pp. 29-39). Boston: Alyson Publications.

Fox, R. C. (1996). Bisexuality in perspective: A review of theory and research. In B. A. Firestein (Ed.), *Bisexuality: The psychology and politics of an invisible minority* (pp. 3-52). Thousand Oaks, CA: Sage.

Freud, S. (1962). *Three essays on the theory of sexuality* (J. Strachey, Trans.). New York: Basic Books. (Original work published 1905).

Herdt, G. (2001). Social change, sexual diversity, and tolerance for bisexuality in the United States. In A. R. D'Augelli and C. J. Patterson (Eds.), *Lesbian, gay, and bisexual identities and youth: Psychological perspectives* (pp. 267-283). New York, NY: Oxford University Press.

Herek, G. M. (1984a). Attitudes toward lesbians and gay men: A factor-analytic study. *Journal of Homosexuality, 10* (1/2), 39-51.

Herek, G. M. (1984b). Beyond "homophobia": A social psychological perspective on attitudes toward lesbians and gay men. *Journal of Homosexuality, 10* (1/2), 1-21.

Herek, G. M. (1994). Assessing heterosexuals' attitudes toward lesbians and gay men. In B. Greene & G. M. Herek (Eds.), *Psychological perspectives on lesbian and gay psychology: Vol 1. Lesbian and gay psychology: Theory, research, and clinical applications* (pp. 206-228). Thousand Oaks, CA: Sage.

Herek, G. M. (2002). Heterosexuals' attitudes toward bisexual men and women in the United States. *The Journal of Sex Research, 39* (4), 264-274.

Hudson, W. W., & Ricketts, W. A. (1980). A strategy for the measurement of homophobia. *Journal of Homosexuality, 5* (4), 357-371.

Hutchins, L., & Ka'ahumanu, L. (Eds.) (1991). *Bi any other name: Bisexual people speak out.* Boston: Alyson Publications.

Mohr, J. J., & Fassinger, R. E. (2000a). Measuring dimensions of lesbian and gay male experience. *Measurement and Evaluation in Counseling and Development, 33* (2), 66-90.

Mohr, J. J., & Fassinger, R. E. (2000b). *Lesbian, Gay, and Bisexual Identity Scale.* Unpublished measure.

Mohr, J. J., Israel, T., & Sedlecek, W. (2001). Counselors' attitudes regarding bisexuality as predictors of counselors' clinical responses: An analogue study of a female bisexual client. *Journal of Counseling Psychology, 48,* 212-222.

Mohr, J. J., & Rochlen, A. B. (1999a). Measuring attitudes regarding bisexuality in lesbian, gay male, and heterosexual populations. *Journal of Counseling Psychology, 46,* 353-369.

Mohr, J. J., & Rochlen, A. B. (1999b, August). Attitudes toward bisexual women and men: Conceptualization, measurement, and correlates. In R. C. Fox (Chair), *Current research on bisexuality.* Symposium conducted at the annual meeting of the American Psychological Association, Boston, MA.

Nagle, J. (1995). Framing radical bisexuality: Toward a gender agenda. In N. Tucker (Ed.), *Bisexual politics: Theories, queries, and visions* (pp. 305-314). Binghamton, NY: Harrington Park Press.

Neisen, J. H. (1990). Heterosexism: Redefining homophobia for the 1990's. *Journal of Gay and Lesbian Psychotherapy, 1* (3), 21-35.

Ochs, R. (1996). Biphobia: It goes more than two ways. In B. A. Firestein (Ed.), *Bisexuality: The psychology and politics of an invisible minority* (pp. 217-239). Thousand Oaks, CA: Sage Publications.

Ponterotto, J. G., Reiger, B. P., Barrett, A., Harris, G., Sparks, R., Sanchez, C. M. et al. (1996). Development and initial validation of the Multicultural Counseling Awareness Scale. In G. R. Sodowsky & J. C. Impara (Eds.), *Multicultural assessment in counseling and clinical psychology* (pp. 247-282). Lincoln, NE: Buros Institute of Mental Measurements.

Ross M. W., & Rosser, B. R. S. (1996). Measurement and correlates of internalized homophobia: A factor analytic study. *Journal of Clinical Psychology, 52* (1), 15-21.

Rust, P. C. (1993). Neutralizing the political threat of the marginal woman: Lesbians' beliefs about bisexual women. *Journal of Sex Research, 30* (3), 214-228.

Rust, P. C. (1995). *Bisexuality and the challenge to lesbian politics: Sex, loyalty, and revolution.* New York: New York University Press.

Rust, P. C. (1996). Monogamy and polyamory: Relationship issues for bisexuals. In B. A. Firestein (Ed.), *Bisexuality: The psychology and politics of an invisible minority* (pp. 127-148). Thousand Oaks, CA: Sage Publications.

Shidlo, A. (1994). Internalized homophobia: Conceptual and empirical issues in measurement. In B. Greene & G. M. Herek (Eds.), *Psychological perspectives on les-*

bian and gay psychology: Vol 1. Lesbian and gay psychology: Theory, research, and clinical applications (pp. 176-205). Thousand Oaks, CA: Sage.

Sodowsky, G. R. (1996). The Multicultural Counseling Inventory: Validity and applications in multicultural training. In G. R. Sodowsky & J. C. Impara (Eds.), Multicultural assessment in counseling and clinical psychology (pp. 247-282). Lincoln, NE: Buros Institute of Mental Measurements.

Sodowsky, G. R., Kuo-Jackson, P. Y., Richardson, M. F., & Corey, A. T. (1998). Correlates of self-reported multicultural competencies: Counselor multicultural social desirability, race, social inadequacy, locus of control, racial ideology, and multicultural training. Journal of Counseling Psychology, 45, 256-264.

Spaulding, L. R., & Peplau, L. A. (1997). The unfaithful lover: Heterosexuals' perceptions of bisexuals and their relationships. Psychology of Women Quarterly, 21 (4), 611-625.

Udis-Kessler, A. (1990). Bisexuality in an essentialist world: Toward an understanding of biphobia. In T. Geller (Ed.), Bisexuality: A reader and sourcebook (pp. 51-63). Ojai, CA: Times Change Press.

Weinberg, G. (1972). Society and the healthy homosexual. New York: St. Martin's Press.

Weise, E. R. (1992). Closer to home: Bisexuality and feminism. Seattle: Seal Press.

Worthington, R. L., Savoy, H. B., & Vernaglia, E. R. (2000, August). Beyond tolerance: Issues in LGB affirmativeness: Theory, research, and measurement. Paper presented at the American Psychological Association Annual Convention, Washington, DC.

Zinik, G. A. (1985). Identity conflict or adaptive flexibility? Bisexuality reconsidered. Journal of Homosexuality, 11 (1/2), 7-19.

Bisexual best case scenario

http://www.haworthpress.com/web/JB
© 2004 by The Haworth Press, Inc. All rights reserved.
Digital Object Identifier: 10.1300/J159v04n01_10

[Haworth co-indexing entry note]: "Bisexual Best Case Scenario." Clurman, Dan. Co-published simultaneously in *Journal of Bisexuality* (Harrington Park Press, an imprint of The Haworth Press, Inc.) Vol. 4, Nos.
1/2, 2004, p. 135; and: *Current Research on Bisexuality* (ed: Ronald C. Fox) Harrington Park Press, an imprint of The Haworth Press, Inc., 2004, p. 135. Single or multiple copies of this article are available for a fee
from The Haworth Document Delivery Service [1-800-HAWORTH. 9:00 a.m. - 5:00 p.m. (EST). E-mail address: docdelivery@haworthpress.com].

Mental Health Services Experiences of Bisexual Women and Bisexual Men: An Empirical Study

Emily H. Page

http://www.haworthpress.com/web/JB
© 2004 by The Haworth Press, Inc. All rights reserved.
Digital Object Identifier: 10.1300/J159v04n01_11

[Haworth co-indexing entry note]: "Mental Health Services Experiences of Bisexual Women and Bisexual Men: An Empirical Study." Page, Emily H. Co-published simultaneously in *Journal of Bisexuality* (Harrington Park Press, an imprint of The Haworth Press, Inc.) Vol. 4, Nos. 1/2, 2004, pp. 137-160; and: *Current Research on Bisexuality* (ed: Ronald C. Fox) Harrington Park Press, an imprint of The Haworth Press, Inc., 2004, pp. 137-160. Single or multiple copies of this article are available for a fee from The Haworth Document Delivery Service [1-800-HAWORTH, 9:00 a.m. - 5:00 p.m. (EST). E-mail address: docdelivery@haworthpress.com].

SUMMARY. Two hundred seventeen women and men participated in the first empirical research on the experiences of self-identified bisexual clients with mental health services. Findings suggest that bisexual women and men seek help for sexual orientation issues less frequently and rate their services as less helpful with sexual orientation concerns than gay and lesbian participants in comparable research. Men experienced more stress in connection with their bisexuality than women, and bisexual issues were more important for men in terms of their initial reasons for seeking mental health services. Women's overall clinical issues were more serious than those of men. Of the more than two-thirds of the sample who disclosed their sexual orientation often or always to a mental health provider, most experienced acceptance from their clinicians. Participants with more serious clinical issues, however, disclosed their bisexuality to clinicians less frequently than those with more moderate clinical issues, and they experienced less acceptance of their sexual orientation upon disclosure and more biased clinical interventions from providers. Overall, participants urged providers to validate bisexuality as legitimate and healthy, to be accurately informed about bisexual issues, and to intervene proactively with bisexual clients. *[Article copies available for a fee from The Haworth Document Delivery Service: 1-800-HAWORTH. E-mail address: <docdelivery@haworthpress.com> Website: <http://www.HaworthPress.com> © 2004 by The Haworth Press, Inc. All rights reserved.]*

KEYWORDS. Bisexuality, homosexuality, sexual orientation, mental health services, psychotherapy, counseling, heterosexual bias, sexual orientation conversion therapy

Empirical research on lesbians, gay men, and mental health services has been ongoing for more than thirty years. Research on the provision of mental health services for bisexual women and bisexual men is just beginning. The current study expands on findings from prior research on lesbian and gay mental health services by inquiring about the specific experiences and needs of bisexual clients in mental health treatment. Important information is provided about the motivations of bisexual clients to seek mental health services, their ratings for the overall helpfulness of services received, as well as their assessment of both positive and problematic aspects of the services they received. In addition, themes of importance to bisexual mental health clients are clarified, and further information is provided about the experiences of bisexual clients in terms of gender, ethnicity, and seriousness of clinical issues.

BACKGROUND

Historical Approaches to Sexual Orientation in Psychology

Until the 1970s, the illness model of homosexuality dominated theory and practice in psychology (Bayer, 1981). Same-sex attractions and behaviors were seen as pathological, and the goal of mental health services for bisexual, gay, and lesbian clients was to promote a transition to an exclusively heterosexual orientation (Drescher, 1998). Some mental health practitioners have continued to offer services based on the illness model, focusing on the elimination of same-sex attractions and behaviors in lesbian, gay and bisexual clients (Socarides et al., 1997). There is no evidence, however, based on carefully conducted empirical research, to support the claims of therapists advocating this approach. In fact, there is evidence that sexual orientation conversion therapy is ineffective and includes violations of ethical guidelines (Shidlo, Schroeder, & Drescher, 2002). There is also evidence that clients for whom this therapy has failed experience depression, low self-esteem, sexual dysfunction, and withdrawal from social support (Haldeman, 2001). Since it is likely that some bisexual women and men have been involved in conversion therapy, this is an important area for further research on issues having to do with mental health services for bisexual clients.

Affirmative Services for Lesbians and Gay Men

Since the early 1970s, all the major professional organizations devoted to mental health services have taken the position that there is nothing inherently unhealthy about same-sex attractions and relationships (American Counseling Association, 1996; American Psychiatric Association, 1974; Conger, 1975). This change in direction away from the illness model has led to a more affirmative approach, focused on assisting individuals to face and overcome the complex effects of social stigma based on sexual orientation and identity. In 1997, the American Psychological Association adopted a resolution, *Appropriate Therapeutic Responses to Sexual Orientation*, supporting the "dissemination of accurate information about sexual orientation, and mental health, and appropriate interventions in order to counteract bias that is based on ignorance and unfounded beliefs about sexual orientation" (American Psychological Association, 1997, p. 2). This resolution was followed in 2000 by the American Psychological Association's adoption of the *Guidelines for Psychotherapy for Lesbian, Gay and Bisexual Clients* and publication of *The Handbook of Counseling and Psychotherapy with Lesbian, Gay, and Bisexual Clients* (Division 44/Committee on Lesbian, Gay, and Bisexual Concerns Joint Task Force on Guidelines for Psychotherapy with Lesbian, Gay, and Bisexual Clients, 2000; Perez, DeBord, & Bieschke, 2000).

Empirical Research on Mental Health Services for Lesbians and Gay Men

A body of theory and research has charted the parameters of this affirmative approach (Perez et al., 2000). Empirical research has found that, compared to their heterosexual counterparts, lesbian and gay clients use psychotherapy and other mental health services in comparatively greater numbers (Cochran, Sullivan, & Mays, 2003), participate in more and lengthier courses of services, and value mental health services more highly (Bieschke, McClanahan, Tozer, Grzegorek, & Park, 2000). Research has also found that lesbian and gay clients give their psychotherapists, counselors, and mental health providers mixed reviews in regard to their level of knowledge, skill, and helpfulness in addressing lesbian and gay issues (Bieschke et al., 2000; Jones & Gabriel, 1999; Lebolt, 1999; Nystrom, 1997).

Empirical Research on Mental Health Services for Bisexual Women and Men

Since it is likely that bisexual women and men have been included in the samples of many of the studies on psychotherapy for lesbians and gay men, it might be assumed that their findings apply, to some degree, to bisexual women and men. Most of these studies, however, failed to report findings taking into consideration differences between bisexual, gay and lesbian participants (Chung & Katayama, 1996).

Two studies have distinguished between responses of bisexual participants and lesbian and gay participants (Lucksted, 1996; Moss, 1994). Both studies found that bisexual participants experienced greater degrees of heterosexual bias from their providers than did lesbian and gay participants. This difference has additional importance in light of recent findings in which bisexual responses were higher for anxiety, depression, suicidality and negative affect than lesbian, gay, and heterosexual responses (Balsam & Rothblum, 2002; Jorm, Korten, Rodgers, Jacomb, & Christensen, 2002). In particular, Jorm et al. (2000) found that, compared to lesbian, gay, and heterosexual participants in their study, the bisexuals in their sample experienced more "current adverse life events, greater childhood adversity, less positive support from family, [and] more negative support from friends . . ." (p. 423). These authors suggest that this disparity in psychosocial stressors is due, in part, to the dual prejudice that bisexual women and men experience: prejudice against bisexuality as well as prejudice against homosexuality. The negative effects of prejudicial attitudes towards bisexual women and men have also been emphasized in discussion of findings from empirical research on bisexual identity (Fox, 1996; Rust, 2001b), professional discussions of bisexuality (Firestein, 1996), and in anecdotal reports about the bisexual experience (Bisexual Anthology Collective, 1995; Hutchins & Kaahumanu, 1991; Orndorff, 1999).

Since research suggests that bisexual women and men may have greater mental health challenges (Balsam & Rothblum, 2002; Jorm et al., 2002) and may be receiving less effective and potentially even more harmful services than those of other sexual orientations (Lucksted, 1996; Moss, 1994), it is important to learn more about the specific mental health care experiences and needs of bisexual women and bisexual men.

STUDY DESIGN

The present study used a 49-item questionnaire, designed by the researcher, which combined multiple-choice and open-ended questions, in order to provide an in-depth impression of bisexual client's clinical experiences. Whereas most previous studies focused either exclusively or primarily on the psychotherapy experiences of lesbians and gay men, this survey invited self-identified bisexual women and men to provide information on the full range of their experiences with mental health services.

Data Collection and Analysis

Questionnaire distribution. A convenience sample was gathered by making the questionnaire available in three formats: an *Internet Website*, with links posted on other Websites related to bisexual or mental health consumer issues; *e-mail*, via announcements on e-mail lists related to gay, lesbian or bisexual issues or mental health consumer issues; and *paper*, distributed at conferences on bisexuality in Boston and Los Angeles, as well as through the researcher's network of professional and personal contacts.

Data analysis. Frequencies of multiple-choice responses were obtained. Responses to open-ended questions were examined by the researcher and sorted into topical groupings as suggested by Miles and Huberman (1994), and six broad themes related to treatment experiences emerged. Comparisons were made between demographic variables and content responses and statistical tests were performed, as appropriate, on the data collected.

The Sample

Demographic characteristics. Participants included 217 self-identified bisexual women (71%) and men (29%) residing in the United States, who responded to the survey via the Internet Website (42%), e-mail (22%), or paper (36%). Half of the participants were under 30 years of age (52%), while another 27% were between 30 and 39 years of age, and the remainder were 40 years of age or older (21%). Most lived in urban (49%) and suburban (36%) settings, and had completed at least two years of college (83%). The sample was predominantly European American (84%). Women and men of color, including small numbers of all racial and ethnic minorities, made up 16% of the sample.

Sexual orientation characteristics. Participants first identified as bisexual before the age of 15 (18%), between the ages of 15 and 19 (39%), between 20 and 29 years of age (30%), between 30 and 39 years of age (11%), or at age 40 or older (3%). Most had considered themselves heterosexual and then bisexual (55%). Other sequences of sexual orientation self-identification included: heterosexual, then lesbian or gay and then bisexual (13%); lesbian or gay, then bisexual (10%); bisexual throughout life (11%); and other multiple self-identification sequences (11%).

Self-identification as bisexual relative to entering treatment. Participants had first self-identified as bisexual before (56%), during (19%), or after (16%) entering mental health treatment. A small proportion (8%) did not recall the timing of coming out as bisexual relative to when they entered mental health services. There was a difference, although not statistically significant, between participants of color and European American participants in regard to when they had come out as bisexual in relationship to the time they entered treatment ($\chi^2 = 6.3604$; $df = 2$; *Fisher's Exact Test*, $p = 0.0608$). Proportionately more European American participants than participants of color came out before beginning mental health treatment (64% vs. 54%), whereas a greater proportion of participants of color than European American participants came out during their participation in mental health services (39% vs.18%). A greater proportion of European American participants than participants of color came out as bisexual after completing treatment (18% vs. 8%).

Relationship status. About a quarter of the sample (25%) were in no relationship at the time of the research. One-third were currently in a monogamous relationship (33%) and another third were in a nonmonogamous relationship (33%). In terms of ideal relationship patterns, 54% preferred nonmonogamous relationships and 33% preferred monogamous relationships.

RESULTS

Use of Mental Health Services

Types of mental health services used. Individual psychotherapy or counseling was the modality used most, either alone (37%) or combined with other modalities (26%), during the time participants responded to the survey. Other modalities included: family or couples therapy only (2%), or with other services (8%); group therapy plus one or more other service (15%); psychopharmacology only (5%), or with other services (13%); and residential, rehabilitation or other services, such as case management or addiction recovery (5%). Nineteen percent had been hospitalized at some point for mental health reasons.

Twenty-six percent were receiving no mental health services at the time of responding to the research.

Overall reasons for seeking mental health services. Participants' reasons for seeking mental health services included: *depression* (40%); *family or relationship problems* (19%); *post-traumatic stress disorder* (10%); *anxiety* (7%); *issues connected to participants' sexual identity* (6%); *an addiction* (4%); *issues connected to participants' gender identity* (3%); *a suicide attempt* (2%); and small proportions of additional reasons (10%).

Clinicians' diagnoses. Participants received a range of diagnoses from their mental health services providers, including *depression* (38%); *generalized anxiety disorder* (10%); *post-traumatic stress disorder* (7%); and *bipolar disorder* (7%). Other diagnoses included: *adjustment disorder; bereavement; sexual or gender dysphoria;* and *borderline personality disorder* (< 3% each). A few reported a diagnosis of a more serious mental illness, i.e. *schizophrenia, schizoaffective disorder,* or *dissociative identity disorder* (< 2% each).

Classification of clinical issues as moderate or more serious. The following experiences were used to catagorize a participant as having more serious mental health issues: a major mental illness diagnosis from the participant's clinician; a suicide attempt; participation in residential, rehabilitation, or day treatment services; or a psychiatric hospitalization. Almost a fifth of the participants had more serious (18%) as opposed to more moderate (72%) mental health issues. There was a significant difference between the level of seriousness of clinical issues for women compared to men ($\chi^2 = 5.370$; $df = 1$; *Fisher's Exact Test, p* = .021). A greater proportion of women than men (33% vs. 17%) had more serious clinical issues.

Motivation to Seek Services for Bisexual Issues

Level of stress in connection with bisexual issues. Participants were asked to respond to the question: *Have you experienced stress or difficulty related to your bisexuality?* Overall, almost two-thirds of participants experienced moderate levels of stress related to their sexual orientation. There were significant differences between women and men in terms of their level of stress about bisexual issues (Table 1). Proportionately more women than men experienced stress.

Importance of bisexual issues in seeking mental health services. Participants were asked to respond to the question: *Have you sought mental health services specifically to assist with stress or difficulty related to your bisexuality.* Overall, more than two-thirds did not include bisexual issues in terms of their reasons for seeking mental health services. There was a statistically significant difference between responses of women and men (Table 2). There was also a difference, though not statistically significant, between responses of participants with more moderate and more serious clinical issues regarding the importance of bisexual issues in terms of seeking mental health services (Table 3).

TABLE 1. Level of Stress in Connection with Bisexual Issues: By Gender

Stress in Connection with Bisexual Issues	Gender					
	Women		Men		Total	
	N	%	N	%	N	%
No stress at all	9	5.9	2	3.2	11	5.1
Only minor stress	37	24.2	11	17.7	48	22.3
Some stress	65	42.5	20	32.3	85	39.5
Quite difficult	37	24.2	23	37.1	60	27.9
The hardest thing in life	5	3.3	6	9.7	11	5.1
Total	153	100.0	62	100.0	215	100.0

(χ^2 = 8.775; df = 4; *Fisher's Exact Test, p* = .0092)

TABLE 2. Importance of Bisexual Issues in Seeking Mental Health Services: By Gender

Importance of Bisexual Issues in Seeking Mental Health Services	Gender					
	Women		Men		Total	
	N	%	N	%	N	%
Never sought help for bisexual issues	60	38.9	17	27.6	77	35.5
Didn't seek help, but bisexual issues came up during services	57	37.0	16	25.4	73	33.6
Sought help for bisexual issues, but other issues were much bigger	15	9.7	8	12.7	23	10.6
Bisexual issues were only or main reasons for seeking mental health services	22	14.3	22	34.9	44	20.3
Total	154	100.0	62	100.0	217	100.0

(χ^2 = 13.5164; df = 4; *Fisher's Exact Test, p* = .0096)

Helpfulness of Mental Health Services

Overall helpfulness with bisexual issues. Participants were asked to rate the degree to which a recent course of mental health services had been helpful with their bisexual issues. Helpfulness ratings were: (1) *extremely unhelpful*

TABLE 3. Importance of Bisexual Issues in Seeking Mental Health Services: By Seriousness of Mental Health Issues

Importance of Bisexual Issues in Seeking Mental Health Services	Seriousness of Mental Health Issues					
	More Moderate		More Serious		Total	
	N	%	N	%	N	%
Never sought help for bisexual issues	47	30.3	30	48.4	77	35.5
Didn't seek help, but bisexual issues came up during services	56	36.1	17	27.4	73	33.6
Sought help for bisexual issues, but other issues were much bigger	16	10.3	7	11.3	23	10.6
Bisexual issues were only or main reasons for seeking mental health services	36	23.2	8	12.9	44	20.3
Total	155	100.0	62	100.0	217	100.0

(χ^2 = 9.735; df = 4; *Fisher's Exact Test, p* = .0502)

(4%); (2) *moderately unhelpful* (12%); (3) *neither helpful nor unhelpful* (35%); (4) *moderately helpful* (25%); and (5) *extremely helpful* (24%). Average helpfulness ratings were halfway between (3) *neither helpful nor unhelpful* and (4) *somewhat helpful* ($N = 212; M = 3.5; SD = 1.11$). There were no significant differences between the responses of women and men or between those with more serious or more moderate mental health issues in terms of the help they indicated they received with their sexual orientation issues.

Disclosure of bisexuality to clinician. Participants were asked: *Do you usually let a mental health practitioner know you are bisexual?* Participants rated their level of disclosure as (1) *never* (11%), (2) *rarely* (6%), (3) *sometimes* (22%), (4) *often* (14%), and (5) *always* (47%). There was a significant difference in terms of openness about their bisexuality with mental health clinicians for participants with more serious clinical issues (M = 3.6774, SD = 1.2251) compared to participants with more moderate clinical issues (M = 4.1871, SD = 1.2421) (*Independent means t-test, t* = 2.758, p = .009). Those with more serious issues were less open about their bisexuality.

Perceptions of clinician's acceptance of participant's bisexuality. Participants were asked: *When you do let practitioners know you are bisexual, how accepting have they been?* Overall responses were: (1) *extremely accepting* (27%); (2) *moderately accepting* (62%); (3) *neither accepting nor unaccepting* (1%); (4) *moderately unaccepting* (8%); and (5) *extremely unaccepting* (2%). There was a significant difference in terms of practitioner acceptance for participants with more serious clinical issues (M = 3.7554, SD = .9502) compared to participants with moderate clinical issues (M = 4.2190, SD = .8464) (*Independent means t-test, t* = −3.201, *p* = .002). Those with more serious clinical issues experienced less acceptance of their bisexuality when they were open about it with their clinicians.

Problematic Experiences Related to Bisexual Issues

Participants provided information about *problematic experiences in treatment related to their bisexual issues* in two ways: (1) Sixty-six participants checked any of six listed *examples of biased interventions* that they had experienced; and (2) Almost all participants provided written descriptions of the *main problems* they faced as bisexual consumers of mental health services.

Examples of biased provider interventions related to bisexual issues. A list of examples of biased interventions was compiled, based on prior research on psychotherapy experiences of lesbian and gay clients (Garnets et al., 1991; Lucksted, 1996) and was expanded to include circumstances specific to the bisexual experience. Participants were asked to check any example that they had experienced while participating in mental health services. Of the 66 (30%) who responded, the two most frequently checked examples of bias were interventions in which the clinician *invalidated* and *pathologized* the sexual orientation of the client in one of two ways (Table 4). Clinicians assumed that the client's bisexuality was connected to clinical issues when the client didn't agree, or assumed that bisexual attractions and behavior would disappear when the client regained psychological health. A greater proportion of those with more serious clinical issues experienced these examples of bias than did those with more moderate clinical issues.

Most important problems as bisexual mental health services consumers. Almost all participants responded to the question: What do you think is the most important issue or problem you face in being both a mental health consumer and a bisexual? (Table 5). The most frequent themes in responses to this question were: (1) *invalidation of bisexuality*, e.g., "I always felt like my therapist was humoring me when we discussed my bisexuality, like she thought it was a phase, despite that I've had long-term relationships with both sexes fairly consistently"; (2) *lack of knowledge about bisexual issues*, e.g., "Finding practitioners who understand the oppression bisexuals get from other queers"; and (3) *interpretation of bisexual attractions or behaviors as unhealthy*, e.g., "I feel I have the most difficulty with being bisexual and polyamorous when trying to find an appropriate therapist [i.e., one that doesn't think these are symptoms of a problem]." Some participants provided examples of (4) *lack of skill in working with bisexual issues*, e.g., "When I mentioned my bisexuality, she didn't seem to know what to say, or any theory at all other than commonsense fake-seeming things to say"; and (5) *lack of*

TABLE 4. Examples of Biased Provider Interventions by Seriousness of Clinical Issues

	Seriousness of Clinical Issues					
	More Moderate		More Serious		Total	
Biased Interventions	N	%	N	%	N	%
Assumption that sexual orientation is connected to clinical goals	29	18.7	26	41.9	55	25.3
"You aren't really bisexual. It's part of your illness"	17	11.0	17	27.4	34	15.7
To get better: Limit interest in the same sex	10	6.5	11	11.3	17	7.8
Attempted conversion to heterosexual	7	4.5	9	14.5	16	7.4
To get better: Limit interest in the other sex	5	3.2	5	8.9	10	4.6
Attempted conversion to lesbian or gay	4	2.6	4	6.5	8	3.7

TABLE 5. Most Important Problems in Services and Top Suggestions to Clinicians

	Most Important Problems in Services		Top Suggestions to Clinicians	
Themes	N	%	N	%
Validation/Invalidation of Bisexuality	92	42.4	121	55.8
Knowledge/Lack of Knowledge of Bisexual Issues	57	26.3	38	17.5
Views/Doesn't View Bisexuality as Healthy Per Se	42	19.4	44	20.3
Proactive Intervention/Lack of Proactive Intervention	14	6.4	7	3.2
Skill/Lack of Skill with Bisexual Issues	3	1.4	7	3.2
General Clinical Skills	0	0.0	0	0.0
Not Indicated	9	4.0	0	0.0
Total	217	100.0	217	100.0

proactive interventions, e.g., "My therapist didn't even attempt to find out my orientation [assumed I was straight] and this made me scared to tell her."

Positive Experiences Related to Bisexual Issues

Participants provided information about *positive mental health experiences related to bisexual issues* in two ways: (1) All participants wrote *sug-*

gestions to clinicians about working with bisexual clients; and (2) Sixty participants wrote descriptions of *exemplary interventions* with bisexual issues that they had experienced during their mental health services.

Suggestions for clinicians. All participants provided up to three suggestions for clinicians, prioritized in order of importance (Table 5). The most frequent of participants' first, second, and third priority suggestions were examples of the clinician (1) *validating bisexuality* (57%, 52%, 56%, respectively), e.g., "Accept *all* of their clients' feelings: same-sex attractions, opposite-sex attractions, shame, fear, anger, pride." Additional themes emphasized by participants were that clinicians (2) *view bisexuality as healthy per se*, e.g., "Bisexuality is not proof or even strong evidence of having been sexually abused as a child"; and that they acquire (3) *knowledge of bisexual issues*, e.g., "Know we aren't sitting on the fence." Some participants offered suggestions that were examples of (4) *skill in working with bisexual issues*, e.g., "Help the patient resolve inner conflicts." Others offered examples of *proactive interventions*, e.g., "Be creative problem solvers and think outside the lines like we do."

Descriptions of exemplary interventions. Participants were also asked to provide examples of exemplary interventions: *If you have experienced a really positive interaction around being a bisexual in the mental health system, please describe one or more time this happened.* Of the 60 participants (28%) who responded, the most frequent examples were experiences of service providers (1) *intervening proactively in affirmation of bisexuality or the bisexual identity of the participant* (n = 18), e.g., "She recommended appropriate support groups, didn't push or pull in any direction, helped me sort out that I was not dealing with 'gender dysphoria,'etc."; (2) *using general clinical skills*, not specific to bisexual issues (n = 13), e.g., "I felt respected and supported in the decisions I have made"; and (3) *validating bisexuality* (n = 10), e.g., "I've never felt that my therapist doubts the authenticity of my bisexual feelings. Our focus is not on the question 'why am I bisexual' but instead 'what does this mean for my life now and in the future?'" In addition some participants provided examples of (4) *skill in working with bisexual issues* (n = 10), e.g., "He never batted an eye . . . he simply took what I had to say according to the pronoun I use." Some contributed examples of *accurate knowledge of bisexual issues* (n = 5), e.g., "My current therapist . . . seems to really understand the fluidity of gender and sexual orientation."

DISCUSSION

Motivation to Seek Services for Bisexual Issues and Help Received

Findings in this study differ from findings of previous research suggesting that lesbian and gay clients value psychotherapy and mental health services highly as a resource for help with their sexual orientation concerns (Bieschke et al., 2000; Jones & Gabriel, 1999). In contrast, more than two-thirds of the participants in this study did not initially seek mental health services for assistance with issues connected to their bisexuality. It may be that bisexual clients do not see mental health providers as being able to help them with issues connected to their sexual orientation to the degree lesbian and gay clients do. For example, some participants indicated that they did not have confidence that mental health providers would be understanding or helpful, saying: "No, I've never brought it up, I never felt like I could"or "I don't really know where to go for help." Others indicated that they did not experience a need for clinical help with their bisexuality: "I never had a problem with being bi. It never was traumatic." Participants in this study also gave a lower rating for the help that they received with their sexual orientation issues than gay and lesbian participants gave in roughly comparable studies (Bieschke et al., 2000; Jones & Gabriel, 1999; Liddle, 1996).

Validation of Bisexuality as Legitimate and Healthy Per Se

Participants in this study strongly urged their clinicians to validate their bisexual orientation and identity as legitimate, healthy per se, and equal in standing to lesbian, gay and heterosexual orientations. This emphasis on the desire for validation of one's bisexuality is mirrored in autobiographical accounts of the bisexual experience (Bisexual Anthology Collective, 1995; Hutchins & Kaahumanu, 1991; Orndorff, 1999) and current clinical theory about affirmative services for bisexuals (Dworkin, 2001; Matteson, 1996). The impact of negative attitudes toward bisexuality on bisexual clients and the importance of acknowledgment and validation are also found in the American Psychological Association's *Guidelines for Psychotherapy with Lesbian, Gay, and Bisexual Clients* (Division 44/Committee on Lesbian, Gay, and Bisexual Concerns Joint Task Force on Guidelines for Psychotherapy with Lesbian, Gay, and Bisexual Clients, 2000):

> Bisexual adults and youth may experience a variety of stressors in addition to the societal prejudice due to same-sex attractions. One such stressor is that the polarization of sexual orientation into heterosexual and homosexual categories invalidates bisexuality. (Eliason, 1997; Fox, 1996; Markowitz, 1995; Matteson, 1996; Ochs, 1996; Paul, 1996; Shuster, 1987). This view has influenced psychological theory and practice as well as societal attitudes and institutions. (p. 1445)

This *Guideline* addressing counseling and psychotherapy with bisexual clients further suggests that validation of only the end points of the sexual orientation spectrum results in inaccurate and pathologizing assessments of bisexual women and men seeking clinical services. Bisexual clients may be seen as in a transitional state, or "as developmentally arrested or in other ways psychologically impaired" (p. 1447). In fact, no evidence of psychopathology or maladjustment based on empirical research has been found for a bisexual identity per se (Fox, 1966). Some studies suggest that bisexual individuals are more resilient (Zinik, 1984), more flexible in relationship roles (Matteson, 1996) and have self-esteem and life satisfaction equal to lesbian, gay and heterosexual counterparts (Balsam & Rothblum, 2002; Jorm et al., 2002).

Descriptive written responses of this study illustrate the impact on clients of invalidating or pathologizing bisexuality. One respondent wrote that a session created "more stress than I had gone in with (though the stress had nothing to do with how I felt about my sexuality, he just made me very angry at how he treated me) . . . this counselor did not even accept the POSSIBILITY [sic] that bisexuality even exists." Another said her clinician "saw it [her bisexuality] as 'illness'/or a medicatable situation, rather than inquiring more and finding the dilemma that 'causes' my feelings of distress." A third respondent wrote simply: "We DO exist!"

The emphasis on basic validation of their sexual orientation by the participants in this study contrasts with findings from prior research on lesbian and gay clients' psychotherapy experiences. In the prior studies, lesbian and gay participants rated training in skills specific to lesbian and gay issues and general therapeutic skills more highly than a practitioner's role in validation of their sexual orientation as real and healthy per se (Lebolt, 1999; Liddle, 1996; Morgan & Eliason, 1992). This may be a reflection of how publicly invisible bisexual issues still are compared with societal awareness of lesbian and gay issues.

Being Knowledgeable and Skillful with Bisexual Issues

Participants' emphasis on the importance of providers having up-to-date information about bisexuality provides further guidance for clinical practice. One participant alluded to the empathy that accurate understanding brings: "I think that most doctors, unless they are bisexual have no idea what it is like. Therefore, how can they help?!" Another respondent urged clinicians to be able to distinguish between the impact of societal stigma on bisexual individuals and psychological difficulties that have nothing to do with sexual orientation: "[Clinicians should] get knowledge and be able to distinguish between problematic areas in functioning–relationship skills, etc., and the basics about the stresses that bisexuals face, so they don't assume all stress means bi is a bad thing."

Beyond just having information about bisexual issues, participants in this study also expressed a desire for clinicians to be skillful in helping their bisexual clients with tasks and challenges connected to their sexual orientation. At one end of the range are comments about issues of counter-transference and self-monitoring by practitioners: "If you're not comfortable with the subject, don't pretend you are, it's really obvious when you're not." Responses at other end of the range include interventions with relationship issues: "[Clinician helped with] my stress about being in a committed relationship with a man, but still being attracted to women. She helped me come up with ideas about being evolved with my sexuality (because it doesn't go away) without having a sexual relationship with another person." Some comments address in a more general way, helpful attitudes toward domains of experience that can make up a bisexual identity: "Be patient about coming out issues"; and "Be understanding about open relationships when they happen."

General Clinical Skills Seen as Helpful with Bisexual Issues

In addition, participants identified basic clinical attitudes and skills that bisexual clients find helpful. An overall attitude of acceptance can provide enough safety to encourage disclosure of sexual orientation issues: "At first I was afraid to tell her for fear of being judged but she seemed really understanding." Openness, combined with an interest in learning can have a great positive impact, even if the clinician is uninformed about sexual minority issues: "Overall she is helpful–bi stuff is new to her, but she's very open–it's a healing experience all the way around." Attending to and valuing what is unique in a client, can have a transformative impact: "My current therapist values me as I am and has helped me to value myself."

Proactive Interventions with Bisexual Issues

In descriptions of exemplary interventions with bisexual issues, participants emphasized the value of a more active role than is the usual clinical approach. This finding parallels theory about affirmative psychotherapy for lesbian and gay clients, which suggests that proactive interventions are needed to counteract the impact of social stigma on sexual minority clients (Browning, Reynolds, & Dworkin, 1991; Fassinger, 2000). Examples of proactive interventions contributed by participants in this study cover the full span of functions enumerated in the literature, including challenging a client's homophobic or biphobic thinking; providing empirical information and community resources; educating heterosexual and lesbian group clients about bisexuality; and advocating for bisexual issues with colleagues and society as a whole.

Some comments illustrate the negative consequences of an overly passive approach. A silent clinician can be assumed to be in agreement with societal bias. For instance, one participant took the silence of a lesbian counselor as tacit disapproval when she discussed her bisexual attractions. Clinicians can also fail to notice stereotypes in their own thinking. "It is too difficult to bring up," a participant wrote. "She [the provider] calls it experimentation and does not take any of it seriously." Sometimes passivity leads to inaccurate diagnosis. One comment described a provider who assumed that a depression was biological in origin. The participant suggested that active inquiry by the provider would have uncovered an endogenous reason for the depression, i.e., the client's struggle to resolve her same-sex and other-sex attractions in the context of her monogamous relationship.

In contrast, some proactive interventions can help clients discover connections between their bisexuality and other aspects of their process. These discoveries lead to insight, self-esteem, resiliency and confidence. These benefits can result from a clinician posing what one participant described as "good serious questions."

Clinical Experiences and Gender, Ethnicity, and Intensity of Participant's Clinical Issues

Gender. Given that male participants experienced bisexual issues as somewhat more stressful than female participants, it may not be surprising that a greater proportion of men than women sought mental health services for help with their bisexual issues. The literature enumerates several factors associated with stress for bisexual men: isolation; loneliness; lack of bisexual community; and reluctance to disclose their sexual identity to gay peers and female relationship partners (Rust, 2001a; Steinman, 2001). Bisexual men experience pressure based on heterosexism, conflict with class and family norms (Appleby, 2001), and unfounded public assumptions that bisexual men transmit AIDS to heterosexuals (Stokes, McKirnan, & Burzette 1993). Empirical studies also describe gay and bisexual men as experiencing a variety of symptoms, including problem drinking, depression, panic attacks, psychological distress, and suicidal ideation related to sexual orientation (Cochran et al., 2003; Cochran & Mays, 2000; Grossman, D'Augelli, & O'Connell, 2001).

Bisexual women have been described as having more nonclinical sources of support for their bisexual concerns than bisexual men (Matteson, 1996; Rust, 2001a; Steinman, 2001), which may explain why female participants in this study reported less stress about bisexual issues than did male participants. An alternate explanation might be that since the overall clinical issues of women were more serious than those of men, women may have needed to devote more of their clinical time to concerns other than those connected to their sexual orientation.

Ethnicity. The literature on ethnicity and sexual orientation suggests several factors that may underlie the finding that participants of color came out as bisexual somewhat later in relationship to the time they entered mental health services. These factors include critical attitudes toward same-sex attractions and behaviors held by several non-European ethnicities (Smith, 1997) and the "cultural strain" (Fukuyama & Ferguson, 2000, p. 100) entailed in participating in two or more minority identities of race, ethnicity, gender, social class, sexual orientation (Greene, 1994; Rust, 1996a). Additional factors are critical attitudes about bisexuality within lesbian and gay communities (Rust, 2001b) and critical attitudes toward mental health services in some non-western cultures (Atkinson, Morten, & Sue, 1993). Nabors et al. (2001) point out that such "multiple oppressions can have a significant impact on [lesbian, gay and bisexual individuals'] adjustment"(p. 101). Due to these multiple pressures, a woman or man of color may delay self-identification as bisexual and/or delay accessing mental health services.

Seriousness of clinical issues. Proportions of participants in this study with more serious mental health issues (29%) were lower than national estimates of mental health services utilization in which consumers are estimated to have moderate and more serious clinical issues in roughly equal numbers (U.S. Department of Health and Human Services, 1999) and also possibly lower than findings of recent studies that found bisexual participants scored higher for mental health risk factors than heterosexual, gay, and lesbian participants (Jorm et al., 2000; Balsam & Rothblum, 2000; Cochran et al., 2003

Findings about differences between experiences of those with moderate and more serious clinical issues amplify findings in prior research. Men and women with serious mental health issues have been the recipients of stigma and bias that affects them personally, professionally and financially (Wahl, 1999). In addition, lesbians, gay men and bisexuals with major mental illness have reported a lack of services specific to their needs (Avery, Hellman, & Sudderth, 2001). Finally, clinicians have often interpreted bisexual attractions and behaviors as symptoms of psychopathology in clients with more serious mental health issues (Zubenko, George, Soloff, & Schulz, 1987).

A number of factors may explain why those with more serious clinical issues sought mental health services for their bisexual issues less often than clients with more moderate clinical issues. Similar to the women in this study, they may have needed more of their clinical hours for their basic mental health challenges. For example, one respondent wrote: "my physical screwed up health and mental health [mean that] bisexuality is a wanna be." On the other hand, many with more serious issues may have perceived the mental health setting as an unsafe environment in which to either disclose or seek help for their sexual orientation issues. One respondent with a major mental illness diagnosis wrote: "No, I've never had a mental health or psychotherapeutic need having to do with my bisexuality" and then commented: "afraid to."

In some cases, clinicians may assume that psychological trauma or serious mental illness is a barrier to full adult development, including participation in sexual and romantic relationships. One participant commented: "My psychotherapist is still unaware and mostly unhelpful. [sic] I cannot tell her because she is very focused on the sexual abuse I sustained as a child. She doesn't yet realize that I can have had that and still have a relationship."

Another participant's observation illustrates the harmful impact that an invalidating attitude can have on clients with more serious clinical issues: "I was at a stage where I needed support in my decision to explore my bisexuality and, for whatever reason this clinician was extremely discouraging–squashed my very fragile courage and it took years to recoup." Because these clients are already at greater risk, they have a greater need for accuracy and sensitivity from their practitioners, rather than the reverse.

Study Limitations and Implications for Further Research

Overall, this sample was similar to samples in prior research on lesbians, gay men and bisexuals. There were more women than men and more European American participants than participants of color. Participants were well-educated and were more concentrated in populated areas. This writer joins others (Bieschke et al., 2000; Fukuyama & Ferguson, 2000; Rust, 2001a) in urging future researchers to strive for greater ethnic, class, and geographic diversity in their samples. This was a volunteer sample and findings cannot be generalized to the population of self-identified bisexual clients in mental health care as a whole. The sample was also similar to samples in studies of gay, lesbian or bisexual identities with one exception. Participants' ages and the ages at which they came out as bisexual were slightly younger in this study than in bisexual identity studies (Fox, 1996) as well as in studies of lesbian and gay mental health care experiences (Bieschke et al., 2000). This difference may be explained, in part, by the use in the current study of Internet and email data collection. It may also be that individuals are self-identifying as bisexual earlier in general (Rust, 2001b).

This was a study that captured information about mental health care experiences at a point in time. Longitudinal studies that allow for comparisons between courses of treatment as well as comparisons between types of services and types of providers would be most useful. Other promising areas for further research include: outcomes and possible negative impacts of sexual orientation conversion therapy; more details of mental health services experiences for women and men who experience same-sex and other-sex attractions; best approaches for men and women who are exploring changes in their sexual attractions or changes in their personal definition of sexual identity. Empirical findings about all aspects of bisexual identity can help mental health clinicians to be most effective with their bisexual clients. Of particular interest are: how bisexual identities are established and successfully maintained (Fox, 1996), patterns of relationship and family (Rust, 1996b), and distinctions between bisexuals in terms of gender, ethnicity, age, education, and class. Research on the effects of multiple minority statuses for bisexual women and men is also recommended. Finally, clinical practice can benefit greatly from empirical research on the impact of social stigma on bisexual women and bisexual men and the ways in which this may be related to the development of mental health problems; and studies to establish an in-depth empirical basis for the inherent psychological health of bisexual attractions and behaviors.

Implications for Mental Health Practice

This study provides important information about what self-identified bisexual women and men need from their clinicians. It suggests that a provider's basic approach toward bisexuality and bisexual identities really matters. The position that all sexual orientations are of equal validity and that a bisexual orientation or identity is healthy per se is extremely important in creating a positive alliance with bisexual clients. In addition, an active clinical approach can result in many benefits for bisexual clients. These benefits can include the creation of a safe environment in which to address sexual orientation topics, elimination of unconscious bias in both the clinician and the client, and enhanced self-esteem and resiliency for bisexual clients. Lastly, many approaches that are beneficial to clients in general can be very beneficial for bisexual clients. Among these skills are: basic respect and acceptance for the client and her unfolding process; approaching each individual as unique; and having confidence that the client's process will lead to successful outcomes.

However, more than just a basic approach is recommended. The participants in this study also suggest that clinicians acquire current and accurate information about the details of their experiences as same- and other-sex-attracted women and men. This includes information about differences by gender, ethnicity, age, education, and class, as well as preferred and actual patterns of intimate and family relationships. It also includes information about the impacts of societal bias, which often views bisexuality as nonexistent, merely a transitional state or a symptom of psychological dysfunction. Information regarding the range of resources about bisexual issues is available in the professional literature (Fox, 2003) and in the Bisexual Resource Center's *Bisexual Resource Guide* (Ochs, 2001).

CONCLUSION

It should be a matter of concern if, as this study suggests, bisexual women and men are not as motivated to seek help from mental health providers with their sexual orientation issues as their lesbian and gay counterparts. By responding to the concerns expressed in this study, mental health providers have an opportunity to make mental health services a vehicle through which bisexual women and men can anticipate and receive real help. One outcome of such a response could be a shift in the emphasis in future bisexual mental health consumer studies. Whereas the main emphasis in this study was whether providers see bisexuality as valid and healthy, emerging themes in future studies might be more focused on accuracy and expertise with bisexual issues. To adapt the words of a respondent in this study: up-to-date and effective clinical skill with bisexual clients shouldn't be "a wanna be."

REFERENCES

American Counseling Association. (1996). ACA code of ethics and standards of practice. In B. Herlihy & G. Corey (Eds.), *ACA ethical standards casebook* (5th ed., pp. 26-59). Alexandria, VA: Author.

American Psychiatric Association. (1974). Position statement on homosexuality and civil rights. *American Journal of Psychiatry, 131,* 497.

American Psychological Association. (1998). Appropriate therapeutic responses to sexual orientation in the proceedings of the American Psychological Association, Incorporated, for the legislative year 1997. *American Psychologist, 53*(8), 882-939.

American Psychological Association Division 44/Committee on Lesbian, Gay, and Bisexual Concerns Joint Task Force on Guidelines for Psychotherapy with Lesbian, Gay, and Bisexual Clients. (2000). Guidelines for psychotherapy with lesbian, gay, and bisexual clients. *American Psychologist, 55*(12), 1440-1451.

Appleby, G. A. (2001). Ethnographic study of twenty-six gay and bisexual working-class men in Australia and New Zealand. *Journal of Gay and Lesbian Social Services: Issues in Practice, Policy & Research, 12*(3/4), 119-132.

Atkinson, D. R., Morten, G., & Sue, D. W. (1993). *Counseling American minorities: A cross-cultural perspective* (4th ed.). Madison, WI: Brown & Benchmark.

Avery, A. M., Hellman, R. E., & Sudderth, L. K. (2001). Satisfaction with mental health services among sexual minorities with major mental illness. *American Journal of Public Health, 91*(6), 990-991.

Balsam, K. F., & Rothblum, E. D. (2002). *Sexual orientation and mental health: A comparison of adult siblings.* Paper presented at the 110th Annual Convention of the American Psychological Association, Chicago, IL.

Bayer, R. (1981). *Homosexuality and American psychiatry: The politics of diagnosis.* Princeton, NJ: Princeton University Press.

Bieschke, K. J., McClanahan, M., Tozer, E., Grzegorek, J. L., & Park, J. (2000). Programmatic research on the treatment of lesbian, gay, and bisexual clients: The past, the present, and the course for the future. In R. M. Perez, K. A. DeBord & K. J. Bieschke (Eds.), *Handbook of counseling and psychotherapy with lesbian, gay and bisexual clients* (pp. 309-336). Washington, D.C.: American Psychological Association.

Bisexual Anthology Collective. (1995). *Plural desires: Writing bisexual women's realities.* Toronto: Sister Vision Black Women & Women of Colour Press.

Browning, C., Reynolds, S. L., & Dworkin, S. H. (1991). Affirmative psychotherapy for lesbian women. *The Counseling Psychologist, 19,* 177-196.

Chung, Y. B., & Katayama, M. (1996). Assessment of sexual orientation in lesbian/gay/bisexual studies. *Journal of Homosexuality, 30*(4) 49-64.

Cochran S. D., & Mays, V. M. (2000). Lifetime prevalence of suicide symptoms and affective disorders among men reporting same-sex sexual partners: Results from NHANES III. *American Journal of Public Health, 90*(4), 573-578.

Cochran, S. D., Sullivan, J. G., & Mays, V. M. (2003). Prevalence of mental disorders, psychological distress, and mental services use among lesbian, gay, and bisexual adults in the United States. *Journal of Consulting & Clinical Psychology, 71*(1) 53-61.

Conger, J. (1975). Proceedings of the American Psychological Association, Incorporated, for the year 1974: Minutes of the annual meeting of the Council of Representatives. *American Psychologist, 30,* 620-651.

Drescher, J. (1998). I'm your handyman: A history of reparative therapies. *Journal of
Homosexuality, 36*(1), 19-42.

Dworkin, S. (2001). Treating the bisexual client. *Journal of Clinical Psychology,
57*(5), 671-680.

Fassinger, R. E. (2000). Applying counseling theories to lesbian, gay and bisexual clients: Pitfalls and possibilities. In R. M. Perez, K. A. DeBord & K. J. Bieschke
(Eds.), *Handbook of counseling and psychotherapy with lesbian, gay and bisexual
clients* (pp. 107-132). Washington, D.C.: American Psychological Association.

Firestein, B. A. (Ed.). (1996). *Bisexuality: The psychology & politics of an invisible minority.* Thousand Oaks, CA: Sage.

Fox, R. C. (1996). Bisexuality in perspective: A review of theory and research. In B. A.
Firestein (Ed.), *Bisexuality: The psychology and politics of an invisible minority*
(pp. 3-50). Newbury Park, CA: Sage.

Fox, R. C. (2003). A readers guide to the social science literature on bisexuality. *The
Journal of Bisexuality 3*(3/4), XX-YY.

Fukuyama, M., & Ferguson, A. (2000). Lesbian, gay and bisexual people of color: Understanding cultural complexity and managing multiple oppressions. In R. M.
Perez, K. A. DeBord & K. J. Bieschke (Eds.), *Handbook of counseling and psychotherapy with lesbian, gay and bisexual clients* (pp. 81-106). Washington, D.C.:
American Psychological Association.

Garnets, L., Hancock, K. A., Cochran, S. E., Goodchilds, J., & Peplau, L. A. (1991). Issues in psychotherapy with lesbians and gay men: A survey of psychologists. *American Psychologist, 46,* 964-972.

Greene, B. (1994). Ethnic minority lesbians and gay men: Mental health and treatment
issues. *Journal of Consulting and Clinical Psychology, 62*(2), 243-251.

Haldeman, D. (2001). Therapeutic antidotes: Helping gay and bisexual men recover
from conversion. *Journal of Gay & Lesbian Psychotherapy, 5*(3/4), 117-130.

Hutchins, L., & Kaahumanu, L. (Eds.). (1991). *Bi any other name: Bisexual people
speak out.* Boston: Alyson.

Jones, M. A., & Gabriel, M. A. (1999). Utilization of psychotherapy by lesbians, gay
men, and bisexuals: Findings from a nationwide survey. *American Journal of
Orthopsychiatry, 69*(2), 209-219.

Jorm, A. F., Korten, A. E., Rodgers, B., Jacomb, P. A., & Christensen, H. (2002). Sexual orientation and mental health: Results from a community survey of young and
middle-aged adults. *British Journal of Psychiatry, 180,* 423-427.

Lebolt, J. (1999). Gay affirmative psychotherapy: A phenomenological study. *Clinical
Social Work Journal, 27,* 355-370.

Liddle, B. J. (1996). Therapist sexual orientation, gender and counseling practices as
they relate to ratings of helpfulness by gay and lesbian clients. *Journal of Counseling Psychology, 43,* 394-401.

Lucksted, A. (1996, March). *Lesbian and bisexual women who are mental health care
consumers: Experiences in the mental health system.* Paper presented at the Annual
Conference of the Association of Women in Psychology, Portland, OR.

Matteson, D. R. (1996). Counseling and psychotherapy with bisexual and exploring clients. In B. A. Firestein (Ed.), *Bisexuality: The psychology & politics of an invisible minority* (pp. 185-213). Thousand Oaks, CA: Sage.

Miles, M. B., & Huberman, A. M. (1994). *Qualitative data analysis: An expanded sourcebook* (2nd ed.). Thousand Oaks, CA: Sage.

Morgan, K. S., & Eliason, M. J. (1992). The role of psychotherapy in Caucasian lesbians' lives. *Women & Therapy, 13*, 27-52.

Moss, J. F. (1994). The heterosexual bias inventory (HBI): Gay, lesbian and bisexual clients' perceptions of heterosexual bias in psychotherapy. (Doctoral dissertation, Michigan State University, Lansing, MI). *Dissertation Abstracts International, 55*(12), 5571-B.

Nabors, N. A., Hall, R. L., Miville, M. L., Nettles, R., Pauling, M. L., & Ragsdale, B. L. (2001). Multiple minority group oppression: Divided we stand? *Journal of the Gay & Lesbian Medical Association, 5*(3), 101-105.

Nystrom, N. M. (1997). Oppression by mental health providers: A report by gay men and lesbians about their treatment. *Dissertation Abstracts International, 58*(6), 2394A.

Ochs, R. (Ed.). (2001). *Bisexual resource guide* (4th ed.). Cambridge, MA: Bisexual Resource Center.

Orndorff, K. (Ed.). (1999). *Bi lives: Bisexual women tell their stories.* Tucson, AZ: See Sharp Press.

Perez, R. M., DeBord, K. A., & Bieschke, K. J. (Eds.). (2000). *Handbook of counseling and psychotherapy with lesbian, gay and bisexual clients.* Washington, D.C.: American Psychological Association.

Rust, P. C. (1996a). Managing multiple identities: Diversity among bisexual women and men. In B. A. Firestein (Ed.), *Bisexuality: The psychology and politics of an invisible minority* (pp. 53-83). Newbury Park, CA: Sage.

Rust, P. C. (1996b). Monogamy and polyamory: Relationship issues for bisexuals. In B. A. Firestein (Ed.), *Bisexuality: The psychology and politics of an invisible minority* (pp. 127-148). Newbury Park, CA: Sage.

Rust, P. C. (2001a). Make me a map: Bisexual men's images of bisexual community. *Journal of Bisexuality, 1*(2/3), 47-108.

Rust, P. C. (2001b). Two many and not enough: The meanings of bisexual identities. *Journal of Bisexuality, 1*(1), 31-68.

Shidlo, A., Schroeder, M., & Drescher, J. (Eds.). (2002). *Sexual conversion therapy: Ethical, clinical and research perspectives.* Binghamton, NY: Harrington Park Press.

Smith, A. (1997). Cultural diversity and the coming-out process: Implications for clinical practice. In B. Greene (Ed.), *Ethnic and cultural diversity among lesbians and gay men* (pp. 279-300). Thousand Oaks, CA: Sage.

Socarides, C., Kaufman, B., Nicolosi, J., Satinover, J., & Fitzgibbons, R. (1997, January 9). *Don't forsake homosexuals who want help.* Retrieved May 6, 2003, from http://www.narth.com/docs/wsjletter01.html

Steinman, E. (2001). Interpreting the invisibility of male bisexuality: Theories, interactions, politics. *Journal of Bisexuality, 1*(2/3),15-45.

Stokes, J. P., McKirnan, D. J., & Burzette, R. G. (1993). Sexual behavior, condom use, disclosure of sexuality, & stability of sexual orientation in bisexual men. *Journal of Sex Research, 30*(3), 203-213.

U. S. Department of Health and Human Services. (1999). *Mental health: A report of the Surgeon General.* Rockville, MD: Author.

Wahl, O. F. (1999). Mental health consumers' experience of stigma. *Schizophrenia Bulletin, 25,* 467-478.

Zinik, G. A. (1984). The relationship between sexual orientation and eroticism, cognitive flexibility, and negative affect (Doctoral dissertation, University of California, Santa Barbara, 1983). *Dissertation Abstracts International, 45*(8), 2707B.

Zubenko, G. S., George, A. S., Soloff, P. H., & Schulz, P. (1987). Sexual practices among patients with borderline personality disorder. *American Journal of Psychiatry, 144,* 748-752.

Bisexuality:
A Reader's Guide
to the Social Science
Literature

Ronald C. Fox

http://www.haworthpress.com/web/JB
© 2004 by Ronald C. Fox. All rights reserved. Used with permission of the author.
Digital Object Identifier: 10.1300/J159v04n01_12

[Haworth co-indexing entry note]: "Bisexuality: A Reader's Guide to the Social Science Literature." Fox, Ronald C. Co-published simultaneously in *Journal of Bisexuality* (Harrington Park Press, an imprint of The Haworth Press, Inc.) Vol. 4, Nos. 1/2, 2004, pp. 161-255; and: *Current Research on Bisexuality* (ed: Ronald C. Fox) Harrington Park Press, an imprint of The Haworth Press, Inc., 2004, pp. 161-255.

SUMMARY. This reading list brings together a wide range of nonfiction books, journal articles, book chapters, theses, and dissertations that will be helpful to readers with an interest in the theoretical, research, clinical and community perspectives that have developed on bisexuality in the last twenty years. During this time, the illness model of homosexuality has been replaced by a more affirmative approach to lesbian, gay, bisexual, transgender, intersex, queer, and questioning people, and the dichotomous model of sexual orientation has been replaced by a multidimensional approach to sexual orientation that has supported the recognition of bisexuality as a valid and distinct sexual orientation and identity. The work cited here represents the efforts of those researchers, clinicians, academicians, and community activists whose contributions to the literature offer a more comprehensive understanding of bisexuality and bisexual people. References are included in the following areas: multidimensional approaches to sexual orientation: bisexual identity, attractions and behavior; bisexual relationships and families; bisexuality and polyamory; bisexual youth and elders, bisexuality and transgender people; bisexuality and ethnic, racial, and cultural diversity; bisexuality and HIV/AIDS; affirmative mental health services for bisexual people; bisexuality and feminism; bisexuality and spirituality; bisexuality and queer theory; prejudice, discrimination, heterosexism, and biphobia; and bisexual politics and community.

KEYWORDS. Bisexuality, homosexuality, bisexual identity, sexual orientation, sexual identity, bisexual behavior, sexual diversity, bisexual women, bisexual men, bisexual relationships, bisexual families, monogamy, nonmonogamy, polyamory, bisexual youth, bisexual elders, bisexuality and ethnicity, HIV/AIDS, mental health services, psychotherapy, counseling, bisexuality and feminism, bisexuality and spirituality, queer theory, cultural criticism, prejudice, discrimination, heterosexism, homophobia, biphobia, bisexual politics, bisexual community

NONFICTION BOOKS SPECIFICALLY ON BISEXUALITY

Aggleton, P. (Ed.). (1996). *Bisexualities & AIDS: International perspectives.* London: Taylor & Francis. Collection of essays and reviews of the research literature on bisexual behavior among men in a number of modern cultures, including Australia, Brazil, Canada, China, Costa Rica, the Dominican Republic, France, India, Mexico, Papua New Guinea, Peru, the Philippines, and the U. K.

Angelides, S. (2001). *A History of Bisexuality*. Chicago: University of Chicago Press. A critical review of how bisexuality has been understood in biology, genetics, psychoanalytic thinking, and queer theory in relationship to heterosexuality and homosexuality.

Bi Academic Intervention (P. Davidson, J. Eadie, C. Hemmings, A. Kaloski, & M. Storr) (Eds.). (1997). *The bisexual imaginary: Representation, identity, and desire*. London: Cassell. Collection of essays on bisexuality in history, literature, film, and cultural studies.

Bisexual Anthology Collective (L. Acharya, N. Chater, D. Falconer, S. Lewis, L. McLannan, & S. Nosov) (Eds.). (1995). *Plural desires: Writing bisexual women's realities*. Toronto: Sister Vision Press. An anthology of writings by a diverse group of Canadian & U.S. women.

Bode, J. (1976). *View from another closet: Exploring bisexuality in women*. New York: Hawthorne. One of the first books on bisexuality, based on the author's interviews with bisexual women.

Bryant, W. (1997). *Bisexual characters in film: From Anaïs to Zee*. New York: Harrington Park Press. Descriptive compilation of films with bisexual characters.

Cantarella, E. (1992). *Bisexuality in the ancient world*. New Haven, CT: Yale University Press. Translated from the Italian. A scholarly examination of bisexuality in ancient classical Greece and Rome.

Deschamps, C. (2002). *Le miroir bisexuel: Une socio-anthropologie de l'invisible*. [The bisexual mirror: A social anthropology of the invisible]. Paris: Balland. An in-depth look at bisexuality in France today, based on the author's study of a Parisian support group for bisexual women and bisexual men.

Falk, R. (1975). *Women loving: A journey toward becoming an independent woman*. New York: Random House. In depth personal account of the author's process of coming to terms with and honoring her bisexuality.

Feldhorst, A. (Ed.). *(1996). Bisexualitäten*. [Bisexualities]. Berlin: Deutsche AIDS-Hilfe. Collection of essays on bisexual identity, relationships, and communities in Germany.

Firestein, B. A. (Ed.). (1996). *Bisexuality: The psychology and politics of an invisible minority*. Thousand Oaks, CA: Sage. A collection of essays that provides the most comprehensive overview and review of bisexuality and psychology to date, with chapters by Ron Fox, Loraine Hutchins, Carol Queen, Maggie Rubenstein, Paula Rust, Robyn Ochs, and others.

Fraser, M. (1999). *Identity without selfhood: Simone de Beauvoir and bisexuality*. New York: Cambridge University Press. The author examines how feminism, queer theory, and post-modern analysis have viewed Simone de

Beauvoir and how the emphasis on deconstruction of Western approaches to sexuality present obstacles to acknowledging and validating bisexuality as a sexual orientation and identity.

Garber, M. (1995). *Vice versa: Bisexuality and the eroticism of everyday life.* New York: Simon & Schuster. If you are interested in an in-depth look at bisexuality in literature, popular culture, or psychoanalysis, this book is for you.

Geissler, S.-A. (1993). *Doppelte Lust: Bisexualität heute–Erfahrungen und Bekenntnisse.* [Dual desire: Bisexuality today: Experiences and confessions]. Munich: Wilhelm Heyne. An exploration of bisexuality in Germany, based on author's interviews with bisexual women and bisexual men.

Geller, T. (Ed.). (1990). *Bisexuality: A reader & sourcebook.* Ojai, CA: Times Change Press. Collection of interviews and articles.

George, S. (1993). *Women and bisexuality.* London: Scarlet Press. An examination of bisexual identity and relationships, based on the author's survey study of 150 self-identified bisexual women in the United Kingdom.

Gooß, U. (1995). *Sexualwissenschaftliche Konzepte der Bisexualität von Männern.* [The concept of bisexuality in scientific discourse about human sexuality]. Stuttgart: Ferdinand Enke. Scholarly examination by a German psychiatrist of the origins and development of the concept of bisexuality in the fields of psychology and sexology, including an overview of current theory and research.

Haeberle, E. J., & Gindorf, R. (Eds.). (1994). *Bisexualitäten: Ideologie und Praxis des Sexualkontes mit beiden Geschlectern.* [Bisexualities: Theory and practice of sexual relations with both sexes]. Stuttgart: Gustav Fischer Verlag. Also published in 1998 in English as: *Bisexualities: The ideology and practice of sexual contact with both men and women.* New York: Continuum. Collection of essays by participants in the 1990 International Berlin Conference for Sexology. Most chapters reflect the beginnings of the shift in scholarly thinking about bisexuality that has come about as a result of subsequent and more current research on bisexuality and bisexual identity.

Hall, D. E., & Pramaggiore, M. (Eds.). (1996). *RePresenting bisexualities: Subjects and cultures of fluid desire.* New York: NYU Press. Collection of essays on bisexuality in queer theory, literature, film, and cultural studies.

Hansson, H. (Ed.). (1990). *Bisexuele levens in Nederland.* [Bisexual lives in the Netherlands]. Amsterdam: Orlando. Portrait of bisexual identity and relationships, based on the author's interviews with bisexual women and men.

Hemmings, C. (2002). *Bisexual spaces: A geography of sexuality and gender.* New York: Routledge. The author of several articles and book chapters on bisexuality and queer theory applies a postmodern perspective sexuality, gender, and bisexual identity through by examining the geography and culture of Northampton, Massachusetts, and San Francisco.

Honnens, B.. (1996). *Wenn die andere ein Mann ist: Frauen als Partnerinnen bisexueller Männer.* [When the other person is a man: Women partners of bisexual men]. Frankfurt: Campus. Explores the experiences of women in marriages with bisexual men in Germany, based on the author's interviews.

Hüsers, F., & König, A. (1995). *Bisexualität.* [Bisexuality]. Stuttgart: Georg Thieme. A sociologist and a psychiatrist provide a comprehensive and affirmative picture of and guide to bisexuality in Germany today.

Hutchins, L., & Kaahumanu, L. (Eds.). (1991). *Bi any other name: Bisexual people speak out.* Boston: Alyson. Diverse collection of 75 essays and autobiographical narratives by bi-identified people from the United States.

Klein, F. (1993). *The bisexual option (2nd ed.).* New York: Harrington Park Press. Second edition of the one of the first affirmatively written books on bisexuality, originally published in 1978 (Charlotte Wolff's 1979 book, listed below, is the other). The author is also the creator of the well-known Klein Sexual Orientation Grid (KSOG), a multidimensional approach to sexual orientation and sexual identity.

Klein, F., & Schwartz, T. (2001). *Bisexual and gay husbands, their stories, their words.* New York: Harrington Park Press. A collection of personal accounts, based on contributions to an online discussion group for gay and bisexual married men.

Klein, F., & Wolf, T. J. (Eds.). (1985). *Two lives to lead: Bisexuality in men and women.* New York: Harrington Park Press. The first published scholarly collection of reports on 1980s research on bisexuality. Originally a special issue of the prestigious *Journal of Homosexuality* (1985, Vol. 11, Issue 1/2).

Kohn, B., & Matusow, A. (1980). *Barry* and *Alice: Portrait of a bisexual marriage.* Englewood Cliffs, NJ: Prentice-Hall. An autobiographical account of the authors' marriage and the impact on their relationship of their coming to terms with their bisexuality.

Kolodny, D. R. (Ed.). (2000). *Blessed bi spirit: Bisexual people of faith.* New York: Continuum. A wide-ranging anthology, with contributions by 31 bisexual people of faith speaking in a most affirmative way about the intersection of spirituality and sexuality in their lives.

Kuppens, A. (1995). *Biseksuele identiteiten: Tussen verlangen en praktijk.* [Bisexual identities: Between desire and behavior]. Nijmegen, Netherlands: Wetenschapswinkel. Theoretical overview and discussion of bisexual identities, based on interviews with bisexual women and bisexual men.

Mendès-Leité, R., Deschamps, C., & Proth, B.-M. (1996). *Bisexualité: Le dernièr tabou.* [Bisexuality: The last taboo]. Paris: Calmann Levy. Portrait of bisexual identity and behavior among bisexual men in France today, based on the authors' interviews.

Ochs, R. (2001). *Bisexual resource guide* (4th ed.). Cambridge, MA: Bisexual Resource Center. Includes reading lists of fiction, nonfiction, biography, and autobiography in books, chapters, and journal articles, a list of recommended films, a merchandise guide, announcements, and listings of more than 1,700 bisexual and bi-inclusive groups & electronic mail lists.

Off Pink Collective. (1988). *Bisexual lives*. London: Off Pink Publishing. Collection of personal narratives by bisexual women and bisexual men in the U. K.

Orndorff, K. (Ed.). (1999). *Bi lives: Bisexual women tell their stories*. Tucson, AZ: See Sharp Press. A collection of very thoughtfully done interviews with a diverse group of 18 women, with a focus on how they became aware of and came to terms with their bisexuality.

Rose, S., Stevens, C., & The Off-Pink Collective. (Eds.). (1996). *Bisexual horizons: Politics, histories, lives*. London: Lawrence & Wishart. Diverse collection of 54 essays and autobiographical narratives by bi-identified people, mostly from the U. K.

Rust, P. C. (1995). *Bisexuality and the challenge to lesbian politics: Sex, loyalty & revolution*. New York: NYU Press. The author traces the origins of the controversy about bisexuality among lesbians to the 1970s lesbian feminist debates, out of which, she argues, developed an environment in which bisexuality inevitably became a challenge to lesbian politics. She also discusses likely for the sexual politics of the future.

Rust, P. C. R. (Ed.). (2000). *Bisexuality in the United States: A social science reader*. New York: Columbia University Press. Comprehensive collection of classic journal articles and book chapters on bisexuality, including many for which the original references are included in this reading list, and as well as in-depth reviews of the literature by the editor preceding each of the books sections.

Storr, M. (Ed.). (1999). *Bisexuality: A critical reader*. London: Routledge. Psychological, sociological, activist, and post-modern/cultural criticism perspectives are all included in this edited volume of previously published articles, book chapters and book excerpts. Features material by Freud, Ellis, and Kinsey, as well as bi authors Fritz Klein, Amanda Udis-Kessler, Sue George, Jo Eadie, Amber Ault, Clare Hemmings, and Ann Kaloski.

Tielman, R. A. P., Carballo, M., & Hendriks, A. C. (Eds.). (1991). *Bisexuality and HIV/AIDS: A global perspective*. Buffalo, NY: Prometheus. Collection of essays and reviews of research on bisexual identity and behavior among men in a number of modern cultures, including Australia, India, Indonesia, Latin America, Mexico, the Netherlands, New Zealand, Sub-Saharan Africa, Thailand, the United Kingdom, and the United States.

Tucker, N., Highleyman, L., & Kaplan, R. (Eds.). (1995). *Bisexual politics: Theories, queeries, and visions*. New York: Harrington Park Press. Diverse collection of essays exploring the history, philosophies, visioning, and strategies of bisexual politics in the United States.

van Kerkhof, M. P. N. (1997). *Beter biseks. Mythen over biseksualiteit ontrafeld*. [Better bisexuality: Myths about bisexuality revealed]. Amsterdam: Schorer Boeken. Examination of bisexual identity and relationships, based on interviews with bisexual women and bisexual men.

Weatherburn, P., Reid, D. S., Beardsell, S., Davies, P. M., Stephens, M., Broderick, P., Keogh, P., & Hickson, F. (1996). *Behaviourally bisexual men in the UK: Identifying needs for HIV prevention*. London: Sigma Research. Results of a government sponsored survey study of sexual behavior and HIV/AIDS awareness.

Weinberg, M. S., Williams, T. J., & Pryor, D. W. (1994). *Dual attraction: Understanding bisexuality*. New York: Oxford University Press. Results of the authors' interview and survey research on bisexual identity and relationships in 1980s San Francisco. Includes personal narratives, the authors' views on how bisexual identity develops, comparison of bisexual, heterosexual, and lesbian/gay patterns of sexual attractions and relationships, and a portrait of the impact of HIV/AIDS on the lives of individuals from their original interviews.

Weise, E. R. (Ed.). (1992). *Closer to home: Bisexuality and feminism*. Seattle: Seal Press. Collection of 23 essays by bisexual feminist women on bisexuality, feminism, and their intersection.

Williams, M. J. K. (1999). *Sexual pathways: Adapting to dual attraction*. Westport, CT: Praeger. A study of bisexual identity and relationships, based on the author's interviews with 30 American bisexual women and men.

Wolff, C. (1979). *Bisexuality: A study*. London: Quarter Books. One of the first books on bisexuality written from an affirmative perspective (Fritz Klein's *Bisexual Option*, listed above, is the other), based on the author's survey research on bisexual women and bisexual men in the U.K.

BI-INCLUSIVE NONFICTION BOOKS

Sexual Orientation: Multidimensional Approaches

Bohan, J. S. (1996). *Psychology and sexual orientation: Coming to terms*. New York: Routledge. Excellent bi-inclusive historical and contemporary overview of the field of sexual orientation and sexual identity.

Bohan, J. S., Russell, G. M., & Cass, V. (1999). *Conversations about psychology and sexual orientation*. New York: New York University Press. Excellent and informative book on psychology and sexual orientation with a chapter by Fritz Klein on the importance of a multidimensional approach to sexual orientation and a chapter by Vivienne Cass, in which she updates her widely known and often cited stage theory of gay and lesbian identity formation with a much more open and inclusive theoretical framework for sexual identity development that acknowledges the multiple pathways that many people take in coming to terms with and potentially changing their sexual identities over time.

Rust, P. C. (Ed.). (1997). *Sociology of sexuality* and *sexual orientation: Syllabi and teaching materials*. Washington, DC: American Sociological Association. Collection of college course syllabi, including the syllabus for Robyn Ochs' course "Contexts and constructs of identity: Bisexuality."

Lesbian, Gay, Bisexual, Transgender, Queer Identities

Atkins, D. (1996). (Ed.). *Looking queer: Body image and identity in lesbian, bisexual, gay and transgender communities*. New York: NYU Press. An excellent collection that includes a number of bi voices (including the editor's): Greta Christina, Kate Woolfe, Catherine Lundoff, Nina Silver, Susanna Trnka, Julie Waters, Morgan Holmes, Raven Kaldera, Laura Cole, Layli Phillips, Ganapati Durgadas and Jill Nagle.

Burch, B. (1994). *On intimate terms: The psychology of difference in lesbian relationships*. (Urbana & Chicago: University of Illinois Press. The author draws a distinction between "primary" and "bisexual" lesbians, positing a complementarity, or attraction, between the two. She sees "bisexual lesbians" as women who identify as lesbian later than "primary lesbians" and may have had significant heterosexual relationships and/or continue to recognize heterosexual relationships as a possibility. Primarily about women who identify as lesbian rather than bisexual, but extensive discussion of bisexuality.

Burch, B. (1997). *Other women: Lesbian/bisexual experience and psychoanalytic views of women*. New York, NY: Columbia University Press. The author's second book focusing on lesbian and bisexual women, their identities and relationships, in the context of classical and contemporary psychoanalytic theory and practice.

D'Augelli, A. R., & Patterson, C. J. (Eds.). (1995). *Lesbian, gay, and bisexual identities over the lifespan: Psychological approaches*. New York: Oxford University Press. Groundbreaking LGB psychology book that includes a chapter by Ron Fox on bisexual identities.

Esterberg, K. G. (1997). *Lesbian* and *bisexual identities: Constructing communities, constructing selves*. Philadelphia: Temple University Press. An in-depth study of lesbian and bisexual identity development, based on the author's interviews with a diverse group of women in a Northeastern community in the U.S.

Johnson, B. K. (1997). *Coming out every day: A gay, bisexual, or questioning man's guide*. Oakland, CA: New Harbinger. The queer man's comprehensive and bi-inclusive guide to coming out and maintaining a positive self-accepting identity.

Norris, S., & Read, E. (1985). *Out in the open: People talking about being gay or bisexual*. London: Pan Books. Collection of personal narratives of women and men describing being gay, lesbian, and bisexual in the U.K.

Savin-Williams, R. C., & Cohen, K. M. (Eds.). (1996). *The lives of lesbians, gays, and bisexuals: Children to adults*. Fort Worth, TX: Harcourt Brace. A bi-inclusive collection addressing developmental issues of lesbians, gay men, bisexual women, and bisexual men over the lifespan.

Wishik, H., & Pierce, C. (1991). *Sexual orientation & identity: Heterosexual, lesbian, gay, and bisexual journeys*. Laconia, NH: New Dynamics. An in-depth and affirmative exploration of sexual orientation and the development of sexual identity with interwoven theory and personal narratives.

Sexuality

Bright, S. (1992). *Susie Bright's sexual reality: A virtual sex world reader*. Pittsburgh, PA: Cleis Press. Collection of bi-affirmative autobiographical essays on sexuality and sexual diversity.

Laumann, E. O., Gagnon, J. H., Michael, R. T., & Michaels, S. (Eds.). (1994). *The social organization of sexuality: Sexual practices in the United States*. Chicago: University of Chicago Press. This interesting and controversial book contains results of the most recent large-scale study of sexuality in the U. S. The study was carried out, with private funding, after United States Congress refused to provide public funding. Chapter 9 titled "Homosexuality" includes the most recent statistics from research of this type on same-sex behavior and relationships, bisexual attractions and behavior, and LGB self-identification.

Marrow, J. (1997). *Changing positions: Women speak out on sex and desire*. Holbrook, MA: Adams Media. Comprehensive and enlightening contemporary portrait of women's sexuality, based on the author's interviews with bisexual, lesbian, and heterosexual women.

Pasle-Green, J., & Haynes, J. (1977). *Hello, I love you: Voices from within the sexual revolution*. New York: Times Change Press. Diverse collection of 1970s personal narratives on sexual behavior, relationships, and bisexuality.

Queen, C., & Schimel, L. (Eds.). (1997). *Pomosexuals: Challenging assumptions about gender and sexuality*. San Francisco: Cleis Press. A bi-affirmative, bi-inclusive collection of essays celebrating gender and sexual diversity.

Relationships, Friendships, and Families

Abbott, D., & Farmer, E. (Eds.). (1995). *From wedded wife to lesbian life: Stories of transformation*. Freedom, CA: Crossing Press. Collection of personal narratives of 43 women about their coming-out experiences.

Buxton, A. P. (1994). *The other side of the closet: The coming out crisis for straight spouses and families*. New York: John Wiley & Sons. An exploration of the issues involved in heterosexual marriages in which of one of the partners comes out as gay or bisexual, with a focus on the experiences of the female spouses of gay and bisexual men.

Cassingham, B. J., & O'Neil, S. M. (Eds.). (1993). *And then I met this woman*. Racine, WI: Mother Courage Press. About previously married women's journeys into same-sex relationships. Most of the women in the book identify as lesbian, a few identify as bisexual. These first person accounts may be helpful for women coming out from heterosexual identities.

Dickens, J., & McKellen, I. (1996). *Family outing: Guide for parents of gay, lesbian, and bisexual people*. London: Dufour Editions. This book from the U.K. focuses on the issues faced by parents and families of LGB people.

Faderman, L. (1991). *Odd girls and twilight lovers*. New York: Penguin. Fascinating history of lesbian life in 20th-century U.S. Includes numerous references to bisexuality, especially in the 1920s and 1980s.

Gochros, J. S. (1989). *When husbands come out of the closet*. New York: Harrington Park Press. Study of the impact of the coming out process on the spouses of gay and bisexual men and their marital relationship.

Kaeser, G., Gillespie, P., & Weston, K. (1999). *Love makes a family: Portraits of lesbian, gay, bisexual, and transgender parents and their families*. Boston: University of Massachusetts Press. A collection of photographs and statements from a diverse group of LGBT persons and their families.

Patterson, C. J., & D'Augelli, A. R. (Eds.). (1998). *Lesbian, gay, and bisexual identities in families: Psychological perspectives*. New York: Oxford University Press. A collection of essays on LGB identities in families.

Strock, C. (1998). *Married women who love women*. New York: Doubleday. Portrait of currently lesbian-identified married women, their attractions and relationships with other women, and the impact of these experiences on their heterosexual marriages. Based on interviews and the author's personal experiences. May be helpful for women with current or past similar experiences.

Whitney, C. (1990). *Uncommon lives: Gay men and straight women*. Penguin: New York. Based on the author's interviews with gay and bisexual men and heterosexual women.

Polyamory

Anapol, D. M. (1997). The new *love without limits: Secrets of sustainable intimate relationships*. San Rafael, CA: IntiNet Resource Center. A bi-inclusive classic on polyamory.

Easton, D., & Liszt, C. A. (1997). *The ethical slut: A guide to infinite possibilities*. San Francisco: Greenery Press. An comprehensive bi-inclusive guide to polyamorous relationships.

Foster, B. M., Foster, M., & Hadady, L. (1997). *Three in love: Menages à trois from ancient to modern times*. New York: Harper Collins. Overview of threesomes throughout history.

Lano, K., & Parry, C. (Eds.). (1995). *Breaking the barriers to desire: Polyamory, polyfidelity and non-monogamy–New approaches to multiple relationships*. Nottingham, England, UK: Five Leaves Publications. Collection of the essays on diverse forms of multiple relationships.

Munson, M., & Stelboum, J. P. (Eds.). (1999). *The lesbian polyamory reader: Open relationships, non-monogamy, and casual sex*. New York: Haworth Press. A collection of essays on polyamory and lesbian and bisexual women.

Nearing, R. (1992). *Loving more: The polyfidelity primer*. Boulder, CO: Loving More. Another classic guide to committed polyamorous relationships.

West, C. (1995). *Lesbian polyfidelity*. San Francisco: Booklegger Press. Comprehensive guide to committed polyamorous relationships among women.

Lesbian, Gay, Bisexual, Transgender, Queer, Questioning Youth

Bass, E., & Kaufman, K. (1996). *Free your mind: The book for gay, lesbian, and bisexual youth–and their allies*. New York: Harper Perennial. A broad-ranging bi-inclusive contemporary guide for LGB youth, allies, and families.

Bernstein, R., & Silberman, S. C. (Eds.). (1996). *Generation Q: Gays, lesbians, and bisexuals born around 1969's Stonewall riots tell their stories of growing up in the age of information*. Boston: Alyson. Diverse collection of personal narratives by gay, lesbian, and bisexual youth.

Findlen, B. (Ed.). (1995). *Listen up: Voices from the next feminist generation*. Seattle: Seal Press. An anthology of autobiographical writings by feminists in their 20s. Several contributors self-identify as bisexual, including

Anastassia Higgenbotham, Laurel Gilbert, Jee Yeun Lee, and Christine Doza.

Gray, M. L. (Ed.). (1999). *In your face: Stories from the lives of queer youth.* New York: Harrington Park Press. An impressive collection of personal perspectives by a diverse group of LGB youth.

Huegel, K., & Cozza, S. (2003). GLBTQ: The survival guide for queer and questioning teens. Minneapolis, MN: Free Spirit Publishing. Written for lesbian, gay, bisexual, transgender, and questioning teens, with personal narratives of LGBTQ youth as well as input from people at PFLAG and GLSEN.

Mastoon, A. (1997). *The shared heart: Portraits and stories celebrating lesbian, gay, and bisexual young people.* New York: William Morrow. A collection of photographs and personal narratives from a diverse group of LGB youth.

Owens, R. E. (1998). *Queer kids: The challenges and promise for lesbian, gay, and bisexual youth.* New York: Haworth Press. Provides an overview of typical issues facing LGB youth, including sexual identity development, coming out, difficult school conditions and situations, parental reactions, LGB youth programs, and counseling issues.

Pollack, R., & Schwartz, C. (1995). *The journey out: A guide for and about lesbian, gay and bisexual teens.* New York: Viking. A bi-inclusive guide to coming out and LGB identity for teenagers, their families, and their friends.

Sanlo, R. L. (1998). *Working with lesbian, gay, bisexual, and transgender college students: A handbook for faculty and administrators.* Westport, CT: Greenwood Press. The Coordinator of the LGBT Student Resources Center at the University of California Los Angeles provides a comprehensive source of information on working with LGBT college students.

Sherrill, J.-M., & Hardesty, C. A. (1994). *The gay, lesbian and bisexual students' guide to colleges, universities, and graduate schools.* New York: NYU Press. Comprehensive guide to LGB affirmative institutions of higher learning.

Transgender Persons and Identities

Blackwood, E., & Wieringa, S. E. (Eds.). (1999). *Female desires: Same-sex relations and transgender practices across cultures.* New York: Columbia University Press. A collection of essays on same-sex and transgender experiences in diverse cultures.

Denny, D. (Ed.). (1998). *Current concepts in transgender identity.* New York: Garland. An up-to-date collection of essays representing emerging affirmative approaches to transgender identities and issues, including chapters on gender identity and sexual orientation by Ira Pauly and Jamison Green.

Wilchins, R. A. (1997). *Read my lips: Sexual subversion and the end of gender.* Ithica, NY: Freehand Books. Collection of autobiographical essays by a bi-identified transgender activist celebrating sexual and gender diversity.

Sexual Orientation and Ethnic, Racial, and Cultural Diversity

Asian & Pacific Islander Wellness Center. (1997). *Understanding Asian and Pacific Islander sexual diversity: A handbook for individuals.* San Francisco: Asian & Pacific Islander Wellness Center. An excellent overview of historical and contemporary sexual diversity in the Asian and Pacific Islander communities, including a list of community organizations and a reading list.

Jacobs, S. E., Thomas, E., & Lang, S. (Eds.) (1997). *Two-spirit people: Native American gender identity, sexuality, & spirituality.* Urbana, IL: University of Illinois Press. An excellent collection of in-depth examinations of gender and sexual diversity of Native American people.

Lim-Hing, S. (Ed.). (1994). *The very inside: An anthology of writing by Asian and Pacific Islander lesbian and bisexual women.* Toronto: Sister Vision Press. A collection of essays and poetry that includes several pieces by bi-identified women.

Ratti, R. (Ed.). (1993). *Lotus of another color: An unfolding of the South Asian lesbian and gay experience.* Boston: Alyson. An anthology that includes three essays by bi-identified people.

Summerhawk, B., McMahill, C., & McDonald, D. (Eds.). (1998). *Queer Japan: Personal stories of Japanese lesbians, gays, transsexuals, and bisexuals.* Norwich, VT: New Victoria. A groundbreaking collection of personal narratives from Japanese LGBT persons.

Note: The following books contain descriptions of individuals and categories of persons with both same-sex and other-sex behavior and relationships in diverse cultures around the world. Although the authors do not generally conceptualize these as examples of bisexuality, there is ample material in these volumes demonstrating that bisexuality has been an accepted and integral part of many cultures both currently and historically.

Brown, L. B. (Ed.). (1997). *Two Spirit people: American Indian lesbian women and gay men.* New York: Harrington Park Press.

Carrier, J. (1995). *De los otros: Intimacy and homosexuality among Mexican men.* New York: Columbia University Press.

Greenberg, D. F. (1988). *The construction of homosexuality.* Chicago: University of Chicago Press.

Herdt, G. H. (1984). *Ritualized homosexuality in Melanesia*. Berkeley, CA: University of California Press.

Herdt, G. H., & Stoller, R. J. (1990). *Intimate communications: Erotics and the study of culture*. New York: Columbia University Press.

Hinsch, B. (1990). *Passions of the cut sleeve: The male homosexual tradition in China*. Berkeley, CA: University of California Press.

Ihara, S. (1972). *Comrade loves of the Samurai*. Rutland, VT: Tuttle.

Leong, R. (Ed.). (1996). *Asian American sexualities: Dimensions of the gay and lesbian experience*. New York: Routledge.

Leupp, G. P. (1995). *Male colors: The construction of homosexuality in Tokugawa Japan*. Berkeley, CA: University of California Press.

Murray, S. O. (1984). *Social theory, homosexual realities*. New York: Gay Academic Union.

Murray, S. O. (Ed.). (1987). *Male homosexuality in Central and South America*. New York: Gay Academic Union.

Murray, S. O. (1992). *Oceanic homosexualities*. New York: Garland Publishing.

Murray, S. O. (1995). *Latin American male homosexualities*. Albuquerque, NM: University of New Mexico Press.

Murray, S. O. (2000). *Homosexualities*. Chicago: University of Chicago Press.

Murray, S. O., & Roscoe, W. (Eds.). (1997). *Islamic homosexualities: Culture, history, and literature*. New York: New York University Press.

Murray, S. O., & Roscoe, W. (Ed.). (1998). *Boy-wives and female-husbands: Studies of African homosexualities*. New York: St. Martins Press.

Ruan, F. F. (1991). *Sex in China: Studies in sexology in Chinese culture*. New York: Plenum Press.

Saikaku, I. (1990). *The great mirror of male love*. (trans., P. G. Schalow). Stanford, CA: Stanford University Press.

Schifter, J. (2000). *Public sex in a Latin society*. New York: Haworth.

Schifter, J., & Pana, J. M. (2000). *The sexual construction of Latino youth: Implications for the spread of HIV/AIDS*. New York: Haworth.

Schmitt, A., & Sofer, J. (Ed.). (1992). *Sexuality and eroticism among males in Moslem societies*. New York: Harrington Park Press.

Schneebaum, T. (1988). *Where the spirits dwell: An odyssey in the jungle of New Guinea*. New York: Grove.

Seabrook, J. (1999). *Love in a different culture: The meaning of men who have sex with men in India*. London: Verso.

Watanabe, T., & Jun'ichi, I. (1987). *The love of the Samurai: A thousand years of Japanese homosexuality* (D. R. Roberts, trans.). London: GMP Publications.

Sexual Orientation and Health Care, Counseling, and Psychotherapy

Appleby, G. A., & Anastas, J. W. (1998). *Not just a passing phase: Social work with gay, lesbian, and bisexual people*. New York: Columbia University Press. A bi-affirmative handbook of social work practice with LGB people, including sections on identity development, community, relationships, LGB families, aging, HIV, and mental health issues.

Cabaj, R. P., & Stein, T. S. (Eds.). (1996). *Textbook of homosexuality and mental health.* Washington, DC: American Psychiatric Press. A groundbreaking LGB-affirmative book, with chapters by Ron Fox (on bisexual identity) and Dave Matteson (on bisexual counseling issues) and other bi-inclusive chapters on a diverse range of LGB psychiatry and psychology issues.

Davies, D., & Neal, C. (Eds.). (1996). Pink therapy: A guide for counsellors and therapists working with lesbian, gay and bisexual clients (pp. 131-148). Buckingham, England, U.K.: Open University Press. A bi-affirmative handbook addressing issues of importance in working with LGBT clients.

Denborough, D. (2002). *Queer counselling and narrative practice.* Adelaide, South Australia, Australia: Dulwich Centre Publications. An excellent bi-inclusive guide to the practice of narrative therapy with LGBTQ people. The publisher also puts out the Dulwich Centre Journal, the first issue of which was titled "Bisexuality: Identity, politics and partnerships" and included a diverse collection of Australian bi voices.

Eliason, M. J. (1996). *Who cares?: Institutional barriers to health care for lesbian, gay, and bisexual persons.* New York: NLN Press. A bi-inclusive thorough examination of obstacles to quality health care for lesbians, gay men, bisexual women, and bisexual men.

Finnegan, D. G., & McNally, E. (2002). *Counseling lesbian, gay, bisexual, and transgendered substance abusers.* New York: Harrington Park Press. A groundbreaking inclusive guide to providing culturally sensitive substance abuse services to LGBT people.

Garnets, L. D., & Kimmel, D. C. (Eds.). (2003). *Psychological perspectives on lesbian, gay, and bisexual experiences.* New York: Columbia University Press. The editors' provide integrative introductions to sections that include essays by a diverse group of authors on sexual orientation, prejudice, identity, diversity, relationships, developmental issues, mental health, research, practice, and public policy, including those on bisexual issues by Ron Fox, Lisa Diamond, Ritch Savin-Williams, and Paula Rust.

Greene, B., & Croom, G. L. (Eds.). (2000). *Education, research, and practice in lesbian, gay, bisexual, and transgendered psychology: A resource manual* (pp. 1-45). Thousand Oaks, CA: Sage. A collection of essays providing an overview of the history, accomplishments, and challenges of an evolving and increasingly inclusive LGBT psychology.

Gruskin, E. P. (1999). *Treating lesbians and bisexual women: Challenges and strategies for health professionals.* Thousand Oaks, CA: Sage. This book provides an overview of the important issues facing health care profession-als in providing affirmative treatment for lesbian and bisexual women.

Hunter, S., Shannon, C., Knox, J., & Martin, J. I. (1998). *Lesbian, gay, and bi-sexual youths and adults: Knowledge for human services practice.* Thousand Oaks, CA: Sage. This bi-affirmative volume provides an overview of knowledge important to providing services to LGB youth and adults.

Kominars, S. B., & Kominars, K. D. (1996). *Accepting ourselves and others: A journey into recovery from addictive and compulsive behaviors for gays, lesbians and bisexuals.* Center City, MN: Hazelden. A bi-inclusive LGB-centered guide to the process of recovery.

Longres, J. F. (Ed.). (1996). *Men of color: A context for service to homosexu-ally active men.* New York: Harrington Park Press. Contributions to this volume focus on how identity, behavior, and community figure into provid-ing affirmative social services for gay and bisexual men of color.

Neal, C., & Davies, D. (Eds.). (2000). *Issues in therapy with lesbian, gay, bi-sexual and transgender clients.* Buckingham, England, U.K.: Open Univer-sity Press. A collection of essays on psychotherapy with LGBT clients, including a contribution by therapists Liz Oxley and Claire Lucius on bi-sexual issues in psychotherapy.

Niesen, J. H. (1994). *Counseling lesbian, gay, and bisexual persons with alco-hol and drug abuse problems.* Arlington, VA: National Association of Al-cohol and Drug Abuse Counselors. A bi-inclusive handbook on alcohol and drug abuse treatment with LGB persons by the director of New Leaf, a San Francisco agency serving the LGBT community.

Perez, R. M., DeBord, K. A., & Bieschke, K. J. (Eds.). (2000). *Handbook of counseling and psychotherapy with lesbian, gay, and bisexual clients.* Wash-ington, DC: American Psychological Association. A well done bi-inclusive volume, with contributions on: LGB identity development; issues of diver-sity in counseling LGB clients; adapting and applying psychological theories to clinical practice; research and training issues; and affirmative approaches to individual, couples, and group counseling with LGB clients.

Whitman, J. S., & Boyd, C. J. (2003). *The therapist's notebook for lesbian, gay, and bisexual clients: Homework, handouts, and activities for use in psychotherapy.* New York: Haworth. A comprehensive and inclusive col-lection of resources to complement the therapist's existing repertoire of ap-proaches of working affirmatively with LGB people.

LGBTQ Persons and Spirituality

Chneer, D., & Aviv, C. (1991). *Queer Jews.* New York: Routledge. An in-depth exploration of spirituality in the lives of lesbian, gay, bisexual, and queer identified Jews.

Conner, R. P., Sparks, D. H., & Sparks, M. (1997). *Cassell's encyclopedia of queer myth, symbol and spirit.* London: Cassell. A wide-ranging bi-affirmative encyclopedia of LGBT spirituality.
Kimball, R. S. (Ed.). (2000). *Our whole lives: Sexuality education for adults.* Boston, MA: Unitarian Universalist Association and United Church Board of Homeland Ministries. Features a section on sexual orientation by bi activists and educators Bobbi Keppel and Alan Hamilton.
Spahr, J. A. (1995). *Called out: The voices of lesbian, gay, bisexual, and transgendered Presbyterians.* Gaithersburg, MD: Chi Rho Press. A view into the spiritual lives of LGBT Presbyterians.
Stuart, E. (1998). *Religion is a queer thing: A guide to the Christian faith for lesbian, gay, bisexual and transgendered people.* New York: Cassell. A comprehensive examination and formulation of an affirmative approach to Christianity for LGBT people.
Sweasey, P. (1997). *From queer to eternity: Spirituality in the lives of lesbian, gay and bisexual people.* New York: Cassell. Exploration of spirituality and LGB people.
Tigert, L. M. (1996). *Coming out while staying in: Struggles and celebrations of lesbians, gays, and bisexuals in the church.* Cleveland, OH: United Church Press. Another volume exploring spirituality in the lives of LGB people.

Queer Theory, Cultural Studies, Post-Modern Perspectives

Beemyn, B., & Eliason, M. (Eds.). (1996). *Queer studies: A lesbian, gay, bisexual, & transgender anthology.* NY: NYU Press. Includes essays by Paula Rust, Amanda Udis-Kessler, Ruth Goldman, Amber Ault, Christopher James, Warren J. Blumenfeld and others. An impressive bi-inclusive mixed-orientation collection, with several chapters on bisexuality in the context of queer studies.

Lesbian, Gay, Bisexual, Transgender, Intersex, and Queer Communities and Politics

Colker, R. (1996). *Hybrid: Bisexuals, multiracials, and other misfits under American law.* New York: NYU Press. An examination of how the legal system treats and mistreats those who don't fit standard categories, including bisexual and multiracial people.
Ellis, A. L., Highleyman, L., Schaub, K., & White, M. (2002). The Harvey Milk Institute guide to lesbian, gay, bisexual, transgender, and queer internet research. New York: Harrington Park Press. A comprehensive guide to using the Internet to locate resources on LGBTQ people and issues.

Gamson, J. (1998). *Freaks talk back: Tabloid talk shows and sexual noncon-formity*. Chicago: University of Chicago Press. Well-written stories about US talk shows and their treatment of lesbian, gay, bi, and transgendered people. Explores the issues from many angles, including how, while being used by talk shows, activists in return use talk shows to educate the public about LGBT issues. Includes substantial discussion of how bi people in particular are treated, including a number of entertaining behind the scenes stories.

Harris, P. (1999). *The queer press guide 2000*. New York: Painted Leaf Press. Comprehensive listing of LGBT newspapers and magazines.

Hertzog, M. (1996). *The lavender vote: Lesbians, gay men, and bisexuals in American electoral politics*. New York: New York University Press. Focus on the impact of LGB people on the electoral process.

Koyama, E. (2001). *Introduction to intersex activism: A guide for lesbian, gay, bisexual, and trans allies*. Petaluma, CA: Intersex Society of North America. A ground-breaking introduction to the experiences and concerns of intersex people and the ways in which LGBTI people can work together to address intersex and common concerns.

Shepard, C. F., Yeskel, F., & Outcalt, C. (1996). *Lesbian, gay, bisexual, and transgender campus organizing: A comprehensive manual*. Washington, DC: National Gay and Lesbian Task Force. Also available online at: <http://www.ngltf.org/>. A guide to LGBT campus organizing.

Stevenson, M. R., & Cogan, J. C. (2003). *Everyday activism: A handbook for lesbian, gay, and bisexual people and their allies*. New York: Routledge. A practical guide to taking action on issues of concern to LGBT people.

Swan, W. (1997). *Gay/lesbian/bisexual/transgender public policy issues: A citizen's and administrator's guide to the new cultural struggle*. New York: Harrington Park Press. Focus on GLBT Public Policy Issues.

Working Group on Funding Lesbian & Gay Issues. (1999). *Funders of les-bian, gay & bisexual programs: A directory for grantseekers* (3rd ed.). New York: Working Group on Funding Lesbian & Gay Issues. Also accessible online at: http://www.workinggroup.org/lgbtfunders/FD/fdirectory.htm

JOURNAL ARTICLES, BOOK CHAPTERS, THESES, AND DISSERTATIONS ON BISEXUALITY

Complete references are provided for all listed journal articles, book chapters, theses, and dissertations, with the exception of chapters that appear in the following anthologies for which complete references are provided in the preceding book section. For the anthology chapters that are listed in the sections below, the authors' names, chapter titles, book editors, book titles, and page numbers are given:

Bernstein & Silberman, *Generation Q*
Bisexual Anthology Collective, *Plural desires*
Findlen, *Listen up: Voices from the next feminist generation*
Hutchins & Kaahumanu, *Bi any other name*
Rose, Stevens, and the Offpink Collective, *Bisexual horizons*
Tucker, *Bisexual politics*
Weise, *Closer to home*

Sexual Orientation: Multidimensional Approaches

Baltar, J. F. (1998). The Baltar Sexual Identity Inventory–Female Form: A multidimensional measure of sexual identity. (Doctoral dissertation, Loyola University of Chicago, 1998). *Dissertation Abstracts International, 58*(12), 6799B.

Bem, D. J. (1996). Exotic becomes erotic: A developmental theory of sexual orientation. *Psychological Review, 103*(2), 320-335.

Berkey, B. R., Perelman-Hall, T., & Kurdek, L. A. (1990). The multidimensional scale of sexuality. *Journal of Homosexuality, 19*(4), 67-87.

Bohan, J. S., & Russell, G. M. (1999). Implications for psychological research and theory building. In J. S. Bohan & G. M. Russell (Eds.), *Conversations about psychology and sexual orientation* (pp. 85-105). New York: New York University Press.

Bohan, J. S., & Russell, G. M. (1999). Conceptual frameworks. In J. S. Bohan & G. M. Russell (Eds.), *Conversations about psychology and sexual orientation* (pp. 11-30). New York: New York University Press.

Cass, V. C. (1990). The implications of homosexual identity formation for the Kinsey model and scale of sexual preference. In D. P. McWhirter, S. A. Sanders, & J. M. Reinisch (Eds.), *Homosexuality/heterosexuality: Concepts of sexual orientation* (pp. 239-266). New York: Oxford University Press.

Cass, V. (1996). Sexual orientation identity formation: A Western phenomenon. In R. P. Cabaj & T. S. Stein (Eds.), *Textbook of homosexuality and mental health* (pp. 227-251). Washington, DC: American Psychiatric Press.

Cass, V. (1999). Bringing psychology in from the cold: Framing psychological theory and research within a social constructionist psychology approach. In J. S. Bohan & G. M. Russell (Eds.), *Conversations about psychology and sexual orientation* (pp. 106-128). New York: New York University Press.

Chung, Y. B., & Katayama, M. (1996). Assessment of sexual orientation in lesbian/gay/bisexual studies. *Journal of Homosexuality, 30*(4), 49-62.

Coleman, E. (1987). Assessment of sexual orientation. *Journal of Homosexuality, 14*(1/2), 9-24.

Coleman, E. (1987). Bisexuality: Challenging our understanding of human sexuality and sexual orientation. In E. E. Shelp (Ed.), *Sexuality and medicine* (pp. 225-242). New York: Reidel.

Ellis, L., Burke, D., & Ames, M. A. (1987). Sexual orientation as a continuous variable: A comparison between the sexes. *Archives of Sexual Behavior, 16*(6), 523-529

Garnets, L. D., & Peplau, L. A. (2001). A new paradigm for women's sexual orientation: Implications for therapy. *Women & Therapy, 24*(1/2).

Gonsiorek, J., & Weinrich, J. D. (1995). Definition and measurement of sexual orientation. *Suicide & Life-Threatening Behavior, 25*(Suppl.), 40-51.

Holden, J. M., & Holden, G. S. (1995). The *Sexual Identity Profile*: A multidimensional bipolar model. *Individual Psychology, 51*(2), 102-113

Keppel, B., & Hamilton, A. (2000). Your sexual orientation: Using the Sexual and Affectional Orientation and Identity Scale to teach about sexual orientation. In R. S. Kimball (Ed.), *Our whole lives: Sexuality education for adults* (pp. 157-161). Boston, MA: Unitarian Universalist Association and United Church Board of Homeland Ministries.

Klein, F. (1990). The need to view sexual orientation as a multi-variable dynamic process: A theoretical perspective. In D. P. McWhirter, S. A. Sanders, & J. M. Reinisch (Eds.), *Homosexuality/heterosexuality: Concepts of sexual orientation* (pp. 277-282). New York: Oxford University Press.

Klein, F. (1999). Psychology of sexual orientation. In J. S. Bohan & G. M. Russell (Eds.), *Conversations about psychology and sexual orientation* (pp. 129-138). New York: New York University Press.

Klein, F., Sepekoff, B., & Wolf, T. J. (1985). Sexual orientation: A multi-variable dynamic process. *Journal of Homosexuality, 11*(1/2), 35-50.

MacDonald, A. P., Jr. (1982). Research on sexual orientation: A bridge that touches both shores but doesn't meet in the middle. *Journal of Sex Education and Therapy, 8*(1), 9-13.

MacDonald, A. P., Jr. (1983). A little bit of lavender goes a long way: A critique of research on sexual orientation. *Journal of Sex Research, 19*(1), 94-100. Reprinted in P. C. R. Rust (Ed.). (2000). *Bisexuality in the United States: A social science reader* (pp. 24-30). Columbia University Press.

McConaghy, N. (1987). Heterosexuality/homosexuality: Dichotomy or continuum. *Archives of Sexual Behavior, 16*(5), 411-424.

Neighbors, C. J. (2001). The construct of sexual orientation in ordinary language. (Doctoral dissertation, University of Nevada, Reno, 1999). *Dissertation Abstracts International, 61*(9), 4997B.

Patterson, C. J. (1995). Sexual orientation and human development: An overview. *Developmental Psychology, 31*, 3-11.

Paul, J. P. (1985). Bisexuality: Reassessing our paradigms of sexuality. *Journal of Homosexuality, 11*(1/2), 21-34.

Peplau, L. A., & Garnets, L. A. (2000). A new paradigm for understanding women's sexuality and sexual orientation. *Journal of Social Issues, 56*(2), 329-350.

Ross, M. W. (1990). Toward a synthetic understanding of sexual orientation. In D. P. McWhirter, S. A. Sanders, & J. M. Reinisch (Eds.), *Homosexuality/heterosexuality: Concepts of sexual orientation* (pp. 267-276). New York: Oxford University Press.

Rothblum, E. D. (2000). Sexual orientation and sex in women's lives: Conceptual and methodological issues. *Journal of Social Issues, 56*(2), 193-204.

Rust, P. C. (1996). Finding a sexual identity and community: Therapeutic implications and cultural assumptions in scientific models of coming out. In E. D. Rothblum, & L. A. Bond (Eds.), *Preventing heterosexism and homophobia* (pp. 87-123). Thousand Oaks, CA: Sage. Reprinted in L. D. Garnets & D. C. Kimmel (Eds.). (2003). *Psychological perspectives on lesbian, gay, and bisexual experiences* (pp. 227-269). New York: Columbia University Press.

Rust, P. C. R. (2000). Alternatives to binary sexuality: Modeling sexuality. In P. C. R. Rust (Ed.), *Bisexuality in the United States: A social science reader* (pp. 33-54). New York: Columbia University Press.

Saliba, P. A. (1980). *Variability in sexual orientation.* Unpublished master's thesis, San Francisco State University, San Francisco.

Sell, R. L. (1996). The Sell Assessment of Sexual Orientation: Background and scoring. *Journal of Gay, Lesbian, & Bisexual Identity, 1*(4), 295-310.

Sell, R. L. (1997). Defining and measuring sexual orientation: A review. *Archives of Sexual Behavior, 26*(6), 643-658.

Shively, M., & DeCecco, J. (1977). Components of sexual identity. *Journal of Homosexuality, 3*(1), 41-48.

Shively, M. G., Jones, C., & DeCecco, J. P. (1983-1984). Research on sexual orientation: Definitions and methods. *Journal of Homosexuality, 9*(2/3), 127-136.

Snell, W. E., Fisher, T. D., & Walters, A. S. (1993). The Multidimensional Sexuality Questionnaire: An objective self-report measure of psychological tendencies associated with human sexuality. *Annals of Sex Research, 6*(1), 27-55.

Storms, M. D. (1980). Theories of sexual orientation. *Journal of Personality and Social Psychology, 38*(5), 783-792.

BISEXUAL IDENTITY

Psychological and Sociological Perspectives

Bell, P. (1998). "Coming out bisexual." In U. Biechele (Ed.), *Identitätsbildung, Identitätsverwirrung, Identitätspolitik: Eine psychologische Standort-*

bestimmung für Lesben, Schwule und andere [Identity development, identity confusion, identity politics: A psychological point of reference for lesbians, gays, and others]. Berlin: Deutsche AIDS-Hilfe e.V.

Berenson, C. (2002). What's in a name: Bisexual women define their terms. *Journal of Bisexuality*, 2(2/3), 9-21.

Berenson, C. A. (1999). Interrogating choice: Bisexual identity and politics. (Master's thesis, University of Calgary, Alberta, Canada, 1999). *Masters Abstracts International*, 37(6), 1706.

Blumstein, P. W., & Schwartz, P. (1977). Bisexuality: Some social psychological issues. *Journal of Social Issues*, 33(2), 30-45. Reprinted in L. D. Garnets & D. C. Kimmel (Eds.). (1993). *Psychological perspectives on lesbian and gay male experiences* (pp. 168-183). New York: Columbia University Press. Also reprinted in P. C. R. Rust (Ed.). (2000). *Bisexuality in the United States: A social science reader* (pp. 339-352). New York: Columbia University Press.

Bower, J., Gurevich, M., & Mathieson, C. (2002). (Con)Tested identities: Bisexual women reorient sexuality. *Journal of Bisexuality*, 2(2/3), 23-52.

Bradford, M. (1997). The bisexual experience: Living in a dichotomous culture. (Doctoral dissertation, The Fielding Institute, Santa Barbara, 1997). *Dissertation Abstracts International*, 58(3), 1520B.

Bradford, M. (2004). The bisexual experience: Living in a dichotomous culture. *Journal of Bisexuality*, 4(1/2), 7-23.

Brown, T. (2002). A proposed model of bisexual identity development that elaborates on experiential differences of women and men. *Journal of Bisexuality*, 2(4), 67-91.

Coleman, E. (1998). Paradigmatic changes in the understanding of bisexuality. In E. J. Haeberle & R. Gindorf (Eds.), *Bisexualities: The ideology and practice of sexual contact with both men and women* (pp. 107-112). New York: Continuum.

Evans, T. (2003). Bisexuality: Negotiating lives between two cultures. *Journal of Bisexuality*, 3(2), 91-108.

Firestein, B. A. (1996). Bisexuality as paradigm shift: Transforming our disciplines. In B. A. Firestein (Ed.), *Bisexuality: The psychology and politics of an invisible minority* (pp. 261-291). Thousand Oaks, CA: Sage.

Fox, R. C. (1995). Bisexual identities. In A. R. D'Augelli & C. J. Patterson (Eds.), *Lesbian, gay, and bisexual identities over the lifespan: Psychological perspectives* (pp. 48-86). New York: Oxford University Press. Reprinted in L. D. Garnets & D. C. Kimmel (Eds.). (2003). *Psychological perspectives on lesbian, gay, and bisexual experiences* (pp. 86-129). New York: Columbia University Press.

Fox, R. C. (1995). Coming out bisexual: Identity, behavior, and sexual orientation self-disclosure. (Doctoral dissertation, California Institute of Integral Studies, 1993). *Dissertation Abstracts International*, *55*(12), 5565B.

Galland, V. R. (1975). Bisexual women. (Doctoral dissertation, California School of Professional Psychology, San Francisco, 1975). *Dissertation Abstracts International*, *36*(6), 3037B.

Hansen, C. E., & Evans, A. (1985). Bisexuality reconsidered: An idea in pursuit of a definition. *Journal of Homosexuality*, *11*(1/2), 1-6.

Harwell, J. L. (1976). Bisexuality: Persistent lifestyle or transitional state? (Doctoral dissertation, United States International University, 1976). *Dissertation Abstracts International*, *37*(4), 2449A.

Little, D. R. (1990). Contemporary female bisexuality: A psychosocial phenomenon. (Doctoral dissertation, The Union for Experimenting Colleges, 1989). *Dissertation Abstracts International*, *50*(11), 5379B.

Macalister, H. E. (2003). In defense of ambiguity: Understanding bisexuality's invisibility through cognitive psychology. *Journal of Bisexuality*, *3*(1), 23-33.

MacDonald, A. P. (1981). Bisexuality: Some comments on research and theory. *Journal of Homosexuality*, *6*(3), 21-35.

Morrow, G. D. (1989). Bisexuality: An exploratory review. *Annals of Sex Research*, *2*, 283-306.

Morse, C. R. (1990). Exploring the bisexual alternative: A view from another closet. (Master's thesis, University of Arizona, 1989). *Masters Abstracts International*, *28*(2), 320.

Oattes, C. A. (1996). Crossing the lines: Bisexuality and the generation of possibilities. (Master's thesis, University of Guelph, Ontario, Canada, 1995). *Masters Abstracts International*, *34*(3), 1057.

Ochs, R. (1997). Contexts and constructs of identity: Bisexuality. In P. Rust (Ed.), *Sociology of sexuality and sexual orientation: Syllabi and teaching materials* (pp. 100-107). Washington, DC: American Sociological Association.

Owen, M. K. (2003). Overstepping the bounds: Bisexuality, gender, and sociology. *Journal of Bisexuality*, *3*(2), 29-39.

Paul, J. P. (1983/1984). The bisexual identity: An idea without social recognition. *Journal of Homosexuality*, *9*(2/3), 45-64.

Paul, J. P. (1996). Bisexuality: Exploring/exploding the boundaries. In R. C. Savin-Williams & K. M. Cohen (Eds.), *The lives of lesbians, gays, and bisexuals: Children to adults* (pp. 436-461). Ft. Worth, TX: Harcourt Brace. Reprinted in P. C. R. Rust (Ed.). (2000). *Bisexuality in the United States: A social science reader* (pp. 11-23). New York: Columbia University Press.

Queen, C. (1995). Sexual diversity and bisexual identity. In *Bisexual politics* (pp. 151-160).

Ronald C. Fox   185

Rust, P. C. (1992). Who are we and where do we go from here? Conceptualizing bisexuality. In *Closer to home* (pp. 281-310).
Rust, P. C. (1996). Sexual identity and bisexual identities: The struggle for
self-description in a changing sexual landscape. In B. Beemyn, & M.
Eliason (Eds.), *Queer studies: A lesbian, gay, bisexual, and transgender
anthology* (pp. 64-86). New York: NYU Press.
Rust, P. C. (2001). Two many and not enough: The meanings of bisexual identities. *Journal of Bisexuality, 1*(1), 31-68.
Rust, P. C. R. (2000). Bisexuality: A contemporary paradox for women. *Jour-
nal of Social Issues, 56*(2), 205-221.
Rust, P. C. R. (2002). Bisexuality: The state of the union. *Annual Review of
Sex Research, 13*, 180-214.
Schwartz, P., & Blumstein, P. (1998). The acquisition of sexual identity: Bi-
sexuality. In E. J. Haeberle & R. Gindorf (Eds.), *Bisexualities: The ideol-
ogy and practice of sexual contact with both men and women* (pp. 182-
212). New York: Continuum.
Shuster, R. (1987). Sexuality as a continuum: The bisexual identity. In The
Boston Lesbian Psychologies Collective (Eds.), *Lesbian psychologies: Ex-
plorations & challenges* (pp. 56-71). Urbana & Chicago, IL: University of
Illinois Press.
Twining, A. (1983). Bisexual women: Identity in adult development. (Doctoral dissertation, Boston University, 1983). *Dissertation Abstracts International, 44*(5), 1340A.
Weinberg, M. S., & Williams, C. J. (1974). Bisexuality. In M. S. Weinberg &
C. J. Williams (Eds.), *Male homosexuals: Their problems and adaptations*
(pp. 207-215). New York: Oxford University Press.
Weinberg, M. S., Williams, C. J., & Pryor, D. W. (1998). Becoming and being
"bisexual." In E. J. Haeberle & R. Gindorf (Eds.), *Bisexualities: The ideology and practice of sexual contact with both men and women* (pp. 169-
181). New York: Continuum.
Weinrich, J. D., & Klein, F. (2002). Bi-gay, bi-straight, and bi-bi: Three bisexual subgroups identified using cluster analysis of the Klein Sexual Orientation Grid. *Journal of Bisexuality, 2*(4), 109-140.

Bisexual Identity in the Context of Theory and Research on LGB Identities

Abrams, M. (1980). Becoming lavender. (Doctoral dissertation, City University of New York, 1980). *Dissertation Abstracts International, 41*(4),
1790A.
Clausen, J. (1990). My interesting condition. *Journal of Sex Research, 27*(3),
445-459.

De Cecco, J., & Shively, M. (1983/1984). From sexual identity to sexual relationships: A contextual shift. *Journal of Homosexuality, 9*(2/3), 1-26.

Derr, L. S. (1992). Leaving the lesbian label behind: Women who change their sexual orientation identity. (Doctoral dissertation, Massachusetts School of Professional Psychology). *Dissertation Abstracts International, 54*(4), 2271B.

Diamond, L. M. (2003). Was it a phase? Young women's relinquishment of lesbian/bisexual identities over a 5-year period. *Journal of Personality and Social Psychology, 84*(2), 352-364.

Eliason, M. J. (1996). Identity formation for lesbian, bisexual, and gay persons: Beyond a "minoritizing" view. *Journal of Homosexuality, 30*, 31-57.

Fassinger, R. E., & Miller, B. A. (1996). Validation of an inclusive model of sexual minority identity formation on a sample of gay men. *Journal of Homosexuality, 32*(2), 53-78.

Fleishman, M. R. (1993). Sexuality is not fixed: A study of thirty women whose sexual orientation changed at mid-life. (Doctoral dissertation, Saybrook Institute, 1992). *Dissertation Abstracts International, 54*(1), 519B.

Freimuth, M. J., & Hornstein, G. A. (1982). A critical examination of the concept of gender. *Sex Roles, 8*(5), 515-532.

Golden, C. (1987). Diversity and variability in women's sexual identities. In The Boston Lesbian Psychologies Collective (Eds.), *Lesbian psychologies: Explorations and challenges* (pp. 18-34). Urbana and Chicago, IL: University of Illinois Press.

Golden, C. (1996). What's in a name? Sexual self-identification among women. In R. C. Savin-Williams & K. M. Cohen (Eds.), *The lives of lesbians, gays, & bisexuals: Children to adults* (pp. 229-249). Ft. Worth, TX: Harcourt Brace.

Hurley, K. W. (1994). A qualitative study of sexual identity among bisexual and lesbian women in a lesbian community. (Master's thesis, University of Victoria, British Columbia, Canada, 1993). *Masters Abstracts International, 32*(3), 866.

Katz, R. E. (1993). A study of sexual fluidity and self-concept: The shift from lesbian to heterosexual object choice. (Doctoral dissertation, The Wright Institute, 1993). *Dissertation Abstracts International, 54*(2), 1077B.

McCarn, S. R., & Fassinger, R. E. (1996). Revisioning sexual minority identity formation: A new model of lesbian identity and its implications. *Counseling Psychologist, 24*(3), 508-534.

Morris, J., & Rothblum, E. (1999). Who fills out a "lesbian" questionnaire?: The interrelationship of sexual orientation, years "out," disclosure of sexual orientation, sexual experience with women, and participation in the lesbian community. *Psychology of Women Quarterly, 23*(3), 537-558.

Reynolds, A. L., & Hanjorgiris, W. F. (2000). Coming out: Lesbian, gay, and bisexual identity development. In R. M. Perez, K. A. DeBord, & K. J. Bieschke (Eds.), *Handbook of counseling and psychotherapy with lesbian, gay, and bisexual clients* (pp. 35-55). Washington, DC: American Psychological Association.

Rust, P. C. (1993). "Coming out" in the age of social constructionism: Sexual identity formation among lesbian and bisexual women. *Gender & Society, 7*(1), 50-77.

Seif, H. (1999). To love women, or to not love men: Chronicles of lesbian identification. In D. Atkins (Ed.), *Lesbian sex scandals: Sexual practices, identities, and politics* (pp. 33-44). New York: Haworth.

Sophie, J. (1985). Stress, social network, and sexual orientation identity change in women. (Doctoral dissertation, New York University, 1985). *Dissertation Abstracts International, 46*(3), 949B.

Suppe, F. (1984). In defense of a multidimensional approach to sexual identity. *Journal of Homosexuality, 10*(3/4), 7-14.

Wishik, H. R. (1996). Life maps: Tracking individual gender and sexual identity construction in the contexts of cultures, relationships, and desires. *Journal of Gay, Lesbian, & Bisexual Identity, 1*(2), 129-152.

Personal and Political Perspectives

Brand, K. (2001). Coming out successfully in the Netherlands. *Journal of Bisexuality, 1*(4), 59-68.

Chater, N., & Finkler, L. (1995). "Traversing wide territories": A journey from lesbianism to bisexuality. In *Plural desires* (pp. 14-36).

Clinton, Michelle T. (1996). Almost a dyke: In search of the perfect bisexual. In M. Daly (Ed.), *Surface tension: Love, sex, and politics between lesbians and straight women* (pp. 160-165). New York: Simon & Schuster.

Cooper, L. A., Hynes, M. E., & Westfall, E. R. (1995). The Kinsey three. In *Plural desires* (pp. 261-275).

Della Rosa, L. (1975). The bisexual potential. In K. Jay & A. Young (Eds.), *After you're out: Personal experiences of gay men and lesbian women* (pp. 62-64). New York: Links Books.

Dobinson, C. (1999). Confessions of an identity junkie. *International Journal of Sexuality and Gender Studies, 4*(3), 265-269.

Eadie, J. (1996). Being who we are (and anyone else we want to be). In *Bisexual horizons* (pp. 16-20).

Fox, A. (1991). Development of a bisexual identity: Understanding the process. In *Bi any other name* (pp. 29-36).

Gibian, R. (1992). Refusing certainty: Toward a bisexuality of wholeness. In *Closer to home* (pp. 3-16).

Hamilton, L. (1996). Deaf bisexuality. In *Bisexual horizons* (pp. 144-148).
Humphreys, L.-Z. (2002). Musing on pain, love, and others. *Journal of Bisexuality*, 2(2/3), 129-141.
JEM. (1975). A Bisexual offers some thoughts on fences. In K. Jay & A. Young (Eds.), *After you're out: Personal experiences of gay men and lesbian women* (pp. 65-67). New York: Links Books.
Kaplan, R. (1995). Your fence is sitting on me: The hazards of binary thinking. In *Bisexual politics* (pp. 267-280).
McKeon, E. (1992). To be bisexual and underclass. In *Closer to home* (pp. 27-34).
Lipstadt, H. (1997). From lesbian to has-bian: Taking the long view of friendship and bisexuality. *In the Family: A Magazine for Gays, Lesbians, Bisexuals and Their Relations*, 2(3), 10-12, 22.
Miller, M., & Solot, D. (1999). Fine art of white picket fence-sitting: Bisexuality, marriage, and family diversity. *Anything That Moves*, (20), 20-22.
Montgomery, M. S. (1996). An old bottle for old wine: Selecting the right label. In *Bisexual horizons* (pp. 21-24).
Queen, C. A. (1991). The queer in me. In *Bi any other name* (pp. 17-21).
Reinhardt, R. U. (2001). From Europe with love: A bisexual biography. *Journal of Bisexuality*, 1(1), 163-172.
Shuster, R. (1992). Bisexuality and the quest for principled loving. In *Closer to home* (pp. 147-154).
Starr, C. (1995). Making a sexual choice. In *Plural desires* (pp. 185-190).
Sumpter, S. F. (1991). Myths/realities of bisexuality. In *Bi any other name* (pp. 12-13).
Udis-Kessler, A. (1996). Challenging the stereotypes. In *Bisexual horizons* (pp. 45-57).
Zipkin, D. (1992). Why bi? In *Closer to home* (pp. 55-73).

BISEXUAL ATTRACTIONS AND BEHAVIOR

Psychological and Sociological Perspectives: Women and Men

Amestoy, M. M. (2001). Research on sexual orientation labels' relationship to behaviors and desires. *Journal of Bisexuality*, 1(4), 91-113.
Bagley, C., & Tremblay, P. (1998). On the prevalence of homosexuality and bisexuality, in a random community survey of 750 men aged 18 to 27. *Journal of Homosexuality*, 36(2), 1-18.
Bell, A. P., & Weinberg, M. S. (1978). Dimensions of sexual experience. In A. P. Bell & M. S. Weinberg, *Homosexualities: A study of diversity among men and women* (pp. 49-61). New York: Simon & Schuster.

Bell, A. P., Weinberg, M. S., & Hammersmith, S. K. (1981). Bisexuality. In A. P. Bell, M. S. Weinberg, & S. K. Hammersmith, *Sexual preference: Its development in men and women* (pp. 200-202). Bloomington: Indiana University Press.

Bhugra, D., & De Silva, P. (1998). Dimensions of bisexuality: An exploratory study using focus groups of male and female bisexuals. *Sexual and Marital Therapy, 13*(2), 145-157.

Blackford, L., Doty, S., & Pollack, R. (1996). Differences in subjective sexual arousal in heterosexual, bisexual, and lesbian women. *Canadian Journal of Human Sexuality, 5*(3), 157-167.

Diamond, M. (1993). Homosexuality and bisexuality in different populations. *Archives of Sexual Behavior, 22*(4), 291-310.

Doll, L. (1997). Sexual behavior research: Studying bisexual men and women and lesbians. In J. Bancroft (Ed.), *Researching sexual behavior: Methodological issues* (pp. 145-158). Bloomington, IN: University of Indiana Press.

Gagnon, J. H. (1990). Gender preference in erotic relations: The Kinsey scale and sexual scripts. In D. P. McWhirter, S. A. Sanders, & J. M. Reinisch (Eds.), *Homosexuality/heterosexuality: Concepts of sexual orientation* (pp. 177-207). New York: Oxford University Press.

Gagnon, J. H., Greenblat, C. S., & Kimmel, M. (1998). Bisexuality: A sociological perspective. In E. J. Haeberle & R. Gindorf (Eds.), *Bisexualities: The ideology and practice of sexual contact with both men and women* (pp. 81-106). New York: Continuum.

Gebhard, P. H. (1976). Incidence of overt homosexuality in the United States and Western Europe. In J. M. Livingood (Ed.), *NIMH Task Force on Homosexuality: Final report and background papers. DHEW Publication No. (HSM) 72-9116* (pp. 22-29). Rockville, MD: National Institute of Mental Health.

Janus, S. S., & Janus, C. L. (1993). Homosexuality. In S. S. Janus & C. L. Janus (Eds.), *The Janus Report on sexual behavior* (pp. 69-71). New York: John Wiley & Sons.

Kaplan, G. T., & Rogers, L. J. (1984). Breaking out of the dominant paradigm: A new look at sexual attraction. *Journal of Homosexuality, 10*(3/4), 71-75.

Laumann, E. O., Gagnon, J. H., Michael, R. T., & Michaels, S. (1994). Homosexuality. In E. O. Laumann, J. H. Gagnon, R. T. Michael, & S. Michaels (Eds.), *The social organization of sexuality: Sexual practices in the United States* (pp. 283-320). Chicago: University of Chicago Press.

McIntosh, M. (1968). The homosexual role. *Social Problems, 16*(2), 182-192. Reprinted in K. Plummer (Ed.). (1981). *The making of the modern homosexual* (pp. 30-44). Totowa, NJ: Barnes & Noble Books.

Messiah, A., & Mouret-Fourme, E. (1993). Homosexualité, bisexualité: Éléments de socio-biographie sexuelle [Homosexuality, bisexuality: Elements of a sexual social biography]. *Population, 48*(5), 1353-1380.

Michaels, S. (1996). The prevalence of homosexuality in the United States. In R. P. Cabaj & T. S. Stein (Eds.), *Textbook of homosexuality and mental health* (pp. 43-64). Washington, DC: American Psychiatric Press.

Moskowitz, K. P. (1981). The relationship of adolescent sexual fantasy to adult sexual orientation and preferences. (Doctoral dissertation, California School of Professional Psychology, Berkeley/Alameda, 1980). *Dissertation Abstracts International, 41*(12), 4678B.

Nurius, P. S., & Hudson, W. W. (1988). Sexual activity and preference: Six quantifiable dimensions. *Journal of Sex Research, 24*, 30-46.

Queen, C. (1996). Bisexuality, sexual diversity, and the sex-positive perspective. In B. A. Firestein (Ed.), *Bisexuality: The psychology and politics of an invisible minority* (pp. 103-124). Thousand Oaks, CA: Sage.

Ross, M. W. (1984). Beyond the biological model: New directions in bisexual and homosexual research. *Journal of Homosexuality, 10*(3/4), 63-70.

Ross, M. W., & Paul, J. P. (1992). Beyond gender: The basis of sexual attraction in bisexual men & women. *Psychological Reports, 71*, 1283-1290. Reprinted in P. C. R. Rust (Ed.). (2000). *Bisexuality in the United States: A social science reader* (pp. 92-98). New York: Columbia University Press.

Rudy, K. (1999). Sex radical communities and the future of sexual ethics. In D. Atkins (Ed.), *Lesbian sex scandals: Sexual practices, identities, and politics* (pp. 133-142). New York: Haworth.

Rust, P. C. R. (2000). Academic literature on situational homosexuality in the 1960s and 1970s. In P. C. R. Rust (Ed.), *Bisexuality in the United States: A social science reader* (pp. 221-249). New York: Columbia University Press.

Rust, P. C. R. (2000). Heterosexual gays, heterosexual lesbians, homosexual straights. In P. C. R. Rust (Ed.), *Bisexuality in the United States: A social science reader* (pp. 279-306). New York: Columbia University Press.

Rust, P. C. R. (2000). Review of statistical findings about bisexual behavior, feelings, and identities. In P. C. R. Rust (Ed.), *Bisexuality in the United States: A social science reader* (pp. 129-184). New York: Columbia University Press.

Rust, P. C. R. (2000). The biology, psychology, sociology, and sexuality of bisexuality. In P. C. R. Rust (Ed.), *Bisexuality in the United States: A social science reader* (pp. 403-470). New York: Columbia University Press.

Sell, R. L., Wells, J. A., & Wypij, D. (1995). The prevalence of homosexual behavior and attraction in the United States, the United Kingdom and France: Results of national population-based samples. *Archives of Sexual Behavior, 24*(3), 235-248.

Tkachuk, J. M. (1999). Sexual behaviours and fantasies in relation to sex and sexual orientation. (Doctoral dissertation, University of Regina, Saskatchewan, Canada, 1998). *Master's Abstracts International, 37*(3), 1031.

Tolman, D. L., & Diamond, L. M. (2001). Desegregating sexuality research: Cultural and biological perspectives on gender and desire. *Annual Review of Sex Research, 12,* 33-74.

Van Wyk, P. H., & Geist, C. S. (1984). Psychosocial development of heterosexual, bisexual, and homosexual behavior. *Archives of Sexual Behavior, 13,* 505-544.

Van Wyk, P. H., & Geist, C. S. (1995). Biology of bisexuality: Critique and observations. *Journal of Homosexuality, 28*(3/4), 357-373.

Weinberg, M. S. (1970). Homosexual samples: Differences and similarities. *Journal of Sex Research, 6,* 312-325.

Weinrich, J. D. (1988). The periodic table model of the gender transpositions: II. Limerent and lusty sexual attractions and the nature of bisexuality. *Journal of Sex Research, 24,* 113-129. Reprinted in P. C. R. Rust (Ed.). (2000). *Bisexuality in the United States: A social science reader* (pp. 78-91). New York: Columbia University Press.

Wellings, K., Wadsworth, J., & Johnson, A. M. (1994). Sexual diversity and homosexual behaviour. In A. M. Johnson, J. Wadsworth, K. Wellings, & J. Field (Eds.), *Sexual attitudes and lifestyles* (pp. 183-224). Oxford: Blackwell Scientific Publications.

Psychological and Sociological Perspectives: Women

Bailey, J. V., Farquhar, C., Owen, C., & Whittaker, D. (2003). Sexual behaviour of lesbians and bisexual women. *Sexually Transmitted Infections, 79*(2), 147-50.

Baumeister, R. F. (2000). Gender differences in erotic plasticity: The female sex drive as socially flexible and responsive. *Psychological Bulletin, 126,* 347-374.

Blumstein, P. W., & Schwartz, P. (1974). Lesbianism and bisexuality. In E. Goode & R. Troiden (Eds.), *Sexual deviance and sexual deviants* (pp. 278-295). New York: Morrow.

Blumstein, P. W., & Schwartz, P. (1976). Bisexuality in women. *Archives of Sexual Behavior, 5*(2), 171-181.

Bressler, L. C., & Lavender, A. D. (1986). Sexual fulfillment of heterosexual, bisexual, and homosexual women. *Journal of Homosexuality, 12*(3/4), 109-122.

Diamond, L. M., & Savin-Williams, R. C. (2000). Explaining diversity in the development of same-sex sexuality among young women. *Journal of Social Issues, 56*(2), 297-313. Reprinted in L. D. Garnets & D. C. Kimmel

(Eds.). (2003). *Psychological perspectives on lesbian, gay, and bisexual experiences* (pp. 130-148). New York: Columbia University Press.

Hedblom, J. I. (1973). Dimensions of lesbian sexual experience. *Archives of Sexual Behavior, 2,* 329-341.

Hite, S. (1976). Lesbianism. In S. Hite, *The Hite report: A nationwide study of female sexuality* (pp. 389-416). New York: Dell.

Kinsey, A. C., Pomeroy, W. B., Martin, C. E., & Gebhard, P. H. (1952). Homosexual responses and contacts. In A. C. Kinsey, W. B. Pomeroy, C. E. Martin, & P. H. Gebhard, *Sexual behavior in the human female* (pp. 446-501) Philadelphia: W. B. Saunders.

Loewenstein, S. F. (1984). On the diversity of love object orientations among women. *Journal of Social Work & Human Sexuality, 3*(2-3). Reprinted in P. C. R. Rust (Ed.). (2000). *Bisexuality in the United States: A social science reader* (pp. 203-216). New York: Columbia University Press.

Rothblum, E. D. (2000). Sexual orientation and sex in women's lives: Conceptual and methodological issues. *Journal of Social Issues, 56*(2), 193-204.

Rust, P. C. (1992). The politics of sexual identity: Sexual attraction and behavior among lesbian and bisexual women. *Social Problems, 39*(4), 366-386.

Schäfer, S. (1976). Sexual and social problems of lesbians. *Journal of Sex Research, 12*(1), 50-79.

Spada, J. (1979). Women. In J. Spada, *The Spada report: The newest survey of gay male sexuality* (pp. 215-245). New York: New American Library.

Psychological and Sociological Perspectives: Men

Appleby, G. A. (2001). Ethnographic study of twenty-six gay and bisexual working-class men in Australia and New Zealand. *Journal of Gay and Lesbian Social Services: Issues in Practice, Policy & Research, 12*(3/4), 119-132.

Billy, J. O. G., Tanfer, K., Grady, W. R., & Klepinger, D. H. (1993). The sexual behavior of men in the United States. *Family Planning Perspectives, 25*(2), 52-60.

Binson, D., Michaels, S., Stall, R., Coates, T. J., Gagnon, J. H., & Catania, J. A. (1995). Prevalence and social distribution of men who have sex with men: United States and its urban centers. *Journal of Sex Research, 32*(3), 245-254.

Blumstein, P., & Schwartz, P. (1976). Bisexuality in men. *Urban Life, 5*(3), 339-358.

Carballo-Diéguez, A. (1997). Sexual research with Latino men who have sex with men. In J. Bancroft (Ed.), *Researching sexual behavior: Methodological issues* (pp. 134-144). Bloomington, IN: University of Indiana Press.

Corzine, J., & Kirby, R. (1977). Cruising the truckers: Sexual encounters in a highway rest area. *Urban Life, 6*(2), 171-192.

Doll, L. S., Petersen, L. R., White, C. R., Johnson, E. S., Ward, J. W., & The Blood Donor Study Group. (1992). Homosexually and nonhomosexually identified men who have sex with men: A behavioral comparison. *Journal of Sex Research, 29*(1), 1-14.

Fay, R. E., Turner, C. F., Klassen, A. D., Gagnon, J. H. (1989). Prevalence and patterns of same-gender sexual contact among men. *Science, 243*, 338-348.

George, S. (2001). Making sense of bisexual personal ads. *Journal of Bisexuality, 1*(4), 33-58.

Gindorf, R., & Warran, A. (1998). Bisexualities: Heterosexual contacts of "gay" men, homosexual contacts of "heterosexual" men. In E. J. Haeberle, & R. Gindorf (Eds.), *Bisexualities: The ideology and practice of sexual contact with both men and women* (pp. 213-220). New York: Continuum.

Gray, J. K. (1989). The tearoom revisited: A study of impersonal homosexual encounters in a public setting. (Doctoral dissertation, Ohio State University, 1988). *Dissertation Abstracts International, 50*(1), 264A.

Harry, J. (1990). A probability sample of gay males. *Journal of Homosexuality, 19*(1), 89-104.

Hite, S. (1981). Men who have sex with both women and men. In S. Hite, *The Hite report on male sexuality* (pp. 857-863). New York: Knopf.

Kinsey, A. C., Pomeroy, W. B., & Martin, C. E. (1948). Homosexual outlet. In A. C. Kinsey, W. B. Pomeroy, & C. E. Martin, *Sexual behavior in the human male* (pp. 610-666). Philadelphia: W. B. Saunders.

Krol, J. F. (1990). Restroom to tearoom, a cultural conversion: A note on Humphreys, Delph, and Swidler. *Deviant Behavior, 11*(3), 273-280.

Lever, J., Rogers, W. H., Carson, S., Kanouse, D. E., & Hertz, R. (1992). Behavior patterns and sexual identity of bisexual males. *Journal of Sex Research, 29*(2), 141-167. Reprinted in P. C. R. Rust (Ed.). (2000). *Bisexuality in the United States: A social science reader* (pp. 185-202). New York: Columbia University Press.

McKirnan, D. J., Stokes, J. P., Doll, L., & Burzette, R. G. (1995). Bisexually active men: Social characteristics and sexual behavior. *Journal of Sex Research, 32*(1), 65-76.

Reiss, A. J., Jr. (1961). The social integration of queers and peers. *Social Problems, 9*, 102-120.

Rogers, S. M., & Turner, C. F. (1991). Male-male sexual contact in the U.S.A.: Findings from five sample surveys, 1970-1990. *Journal of Sex Research, 28*(4), 491-519.

Ross, M. W. (1991). A taxonomy of global behavior. In R. A. P. Tielman, M. Carballo, & A. C. Hendriks (Eds.), *Bisexuality & HIV/AIDS: A global perspective* (pp. 21-26). Buffalo, NY: Prometheus.

Sandfort, T. G. M. (1997). Sampling male homosexuality. In J. Bancroft (Ed.), *Researching sexual behavior: Methodological issues* (pp. 261-275). Bloomington, IN: University of Indiana Press.

Stokes, J. P., Damon, W., & McKiman, D. J. (1997). Predictors of movement toward homosexuality: A longitudinal study of bisexual men. *Journal of Sex Research, 34*, 304-312.

Stokes, J. P., McKirnan, D. J., & Burzette, R. G. (1993). Sexual behavior, condom use, disclosure of sexuality, and stability of sexual orientation in bisexual men. *Journal of Sex Research, 30*(3), 203-213.

Stokes, J. P., Miller, R. L., & Mundhenk, R. (1998). Toward an understanding of behaviourally bisexual men: The influence of context and culture. *Canadian Journal of Human Sexuality, 7*(2), 101-113.

Taywaditep, K. J., & Stokes, J.P. (1998). Male bisexualities: A cluster analysis of men with bisexual experience. *Journal of Psychology and Human Sexuality, 10*, 15-41

Van Wyk, P. H. (1982). Developmental factors associated with heterosexual, bisexual, and homosexual outcomes. (Doctoral dissertation, Illinois Institute of Technology, 1982). *Dissertation Abstracts International, 43*(4), 1033B.

Weatherburn, P., Davies, P. M., Hunt, A. J., Coxon, A. P. M., & McManus, T. J. (1990). Heterosexual behaviour in a large cohort of homosexually active men in England and Wales. *AIDS Care, 2*(4), 319-224.

Weinberg, M. S., & Williams, C. J. (1975). Gay baths and the social organization of impersonal sex. *Social Problems, 23*(2), 124-136.

Wheeler, C. C. (1993). An exploration of the relationship of sexual identity in males to erotic fantasy. (Doctoral dissertation, New York University, 1992). *Dissertation Abstracts International, 53*(8), 4396B.

Personal and Political Perspectives

Barragan III, C. J. (1991). More than a footnote. In *Bi any other name* (pp. 17-21).

Christina, G. (1995). Bi sexuality. In *Bisexual politics* (pp. 161-166).

Farajajé-Jones, E. (2000). Loving "queer": We're all a big mix of possibilities of desire just waiting to happen. *In the Family: A Magazine for Gays, Lesbians, Bisexuals and Their Relations, 6*(1), 6-13.

Field, N. (1996). Trade secrets. In *Bisexual horizons* (pp. 133-141).

Goswami, C. (1991). My underself. In *Bi any other name* (pp. 60-63).

Hutchins, L. (1991). Love that kink. In *Bi any other name* (pp. 335-343).

Johnson, L. (1991). Making my own way. In *Bi any other name* (pp. 40-42).

Klassen, K. (1991). Talking about sex, gender, and desire. In *Bi any other name* (pp. 329-334).

Queen, C. (2002). Lesbian love in the swingin' seventies: A bisexual memoir. *Journal of Bisexuality*, 2(2/3), 193-203.

Ripley, R. (1992). The language of desire: Sexuality, identity and language. In *Closer to home* (pp. 91-102).

Stone, D. (1996). Living with the Janus people. In *Bisexual horizons* (pp. 127-132).

Tan, C. (1995). Bisexuality and S/M: The bi switch revolution. In *Bisexual politics* (pp. 167-170).

Yost, L. (1991). Bisexual tendencies. In *Bi any other name* (pp. 74-76).

BISEXUAL RELATIONSHIPS AND FAMILIES

Psychological and Sociological Perspectives: Women and Men

Constantine, L. L., & Constantine, J. M. (1974). Sexual aspects of multilateral relations. In J. V. Smith, & L. G. Smith (Eds.), *Beyond monogamy* (pp. 268-290). Baltimore: The Johns Hopkins University Press.

Dubé, E. (2000). Same- and cross-gender romantic relationships: Mediating variables between female presence and relationship quality. (Doctoral dissertation, Cornell University, Ithica, NY, 1999). *Dissertation Abstracts International*, 60(8), 4273B.

Engel, J. W., & Saracino, M. (1986). Love preferences and ideals: A comparison of homosexual, bisexual, and heterosexual groups. *Contemporary Family Therapy: An International Journal*, 8(3), 241-250.

Halpern, E. L. (1999). If love is so wonderful, what's so scary about MORE? In M. Munson, & J. P. Stelboum (Eds.), *The lesbian polyamory reader: Open relationships, non-monogamy, and casual sex* (pp. 157-164). New York: Haworth.

Labriola, K. (1999). Models of open relationships. In M. Munson, & J. P. Stelboum (Eds.), *The lesbian polyamory reader: Open relationships, non-monogamy, and casual sex* (pp. 217-226). New York: Haworth.

Matteson, D. R. (1987). The heterosexually married gay and lesbian parent. In F. W. Bozett (Ed.), *Gay and lesbian parents* (pp. 138-161). New York: Praeger.

McLean, K. (2004). Negotiating (non)monogamy: Bisexuality in intimate relationships. *Journal of Bisexuality*, 4(1/2), 83-97.

Pallotta-Chiarolli, M. (1995). Choosing not to choose: Beyond monogamy, beyond duality. In K. Lano & C. Parry (Eds.), *Breaking the barriers to desire: Polyamory, polyfidelity and non-monogamy–New approaches to multiple relationships* (pp. 41-67). Nottingham: Five Leaves Publications.

Pallotta-Chiarolli, M., & Lubowitz, S. (2003). "Outside belonging": Multi-sexual relationships as border existence. *Journal of Bisexuality*, *3*(1), 53-86.

Paul, J. P. (1987). Growing up with a gay, lesbian or bisexual parent: An exploratory study of experiences and perceptions. (Doctoral dissertation, University of California, Berkeley, 1986). *Dissertation Abstracts International*, *47*(7), 2756A.

Peplau, L. A., & Spalding, L. R. (2000). The close relationships of lesbians, gay men, and bisexuals. In C. Hendrick & S. S. Hendrick (Eds.), *Close relationships: A sourcebook* (pp. 111-123). Thousand Oaks, CA: Sage. Reprinted in L. D. Garnets & D. C. Kimmel (Eds.). (2003). *Psychological perspectives on lesbian, gay, and bisexual experiences* (pp. 449-475). New York: Columbia University Press.

Rust, P. C. (1996). Monogamy & polyamory: Relationship issues for bisexuals. In B. A. Firestein (Ed.), *Bisexuality: The psychology and politics of an invisible minority* (pp. 127-148). Thousand Oaks, CA: Sage. Reprinted in L. D. Garnets & D. C. Kimmel (Eds.). (2003). *Psychological perspectives on lesbian, gay, and bisexual experiences* (pp. 475-496). New York: Columbia University Press.

Sears, J. T. (1993-1994). Challenges for educators: Lesbian, gay, and bisexual families. *High School Journal*, *77*(1-2), 138-156.

Solot, D., & Miller, M. (2001). Unmarried bisexuals: Distinct voices on marriage and family. *Journal of Bisexuality*, *1*(4), 81-90.

Stein, T. S. (1996). Lesbian, gay, and bisexual families. In R. P. Cabaj & T. S. Stein (Eds.), *Textbook of homosexuality and mental health* (pp. 503-511). Washington, DC: American Psychiatric Press.

Psychological and Sociological Perspectives: Women

Buxton, A. P. (2004). Works in progress: How mixed-orientation couples maintain their marriages after the wives come out. *Journal of Bisexuality*, *4*(1/2), 57-82.

Coleman, E. (1985). Bisexual women in marriages. *Journal of Homosexuality*, *11*(1/2), 87-99.

Coleman, E. (1989). The married lesbian. *Marriage & Family Review*, *14*(3/4), 119-135.

Dixon, J. K. (1984). The commencement of bisexual activity in swinging married women over age thirty. *Journal of Sex Research*, *20*, 71-90.

Dixon, J. K. (1985). Sexuality and relationship changes in married females following the commencement of bisexual activity. *Journal of Homosexuality*, *11*(1/2), 115-133.

Green, G. D., & Clunis, D. M. (1988). Married lesbians. *Women & Therapy*, 8(1/2), 41-49.

Hays, D., & Samuels, A. (1989). Heterosexual women's perceptions of their marriages to bisexual or homosexual men. *Journal of Homosexuality*, 18(1/2), 81-100.

Kisber, S. L. (2000). A comparison of nonparents, parents, and prospective parents who are Jewish lesbian, bisexual, transgendered, and queer-identified women: Differences in their identities, lifestyles, families, social networks, and received social support. (Doctoral dissertation, California School of Professional Psychology, Berkeley/Alameda, 2000). *Dissertation Abstracts International*, 61(1), 536B.

Oswald, R. F. (2000). Family and friendship relationships after young women come out as bisexual or lesbian. *Journal of Homosexuality*, 38(3), 65-83.

Reinhardt, R. U. (1985). Bisexual women in heterosexual relationships: A study of psychological and sociological patterns. (Doctoral dissertation, The Professional School of Psychological Studies, San Diego, 1985). *Research Abstracts International*, 11(3), 67.

Reinhardt, R. U. (2002). Bisexual women in heterosexual relationships. *Journal of Bisexuality*, 2(2/3), 163-171.

Tuerk, C. (2000). Uncommon wisdom: Help for parents of a bisexual daughter. *In the Family: A Magazine for Gays, Lesbians, Bisexuals and Their Relations*, 5(3), 5, 25.

Psychological and Sociological Perspectives: Men

Bozett, F. W. (1982). Heterogeneous couples in heterosexual marriages: Gay men and straight women. *Journal of Marital and Family Therapy*, 8(1), 81-89.

Brownfain, J. J. (1985). A study of the married bisexual male: Paradox and resolution. *Journal of Homosexuality*, 11(1/2), 173-188.

Büntzly, G. (1993). Gay fathers in straight marriages. *Journal of Homosexuality*, 24(3/4), 107-114.

Buxton, A. P. (2001). Writing our own script: How bisexual men and their heterosexual wives maintain their marriages after disclosure. *Journal of Bisexuality*, 1(2/3), 155-189.

Coleman, E. (1985). Integration of male bisexuality and marriage. *Journal of Homosexuality*, 11(1/2), 189-208.

Deabill, G. I. (1987). *An investigation of sexual behaviors in mixed sexual orientation couples: Gay husband and straight wife.* Unpublished doctoral dissertation, Institute for Advanced Study of Human Sexuality, San Francisco.

Dixon, D. (1985). Perceived sexual satisfaction and marital happiness of bisexual and heterosexual swinging husbands. *Journal of Homosexuality*, *11*(1/2), 209-222.

Edser, S. J., & Shea, J. D. (2002). An exploratory investigation of bisexual men in monogamous, heterosexual marriages. *Journal of Bisexuality*, *2*(4), 5-43.

Gochros, J. S. (1983). When husbands come out of the closet: A study of the consequences for their wives. (Doctoral dissertation, University of Denver, 1982). *Dissertation Abstracts International*, *44*(4), 1207A.

Gochros, J. S. (1985). Wives' reactions to learning that their husbands are bisexual. *Journal of Homosexuality*, *11*(1/2), 101-113.

Gochros, J. S. (1991). Bisexuality & female partners. In R. A. P. Tielman, M. Carballo, & A. C. Hendriks (Eds.), *Bisexuality & HIV/AIDS: A global perspective* (pp. 175-186). Buffalo, NY: Prometheus.

Higgins, D. J. (2002). Gay men from heterosexual marriages: Attitudes, behaviors, childhood experiences and reasons for marriage. *Journal of Homosexuality*, *42*(4) 15-35.

Latham, J. D. (1987). Marital adjustment of heterosexually married homosexuals as explained by reasons for marrying and disclosure of sexuality to spouse. (Master's thesis, California State University, Fullerton, 1986). *Masters Abstracts International*, *25*(1), 135.

Latham, J. D., & White, G. D. (1978). Coping with homosexual expression within heterosexual marriages: Five case studies. *Journal of Sex and Marital Therapy*, *4*(3), 198-212.

Matteson, D. R. (1985). Bisexual men in marriage: Is a positive homosexual identity and stable marriage possible? *Journal of Homosexuality*, *11*(1/2), 149-171.

Peterson, L. W. (2001). The married man on line. *Journal of Bisexuality*, *1*(2/3), 191-209.

Ross, H. L. (1971). Modes of adjustment of married homosexuals. *Social Problems*, *18*, 385-393.

Ross, H. L. (1972). Odd couples: Homosexuals in heterosexual marriages. *Sexual Behavior*, *2*(7), 42-49.

Ross, M. W. (1979). Heterosexual marriage of homosexual males: Some associated factors. *Journal of Sex and Marital Therapy*, *5*, 142-150.

Ross, M. W. (1989). Married homosexual men: Prevalence and background. *Marriage & Family Review*, *14*(3/4), 35-57.

van der Geest, H. (1993). Homosexuality and marriage. *Journal of Homosexuality*, *24*(2/3), 15-123.

Wolf, T. J. (1983). Selected psychological and sociological aspects of male homosexual behavior in marriage. (Doctoral dissertation, United States In-

ternational University, 1983). *Dissertation Abstracts International*, *44*(1), 335B.
Wolf, T. J. (1985). Marriages of bisexual men. *Journal of Homosexuality*, *11*(1/2), 135-148.

Personal and Political Perspectives

Arden, K. (1996). Dwelling in the house of tomorrow: Children, young people and their bisexual parents. In *Bisexual horizons* (pp. 247-257).
Bassein, R. S. (1991). A day in the life. In *Bi any other name* (pp. 171-173).
Bear, P. B. (1997). Bi any other name. *Loving More*, *11*, 32.
Brewer, M. (1991). Two-way closet. In *Bi any other name* (pp. 140-143).
Bryant, W. (1991). Love, friendship, and sex. In *Bi any other name* (pp. 69-73).
Cade, F. (1996). Marriage and bisexuality. In *Bisexual horizons* (pp. 114-118).
Casey, N. (1997). Bisexuality: Myth understanding. *Loving More*, *11*, 21.
Fenario, J. (1996). Dating and the bisexual, single mom. *In the Family: A Magazine for Gays, Lesbians, Bisexuals and Their Relations*, *1*(3), 14-15.
Girard, C. (1991). A few brave and gifted people. In *Bi any other name* (pp. 167-170).
Glenn, R. (1991). Proud father of a bisexual son. In *Bi any other name* (pp. 254-257).
Gonsalves, S. (1992). Where healing becomes possible. In *Closer to home* (pp. 115-125).
Harris, J. (1997). Straight but not narrow: The story of a straight spouse. *In the Family: A Magazine for Gays, Lesbians, Bisexuals and Their Relations*, *2*(4), 19-20.
Hutchins, L. (1997). Bisexuality. *Loving More*, *11*, 8-10.
Jones, B., & Jones, P. (1991). Growing up with a bisexual dad. In *Bi any other name* (pp. 159-166).
Kalamka, J. (1999, Summer). We are family? *Anything That Moves*, *(20)*, 32-35.
Keppel, B. (1999, Summer). Swimming upstream: Queer families and change. *Anything That Moves*, *(20)*, 12-14.
Key, M. (1991). Never, never boring. In *Bi any other name* (pp. 174-176).
Miller, M., & Solot, D. (1999). The fine art of white picket fence-sitting: Bisexuality, marriage, and family diversity. *Anything That Moves*, *(20)*, 20-22.
Montgomery, M. S. (1997). The marrying kind: Bisexual life, partnered identity. *Journal of Gay, Lesbian, and Bisexual Identity*, *2*(1), 77-82.
Nachama. (1991). Double quest. In *Bi any other name* (pp. 79-82).

Norrgard, L. (1991). Can bisexuals be monogamous? In *Bi any other name* (pp. 281-284).

Peter, L., & Owens, R. (2001). Forget 2001, It's 20/10 for us. *Journal of Bisexuality, 1*(1), 71-86.

Randolph, E. (2001). Family secrets, or . . . how to become a bisexual alien without really trying. In M. Bernstein, & R. Reimann (Eds.), *Queer families, queer politics: Challenging culture and the state* (pp. 104-111). New York: Columbia University Press.

Reinhardt, R. U. (2001). From Europe with love: A bisexual biography. *Journal of Bisexuality, 1*(1), 163-172.

Rose, S. (1996). Against marriage. In *Bisexual horizons* (pp. 119-121).

Silver, M. (1997). Was Oprah right? *Loving More, 11*, 4-7.

Silver, N. (1992). Coming out as a heterosexual. In *Closer to home* (pp. 35-46).

Trnka, S. (1992). "A pretty good bisexual kiss there . . ." In *Closer to home* (pp. 103-113).

Weise, E. R. (1991). Bisexuality, *The Rocky Horror Picture Show*, and me. In *Bi any other name* (pp. 134-139).

Yoshizaki, A. (1991). I am who I am–A married bisexual teacher. In *Bi any other name* (pp. 25-26).

BISEXUAL, LESBIAN, AND GAY YOUTH

Psychological and Sociological Perspectives: Bisexual Youth

Hoburg, R., Konik, J., Williams, M., & Crawford, M. (2004). Bisexuality among self-identified heterosexual college students. *Journal of Bisexuality, 4*(1/2), 25-36.

McLean, K. (2001). Living life in the double closet: Bisexual youth speak out. *Hecate, 27*(1), 109-118.

Pope, R. L., & Reynolds, A. L. (1991). Including bisexuality: It's more than just a label. In N. J. Evans, & V. A. Wall (Eds.), *Beyond tolerance: Gays, lesbians, and bisexuals on campus* (pp. 205-212). Alexandria, VA: American College Personnel Association.

Russell, S. T., & Seif, H. (2002). Bisexual female adolescents: A critical analysis of past research, and results from a national survey. *Journal of Bisexuality, 2*(2/3), 73-94.

Identity and Developmental Issues of LGB Youth

D'Augelli, A. R. (1996). Enhancing the development of lesbian, gay, and bisexual youths. In E. D. Rothblum, & L. A. Bond (Eds.), *Preventing heterosexism and homophobia* (pp. 124-150). Thousand Oaks, CA: Sage.

D'Augelli, A. R. (1996). Lesbian, gay, and bisexual development during adolescence and young adulthood. In R. P. Cabaj & T. S. Stein (Eds.), *Textbook of homosexuality and mental health* (pp. 267-288). Washington, DC:
American Psychiatric Press.

Diamond, L. M. (1998). The development of sexual orientation among adolescent and young adult women. *Developmental Psychology, 34,* 1085-1095.

Dube, E. M., & Savin-Williams, R. C. (1999). Sexual identity development
among ethnic sexual-minority male youths. *Developmental Psychology,
35,* 1389-1398.

Fisher, B., & Akman, J. S. (2002). Normal development in sexual minority
youth. In B. E. Jones, & M. J. Hill (Eds.), *Mental health issues in lesbian,
gay, bisexual, and transgender communities* (pp. 1-16). Washington, DC:
American Psychiatric Publishing.

Floyd, F. J., Stein, T. S., Harter, K. S. M., Allison, A., & Nye, C. L. (1999).
Gay, lesbian, and bisexual youths: Separation-individuation, parental attitudes, identity consolidation, and well-being. *Journal of Youth and Adolescence, 28*(6).

Kivel, B. D. (1996). In on the outside, out on the inside: Lesbian/gay/bisexual
youth, identity and leisure. (Doctoral dissertation, University of Georgia,
1996). *Dissertation Abstracts International, 57*(3), 1322A.

Remafedi, G., Resnick, M., Blum, R., & Harris, L. (1992). Demography of
sexual orientation in adolescents. *Pediatrics, 89*(4), 714-721.

Savin-Williams, R. C. (1995). Lesbian, gay male, and bisexual adolescents. In
A. R. D'Augelli & C. J. Patterson (Eds.), *Lesbian, gay, and bisexual identi-
ties over the lifespan: Psychological perspectives* (pp. 165-189). New
York: Oxford University Press.

Savin-Williams, R. C. (1996). Ethnic- and sexual-minority youth. In R. C.
Savin-Williams & K. M. Cohen (Eds.), *The lives of lesbians, gays, and bisexuals: Children to adults* (pp. 393-415). Fort Worth, TX: Harcourt Brace.

Savin-Williams, R. C. (1996). Self-labeling and disclosure among gay, lesbian, & bisexual youths. In J. Laird & R-J. Green (Eds.), *Lesbians and gays
in couples & families: A handbook for therapists* (pp. 153-182). San Francisco: Jossey-Bass.

Savin-Williams, R. C. (2001). A critique of research on sexual-minority
youths. *Journal of Adolescence, 24,* 5-13.

Savin-Williams, R. C., & Diamond, L. M. (2000). Sexual identity trajectories
among sexual-minority youths: Gender comparisons. *Archives of Sexual
Behavior, 29*(6), 607-627.

Stewart, F. J., Mischewski, A., & Smith, A. M. A. (2000). 'I want to do what I
want to do': Young adults resisting sexual identities. *Critical Public
Health, 10*(4), 409-422.

LGB Youth and Their Families

D'Augelli, A. R., Hershberger, S. L., & Pilkington, N. W. (1998). Lesbian, gay, and bisexual youth and their families: Disclosure of sexual orientation and its consequences. *American Journal of Orthopsychiatry, 68*(3), 361-371.
Savin-Williams, R. C. (1998). Lesbian, gay, and bisexual youths' relationships with their parents. In C. J. Patterson & A. R. D'Augelli (Eds.), *Lesbian, gay, and bisexual identities in families* (pp. 75-78). New York: Oxford University Press. Reprinted in L. D. Garnets & D. C. Kimmel (Eds.). (2003). *Psychological perspectives on lesbian, gay, and bisexual experiences* (pp. 299- 326). New York: Columbia University Press.
Savin-Williams, R. C. (1998). The disclosure to families of same sex attractions by lesbian, gay, and bisexual youths. *Journal of Research on Adolescence, 8*(1), 49-68.

LGB Youth and Relationships

Diamond, L. M. (2000). Sexual identity, attractions, and behavior among young sexual-minority women over a 2-year period. *Developmental Psychology, 36*(2), 241-250.
Diamond, L. M., Savin-Williams, R. C., & Dube, E. M. (1999). Sex, dating, passionate friendships, and romance: Intimate peer relations among lesbian, gay, and bisexual adolescents. In E. W. Furman & E. B. B. Brown (Eds.), *The Development of Romantic Relationships in Adolescence* (pp. 175-210). New York: Cambridge University Press.
Russell, S. T., Driscoll, A. K., & Truong, N. (2002). Adolescent same-sex romantic attractions and relationships: Implications for substance use and abuse. *American Journal of Public Health, 92*(2), 198-202.

LGB Youth in High School and College

Evans, N. J., & D'Augelli, A. R. (1996). Lesbians, gay men, and bisexual people in college. In R. C. Savin-Williams, & K. M. Cohen (Eds.), *The lives of lesbians, gays, and bisexuals: Children to adults* (pp. 201-226). Fort Worth, TX: Harcourt Brace.
Green, B. C. (1998). Thinking about students who do not identify as gay, lesbian, or bisexual, but . . . *Journal of American College Health, 47*(2), 89-91.
Harbeck, K. M. (1993). Invisible no more: Addressing needs of gay, lesbian and bisexual youth and their advocates. *High School Journal, 77*(1-2), 169-176.

Jackson, D. F. (1999). Experiences of lesbian, gay, and bisexual youth in high school settings. (Doctoral dissertation, DePaul University, 1999). *Dissertation Abstracts International, 60*(3), 1303B.

Kardia, D. B. (1996). Diversity's closet: Student attitudes toward lesbians, gay men, and bisexual people on a multicultural campus. (Doctoral dissertation, University of Michigan, 1996). *Dissertation Abstracts International, 57*(3), 1090A.

Knight, C. E. (2000). The Triangle Program: Experiences of lesbian, bisexual and gay students in the classroom. (Master's thesis, University of Toronto, Ontario, Canada, 2000). *Master's Abstracts International, 38*(6), 1435.

Uribe, V., & Harbeck, K. M. (1991). Addressing the needs of lesbian, gay, and bisexual youth: The origins of Project 10 and school-based intervention. *Journal of Homosexuality, 22*(3/4), 9-28.

Nichols, S. L. (1999). Gay, lesbian, and bisexual youth: Understanding diversity and promoting tolerance in schools. *Elementary School Journal, 99*(5).

Personal and Political Perspectives

Arnaoot, N. (1996). Me and my gender(s). In *Generation Q* (pp. 221-223).

Arnaoot, N. (1996). Stone. In *Generation Q* (pp. 146-148).

Cooper, C. (1996). Fitting. In *Generation Q* (pp. 59-64).

Doza, C. (1995). Bloodlove. In *Listen up: Voices from the next feminist generation* (pp. 249-257).

Gilbert, L. (1995). You're not the type. In *Listen up: Voices from the next feminist generation* (pp. 102-112).

McDade, P. (1996). A difficult floating garden. In *Generation Q* (pp. 102-105).

Medina, D. (1996). Tune in, get off, come out: California dreamin' and my age of Aqueerius. In *Generation Q* (pp. 59-64).

Pemberton, S. (1996). *Rocky Horror* schoolgirl. In *Generation Q* (pp. 69-72).

OLDER BISEXUAL WOMEN AND BISEXUAL MEN

Psychological and Sociological Perspectives

Boxer, A. M. (1997). Gay, lesbian, and bisexual aging into the twenty-first century: An overview and introduction. *Journal of Gay, Lesbian, & Bisexual Identity, 3* (3/4), 187-197.

Linsk, N. L. (1997). Experience of older gay and bisexual men living with HIV/AIDS. *Journal of Gay, Lesbian, & Bisexual Identity, 3* (3/4), 265-285.

Weinberg, M. S., Williams, C. J., & Pryor, D. W. (2001). Bisexuals at midlife: Commitment, salience, and identity. *Journal of Contemporary Ethnography*, *30*(2), 180-208.

Personal and Political Perspectives

Keppel, B. (1991). Gray-haired and above suspicion. In *Bi any other name* (pp. 154-158).
Utz, C. (1991). Ninety-three people = 110% acceptance. In *Bi any other name* (pp. 22-24).

BISEXUALITY AND TRANSGENDER PERSONS AND IDENTITIES

Psychological and Sociological Perspectives

Bentler, P. M. (1976). A typology of transsexualism: Gender identity theory and data. *Archives of Sexual Behavior, 5*, 567-584.
Chivers, M. L., & Bailey, J. M. (2000). Sexual orientation of female-to-male transsexuals: A comparison of homosexual and nonhomosexual types. *Archives of Sexual Behavior, 29*(3), 259-278.
Coleman, E., Bockting, W. O., & Gooren, L. (1993). Homosexual and bisexual identity in sex-reassigned female-to-male transsexuals. *Archives of Sexual Behavior, 22*(1), 37-50.
Denny, D., & Green, J. (1996). Gender identity and bisexuality. In B. A. Firestein (Ed.), *Bisexuality: The psychology and politics of an invisible minority* (pp. 84-102). Thousand Oaks, CA: Sage.
Devor, H. (1993). Sexual orientation identities, attractions, and practices of female-to-male transsexuals. *Journal of Sex Research, 30*(4), 303-315.
Green, J. (1998). FTM: An emerging voice. In D. Denny (Ed.), *Current concepts in transgender identity* (pp. 145-162). New York: Garland.
Mathy, R. M. (2001). A nonclinical comparison of transgender identity and sexual orientation: A framework for multicultural competence. *Journal of Psychology and Human Sexuality, 13*(1), 31-54.
Pauly, I. B. (1990). Gender identity and sexual preference. In D. Denny (Ed.), *Current concepts in transgender identity* (pp. 237-248). New York: Garland.
Tarver, D. E. (2002). Transgender mental health: The intersection of race, sexual orientation, and gender identity. *Review of Psychiatry, 21*(4), 93-108.
Wilchesky, M., Cote, H., & Betito, L. (1994). Plasticity or stability of sexual orientation in male transsexuals. *Canadian Journal of Human Sexuality, 3*(4), 327-332.

Personal and Political Perspectives

Antoniou, L. (1997). Antivenom for the soul. In C. Queen, & L. Schimel (Eds.), *Pomosexuals: Challenging assumptions about gender and sexuality* (pp. 114-121). San Francisco: Cleis Press.

Franek, H. (1998, Summer). Talking about the issues no one's expressing: Telling it like it is in the world of bi-trans romance. *Anything That Moves, 17,* 28-31.

Harrison, D. (1997). The personals. In C. Queen, & L. Schimel (Eds.), *Pomosexuals: Challenging assumptions about gender and sexuality* (pp. 129-137). San Francisco: Cleis Press.

Hemmings, C. (1996). From lesbian nation to transgender liberation: A bisexual feminist perspective. *Journal of Gay, Lesbian, & Bisexual Identity, 1*(1), 37-60.

Martin-Damon, K. (1995). Essay for the inclusion of transsexuals. In *Bisexual politics* (pp. 241-250).

Michaela-Gonzalez, A. (1998, Summer). It's what you think you see that counts: True tales from the edges of the bi-trans continuum. *Anything That Moves, 17,* 22-25.

Miller, M. (1998, Spring). Transman Matt Rice on the new queer identity. *Anything That Moves, (16),* 42-45.

O'Connor, R. (1996). The transgender identity as a political challenge. In *Bisexual horizons* (pp. 243-246).

Valerio, M. W. (1998, Summer). The joker is wild: Changing sex and other crimes of passion. *Anything That Moves, 17,* 32-36.

Wilchins, R. A. (1997). Lines in the sand, cries of desire. In C. Queen & L. Schimel (Eds.), *Pomosexuals: Challenging assumptions about gender and sexuality* (pp. 138-149). San Francisco: Cleis Press.

BISEXUALITY AND ETHNIC, RACIAL, AND CULTURAL DIVERSITY

Overview

Collins, J. F. (2000). Biracial-bisexual individuals: Identity coming of age. *International Journal of Sexuality & Gender Studies, 5*(3), 221-253.

Collins, J. F. (2004). The intersection of race and bisexuality: A critical overview of the literature and past, present, and future directions of the 'Borderlands.' *Journal of Bisexuality 4*(1/2), 99-116.

Croom, G. L. (2000). Lesbian, gay, and bisexual people of color: A challenge to representative sampling in empirical research. In B. Greene & G. L.

Croom (Eds.), *Education, research, and practice in lesbian, gay, bisexual, and transgendered psychology: A resource manual* (pp. 263-281). Thousand Oaks, CA: Sage.

Dworkin, S. (2002). Biracial, bicultural, bisexual: Bisexuality and multiple identities. *Journal of Bisexuality, 2*(4), 93-107.

Fukuyama, M. A., & Ferguson, A. D. (2000). Lesbian, gay, and bisexual people of color: Understanding cultural complexity and managing multiple oppressions. In R. M. Perez, K. A. DeBord, & K. J. Bieschke (Eds.), *Handbook of counseling and psychotherapy with lesbian, gay, and bisexual clients* (pp. 81-105). Washington, DC: American Psychological Association.

Manalansan, M. F. (1996). Double minorities: Latino, Black, and Asian who have sex with men. R. C. Savin-Williams & K. M. Cohen (Eds.), *The lives of lesbians, gays, and bisexuals: Children to adults* (pp. 393-415). Fort Worth, TX: Harcourt Brace.

Rust, P. C. (1996). Managing multiple identities: Diversity among bisexual women and men. In B. A. Firestein (Ed.), *Bisexuality: The psychology and politics of an invisible minority* (pp. 53-83). Thousand Oaks, CA: Sage.

Smith, A. (1997). Cultural diversity and the coming-out process: Implications for clinical practice. In B. Greene (Ed.), *Ethnic and cultural diversity among lesbians and gay men* (pp. 279-300). Thousand Oaks, CA: Sage.

Steinhouse, K. (2001). Bisexual women: Considerations of race, social justice and community building. *Journal of Progressive Human Services, 12*(2), 5-25.

Bisexuality and African-American Women and Men

Bennett, M., & Battle, J. (2001). "We can see them, but we can't hear them": LGBT members of African American families. M. Bernstein & R. Reimann (Eds.), *Queer families, queer politics: Challenging culture and the state* (pp. 53-67). New York: Columbia University Press.

Carroll, T. (1996). *Invisible sissy: The politics of masculinity in African American bisexual narrative.* In D. E. Hall & M. Pramaggiore (Eds.), *RePresenting bisexualities: Subjects and cultures of fluid desire* (pp. 180-204). New York: New York University Press.

Connerly, G. (1996). The politics of Black lesbian, gay, and bisexual identity. In B. Beemyn & M. Eliason (Eds.), *Queer studies: A lesbian, gay, bisexual, and transgender anthology* (pp. 133-145). New York: New York University Press.

Croom, G. L. (1998). The effects of a consolidated versus nonconsolidated identity on expectations of African-American lesbians selecting mates: A pilot study. (Doctoral dissertation, Illinois School of Professional Psychology, 1993). *Dissertation Abstracts International, 58*(12), 6804B.

Cutts, R. N. (1999). Sexual orientation and racial identity formation in African-American men who engage in same-sex sexual behavior. (Doctoral dissertation, California School of Professional Psychology, Los Angeles, 1998). *Dissertation Abstracts International, 60*(1), 362B.

Farrell, L. D. (2002). African-American gay and bisexual men: Racial identity, sexual orientation, and self-esteem. (Doctoral dissertation, Boston University, 2002). *Dissertation Abstracts International, 63*(2), 1079B.

Greene, B. (2000). African American lesbian and bisexual women. *Journal of Social Issues, 56*(2), 239-250.

Ingram, D. M. (1999). Same gender sexually active Black/African women: Sexual identities, sexual orientations, coping styles, and depression. (Doctoral dissertation, California School of Professional Psychology, Berkeley/Alameda, 1999). *Dissertation Abstracts International, 60*(2), 831B.

Jones, B. E. (1996). African American lesbians, gay men, and bisexuals. In R. P. Cabaj & T. S. Stein (Eds.), *Textbook of homosexuality and mental health* (pp. 549-561). Washington, DC: American Psychiatric Press.

Peterson, J. L. (1992). Black men and their same-sex desires and behaviors. In G. H. Herdt (Ed.), *Gay culture in America: Essays from the field* (pp. 147-164). Boston: Beacon Press.

Wekker, G. (1993). Mati-ism and Black lesbianism: Two idealtypical expressions of female homosexuality in Black communities of the Diaspora. *Journal of Homosexuality, 23*(2/3), 145-158.

Bisexuality and Asian/Pacific Islander-American Women and Men

Chan, C. S. (1995). Issues of sexual identity in an ethnic minority: The case of Chinese American lesbians, gay men, and bisexual people. In A. R. D'Augelli, & C. J. Patterson (Eds.), *Lesbian, gay, and bisexual identities over the lifespan: Psychological perspectives* (pp. 87-101). New York: Oxford University Press.

Liu, P. & Chan, C. S. (1996). Lesbian, gay, and bisexual Asian Americans and their families. In J. Laird & R-J. Green (Eds.), *Lesbians and gays in couples and families: A handbook for therapists* (pp. 137-152). San Francisco: Jossey-Bass.

Masequesmay, G. (2001). Becoming queer and Vietnamese American: Negotiating multiple identities in an ethnic support group of lesbians, bisexual women, and female-to-male transgenders. (Doctoral dissertation, University of California, Los Angeles, 2001). *Dissertation Abstracts International, 61*(12), 4959A.

Minemura, E. (1997). *Asian Pacific Islander lesbian and bisexual women in North America: Activism and politics.* (Master's thesis, Michigan State University, 1996). *Masters Abstracts International, 35*(1), 79.

Tsang, D. C. (1996). Notes on queer 'n' virtual sex. In R. Leong (Ed.), *Asian American sexualities: Dimensions of the gay and lesbian experience* (pp. 153-162). New York: Routledge.

Thompson, B. (2000). Fence sitters, switch hitters, and bi-bi girls: An exploration of Hapa and bisexual identities. *Frontiers: A Journal of Women Studies, 21*(1/2), 171-180.

Bisexuality and Latino(a)/Hispanic-American Women and Men

Almaguer, T. (1993). Chicano men: A cartography of homosexual identity and behavior. In H. Abelove, M. A. Barale, & D. M. Halperin (Eds.), *The lesbian and gay studies reader* (pp. 255-273). New York: Routledge.

Alsonso, A. M., & Koreck, M. T. (1993). Silences: "Hispanics," AIDS, and sexual practices. In H. Abelove, M. A. Barale, & D. M. Halperin (Eds.), *The lesbian and gay studies reader* (pp. 110-126). New York: Routledge.

Carballo-Diéguez, A., & Dolezal, C. (1994). Contrasting types of Puerto Rican men who have sex with men (MSM). *Journal of Psychology & Human Sexuality, 6*(4), 41-67.

Carballo-Diéguez, A. (1995). The sexual identity and behavior of Puerto Rican men who have sex with men. In G. M. Herek, & B. Greene (Eds.), *AIDS, identity, and community: The HIV epidemic and lesbians & gay men* (pp. 105-114). Thousand Oaks, CA: Sage.

Carrier, J. M. (1976). Cultural factors affecting urban Mexican male homosexual behavior. *Archives of Sexual Behavior, 5*, 103-124.

González, F. J., & Espín, O. M. (1996). Latino men, Latina women, and homosexuality. In R. P. Cabaj & T. S. Stein (Eds.), *Textbook of homosexuality and mental health* (pp. 583-601). Washington, DC: American Psychiatric Press.

Morales, E. S. (1996). Gender roles among Latino gay and bisexual men: Implications for family and couple relationships. In J. Laird & R-J. Green (Eds.) *Lesbians and gays in couples and families: A handbook for therapists* (pp. 272-297). San Francisco: Jossey-Bass.

Zamora-Hernandez, C. E., & Patterson, D. G. (1996). Homosexually active Latino men: Issues for social work practice. In John F. Longres (Ed.), *Men of color: A context for service to homosexually active men* (pp. 69-91). New York: Harrington Park Press.

Bisexuality and Native-American Women and Men

Callender, C., & Kochems, L. M. (1985). Men and not-men: Male gender-mixing statuses and homosexuality. *Journal of Homosexuality, 11*(3-4), 165-178.

Kochems, L. M., & Jacobs, S.-E. (1997). Gender statuses, gender features, and gender/sex categories: New perspectives on an old paradigm. In S. E. Jacobs, W. Thomas, & S. Lang (Eds.), *Two-Spirit people: Native American gender identity, sexuality, and spirituality* (pp. 255-264). Urbana, IL: University of Illinois Press.

Lang, S. (1997). Various kinds of Two-Spirit people: Gender variance and homosexuality in Native American Communities. In S. E. Jacobs, W. Thomas, & S. Lang (Eds.), *Two-Spirit people: Native American gender identity, sexuality, and spirituality* (pp. 100-118). Urbana, IL: University of Illinois Press.

Saewyc, E. M., Skay, C. L., Bearinger, L. H., Blum, R. W., & Resnick, M. D. (1998). Demographics of sexual orientation among American Indian adolescents. *American Journal of Orthopsychiatry, 68*(4), 590-600.

Tafoya, T. N. (1996). Native two-spirit people. In R. P. Cabaj & T. S. Stein (Eds.), *Textbook of homosexuality and mental health* (pp. 603-617). Washington, DC: American Psychiatric Press.

Tafoya, T. N. (1997). Native gay and lesbian issues: The two-spirited. In B. Greene (Ed.), *Ethnic and cultural diversity among lesbians and gay men* (pp. 1-9). Thousand Oaks, CA: Sage. Reprinted in L. D. Garnets & D. C. Kimmel (Eds.). (2003). *Psychological perspectives on lesbian, gay, and bisexual experiences* (pp. 401-409). New York: Columbia University Press.

Thomas, W. (1997). Navajo cultural constructions of gender and sexuality. In S. E. Jacobs, W. Thomas, & S. Lang (Eds.), *Two-spirit people: Native American gender identity, sexuality, and spirituality* (pp. 156-173). Urbana, IL: University of Illinois Press.

Williams, W. L. (1996). Two-spirit persons: Gender nonconformity among Native American and Native Hawaiian youths. In R. C. Savin-Williams & K. M. Cohen (Eds.), *The lives of lesbians, gays, and bisexuals: Children to adults* (pp. 416-435). Ft. Worth, TX: Harcourt Brace.

Bisexuality and Homosexuality in the Anthropological Literature

Adam, B. D. (1985). Age, structure, and sexuality: Reflections of the anthropological evidence on homosexual relations. *Journal of Homosexuality, 11*(3/4), 19-34.

Blackwood, E. (1985). Breaking the mirror: The construction of lesbianism and the anthropological discourse on homosexuality. *Journal of Homosexuality, 11*(3/4), 1-18.

Carrier, J. M. (1980). Homosexual behavior in cross-cultural perspective. In J. Marmor (Ed.), *Homosexual behavior: A modern reappraisal* (pp. 100-122). New York: Basic Books.

Davenport, W. (1977). Sex in cross-cultural perspective. In F. A. Beach (Ed.), *Human sexuality in four perspectives* (pp. 115-163). Baltimore: Johns Hopkins University Press.

Herdt, G. H. (1984). A comment on cultural attributes and fluidity of bisexuality. *Journal of Homosexuality, 10*(3/4), 53-62.

Herdt, G. H. (1990). Developmental discontinuities and sexual orientation across cultures. In D. P. McWhirter, S. A. Sanders, & J. M. Reinisch (Eds.), *Homosexuality/heterosexuality: Concepts of sexual orientation* (pp. 208-236). New York: Oxford University Press.

Herdt, G. J. (1991). Commentary on status of sex research: Cross-cultural implications of sexual development. *Journal of Psychology & Human Sexuality, 4*(1), 5-12.

Herdt, G. H. (1996). Issues in the cross-cultural study of homosexuality. In R. P. Cabaj & T. S. Stein (Eds.), *Textbook of homosexuality and mental health* (pp. 65-82). Washington, DC: American Psychiatric Press.

Herdt, G., & Boxer, A. (1995). Bisexuality: Toward a comparative theory of identities and culture. In R. G. Parker, & J. H. Gagnon (Eds.), *Conceiving sexuality: Approaches to sex research in a postmodern world* (pp. 69-83). New York: Routledge.

Murray, S. O. (1992). Homosexuality in cross-cultural perspective. In S. O. Murray (Ed.), *Oceanic homosexualities* (pp. xiii-xi). New York: Garland.

Weinrich, J. D., & Williams, W. L. (1991). Strange customs, familiar lives: Homosexualities in other cultures. In J. D. Weinrich & J. C. Gonsiorek (Eds.), *Homosexuality: Research implications for public policy* (pp. 44-59). Newbury Park, CA: Sage.

Bisexuality in Africa

Aina, T. A. (1991). Patterns of bisexuality in Sub-Saharan Africa. In R. A. P. Tielman, M. Carballo, & A. C. Hendriks (Eds.), *Bisexuality and HIV/AIDS: A global perspective* (pp. 81-90). Buffalo, NY: Prometheus.

Gay, J. (1985). "Mummies and babies" and friends and lovers in Lesotho. *Journal of Homosexuality, 11*(3/4), 97-116.

Stobie, C. (2003). Reading bisexualities from a South African perspective. *Journal of Bisexuality, 3*(1), 33-52.

Bisexuality in Asia and the Pacific Islands

Davenport, W. (1965). Sexual patterns and their regulation in a society of the Southwest Pacific. In F. A. Beach (Ed.), *Sex and behavior* (pp. 164-207). New York: John Wiley & Sons.

De Cecco, J. P. (1998). Bisexuality and discretion: The case of Pakistan. In E. J. Haeberle & R. Gindorf (Eds.), *Bisexualities: The ideology and practice of sexual contact with both men and women* (pp. 152-156). New York: Continuum.

Gray, J. P. (1985). Growing yams and men: An interpretation of Kimam male ritualized homosexual behavior. *Journal of Homosexuality*, *11*(3/4), 55-68.

Harada, M. (2001). Japanese male gay and bisexual identity. *Journal of Homosexuality*, *42*(2), 77-100.

Jenkins, C. L. (1996). The homosexual context of heterosexual practice in Papua New Guinea. In P. Aggleton (Ed.), *Bisexualities and AIDS: International perspectives* (pp. 191-206). London: Taylor & Francis.

Khan, S. (1996). Under the blanket: Bisexualities and AIDS in India. In P. Aggleton (Ed.), *Bisexualities and AIDS: International perspectives* (pp. 161-177). London: Taylor & Francis.

Khan, S. (2001). Culture, sexualities, and identities: Men who have sex with men in India. *Journal of Homosexuality*, 40(3/4), 99-115.

Knauft, B. M. (1986). Text and social practice: Narrative "longing" and bisexuality among the Gebusi of New Guinea. *Ethos*, *14*(3), 252-281.

Kumar, B. (1991). Patterns of bisexuality in India. In R. A. P. Tielman, M. Carballo, & A. C. Hendriks (Eds.), *Bisexuality and HIV/AIDS: A global perspective* (pp. 91-96). Buffalo, NY: Prometheus.

Oetomo, D. (1991). Patterns of bisexuality in Indonesia. In R. A. P. Tielman, M. Carballo, & A. C. Hendriks (Eds.), *Bisexuality and HIV/AIDS: A global perspective* (pp. 119-126). Buffalo, NY: Prometheus.

Sittitrai, W., Brown, T., & Virulrak, S. (1991). Patterns of bisexuality in Thailand. In R. A. P. Tielman, M. Carballo, & A. C. Hendriks (Eds.), *Bisexuality and HIV/AIDS: A global perspective* (pp. 97-118). Buffalo, NY: Prometheus.

Tan, M. L. Silahis: Looking for the missing Filipino bisexual male. (1996). In P. Aggleton (Ed.), *Bisexualities and AIDS: International perspectives* (pp. 207-224). London: Taylor & Francis.

Wong, J. (1998). Bisexuality in early Imperial China: An introductory overview. In E. J. Haeberle & R. Gindorf (Eds.), *Bisexualities: The ideology and practice of sexual contact with both men and women* (pp. 140-151). New York: Continuum.

Bisexuality in Mexico, Central America and South America

Carrier, J. M. (1985). Mexican male bisexuality. *Journal of Homosexuality*, *11*(1/2), 75-86.

Chiñas, B. N. (1995). Isthmus Zapotec attitudes toward sex and gender anomalies. In S. O. Murray (Ed.), *Latin American male homosexualities* (pp. 293-302). Albuquerque, NM: University of New Mexico Press.

de Moya, E. A., & García, R. (1996). AIDS and the enigma of bisexuality in the Dominican Republic. In P. Aggleton (Ed.), *Bisexualities and AIDS: International perspectives* (pp. 121-135). London: Taylor & Francis.

García, M. d. L. G., Valdespino, J., Izazola, J., Palacios, M., & Sepúlveda, J. (1991). Bisexuality in Mexico: Current perspectives. In R. A. P. Tielman, M. Carballo, & A. C. Hendriks (Eds.), *Bisexuality & HIV/AIDS: A global perspective* (pp. 41-58). Buffalo, NY: Prometheus.

Mendès-Leité, R. (1993). A game of appearances: The "ambigusexuality" in Brazilian culture of sexuality. *Journal of Homosexuality, 25*(3), 271-282.

Parker, R. (1985). Masculinity, femininity, and homosexuality: On the anthropological interpretation of sexual meanings in Brazil. *Journal of Homosexuality, 11*(3/4), 155-163.

Parker, R. (1989). Youth, identity, and homosexuality: The changing shape of sexual life in contemporary Brazil. *Journal of Homosexuality, 17*(3/4), 269-289.

Prieur, A. (1998). Machos and mayates: Masculinity and bisexuality. In A. Prieur, *Mema's house, Mexico City: On transvestites, queens, and machos* (pp. 179-233). Chicago: University of Chicago Press.

Schifter, J., Madrigal, J., & Aggleton, P. (1996). Bisexual communities and cultures in Costa Rica. In P. Aggleton (Ed.), *Bisexualities and AIDS: International perspectives* (pp. 99-120). London: Taylor & Francis.

Personal and Political Perspectives

Acharya, L., Amita, A., Doctor, F., & Gogia. (1995). "Purifying" the (identi)ghee: South Asian feminists *Gup-shup*. In *Plural desires* (pp. 101-118).

Alexander, C. (1991). Affirmation: Bisexual Mormon. In *Bi any other name* (pp. 193-197).

Barlow, V. (1996). Bisexuality and feminism: One Black women's perspective. In *Bisexual horizons* (pp. 38-40).

Blasingame, B. (1991). The palmist knew. In *Bi any other name* (pp. 144-146).

Chaudhary, K. (1993). The scent of roses. In R. Ratti (Ed.), *A lotus of another color: An unfolding of the South Asian gay and lesbian experience* (pp. 145-150). Boston: Alyson.

Chaudhary, K. (1993). Some thoughts on bisexuality. In R. Ratti (Ed.), *A lotus of another color: An unfolding of the South Asian gay and lesbian experience* (pp. 54-58). Boston: Alyson.

Chen, S. W.–Andy. (1991). A man, a woman, attention. In *Bi any other name* (pp. 179-180).

Choe, M. M. (1992). Our selves, growing whole. In *Closer to home* (pp. 17-26).

Dajenya. (1991). Sisterhood crosses gender preference lines. In *Bi any other name* (pp. 247-251).

Fehr, T. C. (1995). Accepting my inherent duality. In *Plural desires* (pp. 128-129).

Gollain, F. (1996). Bisexuality in the Arab world: An interview with Muhammed. In *Bisexual horizons* (pp. 58-61).

Gorlin, R. (1991). The voice of a wandering Jewish bisexual. In *Bi any other name* (pp. 252-253).

Jadallah, H., & Saad, P. (1995). A conversation about the Arab Lesbian and Bisexual Women's Network. In *Plural desires* (pp. 252-259).

Kaahumanu, L. (1991). Hapa haole wahine. In *Bi any other name* (pp. 306- 325).

Lakshmi & Arka. (1993). Extended family. In R. Ratti (Ed.), *A lotus of another color: An unfolding of the South Asian gay and lesbian experience* (pp. 265-278). Boston: Alyson.

Lee, J. Y. (1995). Beyond bean counting. In *Listen up: Voices from the next feminist generation* (pp. 205-211).

Leyva, O. (1991). ¿Que es un bisexual? In *Bi any other name* (pp. 201-202).

Matsunaga, K. (1998). A bisexual life. In B. Summerhawk, C. McMahill, & D. McDonald (Eds.), *Queer Japan: Personal stories of Japanese lesbians, gays, transsexuals, and bisexuals* (pp. 37-45). Norwich, VT: New Victoria.

N. (1996). Passing: Pain or privilege? What the bisexual community can learn from the Jewish experience. In *Bisexual horizons* (pp. 32-37).

Paul. (1996). On being bisexual and black in Britain. In *Bisexual horizons* (pp. 95- 99).

Pollon, Z. (1995). Naming her destiny: June Jordan speaks on bisexuality. In *Plural desires* (pp. 77-82).

Prabhudas, Y. (1996). Bisexuals and people of mixed-race: Arbiters of change. In *Bisexual horizons* (pp. 30-31).

Reichler, R. (1991). A question of invisibility. In *Bi any other name* (pp. 77-78).

Rios, J. (1991). What do Indians think about? In *Bi any other name* (pp. 37-39).

Silver, A. (1991). Worth the balancing. In *Bi any other name* (pp. 27-28).

Som, I. C.-L. (1995). The queer kitchen. In *Plural desires* (pp. 84-88).

Uwano, K. (1991). Bi-loveable Japanese feminist. In *Bi any other name* (pp. 185- 187).

Whang, S. J. (1991). [untitled]. In *Bi any other name* (pp. 177-178).

BISEXUALITY AND HIV/AIDS

Psychological, Sociological, and Epidemiological Perspectives: Women and Men

ACSF Investigators. (1992). AIDS and sexual behaviour in France. *Nature, 360*, 407-409.

Bajos, N., Spira, A., Ducot, B., Messiah, A. et al. (1992). Analysis of sexual behaviour in France (ACSF): A comparison between two modes of investigation: Telephone survey and face-to-face survey. *AIDS, 6*(3), 315-323.

Bajos, N., Wadsworth, J., Ducot, B., Johnson, A., Le Pont, F., Wellings, K., Spira, A., & Field, J. (1995). Sexual behaviour and HIV epidemiology: Comparative analysis in France and Britain. The ACSF Group. *AIDS, 9*(7), 735-43.

Boulton, M., & Coxon, T. (1991). Bisexuality in the United Kingdom. In R. A. P. Tielman, M. Carballo, & A. C. Hendriks (Eds.), *Bisexuality and HIV/AIDS: A global perspective* (pp. 65-72). Buffalo, NY: Prometheus.

Chetwynd, J. (1991). Bisexuality in New Zealand. In R. A. P. Tielman, M. Carballo, & A. C. Hendriks (Eds.), *Bisexuality and HIV/AIDS: A global perspective* (pp. 131-138). Buffalo, NY: Prometheus.

Doll, L. S., Myers, T., Kennedy, M., & Allman, D. (1997). Bisexuality and HIV risk: Experiences in Canada and the United States. *Annual Review of Sex Research, VIII*, 102-147.

Lawrence, R. M., & Queen, C. (2001). Bisexuals help create the standards for safer sex: San Francisco, 1981-1987. *Journal of Bisexuality, 1*(1), 145-162.

Messiah, A., & the ACSF Group. (1996). Bisexuality and AIDS: Results from French quantitative studies. In P. Aggleton (Ed.), *Bisexualities and AIDS: International perspectives* (pp. 61-75). London: Taylor & Francis.

Myers, T., & Allman, D. (1996). Bisexuality and HIV/AIDS in Canada. In P. Aggleton (Ed.), *Bisexualities and AIDS: International perspectives* (pp. 23-43). London: Taylor & Francis.

Reinisch, J. M., Sanders, S. A., & Ziemba-Davis, M. (1995). Self-labeled sexual orientation and sexual behavior: Considerations for STD-related biomedical research and education. In M. Stein & A. Baum (Eds.), *Chronic diseases* (pp. 241-258). New York: Lawrence Erlbaum Associates.

Reinisch, J. M., Ziemba-Davis, M., & Sanders, S. A. (1990). Sexual behavior and AIDS: Lessons from art and sex research. In B. R. Voeller, J. M. Reinisch, & M. S. Gottlieb (Eds.), *AIDS and sex: An integrated biomedical and biobehavioral approach* (pp. 37-80). Oxford University Press.

Ross, M. W. (1991). Bisexuality in Australia. In R. A. P. Tielman, M. Carballo, & A. C. Hendriks (Eds.), *Bisexuality and HIV/AIDS: A global perspective* (pp. 127-130). Buffalo, NY: Prometheus.

Ross, M. W., Essien, E. J., Williams, M. L., & Fernández-Esquer, M. E. (2003). Concordance between sexual behavior and sexual identity in street outreach samples of four racial/ethnic groups. *Sexually Transmitted Diseases, 30*(2), 110-113.

Sandfort, T. G. M. (1991). Bisexuality in the Netherlands: Some data from Dutch studies. In R. A. P. Tielman, M. Carballo, & A. C. Hendriks (Eds.),

Bisexuality and HIV/AIDS: A global perspective (pp. 73-80). Buffalo, NY: Prometheus.

Rust, P. C. R. (2000). Bisexuality in HIV research. In P. C. R. Rust (Ed.), *Bisexuality in the United States: A social science reader* (pp. 355-400). New York: Columbia University Press.

Sandfort, T. G. M. (1995). HIV/AIDS prevention and the impact of attitudes toward homosexuality and bisexuality. In G. M. Herek & B. Greene (Eds.), *AIDS, identity, and community: The HIV epidemic and lesbians and gay men* (pp. 32-54). Thousand Oaks, CA: Sage.

Bisexuality, Women, and HIV/AIDS

Bevier, P., Chiasson, M., Heffernan, R., & Castro, K. (1995). Women at a sexually transmitted disease clinics who reported same-sex contact: Their HIV seroprevalence and risk behaviors. *American Journal of Public Health, 85*(10), 1366-1371.

Danzig, A. (1990). Bisexual women and AIDS. In The ACT UP/New York Women & AIDS Book Group (Eds.), *Women, AIDS, and activism*. Boston: South End Press.

Diamant, A. L., Schuster, M. A., McGuigan, K., & Lever, J. (1999). Lesbians' sexual history with men: Implications for taking a sexual history. *Archives of Internal Medicine, 159*(22), 2730-2736.

Einhorn, L., & Polgar, M. (1994). HIV-risk behavior among lesbians and bisexual women. *AIDS Education & Prevention, 6*(6), 514-523.

Gómez, C. A. (1995). Lesbians at risk for HIV: The unresolved debate. In G. M. Herek, & B. Greene (Eds.), *AIDS, identity, and community: The HIV epidemic and lesbians and gay men* (pp. 19-31). Thousand Oaks, CA: Sage.

Gómez, C. A., Garcia, D., Kegebein, V. J., Shade, S. B., & Hernandez, S. R. (1996). Sexual identity versus sexual behavior: Implications for HIV prevention strategies for women who have sex with women. *Women's Health: Research on Gender, Behavior, and Policy, 2*(1/2), 91-110.

Gonzales, V., Washienko, K. M., Krone, M. R., Chapman, L. I., Arredondo, E. M., Huckeba, H. J., & Downer, A. (1999). Sexual and drug-use risk factors for HIV and STDs: A comparison of women with and without bisexual experiences. *American Journal of Public Health, 89*(12), 1841-1846.

Jacobs, B. A. (1993). The AIDS epidemic: Its effect on sexual attitudes and practices among lesbian and bisexual women. (Doctoral dissertation, California School of Professional Psychology, Los Angeles, 1992). *Dissertation Abstracts International, 53*(7), 3775B.

Magura, S., O'Day, J., & Rosenblum, A. (1992). Women usually take care of their girlfriends: Bisexuality and HIV risk among female intravenous drug users. *Journal of Drug Issues, 22*(1), 179-190.

Mays, V. M., Cochran, S. D., Pies, C., Chu, S. Y., & Ehrhardt, A. A. (1996). The risk of HIV infection for lesbians and women who have sex with women: Implications for HIV research, prevention, policy, and services. *Women's Health: Research on Gender, Behavior, and Policy, 2*(1/2), 119-139.

Moore, J., Warren, D., Zierler, S., Schuman, P., Solomon, L., Schoenbaum, E. E., & Kennedy, M. (1996). Characteristics of HIV-infected lesbians and bisexual women in four urban centers. *Women's Health: Research on Gender, Behavior, & Policy, 2*(1/2), 49-60.

Morrow, K. M., & Allsworth, J. E. (2000). Sexual risk in lesbians and bisexual women. *Journal of the Gay & Lesbian Medical Association, 4*(4), 159-165.

Nicely, B. A. (2001). Safer sex practices of behaviorally bisexual women: Influences of partner gender, knowledge, commitment, power, barriers, and self-efficacy. (Doctoral dissertation, The University of Akron, 2000). *Dissertation Abstracts International, 61*(7), 3854B.

Nichols, M. (1990). Women and Acquired Immunodeficiency Syndrome: Issues for prevention. In Voeller, B., Reinisch, J. M., & Gottlieb, M. (Eds.), *AIDS and sex: An integrated biomedical and biobehavioral approach* (pp. 37-80). New York: Oxford University Press.

Richters, J., Bergin, S., Lubowitz, S., & Prestage, G. (2002). Women in contact with Sydney's gay and lesbian community: Sexual identity, practice and HIV risks. *AIDS Care, 14*(2), 193-202.

Rila, M. (1996). Bisexual women and the AIDS crisis. In B. A. Firestein (Ed.), *Bisexuality: The psychology and politics of an invisible minority* (pp. 169-184). Thousand Oaks, CA: Sage.

Scheer, S., Peterson, I., Page-Shafer, K., Delgado, V., Gleghorn, A., Ruiz, J., Molitor, F., McFarland, W., & Klausner, J. (2002). Sexual and drug use behavior among women who have sex with both women and men: Results of a population-based survey. *American Journal of Public Health, 92*(7), 1110-1112.

Young, R. M., Friedman, S. R., Case, P., Asencio, M. W., & Clatts, M. (2000). Women injection drug users who have sex with women exhibit increased HIV infection and risk behaviors. *Journal of Drug Issues, 30,* 499-523.

Young, R. M., Weissman, G., & Cohen, J. B. (1992). Assessing risk in the absence of information: HIV risk among women injection-drug users who have sex with women. *AIDS & Public Policy Journal, 7,* 175-183.

Ziemba-Davis, M., Sanders, S. S., & Reinisch, J. M. (1996). Lesbians' sexual interactions with men: Behavioral bisexuality and risk for sexually transmitted disease (STD) and Human Immunodeficiency Virus (HIV). *Women's Health: Research on Gender, Behavior, and Policy, 2*(1/2), 61-74.

Bisexuality, Men, and HIV/AIDS

Aoki, B., Ngin, C. P., Mo, B., & Ja, D. Y. (1989). AIDS prevention models in Asian-American communities. In V. M. Mays, G. W. Albee, & S. F. Schneider (Eds.), Primary Prevention of AIDS: Psychological Approaches (pp. 290-308). Newbury Park, CA: Sage.

Asthana, S., & Oostvogels, R. (2001). The social construction of male 'homosexuality' in India: Implications for HIV transmission and prevention. Social Science & Medicine, 52, 707-721.

Bennett, G., Chapman, S., & Bray, F. (1989). A potential source for the transmission of the human immuno-deficiency virus in the heterosexual population: Bisexual men who frequent 'beats.' Medical Journal of Australia, 151, 314-318.

Boles, J., & Elifson, K. W. (1994). Sexual identity and HIV: The male prostitute. Journal of Sex Research, 31(1), 39-46.

Boulton, M., & Fitzpatrick, R. (1996). Bisexual men in Britain. In P. Aggleton (Ed.), Bisexualities and AIDS: International perspectives (pp. 3-22). London: Taylor & Francis.

Boulton, M., Hart, G., & Fitzpatrick, R. (1992). The sexual behaviour of bisexual men in relation to HIV transmission. AIDS Care, 4(2), 165-175.

Cáceres, C. F. (1996). Male bisexuality in Peru and the prevention of AIDS. In P. Aggleton (Ed.), Bisexualities and AIDS: International perspectives (pp. 136-147). London: Taylor & Francis.

Carrier, J. M. (1989). Sexual behavior and the spread of AIDS in Mexico. Medical Anthropology Quarterly, 10(2/3), 129-142.

Chetwynd, J., Chambers, A., & Hughes, A. J. (1992). Condom use in anal intercourse amongst people who identify as homosexual, heterosexual or bisexual. New Zealand Medical Journal, 105, 262-264.

Chu, S. Y., Peterman, T. A., Doll, L. S., Buehler, J. W., & Curran, J. W. (1992). AIDS in bisexual men in the United States: Epidemiology and transmission to women. American Journal of Public Health, 82(2), 220-224.

Connell, R. W., Crawford, J., Dowsett, G. W., Kippax, S. et al. (1990). Danger and context: Unsafe anal sexual practice among homosexual and bisexual men in the AIDS crisis. Australian and New Zealand Journal of Sociology, 26(2), 187-208.

Connell, R. W., Davis, M. D., & Dowsett, G. W. (1993). A bastard of a life: Homosexual desire and practice among men in working-class milieux. Australian and New Zealand Journal of Sociology, 29(1), 112-135.

Crawford, J., Kippax, S., & Prestage, G. (1996). Not gay, not bisexual, but polymorphously sexually active: Male bisexuality and AIDS in Australia.

In P. Aggleton (Ed.), *Bisexualities and AIDS: International perspectives* (pp. 44-60). London: Taylor & Francis.

Davis, M., Dowsett, Gary, & Klemmer, U. (1996). On the beat: A report on the Bisexually Active Men's Outreach project. In *Bisexual horizons* (pp. 188-199).

Deren, S., Stark, M., Rhodes, F., Siegal, H., Cottler, L., Wood, M. M. et al. (2001). Drug-using men who have sex with men: Sexual behaviours and sexual identities. *Culture, Health & Sexuality, 3*(3), 329-338.

Diaz, R. M., Morales, E. S., Bein, E., Dilan, E., & Rodriguez, R. A. (1999). Predictors of sexual risk in Latino gay/bisexual men: The role of demographic, developmental, social cognitive, and behavioral variables. *Hispanic Journal of Behavioral Sciences, 21*(4).

Diaz, T., Chu, S. Y., Frederick, M., Hermann, P., Levy, A., Mokotoff, E., Whyte, B., Conti, L., Herr, M., Checko, P. J., Rietmeijer, C. A., Sorvillo, F., & Mukhtar, Q. (1993). Sociodemographics & HIV risk behaviors of bisexual men with AIDS: Results from a multistate interview project. *AIDS, 7*(9), 1227-1232.

Doll, L. S., & Beeker, C. (1996). Male bisexual behavior and HIV risk in the United States: Synthesis of research with implications for behavioral interventions. *AIDS Education and Prevention, 8*(3), 205-225.

Doll, L., Peterson, J., Magaña, J. R., & Carrier, J. M. (1991). Male bisexuality and AIDS in the United States. In R. A. P. Tielman, M. Carballo, and A. C. Hendriks (Eds.), *Bisexuality and HIV/AIDS: A global perspective* (pp. 27-40). Buffalo, NY: Prometheus.

Dowsett, G. W. (1991). Reaching men who have sex with men in Australia: An overview of AIDS education, community intervention and community attachment strategies. *Australian Journal of Social Issues, 25*(3), 186-198.

Earl, W. L. (1990). Married men and same sex activity: A field study on HIV risk among men who do not identify as gay or bisexual. *Journal of Sex and Marital Therapy, 16*(4), 251-257.

Ekstrand, M. L., & Coates, T. J. (1994). Are bisexually identified men in San Francisco a common vector for spreading HIV infection to women? *American Journal of Public Health, 84*, 915-919.

Fitzpatrick, R., Hart, G., Boulton, M., McLean, J., & Dawson, J. (1989). Heterosexual sexual behaviour in a sample of homosexually active men. *Genitourinary Medicine, 65*, 259-262.

Goldbaum, G., Perdue, T., & Higgins, D. (1996). Non-gay-identifying men who have sex with men: Formative research results from Seattle, Washington. *Public Health Reports, 33*, 36-40.

Goldbaum, G., Perdue, T., & Wolitski, R. (1998). Differences in risk behavior and sources of AIDS information among gay, bisexual, and straight-identified men who have sex with men. *AIDS & Behavior, 2*(1), 13-21.

Heckman, T. G., Kelly, J. A., Sikkema, K., Roffman, R. R., Solomon, L. J., Winett, R. A., et al. (1995). Differences in HIV risk characteristics between bisexual and exclusively gay men. *AIDS Education and Prevention, 7*(6), 504-512.

Herek, G. M., & Glunt, E. K. (1995). Identity and community among gay and bisexual men in the AIDS era: Preliminary findings from the Sacramento men's health study. In G. M. Herek & B. Greene (Eds.), *AIDS, identity, and community: The HIV epidemic and lesbians and gay men* (pp. 55-84). Thousand Oaks, CA: Sage.

Hernandez, M., Uribe, P., Gortmaker, S., Avila, C., De Caso, L. E., Mueller, N., & Sepulveda, J. (1992). Sexual behavior and status for Human Immunodeficiency Virus Type 1 among homosexual and bisexual males in Mexico City. *American Journal of Epidemiology, 135*(8), 883-94.

Kahn, J. G., Gurvey, J., Pollack, L. M., Binson, D., & Catania, J. A. (1997). How many HIV infections cross the bisexual bridge? An estimate from the United States. *AIDS, 11*(8), 1031-1037.

Kalichman, S. C., Roffman, R. A., Picciano, J. F., & Bolan, M. (1998). Risk for HIV infection among bisexual men seeking HIV-prevention services and risks posed to their female partners. *Health Psychology, 17*(4), 320-327.

Kegeles, S. M., & Catania, J. A. (1991). Understanding bisexual men's AIDS risk behavior: The risk-reduction model. In R. A. P. Tielman, M. Carballo, & A. C. Hendriks (Eds.), *Bisexuality & HIV/AIDS: A global perspective* (pp. 139-147). Buffalo, NY: Prometheus.

Kelly, J. A., Amirkhanian, Y. A., & McAuliffe, T. L. (2002). HIV risk characteristics and prevention needs in a community sample of bisexual men in St. Petersburg, Russia. *AIDS Care, 14*(1), 63-76.

Kennedy, M., & Doll, L. S. (2001). Male bisexuality and HIV risk. *Journal of Bisexuality, 1*(2/3), 109-135.

Krijnen, P., van den Hoek, J. A., & Coutinho, R. A. (1994). Do bisexual men play a significant role in the heterosexual spread of HIV? *Sexually Transmitted Diseases, 21*(1), 24-25.

Lewis D. K., & Watters, J. K. (1994). Sexual behavior and sexual identity in male injection drug users. *Journal of Acquired Immune Deficiency Syndromes, 7*(2), 190-198.

Liguori, A. L., Block, M. G., & Aggleton, P. (1996). Bisexuality and HIV/AIDS in Mexico. In P. Aggleton (Ed.), *Bisexualities and AIDS: International perspectives* (pp. 76-98). London: Taylor & Francis.

Magaña, J. R, & Carrier, J. M. (1991). Mexican and Mexican American male sexual behavior and spread of AIDS in California. *Journal of Sex Research, 28*(3), 425-441.

220   CURRENT RESEARCH ON BISEXUALITY

Matteson, D. R. (1997). Bisexual and homosexual behavior and HIV risk among Chinese-, Filipino- and Korean-American men. *Journal of Sex Research, 34*(1), 93-104.
Mays, V. M., Cochran, S. D., Bellinger, G., Smith, R. G., & and Others. (1992). The language of Black gay men's sexual behavior: Implications for AIDS risk reduction. *Journal of Sex Research, 29*(3), 425-434.
Messiah, A., & Mouret-Fourme, E. (1995). Sociodemographic characteristics and sexual behavior of bisexual men in France: Implications for HIV prevention. *American Journal of Public Health, 85*(11), 1543-1547.
Miller, M. (2002). "Ethically Questionable?": Popular media reports on bisexual men and AIDS. *Journal of Bisexuality, 2*(1), 93-112.
Morales, E. S. (1990). HIV infection and Hispanic gay and bisexual men. *Hispanic Journal of Behavioral Sciences, 12*(2), 212-222.
Morse, E. V., Simon, P. M., Osofsky, H. J., Balson, P. M., & Gaumer, H. R. (1991). The male street prostitute: A vector for transmission of HIV infection into the heterosexual world. *Social Science and Medicine, 32*(5), 535-539.
Nemoto, T., Wong, F. Y., Ching, A., Chng, C. H., Bouey, P., Henrickson, M., & Sember, R. E. (1998). HIV seroprevalence, risk behaviors, and cognitive factors among Asian and Pacific Islander American men who have sex with men: A summary and critique of empirical studies and methodological issues. *AIDS Education and Prevention, 10*(Supplement A), 31-47.
Pan, S., & Aggleton, P. (1996). Male homosexual behaviour and HIV-related risk in China. In P. Aggleton (Ed.), *Bisexualities and AIDS: International perspectives* (pp. 178-190). London: Taylor & Francis.
Parker, R. G. (1992). Sexual diversity, cultural analysis, and AIDS education in Brazil. In G. Herdt, & S. Lindenbaum (Eds.), *The time of AIDS: Social analysis, theory, and method* (pp. 225-242). Newbury Park, CA: Sage.
Parker, R. G. (1996). Bisexuality and HIV/AIDS in Brazil. In P. Aggleton (Ed.), *Bisexualities and AIDS: International perspectives* (pp. 148-160). London: Taylor & Francis.
Parker, R. G., & Carballo, M. (1990). Qualitative research on homosexual and bisexual behavior relevant to HIV/AIDS. *Journal of Sex Research, 27*(4), 497-525.
Parker, R. G., & Tawil, O. (1991). Bisexual behavior and HIV transmission in Latin America. In R. A. P. Tielman, M. Carballo, & A. C. Hendriks (Eds.), *Bisexuality & HIV/AIDS: A global perspective* (pp. 59-64). Buffalo, NY: Prometheus.
Peterson, J. L. (1995). AIDS-related risks and same-sex behaviors among African American men. In G. M. Herek, & B. Greene (Eds.), *AIDS, identity, and community: The HIV epidemic and lesbians and gay men* (pp. 85-104). Thousand Oaks, CA: Sage.

Prestage, G., & Drielsma, P. (1996). Indicators of male bisexual activity in semimetropolitan New South Wales: Implications for HIV prevention strategies. *Australian and New Zealand Journal of Public Health, 20,* 386-392.

Ramirez, J., Suarez, E., de la Rosa, G., Castro, M. A., & Zimmerman, M. A. (1994). AIDS knowledge and sexual behavior among Mexican gay and bisexual men. *AIDS Education and Prevention, 6*(2), 163-74.

Roffman, R. A., Picciano, J. F., Bolan, M, & Kalichman, S. C. (1997). Factors associated with attrition from an HIV-prevention program for gay and bisexual males. *AIDS & Behavior, 1*(2), 125-135.

Roffman, R. A., Picciano, P., Wickizer, L., Bolan, M., & Ryan, R. (1998). Anonymous enrollment in AIDS prevention telephone group counseling: Facilitating the participation of gay and bisexual men in intervention and research. *Journal of Social Service Research, 23,* 5-22.

Roffman, R. A., Stephens, R. S., Curtin, L., Gordon, J. R., Craver, J. N., Stern, M., Beadnell, B., & Downey, L. (1998). Relapse prevention as an interventive model for HIV risk reduction in gay and bisexual men. *AIDS Education and Prevention, 10*(1), 1-18.

Ross, M. W., Wodak, A., Gold, J., & Miller, M. E. (1992). Differences across sexual orientation on HIV risk behaviours in injecting drug users. *AIDS Care, 4*(2), 139-148.

Ryan, R., Longres, J. F., & Roffman, R. A. (1996). Sexual identity, social support and social networks among African-, Latino-, and European-American men in an HIV prevention program. In J. F. Longres (Ed.), *Men of color: A context for service to homosexually active men* (pp. 1-24). New York: Harrington Park Press.

Stokes, J. P., McKirnan, D. J., Doll, L., & Burzette, R. G. (1996). Female partners of bisexual men: What they don't know might hurt them. *Psychology of Women Quarterly, 20,* 267-284.

Stokes, J. P., & Peterson, J. L. (1998). Homophobia, self esteem, and risk for HIV among African American men who have sex with men. *AIDS Education and Prevention, 10*(3), 278-292.

Stokes, J. P., Taywaditep, K., Vanable, P., & McKirnan, D. J. (1996). Bisexual men, sexual behavior, and HIV/AIDS. In B. A. Firestein (Ed.), *Bisexuality: The psychology and politics of an invisible minority* (pp. 149-168). Thousand Oaks, CA: Sage.

Stokes, J.P., Vanable, P.A., & McKirnan, D. J. (1997). Comparing gay and bisexual men on sexual behavior, condom use, and psychosocial variables related to HIV/AIDS. *Archives of Sexual Behavior, 26,* 377-391.

Tafoya, T. (1989). Pulling coyote's tale: Native American sexuality and AIDS. In V. M. Mays, G. W. Albee, & S. F. E. Schneider (Eds.), *Primary prevention of AIDS: Psychological approaches* (pp. 280-28). Newbury Park, CA: Sage.

Weatherburn, P., Davies, P. M., Hunt, A. J., Coxon, A. P. M., & McManus, T. J. (1990). Heterosexual behaviour in a large cohort of homosexually active men in England and Wales. *AIDS Care, 2*(4), 319-224.

Weatherburn, P., & Reid, D. (1995). Survey shows unprotected sex is a common behaviour in bisexual men. *British Medical Journal, 311*, 1163-1164.

Wold, C., Seage III, G. R., Lenderking, W. R., Mayer, K. H., Bin Cai, Heeren, T., & Goldstein, R. (1998). Unsafe sex in men who have sex with both men and women. *Journal of Acquired Immune Deficiency Syndromes & Human Retrovirology, 17*(4), 361-367.

Wong, F. Y., Chng, C. L., & Lo, W. (1998). A profile of six community based HIV prevention programs targeting Asian and Pacific Islander Americans. *AIDS Education and Prevention, 10*(Suppl. 3), 61-76.

Wood, R. W., Krueger, L. E., Pearlman, T. C., & Goldbaum, C. (1993). HIV transmission: Women's risk from bisexual men. *American Journal of Public Health, 83*(12), 1757-9.

Worth, H. (2003). The myth of the bisexual infector? HIV risk and men who have sex with men. *Journal of Bisexuality, 3*(2) 69-88.

Wright, J. W. (1993). African-American male sexual behavior and the risk for HIV infection. *Human Organization, 52*(4), 431-431.

Bisexual Youth and HIV/AIDS

Bettencourt, T., Hodgins, A., Huba, G. J., & Pickett, G. (1998). Bay area young positives: A model of a youth based approach to HIV/AIDS services. *Journal of Adolescent Health, 23*(2), 28-36.

Cochran, S. D., & Mays, V. M. (1996). Prevalence of HIV-related sexual risk behaviors among young 18- to 24-year-old lesbian and bisexual women. *Women's Health: Research on Gender, Behavior, and Policy, 2*(1/2), 75-90.

Cranston, K. (1991). HIV education for gay, lesbian, and bisexual youth: Personal risk, personal power, and the community of conscience. *Journal of Homosexuality, 22*(3/4), 247-259.

Goodenow, C., Netherland, J., & Szalacha, L. (2002). AIDS-related risk among adolescent males who have sex with males, females, or both: Evidence from a statewide survey. *American Journal of Public Health, 92*(2), 203-210.

Hayes, R. B., & Kegeles, S. M. (1991). HIV/AIDS risks for bisexual adolescents. In R. A. P. Tielman, M. Carballo, & A. C. Hendriks (Eds.), *Bisexuality and HIV/AIDS: A global perspective* (pp. 165-174). Buffalo, NY: Prometheus.

Rosario, M., Meyer-Bahlburg, H. F. L., Hunter, J., & Gwadz, M. (1999). Sexual risk behaviors of gay, lesbian, and bisexual youths in New York City: Prevalence and correlates. AIDS *Education & Prevention, 11*(6).

Rosario, M., Schrimshaw, E. W., Hunter, J., & Gwadz, M. (2002). Gay-related stress and emotional distress among gay, lesbian, and bisexual youths: A longitudinal examination. *Journal of Consulting and Clinical Psychology, 70*(4), 967-975.

Rotheram-Borus, M. J., & Koopman, C. (1991). Sexual risk behavior, AIDS knowledge, & beliefs about AIDS among predominantly minority gay & bisexual male adolescents. *AIDS Education & Prevention, 3*(4), 305-312.

Rotheram-Borus, M. J., Marelich, W. D., & Srinivasan, S. (1999). HIV risk among homosexual, bisexual, and heterosexual male and female youths. *Archives of Sexual Behavior, 28*(2), 159-177.

Rotheram-Borus, M. J., Meyer-Bahlburg, H. F., & Koopman, C. (1992). Lifetime sexual behaviors among predominantly minority male runaways and gay/bisexual adolescents in New York City. *AIDS Education & Prevention* (Suppl.), 34-42.

Rotheram-Borus, M. J., Reid, H., Rosario, M., & Kasen, S. (1995). Determinants of safer sex patterns among gay/bisexual male adolescents. *Journal of Adolescence, 18*(1), 3-16.

Transgender Persons and HIV/AIDS

Bockting, W. O., Robinson, B. E., & Rosser, B. R. S. (1998). Transgender HIV prevention: A qualitative needs assessment. *AIDS Care, 10*, 505-526.

Nemoto, T., Luke, D., Mamo, L., Ching, A., & Patria, J. (1999). HIV risk behaviours among male-to-female transgenders in comparison with homosexual or bisexual males and heterosexual females. AIDS *Care, 11*(3).

Personal and Political Perspectives

Bishop, D. (1991). Another senseless loss. In *Bi any other name* (pp. 258-260).

Danzig, A. (1990). Bisexual women and AIDS. In *The ACT UP/New York Women and AIDS Book Group* (pp. 193-198). Boston: South End Press.

Dutton, J. (1996). It's about numbers. In *Bisexual horizons* (pp. 169-175).

George, S. (1996). HIV, AIDS and safer sex: Introduction. In *Bisexual horizons* (pp. 159-165).

Highleyman, L. (1996). Bisexuals and AIDS. In *Bisexual horizons* (pp. 166-168).

Lawrence, R. M., & Queen, C. (2001). Bisexuals help create the standards for safer sex: San Francisco, 1981-1987. *Journal of Bisexuality, 1*(1), 145-162.

Lourea, D. (1991). Just another lingering flu. In *Bi any other name* (pp. 99-102).
Sands, D. (1996). Tony. In *Bisexual horizons* (pp. 211-213).
Stewart, H. (1991). A healing journey. In *Bi any other name* (pp. 147-150).
Stewart, H. (1994, Spring). Surviving HIV: Some thoughts for my brothers and sisters. *Anything That Moves, (7)*, 41, 42, 51.
Wright, J. (1998, Spring). Surviving the storm: Bisexual men and HIV. *Anything That Moves, 16*, 34-37.

HEALTH CARE, COUNSELING, AND PSYCHOTHERAPY

Affirmative Mental Health Services for Bisexual Women and Bisexual Men

Auerback, S., & Moser, C. (1987). Groups for the wives of gay and bisexual men. *Social Work, 32*(4), 321-25.
Bradford, M. (in press). Bisexual issues in same-sex couples therapy. *Journal of Couple and Relationship Therapy, 3*(3/4).
Butt, J. A., & Guldner, C. A. (1993). Counselling bisexuals: Therapists' attitudes towards bisexuality and application in clinical practice. *Canadian Journal of Human Sexuality, 2*(2), 61-70.
Deacon, S. A., Retake, L., & Viers, D. (1996). Cognitive-behavioral therapy for bisexual couples: Expanding the realms of therapy: *The American Journal of Family Therapy, 24*, 242-258.
Dworkin, S. H. (1996). From personal therapy to professional life: Observations of a Jewish, bisexual lesbian therapist and academic. In N. D. Davis, & E. Cole (Eds.), *Lesbian therapists and their therapy: From both sides of the couch* (pp. 37-46). New York: Harrington Park Press.
Dworkin, S. H. (2001). Treating the bisexual client. *Journal of Clinical Psychology, 57*(5), 671-80.
Elise, D. (1998). Gender repertoire: Body, mind, and bisexuality. *Psychoanalytic Dialogues, 8*(3), 353-371.
Gooß, U. (2003). Konzepte der Bisexualität [Concepts of bisexuality]. *Zeitschrift für Sexualforschung, 16*(1), 51-65.
Guidry, L. L. (1999). Clinical intervention with bisexuals: A contextualized understanding. *Professional Psychology: Research and Practice, 30*(1), 22-26.
Hayes, B. G., & Hagedon, W. B. (2001). Working with the bisexual client: How far have we progressed?. *Journal of Humanistic Counseling and Development, 40*(1), 11-20.

Horne, S., Shulman, J., & Levitt, H. M. (2003). To pass or not to pass: Exploration of conflict splits for bisexual-identified clients. In *The therapist's notebook for lesbian, gay, and bisexual clients* (pp. 32-26). New York: Haworth.

Horowitz, J. L., & Newcomb, M. D. (1999). Bisexuality, not homosexuality: Counseling issues and treatment approaches. *Journal of College Counseling, 2*(2), 148-163.

Layton, L. B. (2000). The psychopolitics of bisexuality. *Studies in Gender and Sexuality: Psychoanalysis, Cultural Studies, Treatment, Research, 1*(1), 41-60.

LeVine, P. (1991). Applications of Morita therapy for clients with a bisexual orientation during the coming-out process. *International Bulletin of Morita Therapy, 4*(1-2), 3-14.

Lourea, D. (1985). Psycho-social issues related to counseling bisexuals. *Journal of Homosexuality, 11*(1/2), 51-62.

Markowitz, L. M. (1995). Bisexuality: Challenging our either/or thinking. *In the Family: A Magazine for Lesbians, Gays, Bisexuals and Their Relations, 1*(1), 6-11, 23.

Markowitz, L. M. (2000). Therapy with bisexuals: An interview with Ron Fox. *In The Family, 6*(2), 6-9, 21.

Mascher, J. (2003). Overcoming biphobia. In J. S. Whitman & C. J. Boyd (Eds.). (2003). In J. S. Whitman & C. J. Boyd (Eds.). (2003). *The therapist's notebook for lesbian, gay, and bisexual clients* (pp. 78-83). New York: Haworth.

Matteson, D. R. (1987). Counseling bisexual men. In M. Scher (Ed.), *The handbook of counseling and psychotherapy with men* (pp. 232-249). Beverly Hills, CA: Sage.

Matteson, D. (1995). Counseling with bisexuals. *Individual Psychology, 51*(2), 144-159.

Matteson, D. R. (1996). Counseling and psychotherapy with bisexual and exploring clients. In B. A. Firestein (Ed.), *Bisexuality: The psychology and politics of an invisible minority* (pp. 185-213). Thousand Oaks, CA: Sage.

Matteson, D. R. (1996). Psychotherapy with bisexual individuals. In R. P. Cabaj & T. S. Stein (Eds.), *Textbook of homosexuality and mental health* (pp. 433-450). Washington, DC: American Psychiatric Press.

Matteson, D. R. (1999). Intimate bisexual couples. In J. Carlson & L. Sperry (Eds.), *The intimate couple* (pp. 439-459). Philadelphia: Brunner/Mazel.

McVinney, D. (2001). Clinical issues with bisexuals. In SAMSHA Center for Substance Abuse Treatment (Ed.), *A provider's introduction to substance abuse treatment for lesbian, gay, bisexual, and transgender Individuals* (DHHS Publication No. SMA 01-3498, pp. 87-90). Rockville, MD: National Clearinghouse for Alcohol and Drug Information.

Myers, M. F. (1991). Marital therapy with HIV-infected men and their wives. *Psychiatric Annals, 21*(8), 466-470.

Nichols, M. (1988). Bisexuality in women: Myths, realities, and implications for therapy. In E. Cole & E. Rothblum (Eds.), *Women and sex therapy: Closing the circle* (pp. 235-252). New York: Harrington Park Press.

Nichols, M. (1994). Therapy with bisexual women: Working on the edge of emerging cultural and personal identities. In M. P. Mirkin (Ed.), *Women in context: Toward a feminist reconstruction of psychotherapy* (pp. 149-169). New York: Guilford.

Oxley, E., & Lucius, C. A. (2000). Looking both ways: Bisexuality and therapy. In C. Neal & D. Davies (Eds.), *Issues in therapy with lesbian, gay, bisexual and transgender clients* (pp. 115-127). Buckingham, England, United Kingdom.

Poelzl, L. (2001). Bisexual issues in sex therapy: A bisexual surrogate partner relates her experiences from the field. *Journal of Bisexuality, 1*(1), 121-142.

Smiley, E. B. (1997). Counseling bisexual clients. *Journal of Mental Health Counseling, 19*(4), 373-382.

Stokes, J. P., & Damon, W. (1995). Counseling and psychotherapy with bisexual men. *Directions in Clinical Psychology, 5*, 3-13.

Weasel, L. H. (1996). Seeing between the lines: Bisexual women and therapy. *Women & Therapy, 19*(2), 5-16.

Wolf, T. J. (1987). Group counseling for bisexual men. *Journal of Homosexuality, 14*(1/2), 162-165.

Wolf, T. J. (1987). Group psychotherapy for bisexual men and their wives. *Journal of Homosexuality, 14*(1/2), 191-199.

Wolf, T. J. (1992). Bisexuality: A counseling perspective. In S. H. Dworkin, & F. J. Gutierrez (Eds.), *Counseling gay men and lesbians: Journey to the end of the rainbow* (pp. 175-187). Alexandria, VA: American Association for Counseling and Development.

Bisexuality in the Context of Mental Health Services for LGBT Clients

Addison, S. M., & Brown, M. M. (2003). Creating a "thicker description": Understanding identity in mixed-identity relationships. In J. S. Whitman & C. J. Boyd (Eds.). (2003). *The therapist's notebook for lesbian, gay, and bisexual clients* (pp. 115-118). New York: Haworth.

Addison, S. M., & Brown, M. M. (2003). Working with couples on ethnicity and sexual identity: The "parts" interview. In J. S. Whitman & C. J. Boyd (Eds.). (2003). *The therapist's notebook for lesbian, gay, and bisexual clients* (pp. 110-114). New York: Haworth.

Barón, A., & Cramer, D. W. (2000). Potential counseling concerns of aging lesbian, gay, and bisexual clients. In R. M. Perez, K. A. DeBord, & K. J. Bieschke (Eds.), *Handbook of counseling and psychotherapy with lesbian, gay, and bisexual clients* (pp. 207-223). Washington, DC:

Brown, M. M., & Addison, S. M. (2003). Knowing you, knowing me: Sexual identity and the couple. In J. S. Whitman & C. J. Boyd (Eds.). (2003). *The therapist's notebook for lesbian, gay, and bisexual clients* (pp. 106-109). New York: Haworth.

Burch, B. (1993). Heterosexuality, bisexuality, and lesbianism: Rethinking psychoanalytic views of women's sexual object choice. *Psychoanalytic Review, 80*(1), 83-99.

Cabaj, R. P. (1989). AIDS and chemical dependency: Special issues and treatment barriers for gay and bisexual men. *Journal of Psychoactive Drugs, 21*(4), 387-393.

Cabaj, R. P. (1996). Substance abuse in gay men, lesbians, and bisexuals. In R. P. Cabaj, & T. S. Stein (Eds.), *Textbook of homosexuality and mental health* (pp. 783-799). Washington, DC: American Psychiatric Press.

Chen-Hayes, S. F. (1998). Counseling lesbian, bisexual, and gay persons in couple and family relationships: Overcoming the stereotypes. *The Family Journal: Counseling and Therapy for Couples and Families, 5*, 236-240.

Chen-Hayes, S. F. (2003). The sexual orientation, gender identity, and gender expression continuum. In J. S. Whitman & C. J. Boyd (Eds.). (2003). *The therapist's notebook for lesbian, gay, and bisexual clients* (pp. 159-165). New York: Haworth.

Clark, W. M., & Serovich, J. M. (1997). Twenty years and still in the dark? Content analysis of articles pertaining to gay, lesbian, and bisexual issues in marriage and family therapy journals. *Journal of Marital and Family Therapy, 23*, 239-253.

Craft, E. M., & Mulvey, K. P. (2001). Addressing lesbian, gay, bisexual, and transgender issues from the inside: One Federal agency's approach. *American Journal of Public Health, 91*(6), 889-891.

Davies, D. (1996). Working with people coming out. In D. Davies & C. Neal (Eds.), *Pink therapy: A guide for counsellors and therapists working with lesbian, gay and bisexual clients* (pp. 66-85). Buckingham, England, U.K.: Open University Press.

Doctor, F. (2003). Examining links between drug or alcohol use and experiences of homophobia/biphobia and coming out. In J. S. Whitman & C. J. Boyd (Eds.). (2003). *The therapist's notebook for lesbian, gay, and bisexual clients* (pp. 262-267). New York: Haworth.

Dworkin, S. H. (2000). Individual therapy with lesbian, gay, and bisexual clients. In R. M. Perez, K. A. DeBord, & K. J. Bieschke (Eds.), *Handbook of counsel-*

ing and psychotherapy with lesbian, gay, and bisexual clients (pp. 157-181). Washington, DC: American Psychological Association.

Dworkin, S. H., & Gutierrez, F. (1987). Counselors beware: Clients come in every size, shape, color, and sexual orientation. *Journal of Counseling and Development, 68*, 6-8.

Falco, K. L. (1996). Psychotherapy with women who love women. In R. P. Cabaj & T. S. Stein (Eds.), *Textbook of homosexuality and mental health* (pp. 397-412). Washington, DC: American Psychiatric Press.

Fassinger, R. E. (2000). Applying counseling theories to lesbian, gay, and bisexual clients: Pitfalls and possibilities. In R. M. Perez, K. A. DeBord, & K. J. Bieschke (Eds.), *Handbook of counseling and psychotherapy with lesbian, gay, and bisexual clients* (pp. 107-131). Washington, DC: American Psychological Association.

Finnegan, D. G., & McNally, E. B. (1996). Chemically dependent lesbians and bisexual women: Recovery from many traumas. In B. L. Underhill, & D. G. Finnegan (Eds.), *Chemical dependency: Women at risk* (pp. 87-107). New York: Harrington Park Press.

Firestein, B. A. (1999). New perspectives on group treatment with women of diverse sexual identities. *Journal for Specialists in Group Work, 24*(3), 306-315.

Grimes, M. L., & Pytluk, S. D. (2003). Assisting gay, lesbian, and bisexual youth in finding a community. In J. S. Whitman & C. J. Boyd (Eds.). (2003). *The therapist's notebook for lesbian, gay, and bisexual clients* (pp. 293-298). New York: Haworth.

Haldeman, D. (1999). The best of both worlds: Essentialism, social constructionism, and clinical practice. In J. S. Bohan & G. M. Russell (Eds.), *Conversations about psychology and sexual orientation* (pp. 57-70). New York: New York University Press.

Haldeman, D. (2001). Therapeutic antidotes: Helping gay and bisexual men recover from conversion. *Journal of Gay & Lesbian Psychotherapy, 5*(3/4), 117-130.

Hart, J. (1984). Therapeutic implications of viewing sexual identity in terms of essentialist and constructionist theories. *Journal of Homosexuality, 9*(4), 39-51.

Iasenza, S. (1999). Who do *we* want you to be? A commentary on essentialist and social constructionist perspectives in clinical work. In J. S. Bohan & G. M. Russell (Eds.), *Conversations about psychology and sexual orientation* (pp. 71-76). New York: New York University Press.

Jackson, J. (1995). Sexual orientation: Its relevance to occupational science and the practice of occupational therapy. *American Journal of Occupational Therapy, 49*(7), 669-679.

Kauth, M. R., Hartwig, M. J., & Kalichman, S. C. (2000). Health behavior relevant to psychotherapy with lesbian, gay, and bisexual clients. In R. M. Perez, K. A. DeBord, & K. J. Bieschke (Eds.), *Handbook of counseling and psychotherapy with lesbian, gay, and bisexual clients* (pp. 435-456). Washington, DC: American Psychological Association.

Klinger, R. L., & Stein, T. S. (1996). Impact of violence, childhood sexual abuse, and domestic violence and abuse on lesbians, bisexuals, and gay men. In R. P. Cabaj, & T. S. Stein (Eds.), *Textbook of homosexuality and mental health* (pp. 801-818). Washington, DC: American Psychiatric Press.

Levitt, H. M., & Raina, K. (2003). Opening the door or locking it tight: The negotiation of a healthy open relationship. In J. S. Whitman & C. J. Boyd (Eds.). (2003). *The therapist's notebook for lesbian, gay, and bisexual clients* (pp. 119-124). New York: Haworth.

Nichols, M. (1989). Sex therapy with lesbians, gay men, and bisexuals. In S. R. Leiblum, & R. C. Rosen (Eds.), *Principles and practice of sex therapy: Update for the 1990s (2nd ed.).* (pp. 269-297). New York: Guilford.

Rabin, J., Keefe, K., & Burton, M. (1986). Enhancing services for sexual-minority clients: A community mental health approach. *Social Work, 31*(4), 294-298.

Russell, G. M., & Bohan, J. S. (1999). Implications for clinical work. In J. S. Bohan & G. M. Russell (Eds.), *Conversations about psychology and sexual orientation* (pp. 31-56). New York: New York University Press.

Sager, J. B. (2001). Latin American lesbian, gay, and bisexual clients: Implications for counseling. *Journal of Humanistic Counseling, Education & Development, 40*(1), 13-33.

Tiefer, L. (1999). Don't look for perfects: A commentary on essentialist and social constuctionist perspectives in clinical work. In J. S. Bohan & G. M. Russell (Eds.), *Conversations about psychology and sexual orientation* (pp. 77-84). New York: New York University Press.

Wright, E., Shelton, C., Browning, M., Orduna, J. M. G., Martinez, V., & Wong, F. Y. (2001). Cultural issues in working with LGBT individuals. In SAMSHA Center for Substance Abuse Treatment (Ed.), *A provider's introduction to substance abuse treatment for lesbian, gay, bisexual, and transgender Individuals* (DHHS Publication No. SMA 01-3498, pp. 15-27). Rockville, MD: National Clearinghouse for Alcohol and Drug Information.

Mental Health Issues and Services for LGBT Youth

D'Augelli, A. R., & Hershberger, S. L. (1993). Lesbian, gay, and bisexual youth in community settings: Personal challenges and mental health problems. *American Journal of Community Psychology, 21*(4), 421-448.

D'Augelli, A. R., Pilkington, M. W., & Hershberger, S. L. (2002). Incidence and mental health impact of sexual orientation victimization of lesbian, gay, and bisexual youths in high school. *School Psychology Quarterly, 17,* 148-167.

Davies, D. (1996). Working with young people. In D. Davies & C. Neal (Eds.), *Pink therapy: A guide for counsellors and therapists working with lesbian, gay and bisexual clients* (pp. 131-148). Buckingham, England, U.K.: Open University Press.

Dempsey, C. L. (1994). Health and social issues of gay, lesbian, and bisexual adolescents. *Families in Society, 75*(3), 160-167.

Freedner, N., Freed, L. H., Yang, Y. W., & Austin, S. B. (2002). Dating violence among gay, lesbian, and bisexual adolescents: Results from a community survey. *Journal of Adolescent Health, 31*(6), 469-474.

Hartstein, N. B. (1996). Suicide risk in lesbian, gay, and bisexual youth. In R. P. Cabaj & T. S. Stein (Eds.), *Textbook of homosexuality and mental health* (pp. 819-837). Washington, DC: American Psychiatric Press.

Hershberger, S. L., & D'Augelli, A. R. (1995). The impact of victimization on the mental health and suicidality of lesbian, gay, and bisexual youths. *Developmental Psychology, 31*(1), 65-74.

Jackson, B. K. (2000). Predictors and outcomes of self-acceptance among lesbian, gay, and bisexual youth. (Doctoral dissertation, University of Denver, 1999). *Dissertation Abstracts International, 60*(9), 4930.

Lock, J., & Steiner, H. (1999). Gay, lesbian, and bisexual youth risks for emotional, physical, and social problems: Results from a community-based survey. *Journal of the American Academy of Child and Adolescent Psychiatry, 38*(3).

MacDonald, R. D. (1997). Study of the perceived social welfare needs of gay, lesbian, and bisexual adolescents. Master's thesis, California State University, Long Beach, 1997). *Masters Abstracts International, 35*(6), 1670.

McFarland, W. P. (1998). Gay, lesbian, and bisexual student suicide. *Professional School Counseling, 1*(3), 26-29.

Moore, C. D., & Waterman, C. K. (1999). Predicting self-protection against sexual assault in dating relationships among heterosexual men and women, gay men, lesbians, and bisexuals. *Journal of College Student Development, 40*(2), 132-141.

Muller, L. E., & Hartman, J. (1998). Group counseling for sexual minority youth. *Professional School Counseling, 1*(3), 38-41.

Nesmith, A. A., Burton, D. L., & Cosgrove, T. J. (1999). Gay, lesbian and bisexual youth and young adults: Social support in their own words. *Journal of Homosexuality, 37*(1).

Proctor, C. D., & Groze, V. K. (1994). Risk factors for suicide among gay, lesbian, and bisexual youths. *Social Work, 39*(5), 504-513.

Remafedi, G., Farrow, J. A., & Deisher, R. W. (1991). Risk factors for attempted suicide in gay and bisexual youth. *Pediatrics, 87,* 869-875. Reprinted in L. D. Garnets & D. C. Kimmel (Eds.). (1993). *Psychological perspectives on lesbian and gay male experiences* (pp. 486-499). New York: Columbia University Press.

Reynolds, A. L., & Koski, M. J. (1993/1994). Lesbian, gay and bisexual teens and the school counselor: Building alliances. *High School Journal, 77*(1/2), 88-94.

Savin-Williams, R. C., & Cohen, K. M. (1996). Psychosocial outcomes of verbal and physical abuse among lesbian, gay, and bisexual youths. R. C. Savin-Williams, & K. M. Cohen (Eds.), *The lives of lesbians, gays, and bisexuals: Children to adults* (pp. 181-200). Fort Worth, TX: Harcourt Brace.

Savin-Williams, R. C., & Rodriguez, R. G. (1993). A developmental, clinical perspective on lesbian, gay male, & bisexual youths. In T. P. Gullotta, G. R. Adams, & R. Montemayor (Eds.), *Adolescent sexuality: Advances in adolescent development, Vol. 5.* (pp. 77-101). Newbury Park, CA: Sage.

Research on Bisexual Health Issues

Bronn, C. D. (2001). Attitudes and self images of male and female bisexuals. *Journal of Bisexuality, 1*(4), 5-29.

Casserly, J. E. (1999). The Internet and social support: A study of bisexual women. (Master's thesis, California State University, Long Beach, 1998). *Master's Abstracts International, 37*(1), 124.

Fox, R. C. (1996). Bisexuality: An examination of theory and research. In R. P. Cabaj, & T. S. Stein (Eds.), *Textbook of homosexuality and mental health* (pp. 147-171). Washington, DC: American Psychiatric Press.

Fox, R. C. (1996). Bisexuality in perspective: A review of theory and research. In B. A. Firestein (Ed.), *Bisexuality: The psychology and politics of an invisible minority* (pp. 3-50). Thousand Oaks, CA: Sage. Reprinted in B. Greene & G. L. Croom (Eds.). (2000). *Education, research, and practice in lesbian, gay, bisexual, and transgendered psychology: A resource manual* (pp. 161- 206). Thousand Oaks, CA: Sage.

Fritz, E. M. (1987). Bisexuals and heterosexuals contrasted on neuroticism and extroversion. (Doctoral dissertation, University of Pittsburgh, 1986). *Dissertation Abstracts International, 47*(7), 3091B.

Galupo, M. P., & St. John, S. (2004). Friendships across sexual orientations: Experiences of bisexual women. *Journal of Bisexuality, 4*(1/2) 37-53.

Harris, D. A. I. (1978). Social-psychological characteristics of ambisexuals (Doctoral dissertation, University of Tennessee, 1977). *Dissertation Abstracts International, 39*(2), 574A.

.

Horowitz, S. M. (2003). Bisexuality and the quality of life. *Journal of Bisexuality, 3*(2).

Lysne, K. A. (1995). Bisexual self-identification: Cognitive and social factors. (Doctoral dissertation, California Institute of Integral Studies, San Francisco). *Dissertation Abstracts International, 56*(5), 2874B.

Moore, D. L. (2000). Empirical investigation of the conflict and flexibility models of bisexuality. (Doctoral dissertation, Georgia State University, 1999). *Dissertation Abstracts International, 61*(3), 1645B.

Rubenstein, M. (1982). *An in-depth study of bisexuality and its relationship to self-esteem.* Unpublished doctoral dissertation, The Institute for Advanced Study of Human Sexuality, San Francisco.

Taub, J. (1999). Bisexual women and beauty norms: A qualitative examination. *Journal of Lesbian Studies, 3*(4), 27-36.

Zinik, G. (1985). Identity conflict or adaptive flexibility? Bisexuality reconsidered. *Journal of Homosexuality, 11*(1/2), 7-19. Reprinted in P. C. R. Rust (Ed.). (2000). *Bisexuality in the United States: A social science reader* (pp. 55- 60). New York: Columbia University Press.

Bisexuality in the Context of Research on LGBT Health Issues

Balsam, K. F. (2003). Traumatic victimization in the lives of lesbian and bisexual women: A contextual approach. *Journal of Lesbian Studies, 7*(1), 1-14.

Berry, D. K. (1988). Early childhood mother-daughter involvement, femininity/masculinity, and erotic orientation in women. (Doctoral dissertation, Michigan State University, 1988). *Dissertation Abstracts International, 49*(5), 1933B.

Bieschke, K. J., McClanahan, M., Tozer, E., Grzegorek, J. L., & Park, J. (2000). Programmatic research on the treatment of lesbian, gay, and bisexual clients: The past, the present, and the course for the future. In R. M. Perez, K. A. DeBord & K. J. Bieschke (Eds.), *Handbook of Counseling and Psychotherapy with Lesbian, Gay and Bisexual Clients* (pp. 309-336). Washington, D.C.: American Psychological Association.

Breslow, N., Evans, L., & Langley, J. (1986). Comparisons among heterosexual, bisexual, and homosexual male sado-masochists. *Journal of Homosexuality, 13*(1), 83-107.

Charmoli, M. C. (1987). Incest in relation to sexual problems, abusive relationships, self-destructive behavior, and sexual orientation: A psychological study of women. (Doctoral dissertation, University of Minnesota, 1986). *Dissertation Abstracts International, 47*(12), 5048B.

Chung, Y. B. (1995). Career decision making of lesbian, gay, and bisexual individuals. *Career Development Quarterly, 44*(2), 178-190.

Cochran, S. D., Sullivan, J. G., & Mays, V. M. (2003). Prevalence of mental disorders, psychological distress, and mental health services use among lesbian, gay, and bisexual adults in the United States. *Journal of Consulting & Clinical Psychology, 71*(1) 53-61.

Dubé, E. M. (2000). Same- and cross-gender romantic relationships: Mediating variables between female presence and relationship quality. (Doctoral dissertation, Cornell University, 1999). *Dissertation Abstracts International, 60*(8), 4273B.

Galupo, M. P., & St. John, S. (2001). Benefits of cross-sexual orientation friendships among adolescent females. *Journal of Adolescence, 24*(1), 83-93.

Gregory, C. J. (1999). Resiliency among lesbian and bisexual women during the process of self-acceptance and disclosure of their sexual orientation. (Doctoral dissertation, University of Rhode Island, 1998). *Dissertation Abstracts International, 60*(2), 829B.

Gruskin, E. P. (1999). Behavioral health characteristics and sexual orientation of women enrolled in a large HMO. (Doctoral dissertation, University of California, Berkeley, 1999). *Dissertation Abstracts International, 60*(5), 2084B.

Hamner, K. M. (1994). Verbal and physical abuse against lesbians, gay men, and bisexuals: Stigma, social identity, and victim impact. (Doctoral dissertation, University of California, Los Angeles, 1993). *Dissertation Abstracts International, 55*(3), 748.

Herek, G. M., Gillis, J. R., & Cogan, J. C. (1999). Psychological sequelae of hate-crime victimization among lesbian, gay, and bisexual adults. *Journal of Consulting and Clinical Psychology, 67*(6), 945-951.

Herek, G. M., Gillis, J. R., Cogan, J. C., & Glunt, E. K. (1997). Hate crime victimization among lesbian, gay, and bisexual adults. *Journal of Interpersonal Violence, 12*(2), 195-215.

Hoburg, R. (2000). Psychosocial and experiential factors relevant to discrepancies among the affective, behavioral and identity components of sexual orientation. (Doctoral dissertation, University of Connecticut, 2000). *Dissertation Abstracts International, 61*(4), 2202.

Horowitz, S. M., Weis, D. L., & Laflin, M. T. (2001). Differences between sexual orientations, behavior groups, and social background, quality of life and health behaviors. *Journal of Sex Research, 38*(3), 205-218.

Hughes, T. L., & Eliason, M. (2002). Substance use and abuse in lesbian, gay, bisexual and transgender populations. *Journal of Primary Prevention, 22*(3), 263-298.

Istvan, J. (1983). Effects of sexual orientation on interpersonal judgment. *Journal of Sex Research, 19*(2), 173-191.

Jones, J. M. (1988). Sexual practices of alcoholic and nonalcoholic women in the '80s. (Doctoral dissertation, Rutgers University, 1987). *Dissertation Abstracts International*, 48(7), 1887A.

Jorm, A. F., Korten, A. E., Rodgers, B., Jacomb, P. A., & Christensen, H. (2002). Sexual orientation and mental health: Results from a community survey of young and middle-aged adults. *British Journal of Psychiatry*, 180, 423-427.

Juul, T. P. (1995). A survey to examine the relationship of the openness of self-identified lesbian, gay male, and bisexual public school teachers to job stress and job satisfaction. (Doctoral dissertation, New York University, 1994). *Dissertation Abstracts International*, 56(2), 416A.

Kase, A. M. (1996). Lesbian and bisexual women: Attitudes, behaviors, and self-esteem related to self-image, weight, and eating. (Master's thesis, Loyola University of Chicago, 1996). *Masters Abstracts International*, 34(3), 1298.

Killpack, L. (1993). How people cope: Relationships among Jungian personality type, gender, sexual orientation, and coping strategies. (Doctoral dissertation, California School of Professional Psychology, Berkeley/Alameda, 1993). *Dissertation Abstracts International*, 54(5), 2800B.

LaTorre, R. A., & Wendenburg, K. (1983). Psychological characteristics of bisexual, heterosexual and homosexual women. *Journal of Homosexuality*, 9(1), 87-97.

Lavender, A. D., & Bressler, L. C. (1981). Nondualists as deviants: Female bisexuals compared to female heterosexuals-homosexuals. *Deviant Behavior*, 2, 155-165.

Ketz, K., & Israel, T. (2002). The relationship between women's sexual identity and perceived wellness. *Journal of Bisexuality*, 2(2/3), 227-242.

Lonborg, S. D., & Phillips, J. M. (1996). Investigating the career development of gay, lesbian, and bisexual people: Methodological considerations and recommendations. *Journal of Vocational Behavior*, 48(2), 176-194.

Markus, E. B. (1981). An examination of psychological adjustment and sexual preference in the female. (Doctoral dissertation, University of Missouri, Kansas City, 1980). *Dissertation Abstracts International*, 41(10), 4338A.

Nurius, P. S. (1983). Mental health implications of sexual orientation. *Journal of Sex Research*, 19(2), 119-136.

Robinson, J. D. (2001). The thematic content categories of lesbian and bisexual women's sexual fantasies, psychological adjustment, daydreaming variables, and relationship functioning. (Doctoral dissertation, California School of Professional Psychology, Los Angeles, 2001). *Dissertation Abstracts International*, 62(2), 1144B.

Samuels, C. H. (1988). The effects of sexual orientation and degree of feminist affiliation among women on their evaluation of men and women. (Doctoral dissertation, Hofstra University, 1987). *Dissertation Abstracts International, 48*(11), 3425B.

Scheer, S., Parks, C. A., McFarland, W., Page-Shafer, K., Delgado, V., Ruiz, J. D., Molitor, F., & Klausner, J. D. (2003). Self-reported sexual identity, sexual behaviors and health risks: Examples from a population-based survey of young women. *Journal of Lesbian Studies, 7*(1), 69-83.

Sell, R. L., & Petrulio, C. (1996). Sampling homosexuals, bisexuals, gays, and lesbians for public health research: A review of the literature from 1990 to 1992. *Journal of Homosexuality, 30*(4), 31-47.

Sell, R. L., & Becker, J. B. (2001). Sexual orientation data collection and progress toward Healthy People 2010. American Journal of Public Health, 91(6), 876-882.

Selvidge, M. M. D. (2001). The relationship of sexist events, heterosexist events, self-concealment and self-monitoring to psychological well-being in lesbian and bisexual women. (Doctoral dissertation, Memphis State University, 2000). *Dissertation Abstracts International, 61*(7), 3861B.

Stokes, K., Kilmann, P. R., & Wanlass, R. L. (1983). Sexual orientation and sex role conformity. *Archives of Sexual Behavior, 12*(5), 427-433.

Taylor, E. B. (1994). Women's friendships: Influence of feminism and sexual orientation on Caucasian women's friendship patterns and emotional well-being. (Doctoral dissertation, University of Wisconsin, Madison). *Dissertation Abstracts International, 54*(8), 4410B.

Tyler, I. M. (1994). A study of self-perceptions among lesbian and bisexual women. (Doctoral dissertation, Walden University, 1993). *Dissertation Abstracts International, 55*(1), 164B.

Vujnovic, Sandra A. (1985). A profile of patients at a community agency serving sexual minorities. (Doctoral dissertation, University of Pittsburgh, 1984). *Dissertation Abstracts International, 46*(3), 950B.

Valanis, B. G., Bowen, D. J., Bassford, T., Whitlock, E., Charney, P., & Carter, R. A. (2000). Sexual orientation and health. *Archives of Family Medicine, 9*, 843-853.

Wayson, P. D. (1983). A study of personality variables in males as they relate to differences in sexual orientation. (Doctoral dissertation, California School of Professional Psychology, San Diego, 1983). *Dissertation Abstracts International, 44*(4), 1039A.

Wayson, P. D. (1985). Personality variables in males as they relate to differences in sexual orientation. *Journal of Homosexuality, 11*(1/2), 63-73.

Zinik, G. A. (1984). The relationship between sexual orientation and eroticism, cognitive flexibility, and negative affect. (Doctoral dissertation, University of California, Santa Barbara, 1983). *Dissertation Abstracts International, 45*(8), 2707B.

Research on Bisexual Clients' Experiences of Health Care Services

Page, E. (2004). Mental health services for bisexual women and bisexual men: An empirical study. *Journal of Bisexuality, 4*(1/2) 137-160.
Page, E. H. (2003). Mental health treatment experiences of self-identified bisexual women and bisexual men. (Doctoral dissertation, Antioch University New England Graduate School, 2002). *Dissertation Abstracts International, 63*(9), 4382B.

Bisexuality in the Context of Research on LGBT Clients' Experiences of Health Care Services

Avery, A. M., Hellman, R. E., & Sudderth, L. K. (2001). Satisfaction with mental health services among sexual minorities with major mental illness. *American Journal of Public Health, 91*(6), 990-991.
Bidol, H. F. (1996). Effects of expectancies and physician verbal messages on gay/lesbian/bisexual patients' satisfaction with the medical consultation. (Master's thesis, Michigan State University, 1996). *Masters Abstracts International, 34*(5), 1728.
Cochran, S. D., & Mays, V. M. (1988). Disclosure of sexual preference to physicians by black lesbian and bisexual women. *Western Journal of Medicine 149*(5), 616-619.
Diamant, A. L., & Wold, C. (2003). Sexual orientation and variation in physical and mental health status among women. *Journal of Women's Health, 12*(1), 41-49.
Diamant, A. L., Wold, C., Spritzer, K., & Gelberg, L. (2000). Health behaviors, health status, and access to and use of health care: A population-based study of lesbian, bisexual, and heterosexual women. *Archives of Family Medicine, 9*(10), 1043-1051.
Eliason, M. J., & Schope, R. (2001). Does "don't ask don't tell" apply to health care? Lesbian, gay, and bisexual people's disclosure to health care providers. *Journal of the Gay & Lesbian Medical Association, 5*(4), 125-134.
Jones, M. A., & Gabriel, M. A. (1999). Utilization of psychotherapy by lesbians, gay men, and bisexuals: Findings from a nationwide survey. *American Journal of Orthopsychiatry, 69*(2), 209-219.
Kaufman, J. S., Carlozzi, A. F., Boswell, D. L., Barnes, L. L. B., Wheeler-Scruggs, K., & Levy, P. A. (1997). Factors influencing therapist selection among gays, lesbians and bisexuals. *Counselling Psychology Quarterly, 10*(3), 287-297.
Kennedy, C., Strathdee, S. A., Goldstone, I. L., Hogg, R. S., O'Shaughnessy, M. V. (1999). "A lot of things I hide": Understanding disclosure in the care

of HIV-positive bisexual men. *Journal of the Gay & Lesbian Medical Association, 3*(4), 119-126.

Liddle, B. J. (1997). Gay and lesbian clients' selection of therapists and utilization of therapy. *Psychotherapy, 34*(1), 11-18.

Liljestrand, P., Gerling, E., & Saliba, P. A. (1978). The effects of social sex-role stereotypes and sexual orientation on psychotherapeutic outcomes. *Journal of Homosexuality, 3*(4), 361-372.

Moss, J. F. (1995). The Heterosexual Bias Inventory (HBI): Gay, lesbian and bisexual clients' perceptions of heterosexual bias in psychotherapy. (Doctoral dissertation, Michigan State University, 1994). *Dissertation Abstracts International, 55*(12), 5571B.

Smith, E. M., Johnson, S. R., & Guenther, S. M. (1985). Health care attitudes and experiences during gynecologic care among lesbians and bisexuals. *American Journal of Public Health, 75*(9), 1085-1087.

Sweet, M. J. (1994). Gay, lesbian, and bisexual young adults: Satisfaction with counseling experiences. (Doctoral dissertation, University of Wisconsin, Madison, 1993). *Dissertation Abstracts International, 54*(8), 4410B.

Walters, K. L., Simoni, J. M., & Horwath, P. F. (2001). Sexual orientation bias experiences and service needs of gay, lesbian, bisexual, transgendered, and two-spirited American Indians. *Journal of Gay & Lesbian Social Services: Issues in Practice, Policy & Research, 13*(1/2), 133-149.

Research on Health Care Professionals' Knowledge and Attitudes About Bisexual Issues

Alley, G. R. (1996). Biphobia in social work education: Social work students knowledge of and attitudes toward working with bisexual clients. (Master's thesis, California State University, Long Beach, 1996). *Masters Abstracts International, 34*(6), 2234.

Butt, J. A. (1993). Counselling bisexuals: A look at therapists' attitudes towards bisexuality and application in clinical practices. (Master's thesis, University of Guelph, Ontario, Canada, 1992). *Masters Abstracts International, 31*(3), 1376.

Mohr, J. J., Israel, T., & Sedlacek, W. E. (2001). Counselors' attitudes regarding bisexuality as predictors of counselors' clinical responses: An analogue study of a female bisexual client. *Journal of Counseling Psychology, 48*(2), 212-222.

Bisexuality in the Context of Research on Health Care Professionals' Knowledge and Attitudes About LGBT Issues

Avery, A. M. (2001). Graduate students' perceptions of the inclusion of gay, lesbian, and bisexual issues during clinical training in practicums and internship. (Doctoral dissertation, Chicago School of Professional Psychology, 2000). *Dissertation Abstracts International, 62*(12), 5953B.

Bidell, M. P. (2002). The development and validation of the Sexual Orientation Counselor Competency Scale (SOCCS). (Doctoral dissertation, University of California, Santa Barbara, 2000). *Dissertation Abstracts International, 62*(2), 1064B.

Bieschke, K. J., & Matthews, C. (1996). Career counselor attitudes and behaviors toward gay, lesbian, and bisexual clients. *Journal of Vocational Behavior, 48*(2), 243-255.

Caisango, T. M. (1997). Perceptions of knowledge, attitude, and atmosphere of mental health professionals toward counseling gay, lesbian, and bisexuals. (Doctoral dissertation, Kent State University, 1996). *Dissertation Abstracts International, 57*(10), 6172B.

Croteau, J. M., & Lark, J. S. (1995). A qualitative investigation of biased and exemplary student affairs practice concerning lesbian, gay, and bisexual issues. *Journal of College Student Development, 36*(5), 472-482.

Eberz, A. B. (2001). A comparison of licensed psychologists' attitudes and clinical evaluations for clients of differing sexual orientations. (Doctoral dissertation, The Pennsylvania State University, 2000). *Dissertation Abstracts International, 61*(12), 6703B.

Finnegan, D. G., McNally, E. B., Anderson, E. B., & Shelton, C. (2001). Counselor competence in treating LGBT clients. In SAMSHA Center for Substance Abuse Treatment (Ed.), *A provider's introduction to substance abuse treatment for lesbian, gay, bisexual, and transgender individuals* (DHHS Publication No. SMA 01-3498, pp. 115-121). Rockville, MD: National Clearinghouse for Alcohol and Drug Information.

Gelberg, S., & Chojnacki, J. T. (1995). Developmental transitions of gay/lesbian/bisexual-affirmative, heterosexual career counselors. *Career Development Quarterly, 43*(3), 267-273.

Houston, A. N. (2000). Lesbian and bisexual therapists' desire for authenticity: Self-disclosure vs. nondisclosure of sexual orientation in therapy and supervision. (Doctoral dissertation, New School for Social Research, 1998). *Dissertation Abstracts International, 60*(8), 4226B.

Hunt, B. B. (1993). Counselor education students: Their knowledge, attitudes, and beliefs regarding gay, lesbian, and bisexual clients. (Doctoral dissertation, University of Virginia, 1992). *Dissertation Abstracts International, 54*(5), 1679A.

Kanner, E. B. (1980). Contemporary standards of gender characteristics of heterosexuals, homosexuals, and bisexuals as evaluated by mental health practitioners. (Doctoral dissertation, Fordham University, 1980). *Dissertation Abstracts International, 40*(12), 5814B.

McGirr, M. V. (1980). Gender characteristics attributed to heterosexual, homosexual, and bisexual persons by therapists and non-therapists. (Doctoral dissertation, Fordham University, 1980). *Dissertation Abstracts International*, *41*(3), 1094B.

Pilkington, N., & Cantor, J. (1996). Perceptions of heterosexual bias in professional psychology programs: A survey of graduate students. *Professional Psychology: Research and Practice*, *27*(6), 604-612.

Prince, J. P. (1997). Assessment bias affecting lesbian, gay male and bisexual individuals. *Measurement and Evaluation in Counseling and Development*, *30*(2), 82-87.

TRAINING ISSUES REGARDING CULTURALLY COMPETENT LGBT HEALTH CARE

Atkins, D. L., & Townsend, M. H. (1996). Issues for gay male, lesbian, and bisexual mental health trainees. In R. P. Cabaj & T. S. Stein (Eds.), *Textbook of homosexuality and mental health* (pp. 645-655). Washington, DC: American Psychiatric Press.

Bohan, J. S. (1997). Teaching on the edge: The psychology of sexual orientation. *Teaching of Psychology*, *24*(1), 27-32.

Browning, C., & Kain, C. (2000). Teaching lesbian, gay, and bisexual psychology: Contemporary strategies. In B. Greene & G. L. Croom (Eds.), *Education, research, and practice in lesbian, gay, bisexual, and transgendered psychology: A resource manual* (pp. 46-58). Thousand Oaks, CA: Sage.

Cabaj, R. P. (1996). Gay, lesbian, and bisexual mental health professionals and their colleagues. In R. P. Cabaj & T. S. Stein (Eds.), *Textbook of homosexuality and mental health* (pp. 33-39). Washington, DC: American Psychiatric Press.

Croteau, J. M., Bieschke, K. J., Phillips, J. C., Lark, J. S., Fischer, A. R., & Eberz, A. B. (1998). Toward a more inclusive and diverse multigenerational community of lesbian, gay, and bisexual affirmative counseling psychologists. *Counseling Psychologist*, *26*(5), 809-816.

Gainor, K. A. (2000). Including transgender issues in lesbian, gay, and bisexual psychology: Implications for clinical practice and training. In B. Greene & G. L. Croom (Eds.), *Education, research, and practice in lesbian, gay, bisexual, and transgendered psychology: A resource manual* (pp. 131-1 60). Thousand Oaks, CA: Sage.

Hancock, K. A. (2000). Lesbian, gay, and bisexual lives: Basic issues in psychotherapy training and practice. In B. Greene & G. L. Croom (Eds.), *Education, research, and practice in lesbian, gay, bisexual, and transgendered psychology: A resource manual* (pp. 91-130). Thousand Oaks, CA: Sage.

Hart, T. (2001). Lack of training in behavior therapy and research regarding lesbian, gay, bisexual, and transgendered individuals. *Behavior Therapist, 24*, 217-218.

Kimmel, D. C. (2000). Including sexual orientation in life span developmental psychology. In B. Greene & G. L. Croom (Eds.), *Education, research, and practice in lesbian, gay, bisexual, and transgendered psychology: A resource manual* (pp. 59-73). Thousand Oaks, CA: Sage.

Mobley, M. (1998). Lesbian, gay, and bisexual issues in counseling psychology training: Acceptance in the millennium? *Counseling Psychologist, 26*(5), 786-796.

Morrow, S. L. (1998). Toward a new paradigm in counseling psychology training and education. *Counseling Psychologist, 26*(5), 797-808.

Iasenza, S. (1989). Some challenges of integrating sexual orientations into counselor training and research. *Journal of Counseling & Development, 68*(1), 73-76.

Israel, T. (1998). Comparing counselor education training models for working with lesbian, gay, and bisexual clients. (Doctoral dissertation, Arizona State University, 1998). *Dissertation Abstracts International, 59*(3), 1368B.

Israel, T., & Selvidge, M. D. (2003). Contributions of multicultural counseling to counselor competence with lesbian, gay and bisexual clients. *Journal of Multicultural Counseling and Development, 31*(2), 84-98.

Lark, J. S., & Croteau, J. M. (1998). Lesbian, gay, and bisexual doctoral students' mentoring relationships with faculty in counseling psychology: A qualitative study. *Counseling Psychologist, 26*(8), 754-776.

McDaniel, J. S., Cabaj, R. P., & Purcell, D. W. (1996). Care across the spectrum of mental health settings: Working with gay, lesbian, and bisexual patients in consultation-liaison services, inpatient treatment facilities, and community outpatient mental health centers. In R. P. Cabaj, & T. S. Stein (Eds.), *Textbook of homosexuality and mental health* (pp. 687-704). Washington, DC: American Psychiatric Press.

Owen, W. F., Jr. (1996). Gay and bisexual men in medical care. In R. P. Cabaj, & T. S. Stein (Eds.), *Textbook of homosexuality and mental health* (pp. 673-685). Washington, DC: American Psychiatric Press.

Phillips, J. C. (2000). Training issues and considerations. In R. M. Perez, K. A. DeBord, & K. J. Bieschke (Eds.), *Handbook of counseling and psychotherapy with lesbian, gay, and bisexual clients* (pp. 337-358). Washington, DC: American Psychological Association.

Phillips, J. C., & Fischer, A. R. (1998). Graduate students' training experiences with lesbian, gay, and bisexual issues. *Counseling Psychologist, 26*(5), 712-734.

Safren, S. (1999). Selected issues: Facing gay, lesbian, and bisexual graduate students in clinical psychological training. *Behavior Therapist, 22,* 189-192.

Stein, T. S., & Burg, B. K. (1996). Teaching in mental health training programs about homosexuality, lesbians, gay men, and bisexuals. In R. P. Cabaj, & T. S. Stein (Eds.), *Textbook of homosexuality and mental health* (pp. 621-631). Washington, DC: American Psychiatric Press.

Townsend, M. H., & Wallick, M. M. (1996). Gay, lesbian, and bisexual issues in medical schools: Implications for training. In R. P. Cabaj, & T. S. Stein (Eds.), *Textbook of homosexuality and mental health* (pp. 633-644). Washington, DC: American Psychiatric Press.

A change-model approach to raising awareness of gay, lesbian, and bisexual issues among graduate students in counseling.

Tyler, J. M., Jackman-Wheitner, L., Strader, S., & Lenox, R. (1997). A change-model approach to raising awareness of gay, lesbian, and bisexual issues among graduate students in counseling. *Journal of Sex Education and Therapy, 22*(2), 37-43.

ETHICAL ISSUES REGARDING CULTURALLY COMPETENT LGBT HEALTH CARE

American Psychological Association Division 44/Committee on Lesbian, Gay, and Bisexual Concerns Task Force on Psychotherapy with Lesbian, Gay, and Bisexual Clients. (2000). Guidelines for psychotherapy with lesbian, gay, and bisexual clients. *American Psychologist, 55*(12), 1440-1451. Reprinted in L. D. Garnets & D. C. Kimmel (Eds.). (2003). *Psychological perspectives on lesbian, gay, and bisexual experiences* (pp. 756-785). New York: Columbia University Press.

Brown, L. S. (1996). Ethical concerns with sexual minority patients. In R. P. Cabaj & T. S. Stein (Eds.), *Textbook of homosexuality and mental health* (pp. 897-916). Washington, DC: American Psychiatric Press.

Brown, L. S. (1996). Preventing heterosexism and bias in psychotherapy and counseling. In E. D. Rothblum & L. A. Bond (Eds.), *Preventing heterosexism and homophobia* (pp. 36-58). Thousand Oaks, CA: Sage.

Cabaj, R. P. (1996). Sexual orientation of the therapist. In R. P. Cabaj & T. S. Stein (Eds.), *Textbook of homosexuality and mental health* (pp. 513-524). Washington, DC: American Psychiatric Press.

Chung, Y. B. (2003). Ethical and professional issues in career assessment with lesbian, gay, and bisexual persons. *Journal of Career Assessment, 11*(1), 96-112.

Conger, J. (1975). Proceedings of the American Psychological Association, Incorporated, for the year 1974: Minutes of the annual meeting of the Council of Representatives. *American Psychologist, 30,* 620-651. Reprinted in B. Greene & G. L. Croom (Eds.). (2000). *Education, research, and practice in lesbian, gay, bisexual, and transgendered psychology: A resource manual* (pp. 310-313). Thousand Oaks, CA: Sage.

Davidson, G. C. (2001). Conceptual and ethical issues in therapy for the psychological problems of gay men, lesbians, and bisexuals. *Journal of Clinical Psychology, 57,* 695-704.

Dworkin, S. H. (1992). Some ethical considerations when counseling gay, lesbian, and bisexual clients. In S. H. Dworkin, & F. J. Gutierrez (Eds.), *Counseling gay men and lesbians: Journey to the end of the rainbow* (pp. 325-334). Alexandria, VA: American Association of Counseling and Development.

Haldeman, D. C. (1991). Sexual orientation conversion therapy: A scientific examination. In J. Gonsiorek & J. Weinrich (Eds.), *Homosexuality: Research implications for public policy* (pp. 149-160). Newbury Park, CA: Sage.

Haldeman, D. C. (1994). The practice and ethics of sexual orientation conversion therapy. *Journal of Consulting & Clinical Psychology, 62*(2), 221-227.

Haldeman, D. C. (2000). Therapeutic responses to sexual orientation: Psychology's evolution. In B. Greene & G. L. Croom (Eds.), *Education, research, and practice in lesbian, gay, bisexual, and transgendered psychology: A resource manual* (pp. 244-262). Thousand Oaks, CA: Sage.

Herek, G. M., Kimmel, D. C., Amaro, H., & Melton, G. (1991). Avoiding heterosexist bias in psychological research. *American Psychologist, 46*(9), 957-963.

Janson, G. R., & Steigerwald, F. J. (2002). Family counseling and ethical challenges with gay, lesbian, bisexual, and transgendered (GLBT) clients: More questions than answers. *Family Journal: Counseling and Therapy for Couples and Families, 10,* 415-418.

Kooden, H. D., Morin, S. F., Riddle, D. I., Rogers, M., Sang, B. E., & Strassburger, F. (1979). *Removing the stigma: Final Report of the Board of Social and Ethical Responsibility for Psychology's Task Force on the Status of Lesbian and Gay Male Psychologists.* Washington, DC: American Psychological Association.

Morrow, S. L. (2000). First do no harm: Therapist issues in psychotherapy with lesbian, gay, and bisexual clients. In R. M. Perez, K. A. DeBord, & K. J. Bieschke (Eds.), *Handbook of counseling and psychotherapy with lesbian, gay, and bisexual clients* (pp. 137-155). Washington, DC: American Psychological Association.

Nabors, N. A., Hall, R. L., Miville, M. L., Nettles, R., Pauling, M. L., & Ragsdale, B. L. (2001). Multiple minority group oppression: Divided we stand? *Journal of the Gay & Lesbian Medical Association, 5*(3), 101-105.

Richardson, D. (1987). Recent challenges to traditional assumptions about homosexuality: Some implications for practice. *Journal of Homosexuality, 13*(4), 1-12.

Schneider, M. S., Brown, L. S., & Glassgold, J. M. (2002). Implementing the resolution on appropriate therapeutic responses to sexual orientation: A guide for the perplexed. *Professional Psychology, 33*(3), 265-276.

Shidlo, A., & Schroeder, M. (2001). Changing sexual orientation: A consumer's report. *Professional Psychology: Research and Practice, 33,* 249-259.

Stein, T. S. (1996). A critique of approaches to changing sexual orientation. In R. P. Cabaj & T. S. Stein (Eds.), *Textbook of homosexuality and mental health* (pp. 525-537). Washington, DC: American Psychiatric Press.

PREJUDICE, DISCRIMINATION, HETEROSEXISM, AND BIPHOBIA

Prejudice and Discrimination

Anastas, J. W. (1998). Working against discrimination: Gay, lesbian and bisexual people on the job. *Journal of Gay & Lesbian Social Services, 8*(3), 83-98.

Anderson, C. W., & Smith, H. R. (1993). Stigma and honor: Gay, lesbian, and bisexual people in the U.S. military. In L. Diamant (Ed.), *Homosexual issues in the workplace* (pp. 65-89). Washington, DC: Taylor & Francis.

Brown, K. K. (1997). Androgyny, perceived prejudice and outness among lesbian and bisexual women. (Master's thesis, Michigan State University, 1997). *Masters Abstracts International, 35*(5), 1538.

Brown, K. K. (2001). Androgyny and coping with prejudice among lesbian and bisexual women. (Doctoral dissertation, Michigan State University, 2000). *Dissertation Abstracts International, 61*(8), 4393B.

Colker, R. (1996). A bi jurisprudence. In R. Colker, *Hybrid: Bisexuals, multiracials, and other misfits under American law* (pp. 15-38). New York: NYU Press.

Croteau, J. M. (1996). Research on the work experiences of lesbian, gay, and bisexual people: An integrative review of methodology and findings. *Journal of Vocational Behavior, 48*(2), 195-209.

Croteau, J. M., & Von Destinon, M. (1994). A national survey of job search experiences of lesbian, gay, and bisexual student affairs professionals. *Journal of College Student Development*, *35*(1), 40-45.

Kass, N. E., Faden, R. R., Fox, R., & Dudley, J. (1992). Homosexual and bisexual men's perceptions of discrimination in health services. *American Journal of Public Health*, *82*(9), 1277-1279.

Mays, V. M. (2001). Mental health correlates of perceived discrimination among lesbian, gay, and bisexual adults in the United States. *American Journal of Public Health*, *91*(11), 1869-1877.

Omoto, A. M. (1999). Lesbian, gay, and bisexual issues in public policy: Some of the relevance and realities of psychological science. In J. S. Bohan & G. M. Russell (Eds.), *Conversations about psychology and sexual orientation* (pp. 165-182). New York: New York University Press.

Onken, S. J. (1998). Conceptualizing violence against gay, lesbian, bisexual, intersexual, and transgendered people. *Journal of Gay & Lesbian Social Services*, *8*(3), 5-24.

Purcell, D. W., & Hicks, D. W. (1996). Institutional discrimination against lesbians, gay men, and bisexuals. In R. P. Cabaj & T. S. Stein (Eds.), *Textbook of homosexuality and mental health* (pp. 763-782). Washington, DC: American Psychiatric Press.

Russell, G. M., & Bohan, J. S. (1999). Implications for public policy. In J. S. Bohan & G. M. Russell (Eds.), *Conversations about psychology and sexual orientation* (pp. 139-164). New York: New York University Press.

Taylor, V., & Raeburn, N. C. (1995). Identity politics as high-risk activism: Career consequences for lesbian, gay, and bisexual sociologists. *Social Problems*, *42*(2), 252-273.

Heterosexism and LGBT People

American Psychological Association Committee on Lesbian and Gay Concerns. (1991). Avoiding heterosexist bias in language. *American Psychologist*, *46*(9), 973-973.

Blasingame, B. M. (1992). The roots of biphobia: Racism and internalized heterosexism. In *Closer to home* (pp. 47-54).

Chan, C. S. (1996). Combating heterosexism in educational institutions: Structural changes and strategies. In E. D. Rothblum, & L. A. Bond (Eds.), *Preventing heterosexism and homophobia* (pp. 20-35). Thousand Oaks, CA: Sage.

Greene, B. (2000). Beyond heterosexism and across the cultural divide: Developing an inclusive lesbian, gay, and bisexual psychology: A look to the future. In B. Greene & G. L. Croom (Eds.), *Education, research, and prac-*

tice in lesbian, gay, bisexual, and transgendered psychology: A resource manual (pp. 1-45). Thousand Oaks, CA: Sage.

Kaplan, R. (1992). Compulsory heterosexuality and the bisexual existence: Toward a bisexual feminist understanding of heterosexism. In *Closer to home* (pp. 269-280).

Schreier, B. A. (1995). Moving beyond tolerance: A new paradigm for programming about homophobia/biphobia and heterosexism. *Journal of College Student Development,* 26(1), 19-26.

Udis-Kessler, A. (1992). Closer to home: Bisexual feminism and the transformation of hetero/sexism. In *Closer to home* (pp. 205-232).

Waldo, C. R. (1999). Working in a majority context: A structural model of heterosexism as minority stress in the workplace. *Journal of Counseling Psychology,* 46(2), 218-232.

Attitudes Toward Bisexual Women and Bisexual Men

Barrios, B. A., Corbitt, L. C., Estes, J. P., & Topping, J. S. (1976). Effect of a social stigma on interpersonal distance. *The Psychological Record, 26,* 343-348.

Eliason, M. (2001). Bi negativity: The stigma facing bisexual men. *Journal of Bisexuality,* 1(2/3), 137-154.

Eliason, M. J. (1996). A survey of the campus climate for lesbian, gay, and bisexual university members. *Journal of Psychology & Human Sexuality, 8,* 39-58.

Eliason, M. J. (1997). The prevalence and nature of biphobia in heterosexual undergraduate students. *Archives of Sexual Behavior, 26*(3), 317-325.

Herdt, G. (2001). Social change, sexual diversity, and tolerance for bisexuality in the United States. In A. R. D'Augelli, & C. J. Patterson (Eds.), *Lesbian, gay, and bisexual identities and youth: Psychological perspectives* (pp. 267-283). New York: Oxford University Press.

Herek, G. M. (2002). Heterosexuals' attitudes toward bisexual men and women in the United States. *Journal of Sex Research, 39*(4), 264-274.

Israel, T., & Mohr, J. J. (2004). Attitudes toward bisexual women and men: Current research, future directions. *Journal of Bisexuality, 4*(1/2), 117-134.

Mohr, J. J., & Rochlen, A. B. (1999). Measuring attitudes regarding bisexuality in lesbian, gay male, and heterosexual populations. *Journal of Counseling Psychology, 46*(3).

Mulick, P. S., & Wright, L. W., Jr. (2002). Examining the existence of biphobia in the heterosexual and homosexual populations. *Journal of Bisexuality, 2*(4), 45-64.

Ochs, R. (1996). Biphobia: It goes more than two ways. In B. A. Firestein (Ed.), *Bisexuality: The psychology and politics of an invisible minority* (pp. 217-239). Thousand Oaks, CA: Sage.

Ochs, R., & Deihl, M. (1992). Moving beyond binary thinking. In W. Blumenfeld (Ed.), *Homophobia: How we all pay the price* (pp. 67-75). Boston: Beacon. Reprinted in M. Adams, W. J. Blumenfeld, R. Castañeda, H. W. Hackman, M. L. Peters, & X. Zúñiga (Eds.). (2000). *Readings for diversity and social justice: An anthology on racism, antisemitism, sexism, heterosexism, ableism, and classism* (pp. 276-280). New York: Routledge.

Rust, P. C. (1993). Neutralizing the political threat of the marginal woman: Lesbians' beliefs about bisexual women. *Journal of Sex Research, 30*(3), 214-228. Reprinted in P. C. R. Rust (Ed.). (2000). *Bisexuality in the United States: A Social Science Reader* (pp. 471-497). New York: Columbia University Press.

Rust-Rodriguez, P. C. (1990). When does the unity of a "common oppression" break down? Reciprocal attitudes between lesbian and bisexual women (Doctoral dissertation, University of Michigan, 1989). *Dissertation Abstracts International, 50*(8), 2668A.

Spalding, L. R., & Peplau, L. A. (1997). The unfaithful lover: Heterosexuals' perceptions of bisexuals and their relationships. *Psychology of Women Quarterly, 21*(4), 611-625.

Udis-Kessler, A. (1991). Present tense: Biphobia as a crisis of meaning. In *Bi any other name* (pp. 350-358).

Udis-Kessler, A. (1996). Challenging the stereotypes. In *Bisexual horizons* (pp. 45-57).

Bisexuality and Feminism

Armstrong, E. (1995). Traitors to the cause? Understanding the lesbian/gay "bisexuality" debates. In *Bisexual politics* (pp. 199-218).

Ault, A. (1996). Ambiguous identity in an unambiguous sex/gender structure: The case of bisexual women. *Sociological Quarterly, 37*(3), 449-463.

Ault, A. (1994). Hegemonic discourse in an oppositional community: Lesbian feminists and bisexuality. *Critical sociology, 20*(3), 107-122. Reprinted in B. Beemyn, & M. Eliason. (Eds.). (1996). *Queer studies: A lesbian, gay, bisexual, and transgender anthology* (pp. 204-216). New York: NYU Press.

Ault, A. L. (1995). Science, sex, and subjectivity: Bisexuals, lesbian, feminist. (Doctoral dissertation, Ohio State University, 1995). *Dissertation Abstracts International, 56*(4), 1550A.

Baker, K. (1992). Bisexual feminist politics: Because bisexuality is not enough. In *Closer to home* (pp. 255-268).

Bisexual Anthology Collective. (1995). Toward a feminist bisexual politic: A discussion. In *Plural desires* (pp. 210-225).

Bloomsbury, A. (1998). The politics of erotics: Bisexuality, feminism and S/M. *In the Family: A Magazine for Gays, Lesbians, Bisexuals and Their Relations, 3*(4), 16-19.

Bower, T. (1995). Bisexual women, *feminist* politics. In *Bisexual politics* (pp. 99-108).

Came, H. (1996). Towards a free and loose future. In *Bisexual horizons* (pp. 25-29).

Choe, M. M. (1992). Our selves, growing whole. In *Closer to home* (pp. 17-26).

Eliott, B. (1991). Bisexuality: The best thing that ever happened to lesbian-feminism? In *Bi any other name* (pp. 324-328).

Eliott, B. (1992). Holly near and yet so far. In *Closer to home* (pp. 233-254).

Friedland, L., & Highleyman, L. A. (1991). The fine art of labeling: The convergence of anarchism, feminism, and bisexuality. In *Bi any other name* (pp. 285-298).

Golden, C. (1994). Our politics and choices: The feminist movement and sexual orientation. In B. Greene & G. M. Herek (Eds.), *Lesbian and gay psychology: Theory, research, and clinical applications* (pp. 54-70). Thousand Oaks, CA: Sage.

Gregory, D. (1983). From where I stand: A case for feminist bisexuality. In S. Cartledge & J. Ryan (Eds.), *Sex and love: New thoughts on old contradictions* (pp. 141-156). London: The Women's Press.

Heldke, L. (1997). In praise of unreliability. *Hypatia, 12*(3), 174-181.

Hemmings, C. (1995). Locating bisexual identities: Discourses of bisexuality and contemporary feminist theory. In D. Bell & G. Valentine (Eds.), *Mapping desire: Geographies of sexualities* (pp. 41-54). London: Routledge.

Higgenbotham, A. (1995). Chicks goin' at it. In *Listen up: Voices from the next feminist generation* (pp. 3-11).

Layton, L. B. 2000). The psychopolitics of bisexuality. *Studies in Gender and Sexuality, 1*(1), 41-60.

Matteson, D. (1991). Bisexual feminist man. In *Bi any other name* (pp. 43-50).

Murray, A. S. (1995). Forsaking all others: A bifeminist discussion of compulsory monogamy. In *Bisexual politics* (pp. 293-304).

Nagle, J. (1995). Framing radical bisexuality: Toward a gender agenda. In *Bisexual politics* (pp. 305-314).

Ochs, R. (1992). Bisexuality, feminism, men and me. In *Closer to home* (pp. 127-132). Reprinted in A. Desselman, L. McNair, & N. Schniedewind (Eds.). (1999). *Women: Images and realities: A multicultural anthology* (pp. 155-157). Mountainview, CA: Mayfield Publishing.

O'Connor, P. (1997). Warning! Contents under pressure. *Hypatia, 12*(3), 193-188.

Parr, Z. (1996). Feminist bisexuals in the U.K.–Caught between a rock and a hard place? In *Bisexual horizons* (pp. 274-280).

Schneider, A. (1991). Guilt politics. In *Bi any other name* (pp. 275-278).

Stone, S. D. (1996). Bisexual women and the 'threat' to lesbian space: Or what if all the lesbians leave? *Frontiers: A Journal of Women's Studies*, *16*(1), 101-116.

Sturgis, S. M. (1996). Bisexual feminism: Challenging the splits. In *Bisexual horizons* (pp. 41-44).

Taub, J. (2003). What should I wear? A qualitative look at the impact of feminism and women's communities on bisexual women's appearance. *Journal of Bisexuality*, *3*(1), 9-22.

Terris, E. (1991). My life as a lesbian-identified bisexual fag hag. In *Bi any other name* (pp. 56-59).

Udis-Kessler, A. (1992). Closer to home: Bisexual feminism and the transformation of hetero/sexism. In *Closer to home* (pp. 205-232).

Uwano, K. (1991). Bi-lovable Japanese feminist. In *Bi any other name* (pp. 185-187).

Weise, E. R., & Bennett, K. (1992). Feminist bisexuality: A both/and option for an either/or world. In *Closer to home* (pp. 205-231).

Yoshino, K. (2000). The epistemic contract of bisexual erasure. *Stanford Law Review*, 52, 353-459.

Yoshizaki, A. (1992). Breaking the rules: Constructing a bisexual feminist marriage. In *Closer to home* (pp. 155-162).

Young, S. (1992). Breaking silence about the "B-word": Bisexual identity and lesbian-feminist discourse. In *Closer to home* (pp. 75-87).

Woodard, V. (1991). Insights at 3:30 a.m. In *Bi any other name* (pp. 83-86).

Zabatinsky, V. (1992). Some thoughts on power, gender, body image and sex in the life of one bisexual lesbian feminist. In *Closer to home* (pp. 133-146).

BISEXUALITY AND SPIRITUALITY

Psychological and Sociological Perspectives

Davidson, M. G. (2000). Religion and spirituality. In R. M. Perez, K. A. DeBord, & K. J. Bieschke (Eds.), *Handbook of counseling and psychotherapy with lesbian, gay, and bisexual clients* (pp. 409-433). Washington, DC: American Psychological Association.

Hutchins, L. (2002). Bisexual women as emblematic sexual healers and the problematics of the embodied sacred whore. *Journal of Bisexuality*, *2*(2/3), 205-226.

Hutchins, L. A. (2001). Erotic rites: A cultural analysis of contemporary United States sacred sexuality traditions and trends. (Doctoral dissertation,

The Union Institute, 2001). *Dissertation Abstracts International, 62*(01), 219A.

Seif, H. H. (1997). A weave of sexuality, ethnicity and religion: Jewish women of the San Francisco Bay area embracing complexity. (Master's thesis, University of Arizona, 1997). *Masters Abstracts International, 35*(6). 1693.

Personal and Political Perspectives

Chapman, G. (1996). Roots of a male bisexual nature. In *Bisexual horizons* (pp. 62-69).

de Sousa, E. (1995). In the spirit of Aloha: To love is to share the happiness of life here & now. In *Plural desires* (pp. 145-149).

Drake, K. (1996). Bisexuality and spirituality. In *Bisexual horizons* (pp. 111-113).

Durgadas, G. S. (1999). Confessions of a tantric androgyne. In C. Lake (Ed.), *ReCreations: Religion and spirituality in the lives of queer people* (pp. 130-035). Toronto: Queer Press.

Ever, A. (1999). My life as a Jewish queer priestess. In C. Lake (Ed.), *ReCreations: Religion and spirituality in the lives of queer people* (pp. 153-156). Toronto: Queer Press.

Farajajé-Jones, E. (1994, Spring). Currents of the spirit. *Anything That Moves, 7,* 8-9.

Fehr, T. C. (1995). Accepting my inherent duality. In *Plural desires* (pp. 128-129).

Frazin, J. (1994, Spring). An interview with Starhawk. *Anything That Moves, 7,* 24-27.

Hain, D. W. (2002). Organizing a GLBT week at a Christian seminary: A bisexual's journey. *Journal of Bisexuality, 2*(4), 141-147.

Hurley, K. (1991). Coming out in spirit and in flesh. In *Bi any other name* (pp. 94-102).

Hutchins, L. (1991). Letting go: An interview with John Horne. In *Bi any other name* (pp. 112-116).

Litman, J. R. (1991). Kol sason v'kol simcha, kol kalah v'kil kalah: Same gender weddings and spiritual renewal. In D. Shneer & C. Aviv (Eds.), *Queer Jews* (pp. 111-118). New York: Routledge.

Nagle, J. (2002). Queer naked Seder and other newish Jewish traditions. In D. Shneer & C. Aviv (Eds.), *Queer Jews* (pp. 70-83). New York: Routledge.

Perlstein, M. (1996). Integrating a gay, lesbian, or bisexual person's religious and spiritual needs and choices into psychotherapy. In C. J. Alexander (Ed.), *Gay and lesbian mental health: A sourcebook for practitioners* (pp. 173-188). New York: Harrington Park Press.

Rose, S. (1996). Against marriage. In *Bisexual horizons* (pp. 119-121).
Starhawk. (1995). The sacredness of pleasure. In *Bisexual politics* (pp. 325-329).
Tirado, L. (1991). Reclaiming heart and mind. In *Bi any other name* (pp. 117-123).
Utter, B. (1999). Bisexuality and the spiritual continuum. In C. Lake (Ed.),
    ReCreations: Religion and spirituality in the lives of queer people
    (pp. 143-146). Toronto: Queer Press.

QUEER THEORY/CULTURAL STUDIES/LITERARY CRITICISM

Anderlini-D'Onofrio, S. (2003). The lie with the ounce of truth: Lillian
    Hellman's bisexual fantasies. *Journal of Bisexuality*, *3*(1), 87-115.
Ault, A. (1996). Hegemonic discourse in an oppositional community: Lesbian
    feminist stigmatization of bisexual women. In B. Beemyn, & M. Eliason
    (Eds.), *Queer studies: A lesbian, gay, bisexual, & transgender anthology*
    (pp. 204-216). New York: New York University Press.
Beemyn, B. (2002). "To say yes to life": Sexual and gender fluidity in James
    Baldwin's *Giovanni's Room* and *Another Country*. *Journal of Bisexuality*,
    2(1), 55-72.
Blumberg, J., & Soal, J. (1997). Let's talk about sex: Liberation and regulation
    in discourses of bisexuality. In A. Levett, A. Kottler, E. Burman, & I.
    Parker (Eds.), *Culture, power, and difference: Discourse analysis in South
    Africa* (pp. 83-95). Capetown: University of Capetown Press.
Bontz, G. D. (1999). Computer-mediated communication (CMC) and bisex-
    ual identity: A rhetorical criticism of discourse communicated by self-iden-
    tified bisexuals. (Master's thesis, Central Missouri State University, 1998).
    Master's Abstracts International, *37*(3), 716.
Burrill, K. G. (2002). Queering bisexuality. *Journal of Bisexuality*, *2*(2/3),
    95-105.
Carroll, T. (1996). Invisible sissy: The politics of masculinity in Afri-
    can American bisexual narrative. In D. E. Hall, & M. Pramaggiore
    (Eds.), *RePresenting bisexualities: Subjects and cultures of fluid de-
    sire* (pp. 180-204). New York: New York University Press.
Connerly, G. (1996). The politics of Black lesbian, gay, and bisexual identity.
    In B. Beemyn, & M. Eliason (Eds.), *Queer studies: A lesbian, gay, bisexual, &
    transgender anthology* (pp. 133-145). New York: New York University
    Press.
du Plessis, M. (1994). Queer pasts now: Historical fictions in lesbian, bisex-
    ual, and gay film. (Doctoral dissertation, University of Southern California,
    1993). *Dissertation Abstracts International*, *54*(8), 3019A.

du Plessis, M. (1996). Blatantly bisexual; or, Unthinking queer theory. In D. E. Hall, & M. Pramaggiore (Eds.), *RePresenting bisexualities: Subjects and cultures of fluid desire* (pp. 19-54). New York: New York University Press.

Eadie, J. (1997). Living in the past: *Savage nights,* bisexual times. *Journal of Gay, Lesbian, and Bisexual Identity,* 2(1), 7-26.

Eadie, J. (2002). In dialogue: Problems and opportunities in *Together Alone*'s visions of queer masculinities. *Journal of Bisexuality,* 2(1), 9-35.

Fraser, M. (1996). Framing contention: Bisexuality displaced. In D. E. Hall, & M. Pramaggiore (Eds.), *RePresenting bisexualities: Subjects and cultures of fluid desire* (pp. 253-271). New York: New York University Press.

Frieden, L. (2002). Invisible lives: Addressing Black male bisexuality in the novels of E. Lynn Harris. *Journal of Bisexuality,* 2(1), 73-90.

Hall, D. E. (1996). Graphic sexuality and the erasure of a polymorphous perversity. In D. E. Hall, & M. Pramaggiore (Eds.), *RePresenting bisexualities: Subjects and cultures of fluid desire* (pp. 99-123). New York: New York University Press.

Hemmings, C. (1993). Resituating the bisexual body: From identity to difference. In J. Bristow, & A. R. Wilson (Eds.), *Activating theory: Lesbian, gay, bisexual politics* (pp. 119-138).

Hemmings, C. (1997). Bisexual theoretical perspectives: Emergent and contingent relationships. In Bi Academic Intervention (Ed.), *Bisexual imaginary: Representation, identity and desire* (pp. 14-31). London: Cassell.

Hemmings, C. (1998). Waiting for no man: Bisexual femme subjectivity and cultural repudiation. In S. R. Munt (Ed.), *Butch/femme: Inside lesbian gender* (pp. 90-100). London: Cassell.

Hostetler, A. J., & Herdt, G. H. (1998). Culture, sexual lifeways, and developmental subjectivities: Rethinking sexual taxonomies. *Social Research,* 65(2), 249-291.

James, C. (1996). Denying complexity: The dismissal and appropriation of bisexuality in queer, lesbian, and gay theory. In B. Beemyn, & M. Eliason (Eds.), *Queer studies: A lesbian, gay, bisexual,* and *transgender anthology* (pp. 217-240). New York: New York University Press.

Kaloski, A. (1997). Bisexuals making out with cyborgs: Politics, pleasure, con/fusion. *Journal of Gay, Lesbian, and Bisexual Identity,* 2(1), 47-64.

Kraft, R. G. (1969). Sherwood Anderson, bisexual bard: Some chapters in a literary biography. (Doctoral dissertation, University of Washington, 1969). *Dissertation Abstracts International,* 30(6), 2489A.

Loftus, B. (1996). Biopia: Bisexuality and the crisis of visibility in a queer symbolic. In D. E. Hall, & M. Pramaggiore (Eds.), *RePresenting bisexualities: Subjects and cultures of fluid desire* (pp. 207-233). New York: New York University Press.

Morris, S., & Storr, M. (1997). Bisexual theory: A bi academic intervention. *Journal of Gay, Lesbian, & Bisexual Identity*, 2(1), 1-6.

Pramaggiore, M. (1996). Straddling the screen: Bisexual spectatorship and contemporary narrative film. In D. E. Hall, & M. Pramaggiore (Eds.), *Re-Presenting bisexualities: Subjects and cultures of fluid desire* (pp. 272-297). New York: New York University Press.

Shugar, D. R. (1999). To(o) queer or not? Queer theory, lesbian community, and the functions of sexual identities. In D. Atkins (Ed.), *Lesbian sex scandals: Sexual practices, identities, and politics* (pp. 11-20). New York: Haworth.

Sikorski, G. (2000). Replacing monosexual epistemologies: Representing bisexuality in twentieth century American narratives (Ernest Hemingway, Carson McCullers, E. Lynn Harris, Alice Walker). (Doctoral dissertation, The Pennsylvania State University, 2000). *Dissertation Abstracts International*, 61(4), 1409A.

Sikorski, G. (2002). Stepping into the same river twice: Internal/external subversion of the inside/outside dialectic in Alice Walter's *The Temple of My Familiar*. *Journal of Bisexuality*, 2(2/3), 53-71.

Steinman, E. (2001). Interpreting the invisibility of male bisexuality: Theories, interactions, politics. *Journal of Bisexuality*, 1(2/3), 15-45.

Storr, M. (1999). Postmodern bisexuality. *Sexualities*, 2(3), 309-325.

White, J. D. (2002). Bisexuals who kill: Hollywood's bisexual crimewave, 1985-1998. *Journal of Bisexuality*, 2(1), 39-54.

Whitney, E. (2002). Cyborgs among us: Performing liminal states of sexuality. *Journal of Bisexuality*, 2(2/3), 109-128.

Yescavage, K., & Alexander, J. (1999). What do you call a lesbian who's only slept with men? Answer: Ellen Morgan. Deconstructing the lesbian identities of Ellen Morgan and Ellen DeGeneres. In D. Atkins (Ed.), *Lesbian sex scandals: Sexual practices, identities, and politics* (pp. 21-32). New York: Haworth.

Young, S. (1997). Dichotomies and displacement: Bisexuality in queer theory and politics. In S. Phelan (Ed.), *Playing with fire: Queer politics, queer theories* (pp. 51-74). New York: Routledge.

BISEXUAL POLITICS AND COMMUNITY

Geographic Bisexual Communities

Barr, G. (1985). Chicago bi-ways: An informal history. *Journal of Homosexuality*, 11(1/2), 231-234.

Berry, D. (1996). A history of the Edinburgh Bisexual Group. In *Bisexual horizons* (pp. 281-286).

Deschamps, C. (2000). Mises en scène visuelles et rapports de pouvoir: Le cas des bisexuals [Visual representations and power struggles: The case of bisexuals]. *Journal des anthropologies, 82-83*, 251-263.

Dworkin, A. S. (2001). Bisexual histories in San Francisco in the 1970s and early 1980s. *Journal of Bisexuality, 1*(1), 87-119.

Esterberg, K. G. (1996). Gay cultures, gay communities: The social organization of lesbians, gay men, and bisexuals. In R. C. Savin-Williams, & K. M. Cohen (Eds.), *The lives of lesbians, gays, and bisexuals: Children to adults* (pp. 337-392). Fort Worth, TX: Harcourt Brace.

Euroqueer, A. (1996). Bisexuality in Brussels. In *Bisexual horizons* (pp. 287-288).

George, S. (2002). British bisexual women: A new century. *Journal of Bisexuality, 2*(2/3), 175-191.

Hüsers, F. (1996). Bisexual associations in Germany. In *Bisexual horizons* (pp. 293-297).

Kaal, W. (1996). A history of the bi movement in the Netherlands. In *Bisexual horizons* (pp. 289-292).

Nathanson, J. (2002). Pride and politics: Revisiting the Northampton Pride March, 1989-1993. *Journal of Bisexuality, 2*(2/3), 143-161.

Mishaan, C. (1985). The bisexual scene in New York City. *Journal of Homosexuality, 11*(1/2), 223-225.

Roberts, B. C. (1997). "The many faces of bisexuality": The 4th International Bisexual Symposium. *Journal of Gay, Lesbian, and Bisexual Identity, 2*(1), 65-76.

Roberts, W. (1996). The making of an Australian bisexual activist. In *Bisexual horizons* (pp. 149-153).

Ross, J. (2001). The San Francisco field of dreams: A history of the San Francisco Bi Film Festival, 1997-1999. *Journal of Bisexuality, 1*(1), 181-185.

Rubenstein, M., & Slater, C. A. (1985). A profile of the San Francisco Bisexual Center. *Journal of Homosexuality, 11*(1/2), 227-230.

Seif, H. (1999). A "most amazing borsht": Multiple identities in a Jewish bisexual community. *Race, Gender, and Class, 6*(4), 88-109.

Sheiner, M. (1991). The foundations of the bisexual community in San Francisco. In *Bi any other name* (pp. 203-204).

Storr, M. (1998). New sexual minorities, opposition and power: Bisexual politics in the UK. In T. Jordan & A. Lent (Eds.), *Storming the millennium: The new politics of change* (pp. 80-106). London: Lawrence & Wishart.

Tucker, N. (1995). Bay Area bisexual history: An interview with David Lourea. In *Bisexual politics* (pp. 47-62).

Weise, B. R. (1996). The bisexual community: Viable reality or revolutionary pipe dream? In *Bisexual horizons* (pp. 303-313).

The Broader Bisexual Community and Bisexual Politics

Arnesen, C. (1991). Coming out to Congress. In *Bi any other name* (pp. 233- 239).

Chandler, P. (1996). Coming in from the cold: Bisexuality and the politics of diversity. In *Bisexual horizons* (pp. 277-235).

Chavny, P. (2001). Bi Focus: On the margins. *Journal of Bisexuality*, *1*(1), 27-28.

D'Augelli, A. R., & Garnets, L. D. (1996). Lesbian, gay, and bisexual communities. In A. R. D'Augelli & C. J. Patterson (Eds.), *Lesbian, gay, and bisexual identities over the lifespan: Psychological perspectives* (pp. 293-320). New York: Oxford University Press.

Donaldson, S. (1995). The bisexual movement's beginnings in the 70s: A personal retrospective. In *Bisexual politics* (pp. 31-46)

Eadie, J. (1993). Activating bisexuality: Towards a bi/sexual politics. In J. Bristow, & A. R. Wilson (Eds.), *Activating theory: Lesbian, gay bisexual politics* (pp. 139-170).

Esterberg, K. G. (1996). Gay cultures, gay communities: The social organization of lesbians, gay men, and bisexuals. In R. C. Savin-Williams, & K. M. Cohen (Eds.), *The lives of lesbians, gays, and bisexuals: Children to adults* (pp. 337-392). Fort Worth, TX: Harcourt Brace.

Farajajé-Jones, E. (1995). Fluid desire: Race, HIV/AIDS, and bisexual politics. In *Bisexual politics* (pp. 119-130).

Hemmings, C., & Blumenfeld. W. J. (1996). Reading "monosexual." *Journal of Gay, Lesbian, & Bisexual Identity*, *1*(4), 311-321.

Highleyman, L. A. (1995). Identity and ideas: Strategies for bisexuals. In *Bisexual politics* (pp. 73-92).

Highleyman, L., Bray, R., Chapman, D., Davis, A., Ka'ahumanu, L., & Ramos E. (1996). Identity and ideas: A roundtable on identity politics. *Journal of Gay, Lesbian, & Bisexual Identity*, *1*(3), 235-253.

Hutchins, L. (1995). Our leaders, our selves. In *Bisexual politics* (pp. 131-142).

Hutchins, L. (1996). Bisexuality: Politics and community. In B. A. Firestein (Ed.), *Bisexuality: The psychology and politics of an invisible minority* (pp. 240-259). Thousand Oaks, CA: Sage.

Jordan, J. (1996). A new politics of sexuality. In *Bisexual horizons* (pp. 11-15).

Ka'ahumanu, L. (1995). It ain't over 'til the bisexual speaks. In *Bisexual politics* (pp. 63-68).

Lano, K. (1996). Bisexual history: Fighting invisibility. In *Bisexual horizons* (pp. 219-226).

Lenius, S. (2001). Bisexuals and BDSM: Bisexual people in a pansexual community. *Journal of Bisexuality*, *1*(4), 69-78.

North, G. (1990). Where the boys aren't: The shortage of men in the bi movement: Interview with Robyn Ochs. T. Geller (Ed.), *Bisexuality: A reader and sourcebook* (pp. 40-46). Ojai, CA: Times Change Press.

Ochs, R. (1995). Bisexual etiquette: Helpful hints for bisexuals working with lesbians and gay men. In *Bisexual politics* (pp. 237-240).

Ochs, R., & Highleyman, L. (1999). Bisexual movement. In B. Zimmerman (Ed.), *The encyclopedia of lesbianism*. New York: Garland.

Orlando, L. (1991). Loving whom we choose. In *Bi any other name* (pp. 223-232).

Pope, R. L., & Reynolds, A. L. (1991). Including bisexuality: It's more than just a label. In N. J. Evans, & V. A. Wall (Eds.), *Beyond tolerance: Gays, lesbians, & bisexuals on campus* (pp. 205-212). Alexandria, VA: American College Personnel Association.

Randen, H. (2001). Bi signs and wonders: Robyn Ochs and the Bisexual Resource Guide. *Journal of Bisexuality, 1*(1), 7-26.

Rust, P. C. (2001). Make me a map: Bisexual men's images of bisexual community. *Journal of Bisexuality, 1*(2/3), 47-108.

Rust, P. C. R. (2000). Popular images and the growth of bisexual community and visibility. In P. C. R. Rust (Ed.), *Bisexuality in the United States: A social science reader* (pp. 537-553). New York: Columbia University Press.

Shuster, R. (1991). Considering next steps for bisexual liberation. In *Bi any other name* (pp. 266-274).

Udis-Kessler, A. (1992). Identity/politics: A history of the bisexual movement. In *Bisexual Politics* (pp. 17-30). Reprinted in B. Beemyn, & M. Eliason (Eds.). (1996). *Queer studies: A lesbian, gay, bisexual, and transgender anthology* (pp. 52-63). New York: New York University Press.

Udis-Kessler, A. (1996). Identity/politics: Historical sources of the bisexual movement. In B. Beemyn, & M. Eliason (Eds.), *Queer studies: A lesbian, gay, bisexual, & transgender anthology* (pp. 52-63). New York: New York University Press.

Vidal, Gore. (1979). Bisexual politics. In L. Richmond, & G. Maguera (Eds.), *The new gay liberation book* (pp. 134-137). Palo Alto: Ramparts Press.

Yescavage, K., & Alexander, J. (2001). Bi/visibility: A call for a critical update. *Journal of Bisexuality, 1*(1), 173-180.

BISEXUAL COMMUNITY RESOURCES ONLINE

Bisexual Resource Center, Boston. Comprehensive Website, including info on bisexuality, bisexual news, bi conferences, the Bi Bookstore, where bi books, including the Bi Resource Guide, can be ordered, and links to other bi community Websites worldwide. http://www.biresource.org/

BI
FILM-VIDEO WORLD
Frida and Oscar

Wayne Bryant

http://www.haworthpress.com/web/JB
© 2004 by The Haworth Press, Inc. All rights reserved.
Digital Object Identifier: 10.1300/J159v04n01_13

[Haworth co-indexing entry note]: "Frida and Oscar." Bryant, Wayne. Co-published simultaneously in *Journal of Bisexuality* (Harrington Park Press, an imprint of The Haworth Press, Inc.) Vol. 4, Nos. 1/2, 2004, pp. 257-262; and: *Current Research on Bisexuality* (ed: Ronald C. Fox) Harrington Park Press, an imprint of The Haworth Press, Inc., 2004, pp. 257-262. Single or multiple copies of this article are available for a fee from The Haworth Document Delivery Service [1-800-HAWORTH, 9:00 a.m. - 5:00 p.m. (EST). E-mail address: docdelivery@haworthpress.com].

SUMMARY. This essay discusses the many films and documentaries which have been made about bisexual artist Frida Kahlo and writer Oscar Wilde. Similarities and differences in their lives and careers are cited. Films include in this article cover the period from 1960 to 2002. *[Article copies available for a fee from The Haworth Document Delivery Service: 1-800-HAWORTH. E-mail address: <docdelivery@haworthpress.com> Website: <http://www.HaworthPress.com> © 2004 by The Haworth Press, Inc. All rights reserved.]*

KEYWORDS. Bisexual, Oscar Wilde, Frida Kahlo, film

FRIDA AND OSCAR

The motion picture industry has for many years had a fondness for filming the lives and adventures of real-life bisexuals, though not always identifying them as such. Biographical movies have been made of many famous bi people: James Dean and Montgomery Clift, Judy Garland and Janis Joplin, Vaslav Nijinsky, Rudolph Valentino, and so on. But two bisexuals whose lives have appeared on film time and again are Oscar Wilde and Frida Kahlo.

Wilde's story is a relatively easy one to develop as a screenplay. A Dublin-born writer living in London, he takes the theatrical and social worlds by storm with his charm, biting satire, flamboyant dress, and memorable one-liners. He then makes the dreadful mistake of suing the father of his lover for defamation, the father having writing that Wilde was "posing as a Somdomite" [sic]. Revelations during the trial cause Wilde to be charged with offenses to minors and he is sentenced to two years hard labor. The experience leaves him a broken man in exile: his wealth, health, family, and friends all taken from him. It is a story with which most literate Americans are at least somewhat familiar.

In contrast, then, how did a girl born in Coyoacán, Mexico, who contracted polio at the age of six and barely survived a crippling traffic accident at eighteen go on to be the legendary figure about whom so many films have been made? During her lifetime Frida was not as well known as her husband, yet she has lived on to become an icon. She is certainly the only foreign-born, Communist, bisexual artist ever to grace a U. S. postage stamp–an honor which outraged American conservatives.

In 1984, director Paul Leduc made a Spanish film called *Frida, Naturaleza Viva*, in which Ofelia Medina plays a terminally ill Frida Kahlo reflecting on her life, her art and her loves. The flashbacks, while powerful and compelling, are in no way a linear retelling of the life of this highly original artist. Scenes with Diego Rivera, the horror of the bus accident, encounters with Leon

Trotsky, endless painful medical procedures and so on are all told as flash-backs. This is a well-made film, but not for those unfamiliar with her story. In addition to relationships with men, one scene shows Frida with an unidentified woman. They first exchange meaningful glances, suck each other's fingers, embrace and finally kiss. A later sequence shows Frida and a nurse caressing each other.

The American independent movie *A Ribbon Around a Bomb* (1991) con-tains no explicit references to female lovers. The film shows Frida attracted to an imaginary female friend and says she had affairs with other men besides Diego. Over the past thirty years roughly ten other films, shorts, documenta-ries, and TV movies have been made about Frida Kahlo in Mexico, the U.S. and various European countries.

The recent film *Frida* (2002) is the creation of Julie Taymor, a highly tal-ented theater director who made her film debut with *Titus*, based on William Shakespeare's *Titus Andronicus*. Shakespeare, of course, was a very success-ful bisexual playwright whose works have been the basis for nearly five hun-dred films. Taymor's cinematography is incredible in both films and the bisexuality in *Frida* is quite explicit. Indeed, the image on the cover of the video shows two Fridas, one dressed as a man and one as a woman, holding hands, with the caption "Prepare to be seduced."

Salma Hayek, in the role of Frida, and Alfred Molina as Diego Rivera are excellent, both physically and as actors in their roles. The film covers Frida's life from her youth as the third daughter of a Mexican woman and a Jewish German immigrant through her painful later years, made worse by doctors at-tempting to ease her back problems. At fifteen we see her first encounter with the famous artist Diego Rivera, who is painting a mural at her school. The scene of the bus and trolley collision at eighteen is the most visually stunning in the movie, contrasting the beauty of gold powder filling the air with the hor-ror of a handrail bar piercing her pelvis.

During her convalescence Frida begins to paint, just to pass the weeks and months. Once she is able, Frida takes her work to Rivera for an expert opinion. They quickly become friends, then lovers, and ultimately engage in a tempes-tuous marriage. When Frida discovers Diego having an affair with her sister, Christina, the marriage quickly finishes unraveling. But the bond between the two artists is never truly broken. In the end it is her health–more than thirty surgeries and months at a time spent in bed–that finally brings Frida down. At forty-five, with only fifteen months to live, Frida attends the opening of her first one-person exhibition by having her bed carried to the gallery in Mexico City.

In like fashion, the story of Oscar Wilde is one of a brilliant talent destroyed before its time. His story was first told in two films from the U.K., both re-leased in 1960. Robert Morley plays the title role in *Oscar Wilde*, directed by Gregory Ratoff. In *The Trials of Oscar Wilde* (also released as *The Man with the Green Carnation*), Peter Finch stars as Wilde and Ken Hughes directs.

Finch later played the gay doctor in *Sunday, Bloody Sunday*. Significantly, both of these biopics were banned in the United States because of Wilde's bisexuality and remain very difficult to find even now.

Aside from a German made-for-TV movie in 1971, the next Wilde picture came when Henry Herbert directed another British film, *Forbidden Passion: Oscar Wilde–The Movie* (1985). For those unfamiliar with the story, Wilde (Michael Gambon) is happily married and the proud father of two children. He also has a taste for young men and is not nearly discrete enough about it for Victorian England. The trouble begins when he has the poor judgment to fall in love with an impetuous Oxford student named Lord Alfred Douglas (Robin Lermitte), better known to Wilde as Bosey. Scandalous news travels fast and the boy's father, Lord Queensbury, begins harassing Wilde and dragging his reputation through the mud. Things might have cooled off over time had Wilde not retaliated by taking Queensbury to court for libel. When Queensbury digs up a few of Wilde's paid companions as witnesses, it becomes clear that things could get out of hand. Wilde drops the suit, but Queensbury does not give up the fight. Soon he has the playwright back in court on morals charges.

The next part of the film deals with Wilde's life in prison for "the love that dare not speak its name." On his release, Wilde is a broken man. He has lost his family, his reputation and his will to write, so he leaves England to live on the continent. He roams around Europe, usually broke and often in poor health. He has a disappointing reunion with Alfred and eventually dies in France in 1900.

Much of this film, produced for television by the BBC, seems like little more than an opportunity to string together a collection of Wilde's witty one-liners. Disappointing, therefore, was the absence of Wilde's alleged last words as he lay dying in a shabby Paris hotel room, "Either this wallpaper goes or I do!"

Oscar Wilde is a character in a fictional film called *Salome's Last Dance* (1987), directed by Ken Russell. The staff and patrons at Wilde's favorite brothel stage a surprise performance of his banned play, *Salomé*. Nickolas Grace plays Wilde, who is cheerfully entertained by Bosey, but who professes also to love his wife and family. Douglas Hodge does double-duty as Bosey and John the Baptist. Glenda Jackson plays the part of Herodias. Imogen Millais-Scott, as the petulant Salome, performs the famous Dance of the Seven Veils. "Bring me the head of John the Baptist" is her favorite and most memorable line. Director Russell can be spotted as the photographer. At the end of the show, Wilde is arrested for corrupting the morals of a minor. He protests, "We've had one melodramatic ending tonight. Two might be an indulgence."

Most recently (1997) another British film, simply called *Wilde*, made the rounds of the mainstream cinemas. Director Brian Gilbert's film followed the same general formula as *Forbidden Passion*, but with better results. Aside from the giving one the urge to reach for a copy of *Bartlett's Familiar Quota-*

tions and check off each Wilde zinger as it appears, the story was well done and the costuming and sets superb. Of the Wilde films, this is the one to see.

Although one lived in England and is known for his clever words while the other resided in Mexico and remembered for her stunning images, Oscar and Frida do have certain similarities. Wilde was forty-six when he died of meningitis. Kahlo passed away only a week past her forty-seventh birthday (and just a few weeks shy of Wilde's hundredth). Oscar's mother was a poet (who claimed to be "above respectability") and clearly influenced her son's love of words. Frida's father was a noted photographer who had a close relationship with his tomboyish daughter and encouraged her love of images. In the end, each has been the subject of numerous biographical films and continues to bring bisexuality to the attention of the world.

BI BOOKS

Bisexual and Gay Husbands: Their Stories, Their Words

Larry W. Peterson

http://www.haworthpress.com/web/JB
Digital Object Identifier: 10.1300/J159v04n01_14

[Haworth co-indexing entry note]: "Bisexual and Gay Husbands: Their Stories. Their Words." Peterson, Larry W. Co-published simultaneously in *Journal of Bisexuality* (Harrington Park Press, an imprint of The Haworth Press, Inc.) Vol. 4, Nos. 1/2, 2004, pp. 263-269; and: *Current Research on Bisexuality* (ed: Ronald C. Fox) Harrington Park Press, an imprint of The Haworth Press, Inc., 2004, pp. 263-269. Single or multiple copies of this article are available for a fee from The Haworth Document Delivery Service [1-800-HAWORTH, 9:00 a.m. - 5:00 p.m. (EST). E-mail address: docdelivery@haworthpress.com].

Bisexual and Gay Husbands: Their Stories, Their Words. Edited by Fritz Klein and Thomas Schwartz. New York, London, Oxford: Harrington Park Press, 2001, ISBN 1-56023-166-1 (hard); 1-56023-167-X (soft).

Bisexual and Gay Husbands is a special contribution to the literature in a number of ways. Fritz Klein, author of *The Bisexual Option* and editor of the *Journal of Bisexuality*, and Thomas Schwartz, a gay married man living in Seattle who has assisted numerous other married men through their coming out to themselves and their family members, arranged over 1,400 posts selected from an e-mail list founded in early 1996. Their arrangement allows the reader to eavesdrop or look over the shoulder of many men as they converse with one another via the Internet.

Schwartz and Klein opted to minimize their involvement with this book and let the men in this list speak for themselves. Thus, the book provides raw data, without interpretation or synthesis. The reader gets a true sense of the joy, pain, challenges, even personalities of the men posting. To see some analysis and synthesis of the content of these posts, please see my own article, "The Married Man Online," published simultaneously in *Journal of Bisexuality* (Volume 1, Numbers 2/3 2001) and in *Bisexuality in the Lives of Men: Facts and Fictions,* edited by Brett Beemyn and Erich Steinman (New York, London, Oxford: Harrington Park Press, 2001). I share my reaction to the editors' decision not to interpret the posts in my conclusion below.

CONTENT AND ORGANIZATION

The book is arranged into nine chapters that are preceded by a lengthy Introduction written by the editors to explain the book's organization and their decision to change all names to protect the confidentiality of the men whose posts they quote. I find the book's Introduction to be a very important read in itself. Fortunately, once a man's name was changed, the new name remains associated with the same man so that the reader can follow the evolution of one man's thinking about a particular topic if the reader so chooses. The chapters are entitled: "Coming Out," "Sexual Orientation," "Male Relationships," "Relationship with Wife," "Our Kids," "Advice and Comments," "Moral Issues," "Miscellaneous," and "Leaving the Marriages." The posts included in this book were transmitted over a period of approximately eighteen months in 1998 and 1999. The original pool of posts numbered about 3,000 written by approximately 350 men. The editors omitted the posts on this list that treated administrative matters, e.g., how to subscribe or unsubscribe or retrieve posts in the archives or posts that were only important at the moment or would not interest someone outside of the list. This list, by the way, still flourishes but its name is not shared to protect its confidentiality. Anyone interested in knowing more about it is welcome to contact me at *peterson@udel.edu.*

The first chapter, "Coming Out," is indeed a good place to begin since some men started their coming-out process via the Internet. The primary thrust of the coming-out stories in the book relate to men revealing their sexuality or their same-sex thoughts to the wife. Although the list from which these posts were taken is a list for men, there are several instances in this chapter where a wive's post is shared by her husband: "James" (see pp. 9-11; 18-21), "Moris" (11-12), "Melissa" (13-18). Two men–"Buck" (24-26) and "Brandon" (26-28)–share coming-out letters written to parents and other men share experiences interacting with their parents after coming out to them. Various aspects of the coming-out process are discussed by the men, including the pros and cons of remaining in a closet, the timing of coming out to family members, as well as the context of choosing when to come out. The special context of these stories is that each man in question is married. One aspect of the chapter that I found very interesting was the sequence where "Gripp" (31-40) shared his coming-out experience with his wife, shared in five different posts spread over several days.

"Sexual Orientation" is the title of the second chapter. The topic of labels and whether a man considers himself to be gay, bisexual, or simply "not straight" is one that has resurfaced annually on this list during its eight years of existence. A label implies certain associations and emotional baggage that is discussed in the 138 posts quoted in Chapter 2. Several of the posts are only one sentence in length. In fact, most of the posts quoted in this chapter are significantly shorter than those in Chapter 1. Chapter 2 has the following subtitles: "You are not alone," "Bisexuality," "Man of parts?," "Salvation?," "How we respond," "Bisexual acceptance," "Dreams," "What do we call ourselves?," "The gay thing, or TGT," "Sexual preference??" and "Early marriages." It is clear that some men within this list identify as gay, others as bisexual, and still others either do not associate themselves with a label or simply do not care about labels.

"Male Relationships," Chapter 3, begins with posts sharing reactions to a gathering of men in the list in the city of Chicago. Although this list includes men in various countries, the first six national gatherings for these men occurred in the USA (Baltimore, Chicago, Chicago, Seattle, Philadelphia). The 2003 gathering is planned this spring for Toronto, which will be the first meeting outside of the US. In Chapter 3, the men are discussing their reactions to meeting and bonding with other men who are bi/gay and married. Other topics discussed include whether it is "correct" to have a sexual relationship with a man who is significantly younger, the challenges and joys of male friendships, the impact that some male relationships have upon one's relationship to the wife, the differences between Internet friends and local friendships. Dating other men is one subsection of this chapter. For men older than 40, this new experience can be both exciting and extremely frustrating. "Delayed adolescence" is at work with some of these men as they learn about themselves as they date others. The posts about dating reveal the variety of dates the men are experiencing and they reveal how useful the Internet can be both to connect to another person and to share experiences with others. Some of the men seek what is becoming known as a "closed loop relationship," Lee, finding another married man to have a secondary monogamous relationship with while still maintaining a primary relationship with ones wife.

Chapter 4, "Relationship with Wife," includes discussions to understanding and developing strong lines of communication with wives. Of the more than thirty subsections, several are special to the ongoing concerns of these men. "Save marriage and maintain our sexuality" treats comments about maintaining one's own self-image as a gay or bisexual while being a good mate within a marriage. "The roller coaster" section relates to a term frequently used by the men in this list. The metaphor of the roller coaster captures the emotional highs and lows that these men feel. Also, it captures the turmoil of ones relationship with the wife. Yet again, it captures how the wife recycles through certain feelings and fears. "Boundaries" is another important concept that describes the decisions that husbands and wives make in a mixed-orientation marriage. What is acceptable to each partner in the marriage? These boundaries may be fluid, may change as either or both partners change with time, they may be carefully negotiated or they may just happen. "Sex with our wives" is another important topic frequently discussed by these men. Some refuse to have intercourse with their wives, others maintain an active sexual relationship. "She wants dinner with my boyfriend" is a title that appears comical but pertains to those marriages where the wife agrees that the husband may have a boyfriend. Having a wife and a "bf" raises many issues. Men learn that "having their cake and eating it too" is a very challenging way to live and may find their lives very compartmentalized. "Trust" is a subsection with only one post but this long post is an excellent one.

"Our Kids," Chapter 5, includes a lengthy quotation from an article by Amity Pierce Buxton, author of *The Other Side of the Closet: The Coming-Out Crisis for Straight Spouses and Families* (New York, Chichester, Brisbane, Toronto, Singapore: John Wiley & Sons, 1994). Amity Buxton was until recently the only female member of the e-mail list represented by this book. She is no longer a member, but while she was, she used material submitted by these men in her research. The article quoted in Chapter 5 (pp. 289-292) is not from her book, however, but from a GAMMA (Gay and Married Men's Association) Newsletter. Her informative article deals with the issue of when and how does a father come out to his child. This chapter is one source among several on the market currently that any parent, or a therapist helping a patient, should find helpful when faced with telling a child that he/she is gay.

Chapter 6, "Advice and Comments" covers many topics. Some of the these include how to meet men; whether a man should seek a male relationship outside of the marriage; guilt, anger, and feeling trapped; and how to proceed once the husband comes to the wife. A number of the posts treat topics also found in other chapters. In defense of the editors, it is difficult to assign some e-mail posts to a particular chapter when its author may have discussed several different topics within it. Printing entire posts proves problematic when organizing a book, yet I support the editors' decision to print entire posts to give the reader the "flavor" of the man's personality and the context of his comments. The first line of one post (336)–"Boy, I'm having such a rough time right now"–captures the spirit of many of the writings in this chapter. With over ninety pages, Chapter 6 is the longest in the book.

"Moral Issues," Chapter 7. The choices expressed in the posts herein are important and difficult. Should the husband remain sexually abstinent with other men? If he has sex with a boyfriend or other men does he share this information with his wife? Does the man renegotiate the marital vows with his wife? Do they have religious beliefs that limit the man acting on his desires? What does the word "monogamy" mean in the context of a mixed-orientation marriage? If the husband seeks to have a sexual relationship with another man, does the wife have the right also to seek a sexual relationship with another man? There are many moving moments to be found within the posts in this chapter.

Chapter 8, "Miscellaneous," includes those posts that did not neatly fit within the other chapters. The subsections are entitled "Acceptance" (here referring to self-image), "Monogamy/bisexuality in another society," "Update" and "Musings" (here referring to two men bringing others up to date on their personal situations), "Re: Hear what I don't say!" (an excellent post about facade and inner fear), and "Re: Emotional Observation" (the ability or inability to cry). This chapter–six pages in length–is the shortest within the book.

"Leaving the Marriage," the final chapter certainly explores the sadness, the guilt, the relief, the sense of failure, the numbness, and other emotions associated with separation and divorce. It may be helpful for the reader to keep a box of tissues nearby when reading the posts within Chapter 9.

CONCLUSION

This book should prove useful for a variety of reasons. To men in a similar situation, it is validating to read other men's experiences and see where parallels exist compared to ones own life. For therapists and others who seek to understand a married man who identifies himself as gay or bi, herein is much material rich in content. The advantage of this book–many posts by men speaking from the heart–is also its disadvantage. It requires much time to read most chapters plus the editors provide no commentary to assist the reader draw conclusions. In the Introduction the editors state (p. 5) that they ". . . have purposely not commented on the e-mails, as we strongly believe they stand on their own and our words would be superfluous and detract from the strength of the men's words and stories." I believe that the book would be even more valuable if Fritz Klein, a noted expert in the field of bisexuality, had expressed some observations at the conclusion of each chapter to heighten the awareness of the reader about certain points that appeared in the preceding chapter. Despite this recommendation, I believe the time required to absorb the content of these posts is time well invested. I am touched by the depth, variety of content, and variety of style of these posts. Reading this book reminds me of the value of the Internet in allowing men to network, support and validate, and learn from one another.

Index

Acquired immunodeficiency syndrome
  (AIDS)
  anxiety, 15
  bisexuality, 4,153
  journal articles, 213
  see also Human immunodeficiency
    virus
Addiction therapy, 143
Adolescent women, sexual orientation,
  41
Africa, bisexuality, 210
African-Americans, bisexuality, 206
Age and aging, 203
American Association for Marriage
  and Family Therapy, 102
American Counseling Association, 102
American Psychiatric Association, 3,102
American Psychological Association,
  102
Anthropology, bisexuality and
  homosexuality, 209
Anxiety
  AIDS patients, 15
  bisexual response, 141
  mental health services, 144
Appropriate Therapeutic Responses to
  Sexual Orientation, 140
Asia, bisexuality, 210
Asian-Americans, bisexuality, 207
Attitudes
  conceptualization, 127
  interventions, 130
  measurement, 127-129
  bisexuality, 119,124
Attitudes Regarding Bisexuality Scale,
  125
Attitudes Toward Lesbians and Gay
  Men Scale, 128

Beemyn, B., 265
Bernstein, L., 109
Best Interest of Children of Gay and
  Lesbian Parents, The
  (Buxton), 61
Biphobia
  attitudes, 120
  dichotomous culture, 15
  early adulthood, 3
  journal articles, 243
Biology, sexual orientation, 10
*Bisexual and Gay Husbands: Their
  Stories, Their Words* (Klein
  and Schwartz), 265
Bisexual husbands
  books, 265-269
  coping strategies, 68
  heterosexual wives, 80
Bisexual men
  African-Americans, 206
  attitudes toward, 119,124,245
  attractions and behavior, 31,188
  Australia, 87-95
  authenticity, 121
  current research, 124-127
  demographics, 126
  empirical research, 141
  friendships, 40
  future research, 127-130
  heterosexual attitudes, 126
  HIV/AIDS, 217
  intimate relationships, 85-96
  mental health services, 139,224
  negative attitudes, 119
  older, 203
  open relationships, 90
  positive attitudes, 123
  problematic experiences, 147

psychology, 188,192,195
psychosocial stressors, 141
relationships, 87-91
self-esteem, 129
self-identification, 143
sociology, 188,192,145
study and results, 142-149
Bisexual Option, The (Klein), 265
Bisexual Resource Directory, 62
Bisexual Resource Guide, 156
Bisexual wives
    coming out, 59
    communication, 64,67
    coping strategies, 64-70
    counseling, 66
    family negativity, 76
    family support, 73
    finances, 72
    guilt feelings, 75
    heterosexual husbands, 60,64
    negative factors, 75
    physical intimacy, 70
    relationship problems, 76
    self-education, 66
    social expectations, 75
    support, 71
Bisexual women
    African-American, 206
    attitudes toward, 119,124,245
    attractions and behavior, 31,188
    Australia, 87
    authenticity, 121
    college students, 29
    coping strategies, 64
    current research, 124-127
    data analysis, 43
    demographics, 51,126
    early adulthood, 39
    education, 51
    empirical research, 141
    ethnic diversity, 43
    experience and identity, 49-51
    friendships, 39
    future research, 51,127
    heterosexual friendships, 45,64,126

HIV/AIDS, 215
interview method, 43
intimate relationships, 85
invisibility, 46
lesbian view, 124
mental health services, 139,224
negative attitudes, 119
older, 203
open relationships, 90
positive attitudes, 123
problematic experiences, 147
psychology, 51,188,195
psychosocial stressors, 141
relationships, 87-91
self-esteem, 129
self-identification, 143
sex of partner, 47
sexual orientation, 39
social support, 50
sociology, 188,191,195
study and results, 42,142
thematic analysis, 44
Bisexual youth
    college students, 202
    families, 202
    high school, 202
    HIV/AIDS, 222
    identity and development, 200
    journal articles, 200
    mental health services, 229
    personal perspective, 203
    political view, 203
    psychology, 200
    relationships, 202
    sociology, 200
Bisexuality
    affirmation, 149
    Africa, 210
    African-Americans, 206
    anthropology, 209
    Asia, 210
    Asian-Americans, 207
    Australia, 87-95
    background, 9-11
    biased interventions, 147

BOOK ORDER FORM!

Order a copy of this book with this form or online at:
http://www.haworthpress.com/store/product.asp?sku=5222

Current Research on Bisexuality

_____ in softbound at $24.95 (ISBN: 1-56023-289-7)
_____ in hardbound at $39.95 (ISBN: 1-56023-288-9)

COST OF BOOKS _____

POSTAGE & HANDLING _____
US: $4.00 for first book & $1.50
for each additional book
Outside US: $5.00 for first book
& $2.00 for each additional book.

SUBTOTAL _____

In Canada: add 7% GST. _____

STATE TAX _____
CA, IL, IN, MN, NY, OH & SD residents
please add appropriate local sales tax.

FINAL TOTAL _____
If paying in Canadian funds, convert
using the current exchange rate.
UNESCO coupons welcome.

❏ BILL ME LATER:
Bill-me option is good on US/Canada/
Mexico orders only; not good to jobbers,
wholesalers, or subscription agencies.

❏ Signature _____

❏ Payment Enclosed: $ _____

❏ PLEASE CHARGE TO MY CREDIT CARD:

❏ Visa ❏ MasterCard ❏ AmEx ❏ Discover
❏ Diner's Club ❏ Eurocard ❏ JCB

Account # _____

Exp Date _____

Signature _____
(Prices in US dollars and subject to change without notice.)

PLEASE PRINT ALL INFORMATION OR ATTACH YOUR BUSINESS CARD

Name

Address

City   State/Province   Zip/Postal Code

Country

Tel   Fax

E-Mail

May we use your e-mail address for confirmations and other types of information? ❏ Yes ❏ No We appreciate receiving
your e-mail address. Haworth would like to e-mail special discount offers to you, as a preferred customer.
We will never share, rent, or exchange your e-mail address. We regard such actions as an invasion of your privacy.

Order From Your **Local Bookstore** or Directly From
The Haworth Press, Inc. 10 Alice Street, Binghamton, New York 13904-1580 • USA
Call Our toll-free number (1-800-429-6784) / Outside US/Canada: (607) 722-5857
Fax: 1-800-895-0582 / Outside US/Canada: (607) 771-0012
E-mail your order to us: orders@haworthpress.com

For orders outside US and Canada, you may wish to order through your local
sales representative, distributor, or bookseller.
For information, see http://haworthpress.com/distributors

(Discounts are available for individual orders in US and Canada only, not booksellers/distributors.)

Please photocopy this form for your personal use.
www.HaworthPress.com

BOF04